SECOND EDITION

ISSUES AND TRENDS IN LITERACY EDUCATION

Edited by

Richard D. Robinson
University of Missouri-Columbia

Michael C. McKenna
Georgia Southern University

Judy M. Wedman
University of Missouri-Columbia

Allyn and Bacon
Boston • London • Toronto • Sydney • Tokyo • Singapore

*The love of books is a love which requires neither
justification, apology, nor defense.*
—*JOHN LANGFORD*

*This book is dedicated to those teachers
who have inspired in their students
an undying love for reading and writing.*

Series editor: Arnis E. Burvikovs
Series editorial assistant: Bridget Keane
Marketing manger: Brad Parkins
Manufacturing buyer: Suzanne Lareau

Copyright © 2000, 1996 by Allyn & Bacon
A Pearson Education Company
Needham Heights, MA 02494

Internet: www.abacon.com

Library of Congress Cataloging-in-Publication Data

Issues and trends in literacy education / [edited by] Richard D.
    Robinson, Michael C. McKenna, Judy M. Wedman. -- 2nd ed.
        p.   cm.
    Includes bibliographical references and index.
    ISBN 0-205-29651-3
    1. Language arts.   2. Reading.   3. English language composition
    and exercises.   4. Literacy.   I. Robinson, Richard David (date).
II. McKenna, Michael C.   III. Wedman, Judy M. (date).
LB1576.I87   2000
372.6'044--dc21   99-17011
                                                                        CIP

Printed in the United States of America

10 9 8 7 6 5 4 3 2   03 02 01 00

CONTENTS

PREFACE

Reading is the sole means by which we
slip, involuntarily, helplessly, into another's
skin, another's voice, another's soul.
—*JOYCE CAROL OATES*

The primary purpose of this book is to help you better study and understand the field of literacy education. What was once a rather limited discipline is today a vast and complicated body of knowledge and field of inquiry, frequently drawing on information from many diverse areas such as psychology, sociology, and linguistics. The individual wishing to investigate a question or topic in literacy today may find the experience a daunting one.

For example, a recent computer search on the subject "reading comprehension" identified over 7,000 references to this one topic. Ranging across a broad spectrum of subtopics, the results of this search clearly showed the diversity that is typical of the literacy field. These results included data-based research studies, classroom observational inquiries, theoretical research papers, as well as personal opinion articles. These references represented the work of university faculty, classroom teachers, commercial publishers, and private individuals. Complicating the situation is the fact that there is not only a great deal of information currently available, but many different opinions and perspectives as well. These viewpoints often range between a single individual's position on a topic and a national movement reflecting the philosophies and attitudes of many thousands of people.

It is with these circumstances in mind that this book was written. We have attempted to identify the most significant issues and trends facing literacy educators today and to locate sources that explain principal viewpoints on these issues. Beyond selecting sources and providing textual aids to promote comprehension and engagement, our contribution has been minimal. We prefer to let the authors speak for themselves.

We have assumed that most readers of this book have had at least some introduction to the study of literacy education. The book has been developed with practicing teachers in mind—practitioners interested in extending their own thinking about the important issues they face in classrooms. We have not attempted to produce an introductory text, but assume that the foundations of literacy instruction—its purposes, concepts, and methods—have already been laid by means of prior coursework and teaching experience.

Organization of the Text

Each chapter is made up of four parts: (1) a brief introduction to the topic, (2) the articles themselves, (3) an annotated bibliography, and (4) suggestions for further involvement.

Chapter Introductions

Each topic is first summarized in a brief section designed both to provide necessary background and to help stimulate thinking related to the topic. Many readers of this book will have—either through previous education classes or classroom teaching experiences—developed ideas and feelings about the topics discussed in this book. We challenge you to keep an open mind about what you currently believe concerning literacy instruction. In many literacy areas, either because of recent research or relevant classroom experiences, instructional strategies that were once considered appropriate are now being challenged by new ideas and pedagogy.

Each chapter introduction concludes with a list of important questions designed to guide your reading and organize your thinking. Actively considering them should give you a better understanding of your current knowledge, beliefs, and feelings about a particular literacy issue.

Articles

Following the introduction are the selections. Our intent is that this section will help familiarize you with important, though sometimes incompatible, views on the chapter topic. Of particular note is the presentation of differing points of view. For some topics, where there is little disagreement or controversy, you will find a general discussion of the literacy trend. You should understand that the selections are never intended to be all-inclusive but rather to introduce the topic and encourage you to pursue further study on your own.

Following the articles are two sections called **Integrating Sources** and **Classroom Implications.** As the headings indicate, the intent is to help you resolve differences between the articles and to consider possible implications for classroom literacy instruction. These sections are purposely designed to be open ended.

Annotated Bibliographies

Although every article has its own reference section, we have attempted to supplement these with a careful selection of sources useful for further reading. In some cases, the material is divided into a historical and a current listing of literacy sources. In these cases, the reader can see the development and changes in thinking on a literacy topic, noting how historical issues and trends have influenced current opinions and practices.

You Become Involved

The final section of each chapter is designed to help you formulate your own views by engaging in activities that encourage independent thought. For each chapter, a range of possibilities is presented. The ideas can be approached individually or in groups and are meant to be undertaken selectively.

For the University Teacher

Today, colleges of education are increasingly faced with issues of accountability related to their preparation of teachers. Whereas some standards, such as those of the National Council for the Accreditation of Teacher Education (NCATE), apply across the general field of education, subject matter organizations have developed guidelines for more specialized teacher preparation. In this respect, the International Reading Association (IRA) has long been involved in the development of standards for the preparation of literacy educators at all levels. The IRA publication, *Standards for Reading Professionals* (Lunsford & Pauls, 1992), was written to guide the preparation and professional development of literacy educators. Emphasized as a fundamental principle throughout this publication is the fact that all educators, whether at the preservice or inservice level, need an extensive conceptual framework related to the field of literacy instruction.

The following specific guidelines are only part of those listed by which university and college programs of teacher education in the field of literacy will be evaluated. They include the following student outcomes:

- Has knowledge of current and historical perspectives about the nature and purposes of reading and about widely used approaches to reading instruction
- Pursues knowledge of reading and learning processes by reading professional journals and publications and participating in conferences and other professional activities
- Employs inquiry and makes thoughtful decisions during teaching and assessment
- Interprets and communicates research findings related to the improvement of instruction to colleagues and the wider community
- Initiates, participates in, or applies research on reading
- Reads or conducts research with a range of methodologies (e.g., ethnographic, descriptive, experimental, or historical)
- Promotes and facilitates teacher-based and classroom-based research

The primary purpose of this book is to assist you in helping your students meet these wide and diverse guidelines for literacy education. Chapter content is designed to encourage further exploration of certain selected topics in literacy education through the effective use of a wide variety of resources and materials. We would hope that the end product of this book and your instruction is an educator who has been made more aware of the prominent issues and trends in the field of literacy education today and who appreciates their implications for practice.

We wish to take this opportunity to thank the following reviewers for their helpful comments: Liqing Tao, Western Kentucky University; Francine Johnston, University of North Carolina at Greensboro; Linda Thistlewaite, Western Illinois University; and Ruth Farrar, Bridgewater State College.

INTRODUCTION TO THE FIELD OF LITERACY EDUCATION

> Books are yours,
> Within whose silent chambers treasure lies
> Preserved from age to age; more precious far
> Than that accumulated store of gold
> And orient gems which, for a day of need,
> The sultan hides deep in ancestral tombs.
> These hoards of truth you can unlock at will
> —*WILLIAM WORDSWORTH, 1802*

The study of literacy today is a vast and often complicated enterprise. In many fields, information is concentrated in a limited number of journals or produced by relatively few individuals; this is certainly not the case in literacy education, however. For example, important literacy research and writing are currently being done by individuals in fields as diverse as linguistics, cognitive psychology, sociology, computer science, anthropology, and education. Even within the general field of education, literacy materials are often indexed under a broad range of descriptors, such as emergent literacy, assessment, materials, teacher training, and so on. This information is frequently reported in a wide variety of outlets—including journals, books, and research reports—and has recently been lodged in huge computer databases. For the literacy educator, this wide spectrum of knowledge and available resources often presents a daunting challenge.

The purpose of this chapter is to facilitate your further study of literacy education. The intent here is to provide specific information that will help you learn more about the most prominent resources and current thinking in the field. You may already be familiar with some of the sources mentioned.

As You Read

Your study of this chapter should prepare you to examine the issues that follow. As you read, keep the following objectives in mind:

1. Describe some effective strategies for literacy research and study.
2. Identify some of the current trends in literacy education.
3. Identify the major national organizations in the field of literacy study.
4. Describe some of the important journals and references in the field of literacy.

Introduction

Edmund Huey, writing early in the twentieth century about the study of the reading process, noted that "to completely analyze what we do when we read would almost be the acme of a psychologist's achievements, for it would be to describe very many of the most intricate workings of the human mind, as well as to unravel the tangled story of the most remarkable specific performance that civilization has learned in all its history" (Huey, 1908, p. 6). This single statement, in many respects, epitomizes even today the ongoing search for a better understanding of the reading process. Although it is true that much has been done in the study of fundamental processes related to literacy as well as in the development of new instructional programs in literacy since Huey wrote, many important questions remain unanswered at the present time.

Current Trends in Literacy Education

Today, as in the past, the literacy community often finds itself split according to philosophies, theories, and/or practical applications. Although terms may have changed, much of what is debated today is often strikingly similar to the substance of past disputes. Issues such as the most appropriate methods and materials to use in the teaching of literacy as well as how to effectively assess what is learned are, after extended controversy, still the center of much of the literacy debate today.

As you continue your study of literacy issues, it is important to be aware that you must inevitably confront divergent viewpoints and opinions. For almost any of these issues, there is a wide range of opinions and feelings. These differences are clearly evident in the available literature on most topics. Expecting them should make you better at identifying and appraising the various viewpoints on each literacy topic.

A preview of some of the most prominent issues facing literacy educators today may well convince you of the range of problems involved. A major issue is that of whole language versus more conventional philosophies to instruction. Related to it is the role of phonics instruction, spelling, and basal readers. The nature of emerging literacy in early childhood has challenged older notions of "readiness," just as research into vocabulary instruction may surprise you with its implications for day-to-day practice. In content area classrooms, new conceptualizations have arisen as to how literacy activities can help students learn. In the larger arena of education, debate over the proper approaches to assessment and the desirability of national standards has spilled over into literacy. Finally, new advances in technology challenge educators to make the best uses of it in developing literate behavior in students. Each of these topics will be covered later in this book, though their interrelatedness will frequently compel you to cross-reference your thinking!

Organizations in Literacy Education

Many professional organizations address literacy issues as part of their programs, but the following are the most prominent:

- *International Reading Association.* The IRA is the largest organization in the literacy field, with a widespread membership that includes teachers at all levels from college and university faculty through elementary teachers. This organization is noted for its many quality literacy publications as well as a structure that invites participation at local, state, regional, national, and global levels. Its periodicals include *The Reading Teacher, Journal of Adolescent and Adult Literacy, Reading Research Quarterly,* and *Lectura y Vida* (Spanish language).
- *National Council of Teachers of English.* The NCTE is a large organization representing teachers interested in language arts instruction. Like the IRA, the NCTE is noted for a variety of publications, including its two principal journals, *Language Arts* and *English Journal.*
- *National Reading Conference.* This organization is primarily comprised of college and university faculty interested in all types of literacy research. Its periodical is the *Journal of Literacy Research,* and its yearbook also presents research on a wide variety of literacy-related topics.
- *College Reading Association.* Members of this organization are primarily college and university faculty. CRA publishes a journal, *Reading Research and Instruction,* as well as a yearbook.

Leading Journals in the Field of Literacy

The following journals are among the most prominent:

- *The Reading Teacher.* This journal, published by the International Reading Association, includes articles primarily related to the teaching of literacy in the elementary school.
- *Journal of Adolescent and Adult Literacy.* This journal, formerly titled *Journal of Reading,* is published by the International Reading Association with emphasis on literacy education in the content areas as well as on middle, high school, and adult education.
- *Reading Research and Instruction.* Formerly *Reading World,* this journal combines research reports with articles that suggest ideas. It is published by the College Reading Association.

- *Reading Research Quarterly.* This is the leading journal of literacy research. The articles published in this journal consistently represent important contributions to the field of literacy research. Often, the articles published in the *Reading Research Quarterly* include extensive bibliographies of related materials and thus are excellent sources for further study. This journal is a publication of the International Reading Association.
- *Reading Horizons.* This journal is intended primarily for classroom teachers and typically publishes articles related to classroom applications of new literacy research.
- *Journal of Literacy Research.* Primarily a literacy research journal published by the National Reading Conference, this publication also presents position papers and issues-oriented commentary.
- *Reading Psychology.* This journal contains a wide variety of literacy articles, including research, opinion pieces, and suggestions for practice.
- *Language Arts.* This journal is published by the National Council of Teachers of English. Although areas of the language arts curriculum are included, there is a substantial number directly related to literacy concerns. The primary orientation of the journal is toward elementary instruction.
- *English Journal.* Published by the National Council of Teachers of English, this journal addresses the concerns of teachers serving adolescent and older populations.

References in the Study of Literacy Education

Although a seemingly endless flow of new titles enters the field of literacy education, the following books have been selected as important sources for further study. They have been chosen on the basis of their importance to the field and should be excellent starting points for further study.

Reference Materials

Adams, M. J. (1990). *Beginning to read: Thinking and learning about print.* Cambridge, Massachusetts: MIT Press.

This important and scholarly reference reflects the continuing interest in the study of the sound/symbol relationships related to word analysis. Comprehensive synthesis of research in the areas of cognitive and developmental psychology, instructional methodology, and related areas is included.

Flood, J., et al. (Eds.). (1991). *Handbook of research on teaching the English language arts.* New York: Macmillan.

This collection of research reviews focuses on topics broadly ranging across the language arts.

Goodman, K. (1986). *What's whole in whole language?* Portsmouth, New Hampshire: Heinemann.

A thorough discussion of the philosophical foundations of the whole language movement is provided.

Kamil, M., & Langer, J. A. (1985). *Understanding research in reading and writing.* Boston: Allyn and Bacon.

This book is a discussion of the uses of various research methodologies and their specific application to the study of literacy. For those interested in the development of a research design related to literacy, this is an excellent reference.

Pearson, P. D., et al. (1984). *Handbook of reading research.* White Plains, New York: Longman.

Barr, R., et al. (1991). *Handbook of reading research, Part II.* White Plains, New York: Longman.

Both of these volumes are important resources in the study of literacy education. They contain inclusive reviews of important issues in the field as well as extensive bibliographies of related materials. They should be excellent starting points for most studies in the field of literacy education.

Samuels, J., & Farstrup, A. (1992). *What reading research has to say about reading instruction.* Newark, Delaware: International Reading Association.

This is a series of articles written by noted literacy authorities on how current research informs several important issues in the field.

Historical Materials

The following references have been selected to provide a historical perspective on the research and teaching of literacy They should provide you with information on important past work done by noted authorities in the field.

Altick, R. D. (1963). *The art of literacy research.* New York: W. W. Norton.

This cornerstone work on the research methods in literacy anticipates many of the present-day concerns of qualitative researchers.

Anderson, I. H., & Dearborn, W. F (1952). *The psychology of reading.* New York: Roland Press.

This is an important reference in the early study of the psychology of literacy processes.

Betts, E. A. (1946). *Foundations of reading instruction.* New York: American Book Company.

Written for preservice teachers on the teaching of literacy in the elementary grades, this important reference is excellent for comparison with current methods texts.

Dolch, E. W. (1939). *A manual for remedial reading.* Champaign, Illinois: Garrard Press.

This is one of the first references written on the topic of the remediation of reading difficulties.

Gates, A. I. (1929). *The improvement of reading.* New York: Macmillan.

This is one of the first textbooks in elementary literacy instruction.

Gray, W. S. (1948). *On their own in reading.* Chicago: Scott Foresman.

Written by one of the early leaders in the study of literacy, this important reference focuses on the study and classroom use of the sound/symbol relationships.

Huey, E. B. (1908). *The psychology and pedagogy of reading.* Cambridge, Massachusetts: MIT Press.

> *This is an early exploration of cognitive processes that underlie reading. It is famed for the later substantiation through research of many of the author's premises.*

National Society for the Study of Education Yearbooks. Chicago: University of Chicago Press.

> *This series of landmark books deals with important issues in the field of education. These books contain important articles that were often instrumental in the development of later reading policies and research. The following editions deal with the study of literacy: 20th (1921), 24th (1925), 36th (1937), 47th (1948), 48th (1949), 55th (1956), 60th (1961), 67th (1968), 83rd (1984).*

Robinson, H. M. (1946). *Why pupils fail in reading.* Chicago: University of Chicago Press.

> *This is a foundation report in the clinic approach to the study of reading disabilities in children.*

Smith, N. B. (1934). *American reading instruction.* New York: Silver, Burdett.

> *This is a classic in the study of the historical foundations of the study of literacy and of reading instruction from colonial times forward.*

Strategies for Literacy Research

For most readers of this book, a literacy study will begin with a question about a particular concern or interest in this area. This question may arise in response to an assignment in a graduate class in literacy education or as the result of a personal interest in a literacy topic. It also might be initiated by a need to solve a classroom problem related to literacy, such as finding out more about a specific teaching technique or the background related to new commercial materials. For whatever reason, the formation of a question is a very important first step in any literacy study (Altick, 1963).

Unfortunately, it is at this point that many individuals begin to have varying degrees of difficulty. Frequently, initial questions are far too general to be answered in a realistic and effective manner. For example, questions such as the following are almost unanswerable:

- What causes literacy problems?
- What are effective literacy materials?
- What is the best method of teaching literacy skills?

These examples could be improved considerably by narrowing their scope:

- Does the home environment of a child have a lasting effect on literacy development?
- What is the influence of library books on the development of literacy skills?
- Has the use of language experience been shown to be superior to the use of the basal reader in first-grade literacy development?

The degree of specificity of any question will largely be determined by the background knowledge and purposes of each individual.

Once the question has been formulated, the investigator needs to propose a possible answer, sometimes with limited information, but always on the basis of theory. Continuing with the previous examples, the projected answers might look like these:

- The home environment of a child, especially parents reading to their children, does have a positive and long-term effect on literacy development.
- Library books are best used under the direction of a professional librarian rather than the classroom teacher.
- First-grade teachers find language experience instruction to be better suited to disadvantaged students than the use of the basal reader.

Each of these statements may or may not be true. It then becomes the goal of the investigator to find information either to support or to refute these tentative conclusions. In accomplishing this objective, the literacy researcher needs to be aware of a number of potential difficulties. The first is the typically large amount of information available on almost every aspect of literacy education. In the area of literacy education, the question frequently is not "Can I find information on my topic?" but rather "How can I select from the voluminous material available?" The second problem is the wide diversity of sources. Not only are there prominent journals and references in the field, there are also many other resources that publish literacy-related information. These sources include journals, books, research and development reports, newspaper articles, and so forth. Finally, one must consider the fact that for many issues in literacy education, there are widely differing opinions. Thus, for many literacy issues, you should expect to find various personal opinions as well as research results—and differing opinions on what the results mean!

With these obstacles in mind, it may seem an almost impossible task to find an answer to any literacy question. Yet the careful and thorough process of investigation should, in most cases, prove to be successful. Altick (1963), in summarizing this approach to scholarship, noted a pair of elementary principles: "(1) collect all the evidence, internal and external, that has any connection with your hypothesis, and (2) give as much consideration to evidence that weighs against the hypothesis, or that tends to support an alternative one, as to the substantiating kind. And maintain the critical attitude to the very end; the collapsible premise and the spurious fact are always lurking in the path of the unwary" (p. 122). Hopefully, with these thoughts in mind, you should be able to successfully begin, work through, and produce an effective literacy study into a topic of particular interest to you.

References

Altick, R. D. (1963). *The art of literacy research.* New York: W. W. Norton.
Huey, E. B. (1908). *The psychology and pedagogy of reading.* Cambridge, MA: MIT Press.
Wordsworth, W. (1994). *The excursion: Book 4. Dispondency corrected. The works of William Wordsworth.* Ware, Hertfordshire, England: Wordsworth Editions, Ltd.

1

BALANCE

After experimenting with every [reading] scheme, I
believe we shall be driven back to a single resource....
Language needs to be learned, where it is used...by
the daily reading of such books, as, with the aid of free
questioning on the part of the pupil, and full explanations
on the part of the teacher, can be thoroughly mastered.
—*HORACE MANN (1838)*

Learning to read is an individual matter.... All
conventional methods of teaching reading have their
strengths and weaknesses.... Reading might
best be taught by a combination of methods.
—*I. H. ANDERSON AND W. F. DEARBORN (1952)*

In classrooms in which teachers use effective
teaching and organizational strategies and appropriate materials most children make progress.
—*NATIONAL ACADEMY OF SCIENCES (1998)*

A Key to Literacy Instruction

The dictionary defines the word *balance* as being "a state of equilibrium or stabil-
ity." When this term is applied to the teaching of reading it suggests that the classroom teacher is following an eclectic or multifaceted approach to reading. This is
in opposition to the emphasis placed on one approach or method as being the
dominant method of reading instruction.

The key word today in reading instruction is balance. In a recent article,
Cassidy and Wenrich (1998) note that "balanced reading instruction" is currently
the key topic in reading education. They base this conclusion on a series of interviews with leading authorities in the field of reading education, asking them "Which
reading topics did they feel were hot and which were not?" The only topic which

was agreed on by the entire panel of experts as being hot was balanced reading instruction.

Observation of classroom reading practices (May, 1998; Robinson, 1991) has shown that many teachers tend to follow a balanced reading approach, despite whatever the current fad may be in reading instruction. Teachers typically select those aspects of a variety of reading approaches that they find effective, using these ideas and ignoring the remaining parts of these programs.

As You Read

Cassidy and Wenrich (1998) conducted a survey of 25 national/international literacy leaders to identify key topics in reading research and practice. All of the respondents identified balanced reading instruction as an "extremely hot" topic. At this point in literacy history, the research and discussion around balanced instruction is only beginning to appear in the literature. The first article by Pressley, Rankin, and Yokoi (1998) is a research study that examines and delineates the effective literacy practices of primary teachers. The identified practices are related to balanced instruction and implications for teacher education. Second, a literacy curriculum framework is presented by Au, Carroll, and Scheu (1997), which teachers can use to achieve balance. As you read these two articles, consider the following:

1. What is balanced instruction?
2. Why is balanced instruction an important topic in literacy history?
3. How do nationwide curricular and social issues influence literacy instruction? What influences may be attributed to the recent interest in balanced instruction?

References

Anderson, I. W., & Dearborn, W. F. (1952). *The psychology of teaching reading.* New York: Roland Press.

Au, K., Carroll, J., & Scheu, J. (1997). The six aspects of literacy: A curriculum framework. *Balanced literacy instruction: A teacher's resource book.* Norwood, MA: Christopher-Gordon. 4–9.

Cassidy, J., & Wenrich, J. K. (1998, February/March). What's hot, what's not for 1998: Second annual survey examines key topics in reading research and practice. *Reading Today, 15*, 1, 28.

Mann, H. (1838). *The Common School Journal, 1*, 19.

May, F. B. (1998). *Reading as communication.* Upper Saddle River, NJ: Merrill.

National Academy of Sciences. (1998). *Preventing Reading Difficulties.* Washington: National Academy of Sciences.

Pressley, M., Rankin, J., & Yokoi, L. (1996). A survey of instructional practices of primary teachers nominated as effective in promoting literacy. *Elementary School Journal, 96*, 333–384.

Robinson, R. D. (1991). *Teacher effectiveness and reading instruction.* Bloomington, IN: ERIC Clearinghouse on Reading and Communication Skills.

A Survey of Instructional Practices
of Primary Teachers Nominated as Effective
in Promoting Literacy

MICHAEL PRESSLEY
University at Albany,
State University of New York

LINDA YOKOI
University at Albany,
State University of New York

JOAN RANKIN
University of Nebraska

Abstract. *Kindergarten (N = 23), grade 1 (N = 34), and grade 2 (N = 26) teachers, who were nominated by their supervisors (N = 45) as effective in educating their students to be readers and writers, responded to 2 questionnaires about their practice. As expected, there were shifts in reported practices between kindergarten and grade 2, although there was much more similarity than difference in the reports of kindergarten, grade 1, and grade 2 teachers. The teachers claimed commitments to* (a) *qualitatively similar instruction for students of all abilities, along with additional support for weaker readers;* (b) *literate classroom environments;* (c) *modeling and teaching of both lower-order (e.g., decoding) skills and higher-order (e.g., comprehension) processes;* (d) *extensive and diverse types of reading by students;* (e) *teaching students to plan, draft, and revise as part of writing;* (f) *engaging literacy instruction (i.e., instruction motivating literate activities); and* (g) *monitoring of students' progress in literacy.*

What is the nature of effective primary literacy instruction? Many theories and models have been proposed in response to this question (Chall, 1967; Flesch, 1955; K. S. Goodman & Y. M. Goodman, 1979), each emphasizing particular processes and instruction stimulating those processes. Invariably, advocates of a model hypothesize that children will be more literate if they experience the model that they espouse rather than other forms of literacy instruction. Such hypotheses have led to tests of various types of primary-level literacy instruction (Barr, 1984).

The most famous set of such evaluations was the "first-grade studies" in the 1960s, sponsored by the U.S. Office of Education (Adams, 1990, chap. 3; Barr, 1984; Bond & Dykstra, 1967). A strength of these studies was that each of various approaches to reading instruction was tested in several different experiments and, typically, by different research

Source: From "A Survey of Instructional Practices of Primary Teachers Nominated as Effective in Promoting Literacy" by Michael Pressley, Joan Rankin, and Linda Yokoi, 1996, *Elementary School Journal, 1996,* pp. 333–384. © 1996 by the University of Chicago Press. Reprinted by permission.

teams. By most accountings, however, there was no clear overall winner in the first-grade studies (Barr, 1984; Bond & Dykstra, 1967), nor in extensions of the comparisons to grade 2 level (Dykstra, 1968). Although word reading sometimes was improved in programs targeted at increasing decoding skills and knowledge of letter-sound consistencies in words, vocabulary and comprehension were affected little by alternatives to the traditional basal approach. (See Guthrie and Tyler, 1978, for a more optimistic appraisal of the linguistic and the phonics plus basal approaches, which they concluded produced at least slightly greater reading achievement than the alternatives.) Given the ambiguity in the results of the first-grade studies, the great debate about the nature of the optimal beginning reading instruction raged on (Chall, 1967).

The models in the debate have shifted since the late 1960s, however. A popular contemporary approach, whole language, emphasizes language processes and the creation of learning environments in which students experience authentic reading and writing (Weaver, 1990). Both linguistic and cognitive development are presumed to be stimulated by experiencing good literature and attempting to compose new meanings (e.g., see Y. M. Goodman, 1990). There is opposition to explicit, systematic teaching of reading skills, especially elements of decoding (e.g., see King & K. S. Goodman, 1990). According to whole-language theorists, any skills instruction that occurs should be in the context of natural reading and only as needed by individual readers consistent with psycholinguistic models of development, whole-language advocates believe that the development of literacy is a natural by-product of immersion in high-quality-literacy environments.

In contrast, other reading educators argue that learning to break the code is a critical part of primary-level reading and that breaking of the code is most likely when students are provided systematic instruction in decoding (e.g., see Chall, 1967). There is a growing data base showing that such instruction increases reading competence (Adams, 1990), especially for students who experience difficulties in learning to read when instruction is less explicit (Mather, 1992; Pressley & Rankin, 1994).

Increasingly, explicit decoding instruction is conceived in cognitive-science terms, largely because much recent evidence supporting it has been generated by cognitive psychologists and cognitively oriented reading researchers. For example, some cognitive scientists believe that the development of strong and complex connections between words and their components (Adams, 1990; Foorman, 1994) follows from explicit instruction in phonemic awareness, letter recognition, attention to the sounds of words, blending of sounds, and practice in reading and writing words, to the point that they are automatically recognized and produced. Beyond word-level decoding, many cognitive scientists conceive of text comprehension as the application of particular information processes to text (e.g., relating new text to prior knowledge, asking questions in reaction to text, visualizing text content, and summarizing). Skilled comprehension requires self-regulated use of such information processes. A start on the development of such self-regulation is teaching of comprehension strategies that stimulate processes used by good comprehenders, for example, instruction of prior knowledge activation as a prereading strategy, self-questioning during reading, construction of mental images capturing the ideas covered in text, and finding main ideas (Brown, Bransford, Ferrara, & Campione, 1983; Pressley et al., 1992).

There has been much research about the effectiveness of whole language, traditional decoding, and cognitive science-inspired primary-level instruction. The evidence is growing that whole language experiences stimulate children's literate activities and positive attitudes toward literacy, as well as increased understanding about the nature of reading and writing (e.g., see Graham & Harris, 1994; Morrow, 1990, 1991, 1992; Neuman & Roskos, 1990, 1992). Even so, a disturbing finding is that, compared with conventional instruction, whole language programs do not seem to have much of an effect on early reading achievement as measured by standardized tests of decoding, vocabulary, comprehension, and writing (Graham & Harris, 1994; Stahl, McKenna, & Pagnucco, 1994; Stahl & Miller, 1989). In contrast, programs explicitly teaching phonemic awareness, phonics, and letter-sound analysis have promoted standardized-test performance and have proved superior to programs, such as whole language, that emphasize meaning-making (Adams, 1990; Pflaum, Walberg, Karegianes, & Rasher, 1980). In addition, reading programs that explicitly teach students to use repertoires of comprehension strategies have proved their worth in promoting understanding of text (Bereiter & Bird, 1985; Palincsar & Brown, 1984), including when this is measured by standardized assessments (e.g., see Brown, Pressley, Van Meter, & Schuder, 1995).

The hypothetico-deductive studies comparing various types of primary reading instruction with traditional instruction, however, have not provided a satisfactory answer to the question posed in the first line of this article, "What is the nature of effective primary reading instruction?" Most critically, close examination of many recent studies supporting explicit teaching of decoding and instruction of comprehension strategies reveals that there are often many elements of whole language in such teaching, including the reading of outstanding children's literature and daily writing (Pflaum et al., 1980; Pressley et al., 1991, 1992). What has emerged in recent years, in part from the realization that explicit decoding and comprehension instruction typically occur in the context of other components, is a new hypothesis: Effective primary literacy instruction is multifaceted rather than based on one approach or another (e.g., see Adams, 1990; Cazden, 1992; Delpit, 1986; Duffy, 1991; Fisher & Hiebert, 1990; McCaslin, 1989; Pressley, 1994; Stahl et al., 1994). On the basis of available data, however, few details can be added to the generalization that effective instruction often integrates whole language, letter- and word-level teaching, and explicit instruction of comprehension processes. The investigation reported here was designed to provide a window on the details.

We used a research method very different from the hypothetico-deductive approach that has predominated in prior research in this area. Our assumption, consistent with expert theory (Chi, Glaser, & Farr, 1988; Ericsson & Smith, 1991; Hoffmann, 1992), was that effective primary reading teachers would have a privileged understanding of literacy instruction. That is, they would be aware of the elements of their teaching, in part because their teaching is the result of many decisions about what works in their classrooms and what does not. Moreover, we expected that such teachers would be able to relate their knowledge of teaching in response to focused questions, just as other professionals can relate their expertise when questioned (Diaper, 1989; Meyer & Booker, 1991; Scott, Clayton, & Gibson, 1991). Thus, in this study we pursued a detailed description of effective primary reading instruction by surveying reputationally effective primary reading teachers about their instruction.

In doing so, we begin to fill a somewhat surprising gap in the literature. We could find no systematic study of effective primary reading teachers' knowledge about the components that need to be included in primary literacy instruction. There are testimonials about the practice and power of particular approaches to reading instruction, most notably, about whole language (e.g., see Ohanian, 1994; Shannon, 1994; Weaver, 1990; Whitmore & Y. M. Goodman, 1992; see the bibliography in Smith, 1994, for many examples). And entire practitioner journals, such as *Reading Teacher* and *Journal of Reading,* regularly publish the perspectives of certain teachers about specific reading instructional methods. Still, those providing testimonies about or descriptions of particular methods were not selected because of their effectiveness as teachers but, rather, because of the methods that they used in their classrooms. In contrast, in this study a number of teachers were selected on the basis of their perceived effectiveness.

Method

Participants

Our goal in selecting participants was to identify a sample of effective primary-level literacy teachers. We included participants from across the country, to avoid local and regional biases. Fifty reading supervisors were selected randomly from the International Reading Association's list of elementary language arts supervisors. In a letter, they were asked to identify the most effective kindergarten, grade 1, and grade 2 literacy educators in their jurisdiction, with "effective" defined as "successful in educating large proportions of their students to be readers and writers." Forty-five of the supervisors replied to this request, with each nominating one kindergarten, one grade 1, and one grade 2 teacher. As part of the nomination process, the reading supervisors were asked to specify indicators and sources of information informing their opinions of nominated teachers. The possibilities included the following: (a) achievement records of students within a teacher's classes (58% of nominees), (b) conversations in which the nominated teacher has described sound teaching philosophy and practices that the teacher has used in the classroom (96% of nominees), (c) direct observations of the teacher's teaching (88% of nominees), (d) interactions with the teacher during in-service sessions that suggested that the teacher can integrate and apply sound principles of reading instruction (89% of nominees), and (e) positive comments, from other teachers, administrators, or parents, regarding the skills and effectiveness of the teacher (94% of nominees). Nominating supervisors were encouraged to provide additional explanation supporting their positive view of the teacher and were asked to rate their confidence in their evaluation of the teacher, by indicating whether they were (a) absolutely certain, (b) highly confident, (c) confident, (d) somewhat confident, or (e) not confident in their opinion. For all teachers in the study, the nominators supported their nomination with at least three of the indicators and rated their confidence in the nomination as being "absolutely certain" or "highly confident."

Of the 135 teachers nominated, 113 replied to the first-round, short questionnaire sent to them in this study; 86 of these 113 replied to the second and final questionnaire, with 83 of the 86 providing usable responses. The first questionnaire was completed in fall 1992; the second was completed in spring 1993.

Teacher Characteristics

The 83 participants who provided usable responses to the final questionnaire (23 kindergarten teachers, 34 grade 1 teachers, and 26 grade 2 teachers) came from 23 states and represented all major geographic regions of the United States. Forty-two participants held a bachelor's degree only; 41 also held a master's degree. The teachers were generally experienced, with 3–35 years of teaching and a mean of 16.7 years.

School Characteristics

The schools in which participants worked included the diversity of the 1990s American population of school children. For example, the percentage of students in a teacher's school who qualified for free lunch ranged from 0% to 95% (mean = 38%). The percentage of students receiving special education services in these classrooms ranged from 0% to 36% (mean = 10%). Across all of the schools served by participating teachers, 17% of students in the schools in which the teachers taught were African American (classroom range = 0%–100%; eight teachers from majority African American schools), 9% were Mexican American (school range = 0%–81%; four teachers from majority Mexican American schools), 6% were Asian American (school range = 0%–100%), and 7% were native American (school range = 0%–100%; four teachers served majority Native American schools).

Questionnaire

First Short Questionnaire

The overarching goal of the study was to solicit information from the teachers about their literacy instruction. First, all nominated teachers were asked to respond to a short questionnaire requesting three lists of 10 practices that they believed to be "essential in their literacy instruction." Each teacher generated one list for good readers, one for average readers, and one for weaker readers. A letter accompanying this short questionnaire emphasized that the recipients were among a select sample of teachers who had been identified as effective primary reading teachers by their supervisors, and it stated that we were seeking insights into what actually occurs in their classrooms. The response rate to this request was more than 83%: 113 of the 135 nominated teachers responded.

Final Questionnaire

The 300 practices that the teachers cited in response to the short questionnaire were categorized. Some practices were logically related to one another, however—such as some teachers reporting that phonics should never be taught in isolation and others arguing for daily phonics instruction based on workbook exercises. We used all 300 practices to develop a final questionnaire assessing reading and writing instruction, items that teachers could respond to objectively (e.g., measuring the frequency of the teacher's use of an instructional practice, on a seven-point Likert scale from never to several times daily). Every practice cited in response to the initial questionnaire was represented on the final questionnaire. As a means of broadening the categories of response with respect to educational practices that might be targeted at weaker students, we also sent a short survey to a sample of special educators. The special education teachers mentioned a few instructional practices that the regular education teachers did not cite, such as varying instruction with learning style and teaching attending skills. These practices were also assessed on the final questionnaire.

The final questionnaire requested 436 responses of various kinds. It was 27 pages long and was sent to the 113 teachers who responded to the initial questionnaire. The teachers were informed that the survey would require about 45 minutes to complete and were asked to return it within 3 weeks of receiving it. After 3 weeks, we sent a postcard reminder.

The general directions accompanying the questionnaire were the following:

> Many thanks for your reply to the initial round of our survey. The responses we received were exceptionally illuminating. There were so many elements of effective instruction mentioned by teachers, however, that we need to ask more focused questions in order to produce quantifiable data for the survey. The enclosed items are intended to be answered quickly. All of these items are tapping what you know very well, your own instructional practices and thus, we suspect most items will be answered without hesitation on your part. This knowledge that you possess about your primary reading instruction is extremely valuable.

A total of 86 questionnaires were returned (76% response rate). Three returned questionnaires were not usable, however, because they were provided by teachers with teaching assignments other than kindergarten, grade 1, *or* grade 2 (e.g., teaching a combined grades 1–3).

A variety of question types were used, in order to have questions sensitively tapping each practice suggested in the responses to the first questionnaire. In designing questions, we tried to describe practices by using terms that appeared in the responses to the first questionnaire.

Two hundred thirty-one times teachers were asked to check a particular strategy, emphasis, practice, technique, or material if it was present in their classroom. For example, if teachers indicated that they taught concepts of print, they responded to a follow-up item of this type:

> Which of the following concepts of print do you teach? ____none, ____ directionality of print, ____concept of a letter, concept of a word, ____ punctuation, ____ parts of a book, ____ sounds are associated with print. [Such items involving numbers of teachers reporting a practice were analyzed nonparametrically.]

Sixty-six items asked teachers to indicate the frequency of an instructional technique or area of emphasis on eight-point rating scales (e.g., from 0 = never to 7 = several times a day, with midpoint 4 = weekly):

> Do you use "big books"? [scale: never to several times a day]
> After a story, do you ask students "comprehension questions"? [scale: not at all to all stories] [Such items involving numerical values generated by teachers, one value per teacher, were analyzed parametrically.]

Another 65 items asked teachers to estimate the percentage of time or the number of minutes allocated to an activity, as in the following example:

> What percentage of the material read by your students is outstanding children's literature? . . . written at a "controlled" reading level? . . . written to provide practice in phonetic elements and/or patterns . . . high interest, low vocabulary materials?

Thirty-three items requested teachers to categorize their use of instructional practices as "always, sometimes, or never" or "regularly, occasionally, or never," as in the following examples:

> Which of the following extension activities do you use regularly, occasionally, or never?: arts/crafts with print attached, cooking activities, dramatics or puppet plays, drawing or illustrating stories, movement activities, field trips, games.
>   Are home/parents involved in your reading instruction for good readers? . . . average readers? . . . weaker readers?

Forty-three items, such as the following questions, required yes/no responses:

> Do you teach reading across the curriculum?
> Do you teach critical thinking skills?

Sixteen items required a written explanation or clarification of a response, with most of these items requesting "other" responses. (These "other" responses were not informative, for the most part, and they are not included in the results section.) A few of these open-ended questions probed issues that we considered especially important to illuminate, on the basis of review of the first-round lists generated by the teachers. These probes included the following:

> If you consider yourself only somewhat consistent with whole language, please clarify.
>   If . . . .[you teach reading across the curriculum], please describe your practice.
>   [Such items were analyzed both quantitatively and qualitatively.]

For 22 of the items, teachers were required to respond separately for good, average, and weaker students, as illustrated by this example:

> How much of your instructional time in reading involves individual oral reading by students? [Teachers were asked to respond, in terms of minutes, for good, average, and weaker readers.]

Results

We recognized from the outset that the diverse question types on our instrument would preclude many traditional approaches to analyzing questionnaire data, especially ones aggregating over items that assessed related issues. The response distributions to many of the items made aggregation over items untenable anyway (e.g., a number of elements of instruction were endorsed either by most teachers or few teachers, so that responses to the items were not normally distributed). Thus, here in the Results section, we focus on analysis of individual items.

More positively, the responses were striking and orderly for many items—that is, responses did not have the randomness associated with unreliability. In addition, there were many indications that the teachers took great care in responding to the items (e.g., explanations offered about responses in the margins of the questionnaire, all questions answered by most teachers, and extreme neatness in responses). Thus, we concluded that some important sources of error (e.g., carelessness) were probably minimized.

This Results section is organized around issues addressed in the questionnaire, with many issues addressed by several questions and different types of questions. A number of findings are described prosaically in what follows, on the basis of Likert means (e.g., an instructional practice rated 6.72 on a "never" [0] to "several times a day" [7] scale is reported as occurring "several times a day," the whole-number value closest to 6.72).

On the basis of responses to the first, short questionnaire, we expected that the reports would vary by grade level, and they did somewhat. That is, items were analyzed either parametrically or nonparametrically, depending on the type of item, with respect to grade level ($p < .05$ for grade-level effects and all other effects taken up in Results). The most important grade-level differences are summarized in Tables 1 and 2. In general, with increasing grade level, and as students master prereading skills and learn to decode, instruction of higher-

TABLE 1   Classroom Characteristics and Instructional Practices Reported Less Often with Increasing Grade Level

	Kindergarten	Grade 1	Grade 2
Learning Environment:			
Signs and labels (% of teachers)	78	76	46
Learning centers (% of teachers)	100	85	73
General Teaching Processes:			
Letter-recognition drills (% of teachers)	65	26	8
Small-group work and instruction (% of instruction)	....	33	17
Songs (e.g., Alphabet Song) (% of teachers)	100	79	73
Teaching of Reading:			
Teaching Letter Recognition (% of teachers)	100	91	50
Copying/tracing letters (% of instruction)	...	13	2
Teaching alphabetic principle:			
Good readers (% of teachers)	90	75	43
Average readers (% of teachers)	95	81	67
Teaching focusing on sounds of words (% of teachers)	100	85	65
Teaching concepts of print:	Daily	Daily	Weekly
Concept of a letter (% of teachers)	100	85	42
Directions of print (% of teachers)	96	82	42
Phonics drills (% of teachers)	43	21	12
Teaching of phonics using games and puzzles (% of teachers)	91	56	50

Continued

TABLE 1   *Continued*

	Kindergarten	Grade 1	Grade 2
Letter of day/week (% of teachers)	57	18	8
Decoding strategies instruction to weaker readers	...	Daily	Several times a week
Explicit attempts to develop sight word vocabulary:			
Good readers (% of teachers)	...	79	54
Average readers (% of teachers)	83	82	54
Teacher rereading stones	Several times a week	Weekly	Several times year to monthly
Shared big-book reading	Several times a week	Several times a week	Several times a year
Rereading of Big Books:			
Good readers (% of teachers)	100	85	50
Average readers (% of teachers)	100	91	75
Chart stories and poems	...	Several times a week	Monthly
Picture books (% of materials)	46	30	...
Patterned books (% of materials)	32	27	11
	Several times a week	Weekly to several times a week	Monthly
Reading aloud of patterned books (% of teachers)	85	82	54
Controlled reading-level materials	...	40	22
Materials providing practice in reading specific phonetic elements (% of materials)	...	28	8
"Easy" reading (% of reading)	54	33	31
"Frustration"-level reading:			
Good readers	20	11	11
Average readers	21	12	12
Teaching of Writing:			
Student dictation of stories to adults (including whole-class dictation to teacher)	Monthly	Several times a year	Each semester
Shared writing	...	Several times a week	Monthly
Accountability:			
Parent conferences	...	Several times a year	Each semester

*Note: $p < .05$ for each effect summarized in this table. When only two grade levels are indicated in the table, the trend involving third-grade level was in the other direction and not statistically significant.

TABLE 2 Classroom Characteristics and Instructional Practices Reported More Often with Increasing Grade Level

	Kindergarten	Grade 1	Grade 2
General Teaching Processes:			
Round-robin reading	Each semester	Each semester	Several times a year
Individually guided reading for weaker readers (% of reading)	33	53	52
Teaching of Reading:			
Teaching decoding strategies to weaker readers	Several times a week	Daily	. . .
Teaching use of syntax cues for decoding (% of teachers)	35	88	81
Teaching common phonics rules (% of teachers)	13	71	85
Teaching morphemic-structural analysis for decoding (% of teachers)	17	76	92
Teaching syllabification rules for decoding (% of teachers)	0	29	46
Spelling drills (% of teachers)	9	41	69
Spelling tests (% of teachers)	0	65	88
Sight word drills (% of teachers)	35	50	. . .
Teaching comprehension strategies:			
Activating prior knowledge (% of teachers)	70	91	92
Question generation (% of teachers)	57	82	100
Finding main ideas (% of teachers)	61	85	100
Summarization (% of teachers)	70	76	100
Using story grammar cues (% of teachers)	22	58	58
Teaching of the critical thinking skills:			
Webbing (% of teachers)	61	88	96
Identifying causes and effects (% of teachers)	61	94	100
Preteaching of vocabulary (% of teachers)	30	68	69
Choral reading (% of teachers)	57	82	92
Homework (% of teachers)	32	79	85
Student reading aloud to other people	Weekly	Several times a week	Several times a week
Student reading aloud:			
Poetry (% of teachers)	60	85	88
Trade books (% of teachers)	40	91	. . .
Basal stories (% of teachers)	10	67	73
Silent reading	11 minutes daily	17 minutes daily	21 minutes daily
Chapter books (% of materials)	3	7	12

Continued

TABLE 2   *Continued*

	Kindergarten	Grade 1	Grade 2
Basal use (frequency, % of materials)	Each semester, 2	Monthly 22	Monthly 21
Controlled-reading level materials (% of materials)	24	40	...
Materials providing practice with specific phonetic elements (% of materials)	10	28	...
"Instructional"-level reading:			
Average readers (% of reading)	45	60	...
Weaker readers (% of reading)	40	50	55
Teaching of Writing:			
Student story writing (% of teachers)	61	94	96
Writing in response to reading	Several times a year	Weekly	Weekly
Planning before writing (% of teachers)	48	82	92
Revising during writing (% of teachers)	13	71	88
Publishing story collections (% of teachers)	27	59	69
Teaching punctuation:	52	88	96
Out of context (% of all teaching of punctuation)	5	9	27
Accountability:			
Writing portfolios (% of teachers)	48	79	85

Note: $p < .05$ for each effect summarized in this table. When only two grade levels are indicated in the table, the trend involving third-grade level was in the other direction and not statistically significant.

order competencies was reported more often. Analogously, reports of picture books and patterned books gave way to reports of more sophisticated materials with advancing grade. Also, teachers claimed greater attention to mechanics, such as punctuation and spelling, with grades 1 and 2 students than with kindergarten students. There was also increased reporting of planning and editing of writing, from kindergarten to grade 2. Although, with increasing grade, there were more reports of traditional approaches to instruction—such as round-robin reading, use of basals, spelling tests, and homework—the teachers did not report these approaches as predominating in their classrooms but, rather, as blended with many other components. Important differences in grade-level reports are highlighted in what follows.

In responses to the first questionnaire, there were reports of some differences in the explicitness and extensiveness of instruction, as a function of student reading achievement. Thus, 32 of the final survey items requested teachers to estimate the explicitness and/or extensiveness of their instruction, separately for good, average, and weaker readers. For the most part, statistical analyses of these items suggested similar instruction for students, regardless of ability, although there were also some differences as a function of student ability, summarized in Table 3. In general, more explicit/extensive instruction was reported

TABLE 3   Instructional Practices Reported as More Explicit/Extensive for Weaker Compared to Stronger Readers

	Good	Average	Weaker
Grade 1:			
Activities requiring students to focus on the sounds of words	Weekly	Weekly	Several times a week
Teaching of letter-sound associations (% of teachers)	71	85	97
Individually guided writing (% of teachers)	25	31	37
Decoding-strategies instruction	Several times a week	Several times a week	Daily
Grades 1 and 2:			
Teaching of the alphabetic principle (% of teachers):			
Grade 1	71	76	100
Grade 2	35	54	77
Teaching of visual discrimination (% of teachers):			
Grade 1	65	74	85
Grade 2	65	88	92
Teaching of alphabetic recognition (% of teachers):			
Grade 1	35	50	91
Grade 2	12	15	46
Grade 2:			
Teaching of auditory discrimination (% of teachers)	65	88	92
Development of sight vocabulary (% of teachers)	54	54	85
Rereading of big books (% of teachers)	46	69	77
Individual oral reading	16 minutes daily	16 minutes daily	25 minutes daily

Note: $p < .05$ per effect.

for weaker readers, with respect to letter- and word-level skills such as decoding and sight word learning. Nonetheless, we emphasize that the reported instruction differences as a function of reader ability were few.

General Characteristics of Learning Environments

Teachers described classrooms filled with print. All teachers in the sample indicated that they attempted to create a literate environment in their classrooms, including an in-class library. All but one claimed to display student work in the room. All but three teachers reported chart stories and chart poems. Most (71%) reported posting of word lists and use of signs/labels in the classroom (67%; for grade-level differences, however, see Table 1). The teachers reported learning centers (i.e., listening, reading, or writing centers), although their use declined with advancing grade level.

These classrooms were rich with stories. On average, the teachers reported reading to their students daily, with rereading less common and decreasing with increasing grade level. The teachers reported telling stories to students, weekly on average. Sixty-six percent reported audiotaped stories, and 33% prerecorded videotaped stories.

When asked whether they were whole language teachers, 54% responded yes and 43% claimed that they were somewhat whole language teachers. One possibility that we explored was that reported instruction might have been different among those teachers claiming to be wholly committed to whole language than among teachers less committed. For each grade level, we examined the correlations between teacher commitment to whole language and all other variables. There was one striking, consistent correlation, across grades, between commitment to whole language and reported practice: Fully committed whole language teachers were less likely to use basals than were less committed teachers, $r = .49$ at kindergarten, $r = .59$ at grade 1, and $r = .66$ at grade 2.

General Teaching Processes

Participants in this study reported applying many effective conventional instructional methods in the service of literacy education.

Modeling
The teachers reported overt modeling of reading for students on a daily basis; that is, they reported reading aloud for students, making clear to them what is meant by reading. They also reported overt modeling of comprehension strategies several times a week, and modeling of the writing process weekly. The love of reading was reported as modeled daily, the love of writing as modeled weekly.

Practice and Repetition
Practice of isolated skills (e.g., on a computer, skill sheets, workbooks, and songs) was estimated as averaging 13% of the literacy instructional day. The majority (59%) of the sample reported using drills, with drilling for letter recognition—which decreased with increasing grade level—and for phonics/letter-sound association, and spelling—which increased with increasing grade level.

Grouping
The teachers reported a combination of whole-group, small-group, and individual instruction, as well as individual seatwork, as part of the literacy instructional day. More whole-group instruction (about half of total instruction) was reported than small-group instruction, which varied with grade level—it was about a third of instruction at kindergarten and grade 1 and about a sixth of instruction at grade 2. More small-group instruction was claimed than individual instruction, reported as about one-sixth of total literacy instruction. The teachers

believed that only about 10% of their students' time was spent in seatwork. They reported cooperative grouping for 46% of their instruction on average.

Notably, some traditional approaches to primary literacy grouping were not endorsed. Of the 55 teachers indicating use of ability grouping, only 19 reported use of the traditional three-group approach (i.e., high, medium, and low reading groups). Round-robin reading was reported as occurring rarely (i.e., once a month), although slightly more in grades 1 and 2 than in kindergarten.

Sensitivity to Students and Individual Student Needs

The teachers claimed sensitivity to student needs. For instance, 96% of the teachers indicated that they permitted progress in literacy at students' own paces, with 89% reportedly attempting to assess the learning styles of their students and with 92% reportedly attempting to adjust instruction to students' learning style. The teachers claimed that 46% of their total instructional time involved mini lessons, targeted at "things students needed to know at this moment." The teachers estimated that they spent 17% of their instructional time in reteaching the entire class and 21% of their instructional time in reteaching small groups or individual students. Grades 1 and 2 teachers reported that, for weaker students, the majority of instruction involved individually guided reading.

Integration with Other Curricula and Activites

The teachers reported that literacy instruction was integrated with the rest of the curriculum: 93% indicated that reading instruction occurred across the curriculum; the corresponding figure for writing was 88%; for listening, 88%; and for speaking, 75%. Ninety-four percent reported the use of themes extending to other parts of the curriculum to organize reading and writing instruction. In response to an open-ended question, teachers mentioned reading as part of science instruction (35%), social studies (31%), and math (23%), with another 11% simply claiming that reading instruction occurred in all content areas.

All teachers reported using extension activities. These included arts and crafts associated with print experiences, illustration of stories read, games, cooking, and movement activities.

Teaching of Reading

What Is Taught

When asked to divide a total of 100% of their literacy instruction into the percentage dedicated to meaning-making versus decoding, meaning-making predominated, by 71%–27%. This translated into the teaching of the content and processes summarized in this subsection.

Thus, more than 89% of the teachers reported teaching skills and knowledge prerequisite to reading, such as auditory discrimination skills, visual discrimination skills, concepts of print (e.g., punctuation, print-sound association, parts of a book, concept of a word; see Table 1 for grade-level differences, however), and letter-sound associations. Some very basic skills were taught by most kindergarten teachers but were much less prominent with increasing grade. These included letter-recognition activities and copying/tracing of letters. Especially important, the proportion of teachers claiming to teach the alphabetic principle—that all 26 letter symbols are worth learning because each stands for sounds in spoken words (Adams, 1990)—declined with increasing grade. Consistent with the decline with increasing grade in teaching of the alphabetic principle, with advancing grade level there were fewer reports of activities requiring focus on the sounds of words.

An important finding was that, for every basic skill, the majority of teachers who reported teaching it claimed to do so in the context of actual reading and writing. Even so, for every basic skill except concepts of print, at least 88% of the teachers who reported teaching the skill also reported some isolated skills instruction, most often involving games and puzzles to teach the skill or to provide practice with it.

The teachers reported that teaching of decoding strategies and word-level skills and knowledge occurred at least several times a week. Several decoding strategies were reported as taught by most teachers: using context cues to decode words (98% of teachers), using picture cues to decode words (96%), and sounding out words by using letter-sound knowledge (92%). Other strategies were taught little in kindergarten but much more by grade 2: (a) using syntax cues to decode words; (b) using common phonics rules; (c) using morphemic structural analysis clues, including prefixes, suffixes, and base words; and (d) syllabification rules.

The commitment to teaching decoding also came through in the response to questions about the explicit teaching of phonics, which 95% of the teachers said they did. Teachers reported that they used a variety of procedures for doing so, most prominently (a) in the context of real reading (90% of teachers), (b) during discussion of sounds as part of writing (84%), and (c) through invented spelling (84%). Teaching of phonics outside the context of natural reading was reported as well, however, with 43% of the teachers claiming use of workbooks and skill sheets and with 32% reporting use of a phonics program. At least half of teachers at each grade reported use of games and puzzles to teach phonics, although the proportions of teachers claiming to do so decreased with advancing grade. Only at kindergarten level was use of the letter-of-the-day or -week approach reported by a majority of teachers. The teachers decided which phonics elements to teach either according to class/small-group needs (77% of teachers), individual student needs (74%), the sequence prescribed in a basal series or phonics program (40%), or the sequence in a scope-and-sequence chart (14%). In short, there was much more commitment to teaching of phonics in ways that were consistent with ongoing reading and writing and with students' needs during reading and writing than to teaching phonics in isolation, although there were reports of phonics instruction in isolation and/or as prescribed by a standard approach.

The reported explicit teaching of spelling increased with grade level, for example, as reflected in increased reporting of spelling drills and tests with advancing grade. Grades 1 and 2 teachers indicated diverse sources for words tested, including published spelling curricula (38% of teachers), words selected from basal or other stories (33%), items selected from students' writing (30%), lists (Dolch or Chall) of frequently used words (27%), a district-developed spelling program (17%), and student self-selected words (14%). When teachers were asked to respond to the open-ended item "How do you react to children's invented spellings?" all teachers indicated at least acceptance of invented spellings much of the time. Even so, at times, correct spellings were expected. Thus, 11 of the grade 2 teachers indicated, in response to an open-ended question about spelling, that correct spelling (e.g., of high-frequency words) was expected in final drafts of writing for publication.

The teachers (96%) reported explicitly attempting to develop new vocabulary. Most (95%) reported that they did so in the context of other reading and writing, a claim consistent with other claims, including 93% of the teachers reporting that new vocabulary came from stories read in class and 65% of the teachers reporting instruction of vocabulary that students wanted to use in their writing.

Most teachers reported attempting explicitly to develop sight word vocabulary, although less so for good and average readers with advancing grade level. Most teachers (87%) who attempted to develop sight word competence reported doing so in the context of other reading and writing activities. Nonetheless, there were also reports of isolated development of vocabulary, for example, by sight word drilling, which was reported more by grade 1 teachers than by kindergarten teachers.

Critical to meaning-making is comprehension, including understanding of text elements, with 96% of the teachers reporting that they taught text elements and with at least three-quarters of the teachers reporting instruction in each text element (i.e., theme/main idea, details vs. main idea, plot, sequencing, cause-and-effect relations in stories, story mapping/webbing, character analysis, and the idea of the illustrator as an interpreter of a story).

All teachers reported that they taught comprehension strategies, with this commitment holding for readers of all ability levels. A dramatic finding was that all teachers at all grades reported teaching prediction. Seventy-three percent reported teaching visualization as a strategy. Other comprehension strategies (i.e., activating prior knowledge, asking questions, delineating the main idea, summarization, and looking for story grammar elements) were reported more frequently with advancing grade.

All teachers claimed to teach critical thinking strategies. More than 93% reported teaching brainstorming, categorizing, and recalling details. At least the majority reported teaching students how to make distinctions, how to make evaluations, webbing, and identifying causes and effects, with the latter two strategies increasingly endorsed with increasing grade.

Because possession of background knowledge is critical to understanding text, it is notable that teachers reported that they attempted to develop students' background knowledge, on average, for more than half the stories that they covered (i.e., through prereading discussion, related reading, hands-on experiences, or videos/movies). They indicated developing students' understanding of important concepts (e.g., through preteaching of vocabulary) before or as they encountered them in a story, again for more than half the stories on average. The proportion of teachers endorsing such preteaching increased with advancing grade.

Types of Reading and Reading-Related Activities

Teachers reported involving students in many types of reading experiences. The percentage of teachers reporting choral reading increased with grade, as did the percentage of teachers assigning reading homework. Most (i.e., 90% or more) of the teachers reported the following activities: shared reading, including reading along with big books (see Table 1, however, for evidence of grade-level differences); student read-alouds to peers, teachers, other adults, or older and younger children—an activity increasing in frequency with advancing grade level—of poetry, trade books, and basals; student rereadings of stories, books, and big books; silent reading (increasing in frequency with advancing grade level); and student discussions of stories and literature. Many teachers (69%) reported student book sharing as part of literacy instruction—for example, in the form of book reports or informal comments to other students about books that they have read.

What Is Read

The teachers on average reported that 73% of the reading in their classrooms was of out-standing children's literature. In contrast, only 6% was described as expository material, reflecting a heavy bias toward narratives and other clearly literary genres. The teachers reported that a mean of 12%, of their reading was of poems.

Picture books and predictable books declined in prominence with advancing grade. Chapter books increased in occurrence, from kindergarten to grade 2, as did the percentage of reading from basal materials. Reported basal use was highly variable, however, ranging from no use of basals to daily use of them. (See the earlier result relating basal use to whole-language commitment.) Consistent with the reported use of basals, which often attempt to use controlled vocabulary and provide practice in specific phonetic elements, the teachers reported that a nontrivial proportion of reading was of materials with a controlled reading level: 24% of reading materials in kindergarten, 40% in grade 1, and 22% in grade 2. The teachers also reported some reading of material designed to provide practice with specific phonetic elements: 10%, of the materials read in kindergarten, 28% in grade 1, and 8% in grade 2.

In this study, one traditional way of classifying what students read was telling—the percentage of easy, instruction-, and frustration-level reading. In general, the percentage of easy reading decreased with increasing grade level. Although there was relatively little frustration-level reading reported, also reported were decreases in frustration-level reading with increasing grade. Reports of instruction-level reading increased with grade.

The teachers indicated that they used author studies (i.e., several pieces by the same author, with background information about the author, author's style, etc.), but for less than half of what is read. Ninety-four percent of the teachers indicated that they tried to teach their students about the illustrators of stories and texts.

Teaching of Writing

Types of Writing

Most teachers (86%) reported that their students wrote stories and developed written responses to readings, with both of these responses increasing in frequency with increasing grade level. Eighty-seven percent of the teachers reported journal writing by their students, several times a week on average. Students were reported as writing poems only a few times a year.

Composition activities were not precluded in kindergarten simply because students lacked translation skills: kindergarten teachers reported that student dictation of stories to other people occurred once a month on average. They also reported that whole-class dicta-tion of stories to the teacher as scribe occurred about once a month on average. Such dicta-tions were reported as less frequent in grades 1 and 2.

Just as shared reading was reported, so was shared writing (see Table 1). A majority of the teachers reported that they encourage home reading, and 59%, reported that they encourage home writing.

Teaching the Writing Process

Teachers claimed to encourage planning before writing, increasingly from kindergarten to grade 2. Teaching of revising—for example, through student-teacher and peer editing conferences—was also reported more often with advancing grade level. All but one kindergarten teacher and five grade 1 teachers reported some publication of students' work.

The majority of respondents at each grade level reported teaching mechanics, for example, punctuation, with such teaching reported more frequently with advancing grade. Most teaching of punctuation was reported as occurring in context, with the percentage of out-of-context instruction of punctuation increasing with advancing grade, however. A minority (30%) of teachers reported using the computer as part of writing instruction.

Making Literacy and Literacy Instruction Motivating

The teachers reported extensive efforts to make literacy and literacy instruction motivating. In general, the teachers strongly endorsed (i.e., there was a mean rating of at least 5 on a seven-point scale) the following practices: (a) classroom as a risk-free environment; (b) positive feedback; (c) conveying the importance of reading/writing in life; (d) setting an exciting mood for reading, adding color and humor, and so on; (e) encouraging an, "I can read, I can write" attitude; (f) accepting where the child is right now and working to improve literacy from that point, (g) conveying the goal of every lesson and why the lesson is important to students; (h) encouraging students to find and read stories/books that they like, as part of the literacy program (i.e., self-selection of materials that are read); (i) encouraging students' ownership of their reading, by having them make for themselves many decisions about what to read; (j) encouraging personal interpretations of text; (k) selecting class reading materials on the basis of students' interest; and (l) encouraging student ownership of writing (e.g., students' selection of writing topics).

Accountability

Most teachers (i.e., more than 88%) reported regular checks of student comprehension of stories heard and read, by asking students questions after most readings and by requesting students to retell stories. Reading portfolios were reported by 34% of the teachers. Writing portfolios were reported by many more teachers, however, and were reported increasingly with advancing grade level. On average the teachers claimed to communicate with home about student literacy progress once a month. All but three of the teachers reported regular conferences with parents (i.e., at least two a year; see Table 1).

Discussion

The teachers in this study reported an integration of literacy instructional components, many of which enjoy empirical support as improving particular aspects of literacy: it is notable that the teachers reported doing much to create classroom environments supportive of literacy, because placing young children in environments that invite and support literacy stimulates them to do things that are literate (e.g., see Morrow, 1990, 1991; Neuman & Roskos, 1990, 1992). The teachers' claimed commitments to outstanding literature are sensible, given the increasing evidence that, when such literature drives instruction, there are positive effects on students' autonomous use of literature and on their attitudes toward reading (e.g., see Morrow, 1992; Morrow, O'Connor, & Smith, 1990). The literature emphasis reported by the teachers in this study is also striking in light of increasing evidence (e.g., see Feitelson, Kita, & Goldstein, 1986; Morrow, 1992) that consistent experiences with high-quality literature foster growth in understanding the structure of stories, which improves both comprehension and writing, as well as the sophistication of children's language. Just as broad reading expands the knowledge of adults (Stanovich & Cunningham, 1993), extensive experiences with stories expand children's knowledge of the world, as reflected, for example, by breadth of vocabulary (e.g., see Elley, 1989; Robbins & Ehri, 1994).

The claimed attention to the alphabetic principle, development of letter-sound associations, and activities focusing on the sounds of words makes sense in view of the clear associations between such instruction and success in reading (Adams, 1990) and other competencies, such as spelling (e.g., see Ball & Blachman, 1991; Lie, 1991; Nelson, 1990; Tangel & Blachman, 1992; Uhry & Shepherd, 1993). The respondents' reported modeling and explaining of literacy skills and strategies are also sound, for consistent use of these techniques has long-term positive effects on literacy achievement (Duffy et al., 1986, 1987; Duffy, Roehler, & Herrmann, 1988).

That writing was reported as involving instruction to plan, draft, and revise also is sensible: a growing body of data substantiates that children's composing abilities and understanding of writing increase substantially as a function of such instruction (Graham & Harris, 1994).

Primary-level language arts classrooms vary greatly in the extent to which they motivate children's literacy (e.g., see Turner, 1993). Thus, it is striking that sample teachers reported great commitment to motivation of literacy. Each of the 12 items on the final questionnaire pertaining to motivation of literacy received a mean rating near the top of the scale on which it was rated, with very low variability. That is, this sample of teachers claimed to do much to stimulate their students' engagement in reading and writing, from providing immediate positive feedback to fostering long-term beliefs that students can become good readers and writers.

What is also interesting is what was downplayed. Some common classroom instructional elements that have been criticized as potentially undermining reading achievement (e.g., see Allington, 1983; Hiebert, 1983) were reported as infrequent by the sample. For example, little ability-based reading grouping was reported, a practice that probably does not promote student achievement (Slavin, 1987) and that can, in some cases, affect it adversely during the primary years (e.g., see Juel, 1990). Also, the survey teachers did not report round-robin reading as the predominant type of reading but, rather, claimed a variety of types of reading, consistent with the perspective that different types of classroom reading stimulate improvements in different abilities (e.g., see Freppon, 1991; Hoffman, 1987; Reutzel, Hollingsworth, & Eldredge, 1994).

In short, a number of contemporary reading-instructional theorists have argued for balanced reading instruction, meaning the meshing of holistic literacy experiences and skills instruction (e.g., see Adams, 1990; Cazden, 1992; Delpit, 1986; Duffy, 1991; Fisher & Hiebert, 1990; McCaslin, 1989; Pressley, 1994; Stahl et al., 1994). Consistent with that outlook, the teachers in this study depicted their classrooms as integrating the attractive features of whole language with explicit skills. (See Groff, 1991, for complementary data.)

Education of Students Experiencing Difficulties

Although the teachers reported delivering a common curriculum to their students, they also claimed to tailor instruction to individual differences. The teachers' commitment to meeting the needs of individual students came through most clearly with respect to their stance on the literacy education of students experiencing difficulties in learning to read and write. In recent years the literacy instruction offered to weaker readers has been criticized, with observers such as Allington (1991) arguing that weaker readers are often given heavy doses of lower-order, skills-oriented instruction aimed at improving decoding only, with a concomitant reduction in instruction aimed at promoting higher-order meaning-making (e.g., see Bean, Cooley, Eichelberger, Lazar, & Zigmond, 1991). Such compensatory instruction is often disconnected from the curriculum that stronger students experience.

That is not what this sample of teachers claimed to do for their weaker students, however. Although the teachers reported attending more to lower-order skills with weaker readers compared with good readers, there were few differences in instruction reported for good, average, and weaker readers. The teachers depicted their instruction as providing the more explicit lowerorder (i.e., letter- and word-level) instruction that weaker students need without sacrificing weaker students' exposure to and experiences with good literature or their introduction to higher-order skills and strategies. Compensatory instruction for weaker students was described as integrated with the curriculum received by all students. (See Wendler, Samuels, & Moore, 1989, for complementary data that exceptional literacy teachers are especially attuned to providing assistance to students on an as-needed basis.)

Implications for Teacher Education

On the basis of the data reported here, a case can be made that a teacher's education should include exposure to a number of approaches and practices intermingling different types of instruction. As Duffy (1991, pp. 13–14) put it: "I think we do better by teaching teachers multiple alternatives, by teaching them how to network these so they can be accessed appropriately when needed, and by helping them understand that teaching demands fluid, multiple-dimensional responses to an infinite number of classroom situations, not narrow, uni-directional responses.... I want [teachers]... to select among theories and procedures according to their judgement about what the situation calls for." Duffy (1991) came to this conclusion after his immersion in an elementary teaching community for a year, as he studied teaching and teacher change. His perspective was informed by classroom observations and interviews with teachers. We come to the same conclusion, on the basis of information from the participants in the detailed survey summarized here.

Caveats, Potential Limitations, and Future Research

The data obtained in this survey were very orderly. Such orderliness is striking, in light of potential criticisms of a survey of instruction conducted at a distance from actual teaching. First, it could be argued that the criteria for selecting teachers would translate differently in different settings. If our selection criteria had been ineffective, what would be expected would be a sample of teachers widely varying in ability and effectiveness. Such a variable sample might be expected to produce highly variable outcomes, which is not what we obtained. A similar criticism that could be made is that some terms of reference in the survey—terms such as "whole language" and "good," "average," and "weaker" readers—might have had different meanings for different participants. Such a criticism is not consistent, however, with outcomes obtained here. For example, teachers identifying themselves as fully committed to whole language reported that they do not use basals as much as do those teachers who were somewhat committed to whole language, an outcome that would be expected. Our use of the terms "good," "average," and "weaker" readers was not so ambiguous as to preclude teachers from reporting more explicit and extensive teaching of lower-order skills to weaker compared with other readers, consistent with many observations in the reading-instructional literature (e.g., see Harris & Sipay, 1990). In short, although there was certainly some fuzziness in the meanings of some terms in this survey, that is because ideas such as whole language and reading ability classifications are fuzzy concepts. Fuzzy concepts typically can be understood, however, even if precise meanings are elusive (e.g., see Mancuso & Eimer, 1982), and we believe that the orderliness in outcomes obtained in this study suggests that teachers understood the terms in the survey. We carefully designed the questions to describe practices as the teachers themselves, in response to the first, open-ended questionnaire, described the practices.

Another potential concern is that, by relying on nominations from supervisors who are members of the International Reading Association (IRA), the bias would be too much in favor of some literacy perspectives that the supervisors perceived to be favored by the IRA—whole language philosophy in particular. Three realities must be confronted in reflecting on this criticism. First, without a doubt, whole language is one of the main conceptions of reading that is driving primary literacy instruction in North America in the 1990s (see Symons, Woloshyn, & Pressley, 1994), and thus it is hard to imagine a sampling procedure that would not produce many supervisors or teachers who were not extensively exposed to whole language and frequently committed to some version of it. Second, the members of the IRA are diverse in their outlook. The IRA includes the most prominent proponents of a number of instructional practices and perspectives that conflict with the tenets of whole language. Moreover, publications of the IRA reflect diversity of perspective about literacy instruction, more than unanimity with respect to any one stance, including whole language. Our interaction with professionals working in schools who are members of the IRA, most of whom are language arts supervisors, indicates that the grass-roots members are analogously diverse in their outlooks. Third, the criticism that this study may have been biased toward extremism of any type would have to explain away one of the principal findings—that there was balance in perspective, reflected throughout the reports. The teachers in this survey reported integration of diverse practices as part of literacy instruction. Moreover, the teachers claimed many instructional practices not consistent with whole language philosophy, such as isolated skills instruction and, for many, some use of basal readers (e.g., see Weaver, 1990).

One strength of the survey approach used here was that the questions on the final instrument were based on teachers' responses to the initial survey. That is, all practices probed on the final survey were mentioned in responses to the preliminary survey. A weakness of this approach is that there were other practices that teachers did not cite initially, ones that are common in education but that are not considered effective by outstanding teachers. For example, in the preliminary round, no teachers cited pull-out remediation instruction as important in their instruction of weaker readers. It seems likely that such instruction occurs in at least some of the classrooms served by the teachers participating in this survey study. We expect that our future final surveys will largely be teacher driven but that we will also be more proactive in attempting to generate potential teaching elements not identified initially by teachers, in order to tap a fuller range of issues about instruction than we tapped in this survey.

Surveying can provide information about many elements of instruction—but not much insight into teachers' unique implementations of the elements: Might effective teachers be especially talented at story telling, modeling reading and writing processes, communicating with parents, or any of the other elements of instruction? Surveying also does not generate much information about how elements of instruction are blended—either how teachers plan their lessons and, hence, anticipate mixing elements or how they make instructional decisions while they teach and, thus, combine the elements of instruction from minute to minute. Finally, some who remain unconvinced that verbal reports can reflect actual behavior well are reluctant to make *any* inferences about teaching that are based on teachers' questionnaire responses.

For all of those reasons, we are now observing and interviewing a smaller sample of effective primary literacy teachers. What is reported here is the first of what we hope will be converging data about effective primary literacy instruction, data generated by using multiple methods, What the methods across this program of research will have in common, however, will be a focus on effective literacy teachers. With regard to beginning reading instruction, we believe that the great debates to come will be better informed than the great debates of the past— if the debaters know a great deal about the teaching of effective literacy teachers.

Note.   *This research was funded in part by the National Reading Research Center, an Office of Educational Research and Improvement, U.S. Department of Education, research and development center, headquartered at the University of Maryland and the University of Georgia. Authors Pressley and Rankin are principal investigators of the center. Additional funding was provided by the University at Albany, State University of New York (in the form of a graduate stipend and tuition for Linda Yokoi), and the University of Nebraska. The opinions in this article are ours and do not represent the views of the funding agencies. Nazy Kaffashan assisted with the data analysis, and Jennifer Mistretta and Ruth Wharton-McDonald commented on the manuscript as it was being prepared, in part as they prepared to conduct follow-up research documenting effective grade 1 literacy instruction more fully. Correspondence regarding this article and the research program in general can be directed to Michael Pressley, Department of Educational Psychology and Statistics, University at Albany, SUNY, Albany, NY 12222.*

References

Adams, M. J. (1990). *Beginning to read.* Cambridge MA: Harvard University Press.

Allington, R. L. (1983). The reading instruction provided readers of differing reading abilities. *Elementary School Journal, 83,* 548–559.

Allington, R. L. (1991). The legacy of "Slow it down and make it more concrete." In J. Zutell & S. McCormick (Eds.), *Learner factors/ teacher factors: Issues in literacy research and instruction: Fortieth yearbook of the National Reading Conference* (pp. 19–29) Chicago: National Reading Conference.

Ball, E. W., & Blachman, B. A. (1991). Does phoneme awareness training in kindergarten make a difference in early word recognition and developmental spelling? *Reading Research Quarterly, 26,* 49–66.

Barr, R. (1984). Beginning reading instruction: From debate to reformation. In P. D. Pearson (Ed.), *Handbook of reading research* (pp. 545–581). New York: Longman.

Bean, R. M., Cooley, W. W., Eichelberger, T., Lazar, M. K., & Zigmond, N. (1991). In class or pullout: Effects of setting on the remedial reading program. *Journal of Reading Behavior, 23,* 445–464.

Bereiter, C., & Bird, M. (1985). Use of thinking aloud in identification and teaching of reading comprehension strategies. *Cognition and Instruction, 2,* 131–156.

Bond, C. L., & Dykstra, R. (1967). The cooperative research program in the first-grade reading instruction. *Reading Research Quarterly, 2,* 5–142.

Brown, A. L., Bransford, J. D., Ferrara, R. A., & Campione, J. C. (1983). Learning, remembering, and understanding. In J. H. Flavell & E. M. Markman (Eds.), *Handbook of child psychology,* Vol. **3.** *Cognitive development* (pp. 77–166). New York: Wiley.

Brown, R., Pressley, M., Van Meter, P., & Schuder, T. (1995). *A quasi-experimental validation of transactional strategies instruction with previously low-achieving grade-2 readers.* Manuscript submitted for publication, University at Buffalo, State University of New York, Department of Educational and Counseling Psychology.

Cazden, C. (1992). *Whole language plus: Essays on literacy in the United States and New Zealand.* New York: Teachers College Press.

Chall, J. S. (1967). *Learning to read: The great debate.* New York: McGraw-Hill.

Chi, M. T. H., Glaser, R., & Farr, M. J. (Eds.). (1988). *The nature of expertise.* Hillsdale, NJ: Erlbaum.

Delpit, L. D. (1986). Skills and other dilemmas of a progressive black educator. *Harvard Educational Review, 56,* 379–385.

Diaper, D. (Ed.). (1989). *Knowledge elicitation: Principles, techniques, and applications.* New York: Wiley.

Duffy, G. G. (1991). What counts in teacher education? Dilemmas in educating empowered teachers. In J. Zutell & S. McCormick (Eds.), *Learner factors/teacher factors: Issues in literacy research and instruction: Fortieth yearbook of the National Reading Conference* (pp. 1–18). Chicago: National Reading Conference.

Duffy, C., Roehler, I., & Herrmann, G. (1988). Modeling mental processes helps poor readers become strategic readers. *Reading Teacher, 41,* 762–767.

Duffy, G. G., Roehler, L. R., Meloth, M., Vavrus, L., Book, C., Putnam, J., & Wesselman, R. (1986). The relationship between explicit verbal explanation during reading skill instruction and student awareness and achievement: A study of reading teacher effects. *Reading Research Quarterly, 21,* 237–252.

Duffy, G. G., Roehler, L. R., Sivan, E., Rackliffe, G., Book, C., Meloth, M., Vavrus, L., Wesselman, R., Putnam, J., & Bassiri, D. (1987). Effects of explaining the reasoning associated with using reading strategies. *Reading Research Quarterly, 22,* 347–368.

Dykstra, R. (1968). Summrary of the second grade phase of the Cooperative Research Program in primary reading instruction. *Reading Research Quarterly, 4,* 49–70.

Elley, W. B. (1989). Vocabulary acquisition from listening to stories. *Reading Research Quarterly, 24,* 174–187.

Ericsson, K. A., & Smith, J. (Eds.). (1991). *Toward a general theory of expertise.* Cambridge: Cambridge University Press.

Feitelson, D., Kita, B., & Goldstein, Z. (1986). Effects of listening to series stories on first graders' comprehension and use of language. *Research in the Teaching of English,* **20,** 339–356.

Fisher, C. W., & Hiebert, E. H. (1990). Characteristics of tasks in two approaches to literacy instruction. *Elementary School Journal, 91,* 3–18.

Flesch, R. (1955). *Why Johnny can't read.* New York: Harper & Row.

Foorman, B. R. (1994). The relevance of a connectionist model of reading for "The great debate." *Educational Psychology Review, 6,* 25–47.

Freppon, P. A. (1991). Children's concepts of the nature and purpose of reading in different instructional settings. *Journal of Reading Behavior, 23,* 139–163.

Goodman, K. S., & Goodman, Y. M. (1979). Learning to read is natural. In L. B. Resnick & P. A. Weaver (Eds.), *Theory and practice of early reading* (Vol. **1,** pp. 137–154). Hillsdale, NJ: Erlbaum.

Goodman, Y. M. (Ed.). (1990). *How children construct literacy: Piagetian persrectives.* Newark, DE: International Reading Association.

Graham, S., & Harris, K. R. (1994). The effects of whole language on children's writing: A review of literature. *Educational Psychologist, 29,* 187–192.

Groff, P. (1991). Teachers' opinions of the whole language approach to reading instruction. *Annals of Dyslexia, 41,* 83–95.

Guthrie, J. T., & Tyler, S. J. (1978). Cognition and instruction of poor readers. *Journal of Reading Behavior, 10,* 57–78.

Harris, A. J., & Sipay, E. R. (1990). *How to increase reading ability: A guide to developmental and remedial methods.* New York: Longman.

Hiebert, F. H. (1983). An examination of ability grouping for reading instruction. *Reading Research Quarterly, 18,* 231–255.

Hoffman, J. V. (1987). Rethinking the role of oral reading in basal instruction. *Elementary School Journal, 87,* 367–373.

Hoffmann, R. R. (1992). *The psychology of expertise: Cognitive research and empirical AI.* New York: Springer-Verlag.

Juel, C. (1990). Effects of reading group assignment on reading development in first and second grade. *Journal of Reading Behavior, 22,* 233–254.

King, D. F., & Goodman, K. S. (1990). Whole language: Cherishing learners and their language. *Language, Speech, and Hearing Services in Schools, 21,* 221–227.

Lie, A. (1991). Effects of a training program for stimulating skills in word analysis in firstgrade children. *Reading Research Quarterly, 26,* 234–250.

Mancuso, J. C., & Eimer, B. N. (1982). Fitting things into categories. In J. C. Mancuso & J. R. Adams-Webber (Eds.), *The construing person* (pp. 130–151). New York: Praeger.

Mather, N. (1992). Whole language reading instruction for students with learning disabilities: Caught in the cross fire. *Learning Disabilities Research & Practice, 7,* 87–95.

McCaslin, M. M. (1989). Whole language: Theory, instruction, and future implementation. *Elementary School Journal, 90,* 223–229.

Meyer, M., & Booker, J. (1991). *Eliciting and analyzing expert judgement: A practical tour.* London: Academic Press.

Morrow, L. M. (1990). Preparing the classroom environment to promote literacy during play. *Early Childhood Research Quarterly, 5,* 937–554.

Morrow, L. M. (1991). Relationships among physical designs of play centers, teachers' emphasis on literacy in play, and children's literacy behaviors during play. In J. Zu-tell & S. McCormick (Eds.), *Learner factors/teacher factors: Issues in literacy research and instruction: Fortieth yearbook of the National Reading Conference* (pp. 127–140). Chicago: National Trading Conference.

Morrow, L. M. (1992). The impact of a literature-based program on literacy achievement, use of literature, and attitudes of children from minority backgrounds. *Reading Research Quarterly, 27,* 251–275.

Morrow, L. M., O'Connor, E. M., & Smith, J. K. (1990). Effects of a story reading program on the literacy development of at-risk kindergarten children. *Journal of Reading Behavior, 22,* 255–275.

Nelson, L. (1990). The influence of phonics instruction on spelling progress. In J. Zutell & S. McCormick (Eds.), *Literacy theory and research: Analyses from multiple paradigms* (pp. 241–247). Chicago: National Reading Conference.

Neuman, S. B., & Roskos, K. (1990). The influence of literacy-enriched play settings on preschoolers' engagement with written language. In J. Zutell & S. McCormick (Eds.), *Literacy theory and research: Analyses from multiple paradigms* (pp. 179–188). Chicago: National Reading Conference.

Neuman, S. B., & Roskos, K. (1992). Literacy objects as cultural tools: Effects on children's literacy behaviors in play. *Reading Research Quarterly, 27,* 203–225.

Ohanian, S. (1994). "Call me teacher" and "Who the hell are you?" In C. B. Smith (Moderator), *Whole language: The debate* (pp. 1–15, 58–61). Bloomington, IN: ED-INFO Press.

Palincsar, A. S., & Brown, A. L. (1984). Reciprocal teaching of comprehension-fostering and comprehension-monitoring activities. *Cognition and Instruction, 1,* 117–175.

Pflaum, S. W., Walberg, H. J. Karegianes, M. L., & Rasher, S. P. (1980). Reading instruction: A quantitative analysis. *Educational Researcher, 9(7),* 12–18.

Pressley, M. (1994). Commentary on the ERIC whole language debate. In C. B. Smith (Moderator), *Whole language: the debate* (pp. 155–178). Bloomington, IN: ERIC/REC.

Pressley, M., El-Dinary, P. B., Gaskins, I., Schuder, T., Bergman, J. Almasi, L., & Brown, R. (1992). Beyond direct explanation: Transactional instruction of reading comprehension strategies. *Elementary School Journal, 92,* 511–554.

Pressley, M., Gaskins, I. W., Cunicelli, E. A., Burdick, N. J., Schaub-Matt, M., Lee, D. S., & Powell, N. (1991). Strategy instruction at Benchmark School: A faculty interview study. *Learning Disability Quarterly, 14,* 19–48.

Pressley, M., & Rankin, J. (1994). More about whole language methods of reading instruction for students at risk for early reading failure. *Learning Disabilities Research & Practice, 9,* 156–167.

Reutzel, D. R., Hollingsworth, P. M., & Eldredge, J. L. (1994). Oral reading instruction: The effect on student reading development. *Reading Research Quarterly, 29,* 40–59.

Robbins, C., & Ehri, L. C. (1994). Reading storybooks to kindergartners helps them learn new vocabulary words. *Journal of Educational Psychology, 86,* 54–64.

Scott, A. C., Clayton, J. E., & Gibson, F. L. (1991). *A practical guide to knowldge acquisition.* Reading, MA: Addison-Wesley.

Shannon, P. (1994). "The answer is yes . . . " and "People who live in glass houses . . . " In C. B. Smith (Moderator), *Whole language: The debate* (pp. 48–51, 81–99). Bloomington, IN: EDINFO Press.

Slavin, R. E. (1987). Grouping for instruction in the elementary school. *Educational Psychologist, 22,* 109–128.

Smith, C. B. (Moderator). (1994). *Whole language: The debate.* Bloomington, IN: EDINFO Press.

Stahl, S. A., McKenna, M. C., & Pagnucco, J. R. (1994). The effects of whole language instruction: An update and reappraisal. *Educational Psychologist, 29,* 175–186.

Stahl, S. A., & Miller, P. D. (1989). Whole language and language experience approaches for beginning reading: A quantitative research synthesis. *Review of Educational Research, 59,* 87–116.

Stanovich, K. E., & Cunningham, A. E. (1993). Where does knowledge come from? Specific associations between print exposure and information acquisition. *Journal of Educational Psychology, 85,* 211–229.

Symons, S., Woloshyn, V. E., & Pressley, M. (Guest eds.). (1994). Scientific evaluation of whole language (Special issue]. *Educational Psychologist, 29*(4).

Tangel, D. M., & Blachman, B. A. (1992). Effect of phoneme awareness instruction on kindergarten children's invented spelling. *Journal of Reading Behavior, 24,* 233–261.

Turner, J. C. (1993). Situated motivation in literacy instruction. *Reading Research Quarterly, 28,* 288–290.

Uhry, J. K., & Shepherd, M. J. (1993). Segmentation/spelling instruction as part of a first-grade reading program: Effects on several measures of reading. *Reading Research Quarterly, 28,* 218–233.

Weaver, C. (1990). *Understanding whole language: Front principles to practice.* Portsmouth, NH: Heinemann.

Wendler, D., Samuels, S. J., & Moore, V. K. (1989). Comprehension instruction of awardwinning teachers, teachers with master's degrees, and other teachers. *Reading Research Quarterly, 24,* 382–401.

Whitmore, I. F., & Goodman, Y. M. (1992). Inside the whole language classroom. *School Administrator, 49*(5), 20–26.

The Six Aspects of Literacy

A Curriculum Framework

K. AU   *J. SCHEU*
J. CARROLL

A balanced approach to literacy instruction calls for a curriculum framework that gives reading and writing equal status. Such a framework recognizes the importance of both the cognitive and affective dimensions of literacy. It acknowledges the meaning-making involved in the full processes of reading and writing, while recognizing the importance of the strategies and skills used by proficient readers and writers.

A curriculum framework with these characteristics is presented in Figure 1. This framework can also be called a *whole literacy* curriculum (Au, Scheu, Kawakami, & Herman, 1990). The *whole* part of this label recognizes the importance of students' engagement in the full processes of reading and writing in the authentic contexts for learning provided by the readers' and writers' workshops. The *literacy* part of the label refers to the curriculum's emphasis on reading and writing. Of course, speaking and listening are central to the development of literacy and to activities in the readers' and writers' workshops. Oral language and listening comprehension are fully integrated with reading and writing, since students at all grade levels are expected to share their own ideas and respond to the ideas of others. This approach is consistent with research in emergent literacy, which supports the view that literacy does not wait on oral language development (Teale, 1987).

As shown in Figure 1, the overall goal of the curriculum is to promote students' ownership of literacy. . . . Ownership involves students' valuing of their own ability to read and write. Students who own literacy are those who choose to use literacy for purposes they have set for themselves, at home as well as at school. For example, students choose to read a book in their spare time or to write a letter to a grandparent. Ownership develops best in classrooms in which students and teachers form a community of learners (Cairney & Langbien, 1989). Students within this community are recognized for their accomplishments as readers and writers and strive to support one another's literacy learning (Blackburn, 1984).

The next two aspects of literacy, reading comprehension and the writing process, are listed below ownership in Figure 1. Reading comprehension is at the heart of the readers' workshop, while the writing process serves as the focus for the writers' workshop. The remaining three aspects of literacy—language and vocabulary knowledge, word reading and spelling strategies, and voluntary reading—are all developed within both the readers' and the writers' workshops.

Source: From *Balanced Literacy Instruction: A Teacher's Resource Book* (pp. 4–9) by K. H. Au, J. H. Carroll, and J. A. Scheu, 1997, Norwood, MA: Christopher Gordon. Reprinted by permission.

FIGURE 1   **The Six Aspects of Literacy**

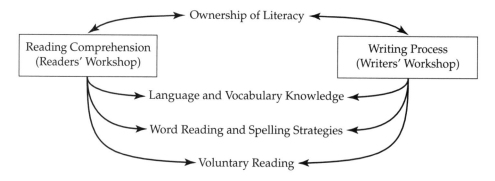

Reading Comprehension

Reading comprehension involves the ability to construct meaning from and to respond to text, using background knowledge as well as printed information. Reading is viewed as the dynamic interaction among the reader, the text, and the situation or social context in which reading takes place (Wixson, Peters, Weber, & Roeber, 1987). In this perspective, a text may have different interpretations, depending on the background knowledge the reader brings to it (Anderson & Pearson, 1984). The social context also influences the process of constructing meaning from text. For example, a reader's interpretation of a novel might differ depending on whether she will be discussing the novel in class or is reading purely for her own enjoyment (Purves, 1985).

Reader response theory . . . plays an important part in a balanced approach to literacy instruction. According to Rosenblatt (1978), more emphasis needs to be placed on the enjoyment of the reading experience, rather than on reading to gather facts or details from the text. Traditional instruction in reading comprehension was largely based on quizzing students about details in the text. According to Rosenblatt and others, an overemphasis on low-level questions detracts from students' efforts to appreciate the novel or other text as a whole and to draw relationships between the text and their own lives. In keeping with reader response theory, teachers might ask students to discuss their feelings about a text, its possible themes, and connections between the text and their own lives. . . .

Writing Process

Writing involves a process of using print (or for younger children. drawing) to construct meaning and communicate a message. Students experience ownership of writing when they write on self-selected topics and come to see themselves as authors. In a balanced literacy curriculum, writing is viewed as a dynamic, nonlinear process. This process includes planning, drafting, revising, editing, and publishing (Graves, 1983). . . .

Typically, writers go back and forth among these different activities. While drafting, for example, the writer may decide to abandon the piece and begin planning a new one. This thoughtful and deliberate shifting from one activity to another is characteristic of good writers. Good writers pay attention mainly to the overall shape and message of the piece. In contrast, poor writers often become overly concerned with the mechanics of writing, such as spelling and punctuation, rather than with the flow of ideas.

Language and Vocabulary Knowledge

This aspect of literacy concerns students' ability to understand and use appropriate terms and structures in both spoken and printed English. The approach to language development in a balanced literacy curriculum is based on the idea that children learn language by using it for real purposes in social situations (Pinnell & Jaggar, 1991). For example, children can develop oral language through small group, teacher-guided discussions in which they share their responses to an interesting book. Teachers foster children's language development by providing them with many opportunities for authentic communication. Through these opportunities, children gain communicative competence, the ability to use language to express themselves appropriately in a variety of social contexts, and the ability to use language as a tool for learning.

The approach to vocabulary taken in a balanced literacy approach is based on the *knowledge hypothesis* (Mezynski, 1983), the idea that vocabulary represents the knowledge a person has of particular topics, not just dictionary definitions. The meaning of a new word is acquired gradually, through repeated encounters with that word (Nagy, Herman, & Anderson, 1985). Teachers can build students' vocabulary knowledge by heightening their interest in words, by teaching them strategies for inferring word meanings from text, and by encouraging them to do wide independent reading.

Word Reading and Spelling Strategies

Many children first learn to deal with print through home experiences with literacy (Taylor, 1983), especially storybook reading. Through storybook reading, children learn concepts about print, for example, that the left page is read before the right and that words run from left to right. Learning concepts about print give children the foundation for developing word reading and spelling strategies.

Students need to have word reading and spelling strategies if they are to read words accurately and quickly. *Fluent readers,* those who experience a smooth and easy flow through the text, integrate knowledge of meaning, structure, and visual cues (Clay, 1993) and decode by analogy (by comparing the unknown word to known words with the same spelling patterns; Cunningham, 1975–1976. . . .) Instruction in word reading strategies involves helping students to use the three cue systems mentioned above in a balanced manner. Students must learn to check their guesses about words by using not just one but all three cue systems, and then to correct their guesses. Once students learn to use the three cue systems in a balanced manner, they usually stumble only over multisyllabic words. At this point, they can benefit from learning about base words and affixes, including plural endings, prefixes, and suffixes.

Teachers can help students to develop word reading strategies by teaching them to apply knowledge of the three cue systems when reading.... Many students benefit from specific instruction in word reading strategies, including phonics.... In addition to teaching word reading strategies, teachers can make sure children receive ample opportunity to read and reread favorite books. Through reading and rereading, students learn to apply knowledge of the three cue systems in a fluent, coordinated manner. Writing, especially invented spelling, provides children with an excellent opportunity to learn about sound-symbol relationships....

Voluntary Reading

In *voluntary reading,* students select the materials they want to read, either for information or for pleasure (Spiegel, 1981). Students read to fulfill their own goals, not just to meet the expectations of the teacher and other adults. Ideally, students choose the times when they will read. Voluntary reading is one way that students demonstrate their ownership of literacy....

Students' voluntary reading is promoted if they become part of a community of readers. In a community of readers, students and teachers give book talks and otherwise share their reading with one another. Students' voluntary reading is supported because they receive recognition and support for their reading and gain ideas about what they would like to read next. Of course, students must also have ready access to books, preferably through an inviting and well stocked classroom library (Morrow & Weinstein, 1986).

Conclusion

In a balanced literacy curriculum, teachers attend to all six aspects of literacy. Two aspects, ownership and voluntary reading, are affective, while the others are cognitive. Two aspects, reading comprehension and the writing process, focus on complex, higher level thinking and meaning making. The final two aspects, language and vocabulary knowledge and word reading and spelling strategies identification, attend to the supporting skills students need to become proficient readers and writers.

References

Anderson, R. C., & Pearson, R. D. (1984). A schema-theoretic view of basic processes in reading comprehension. In P. D. Pearson (Ed.), *Handbook of reading research.* New York, NY: Longman.

Au, K. H., Scheu, J. A., Kawakami, A. J., & Herman, P. A. (1990). Assessment and accountability in a whole literacy curriculum. *The Reading Teacher, 43* (8), 574–578.

Blackburn, E. (1984). Common ground: Developing relationships between reading and writing. *Language Arts, 61,* 367–375.

Cairney, T., & Langbien, S. (1989). Building communities of readers and writers. *The Reading Teacher, 42* (8), 560–567.

Clay, M. M. (1993). *Reading recovery: A guidebook for teachers in training.* Portsmouth, NH: Heinemann.

Cunningham, P. (1975-1976). Investigating a synthesized theory of mediated word recognition. *Reading Research Quarterly, 11,* 127–143.

Graves, D. (1983). *Writing: Teachers and children at work.* Exeter, NH: Heinemann.

Mezynski, K. (1983). Issues concerning the acquisition of knowledge: Effects of vocabulary training on reading comprehension. *Review of Educational Research, 53,* 253–279.

Morrow, L. M., & Weinstein, C. S. (1986). Encouraging voluntary reading: The impact of a literature program on children's use of library centers. *Reading Research Quarterly, 21* (3), 330–346.

Nagy, W. E., Herman, P., & Anderson, R. C. (1985). Learning words from context. *Reading Research Quarterly, 20,* 233–253.

Pinnell, G. S., & Jaggar, A. M. (1991). Oral language: Speaking and listening in the classroom. In J. Flood, J. M. Jensen, D. Lapp, & J. R. Squire (Eds.), *Handbook of research on teaching the English language arts* (pp. 691–720). New York: Macmillan.

Purves, A. C. (1985). That sunny dome: Those caves of ice. In C. R. Cooper (Ed.), *Researching response to litera-ture and the teaching of literature: Points of departure* (pp. 54–69). Norwood, NJ: Ablex.

Rosenblatt, L. (1978). *The reader, the text, the poem: The transactional theory of the literary work.* Carbondale: Southern Illinois University Press.

Spiegel, D. L. (1981). *Reading for pleasure: Guidelines.* Newark, DE: International Reading Association.

Taylor, D. (1983). *Family illiteracy: Young children learning to read and write.* Portsmouth, NH: Heinemann.

Teale, W. H. (1987). Emergent literacy: Reading and writing development in early childhood. In J. E. Readence & R. S. Baldwin (Eds.), *Research in literacy: Merging perspectives.* Thirty-sixth Yearbook of the National Reading Conference (pp. 45–74). Rochester, NY: National Reading Conference.

Wixson, K. K., Peters, C. W., Weber, E. M., & Roeber, E. D. (1987). New directions in statewide reading assessment. *The Reading Teacher, 40* (8), 749–754.

Children's Books Cited

Louie, A. (1982). *Yen-Shen: A Cinderella story from China.* New York, NY: Philomel.

Smith, D. B. (1973). *A taste of blackberries.* New York, NY: HarperCollins

Steptoe, J. (1987). *Mufaro's beautiful daughters.* New York, NY: Lothrop, Lee & Sheperd.

Integrating Sources

1. The articles in this section cover what the authors believe to be a *balanced* approach to reading instruction. How would you define balance in the literacy program and what are the important characteristics of this philosophy?

2. Pressley, Rankin, and Yokoi describe what types of instructional practices? What are some of the important characteristics of these classroom teachers and how do they fit a definition of a balanced approach to reading?

3. Describe the six aspects of a curriculum framework as described by Au, Carroll, and Scheu. How do these ideas compare or contrast with a balanced view of reading instruction?

Classroom Implications

Examine your own classroom reading program in light of how you feel it compares to balanced instruction. How is your teaching the same and how is it different from what has been defined as a balanced approach to reading? What are some aspects of your reading instruction you would like to change based on the information in this chapter?

Annotated Bibliography

Au, K., Carroll, J., & Scheu, J. (1997). *Balanced literacy instruction: A teacher's resource book.* Norwood, MA: Christopher-Gordon.

This is an excellent book on how classroom teachers can implement balanced instruction in their classroom teaching of reading.

Baltas, J., & Shafer, S. (Eds.). (1996). *Scholastic guide to balanced reading K–2: Making it work for you.* Jefferson City, MO: Scholastic.

An edited book that provides teachers with a theoretical base for providing a balanced reading program, and classroom examples of effective programs. Each chapter includes a theoretical article written by an academic expert, an article written by a classroom teacher, a tool that can be used to see if the classroom fits the approach, and suggestions for implementing the approach.

Baltas, J., & Shafer, S. (Eds.). (1996). *Scholastic Guide to Balanced Reading 3–6: Making It Work for You.* Jefferson City, MO: Scholastic.

An edited book that provides teachers with a theoretical base for providing a balanced reading program, and provides classroom examples of effective programs. Each chapter includes a theoretical article written by an academic expert, an article written by a classroom teacher, a tool that can be used to see if the classroom fits the approach, and suggestions for implementing the approach.

Baumann, J. F., & Ivy, G. (1997). *Delicate balances: Striving for curricular and instructional equilibrium in a second-grade literature/strategy based classroom* (Report No. 83). Athens, GA: National Reading Research Center.

A qualitative case study that explored what second graders learned about reading, writing, and literature through a literacy program that integrated strategy instruction into a rich literature-based environment.

Glazer-Mandel, S. (1996). *Have you assessed the balance in your reading program? Teaching PreK-8, 26* (6), 92–93.

A short article that emphasizes the importance of attending to all aspects of reading and language when using a literature-based reading program.

Strickland, D. S. (1997). Teach the skills and thrills of reading. *Instructor, 106* (8), 42–45.

The article lists five "rules of thumb" for attaining a balanced reading program. Discusses issues related to teaching basic skills with literature, grouping, planning, content, and assessment.

Wharton-McDonald, R., et al. (1997). *Outstanding literacy instruction in first grade: Teacher practices and student achievement* (Report No. 81). Athens, GA: National Reading Research Center.

A research study that identifies a cluster of beliefs and practices that were found to distinguish outstanding teaching practice from more typical practice. The cluster includes a balance of skills and high-quality reading and writing experiences.

You Become Involved

Good teachers of reading have long used a variety of approaches to the teaching of reading. This instructional view of what needs to be done in the classroom has only been recently described as a balanced approach to reading. Using your teaching experience and the material in this section consider the following:

1. Describe a fellow teacher who strongly supports the following reading philosophies or definitions:

    a. Whole language

    b. Basal reader

    c. Phonics

    d. Literature-based

    e. Skills model

    How do these teachers compare and contrast in what they do in their reading instruction? What specific changes would each of these teachers need to make to become a balanced teacher of reading?

2. Define balanced reading instruction with specific application of your definition to your current instructional situation.

2

PHONICS

The ordinary way to teach children to read is, after they have
got some knowledge of their letters, & a smattering of some
syllables and words in the horn-book, to turn them into the
A B C Prime, and therein to make them name the letters,
and spell the words, till by often use they can pronounce
(at least) the shortest words at the first sight.
—C. H. (1659)

When put to learning the letters of the alphabet first,
the child has no acquaintance with them, either by eye,
the ear, the tongue, or the mind; but if put to learning
familiar words first, he already knows them. . . . It can hardly
be doubted therefore, that a child would learn to name any
twenty-six familiar words, sooner than the twenty-six unknown, unheard, and unthought of letters of the alphabet.
—HORACE MANN (1838)

Adequate progress in learning to read English beyond the
initial level depends [partially] on having established a working
understanding of how sounds are represented alphabetically.
—C. E. SNOW ET AL. (1998)

The debate over phonics and its proper role in reading instruction, seemingly never
ends. As early as 1659 (see previous quotation), teachers were concerned about
phonics-related issues. Throughout this long history of discussion and debate, various positions have been advocated, ranging from programs built entirely on phonics skills, through other language approaches that had no phonics instruction at all.
As you read and consider the debates of the past and compare them to much of
the current controversy on the effective use of phonics, you as a professional educator need to carefully consider these varying viewpoints related to phonics, and
then develop your own personal position on this important reading issue.

Current Controversy on Phonics

It is often heard from the general public in the return to the basics movement, "If schools would only teach phonics there would be no more reading problems!" Implied in this statement are two fundamental ideas: the first being that if teachers incorporated phonics as a total program, they would solve all reading problems; and secondly, teachers know how to do a better job, but are not doing it!

In our opinion, both of these statements are wrong. Most classroom reading programs, no matter the philosophical orientation, do teach phonics. Where once phonics and reading were two separate subjects, they are today incorporated together in language arts/literacy instruction. The second assumption is, by implication, that the teaching profession is inept, which we deny completely. Teachers tend to be very pragmatic and do what works, which includes varying degrees of phonics education.

In a recent article on the key topics in reading research and practice that concern teachers, phonics was one of the most often cited concerns (Cassidy & Wenrich, 1998). This renewed interest in phonics is evident in the number of new books recently published, as well as the many national, state, and local presentations on this topic. For instance, the national meetings of the International Reading Association as well as the National Reading Conference have had significant increases in presentations on various aspects of phonics ranging between theoretical research to the practical application of phonics principles.

Approaches to Phonics

Merely concluding that phonics is important says little about how it should be approached in primary classrooms. Two major issues arise with respect to phonics instruction: How such instruction should be organized and how it should be carried out.

Organizing phonics instruction obliges a teacher to make curricular decisions about what shall be taught and how. At some risk of oversimplifying the matter, we suggest that there are four basic positions on this issue. (1) Instruction in phonics is largely, if not entirely, unnecessary because children will "naturally" infer letter/sound correspondences from extensive reading. (2) Instruction should be fully contextualized within actual reading and thus involve "teachable moments." (3) Teachable moments are not sufficiently dependable, so a more systematic (though not necessarily sequential) approach is called for to ensure that appropriate instruction occurs in the most timely way. (4) Phonics instruction should be both systematic and sequential.

The second question—that of how phonics instruction should be carried out—has a long history. The two principle positions involve *synthetic* (or explicit) phonics, in which children are taught to blend individual sounds in attacking unfamiliar words, and *analytic* (or implicit) phonics, in which whole words are used to emphasize spelling patterns representing sounds reliably.

Teacher's Goals for the Effective Use of Phonics

The critical role for you as a teacher in considering the use of phonics is to carefully evaluate the various positions on this topic and then to develop your own philosophy as well as teaching strategies for this aspect of reading. Rather than just accept this "changing pendulum" of views and opinions on phonics, you as a knowledgeable professional educator need in the end to form your own opinion.

As You Read

The two articles that follow should provide a good basis for thinking through instructional issues surrounding effective phonics instruction. Stahl, Duffy-Hester, and Stahl (1998) conclude that a systematic phonics instruction is necessary and describe the attributes of an ideal program.

You will find that many of the important questions related to phonics knowledge are connected to other issues examined in this book, such as emergent literacy, and the effective use of various literacy materials. As you consider the following questions, your knowledge of these interrelated issues will be useful:

1. For what reason has phonics instruction been the source of contention?
2. Are there teaching techniques for phonics that seem especially useful in the classroom reading program? If so, which ones and for what reason?
3. To what extent should phonics instruction allow for (a) introduction of skills in isolation? (b) practice of skills in isolation? and (c) learning to occur in the context of connected text or whole text?

References

Adams, M. J., & Bruck, M. (1995). Resolving the "Great Debate." *American Educator, 19,* 7–20.

Cassidy, J., & Wenrich, J. K. (1998). What's hot, and what's not for 1998. *Reading Today.* Newark, DE: International Reading Association.

C. H. (1659). *The Petty-School shewing a way to teach little children to read English with delight and profit. (especially according to the New Primer).* London: Printed by J. T. for Andrew Crook, at the Green Dragon in Pauls Church Yard.

Mann, H. (1838). *Common School Journal, 1,* 326.

Moats, L. C. (1998). Teaching decoding. *American Educator, 22,* 42–49, 95.

Smith, F. (1997). *Reading without nonsense.* (3rd ed.). New York: Teachers College, Columbia University. 42–57.

Snow, C. E., Burns, M., & Griggin, S. (Eds.). (1998). *Prevention of reading difficulties in young children.* Washington: National Academy Press.

Stahl, S. A., Duffy-Hester, A. M., & Stahl, K. A. D. (1998). Theory and research into practice: Everything you wanted to know about phonics (but were afraid to ask). *Reading Research Quarterly, 33,* 338–355.

Everything You Wanted to Know about Phonics (But Were Afraid to Ask)

STEVEN A. STAHL
University of Georgia, Athens

KATHERINE ANNE DOUGHERTY STAHL
Clarke County Public Schools, Georgia

ANN M. DUFFY-HESTER
University of Georgia, Athens

It is difficult to talk about phonics. Regie Routman (1996) used to say that "Phonics is a lot like sex. Everyone is doing it behind closed doors, but no one is talking about it" (p. 91). This has changed. People are talking about it, mostly in confusion about how to do it (phonics, that is). This is true in the media (e.g., Collins, 1997; Levine, 1994) as well as among teachers we talk to. In California, a bellwether state in education, a new report from the California Task Force on Reading (California Department of Education, 1995) recommended that "every school and district must organize and implement a comprehensive and balanced reading program that is research-based and combines skill development with literature and language-rich activities," and asserted that "the heart of a powerful reading program is the relationship between explicit, systematic skills instruction and literature, language and comprehension. While skills alone are insufficient to develop good readers, no reader can become proficient without those foundational skills" (p. 3).

There is a consensus of belief that good reading instruction includes some attention to decoding. Whole language advocates such as Church (1996) and Routman (1996) devoted chapters of their recent books to teaching phonics, and Goodman (1993) wrote a book devoted entirely to phonics. These whole language advocates argued that whole language teachers should be teaching phonics and that decoding instruction had always been part of whole language teaching. To quote Routman again:

> *It would be irresponsible and inexcusable not to teach phonics. Yet the media are having a field day getting the word out that many of us ignore phonics in the teaching of reading. It just isn't so. Some of us may not be doing as good a job as we need to be doing, but I don't know a knowledgeable teacher who doesn't teach phonics. (1996, p. 91)*

Results of a recent U.S. national survey of elementary school teachers indicated that 99% of K–2 teachers consider phonics instruction to be essential (67%) or important (32%) (Baumann, Hoffman, Moon, & Duffy-Hester, 1998).

Beliefs and Phonics

A lot of people are talking about phonics but in different ways. How people talk about phonics depends on their belief systems about reading in general. Different people have different beliefs about how reading should be defined (DeFord, 1985; Stahl, 1997), which might affect how they think about phonics instruction. Some people believe that if one can recognize all of the words in a text quickly and accurately, one will be able to understand and appreciate that text. Therefore, the primary task in teaching reading for people who hold this belief is to teach students how to recognize words (e.g., Gough & Hillinger, 1980). Others believe that reading should begin with interpretations of whole texts, and that phonics should be used only to support the reader's need to get meaning from text (e.g., Goodman, 1993). It is not difficult to see how these different belief systems might lead to different forms of phonics instruction.

The whole language movement helped to change the way we talk about phonics. This movement exploded onto the educational scene, rapidly changing basic beliefs about education (Pearson, 1989) and basal reading programs (Hoffman et al., 1994), as well as views on reading and reading instruction, and focusing on uses of written language for communication and on individual responses to literature and exposition (e.g., Goodman, 1986). Whole language advocates generally include phonics (or graphophonemics) as one of the cuing systems used in identifying words. Their model of reading is partially based on Goodman (1976) who suggested that readers use three cuing systems—graphophonemic, syntactic, and semantic—to identify words as they encounter them in meaningful text.

Goodman based his model on his work with miscue analysis (e.g., Goodman & Goodman, 1977), or the analysis of oral reading miscues that readers make during reading. Whole language teachers have advocated teaching children about letter-sound correspondences, but *only as an aid to a child's ongoing process of getting meaning from a text or producing a text*, and *only as needed*. In some instructional programs based on the whole language philosophy, the teacher does not teach from a predetermined scope and sequence but instead gives children the information they need to understand texts.

Although the issue should never have been whole language versus phonics but instead issues of how best to teach children to decode, the polarizing rhetoric used by some on the whole language movement seems to have convinced people that whole language and phonics are opposed to each other (McKenna, Stahl, & Reinking, 1994; Moorman, Blanton, & McLaughlin, 1994). Many teachers adopting a whole language philosophy perceived that they should never teach words in isolation, should provide phonics instruction only when students demonstrate the need for this instruction, and should never use unauthentic literature, such as books chosen for spelling patterns, in instruction. Although these rules are often violated by knowledgeable whole language teachers (see McIntyre & Pressley, 1996; Mills, O'Keefe, & Stephens, 1992; Pressley, Rankin, & Yakoi, 1996), they were nonetheless somehow communicated to many others.

These (mis)perceptions of whole language teaching resulted in confusion for many whole language teachers. Further, when some teachers (or their administrators) perceived a need for phonics instruction, they added on a program unrelated to their regular, literature-based program. These *Frankenclasses* were stitched together, with neither part of the curriculum informing the other. Such a curriculum may be no more desirable than the omission of phonics instruction.

In this article, we will review basic principles underlying word learning and phonics instruction. These principles are applicable in many primary-grade classrooms. Next, we will discuss approaches to teaching phonics. Finally, we will draw some tentative conclusions on how an integrated language arts program that includes phonics instruction may look in first-grade classrooms.

Understanding Phonics Instruction

When evaluating phonics instruction, we can rely on a research base going back to the 1920s for some empirical principles, but we also need to rely on some common sense. Research tells us that an early and systematic emphasis on teaching children to decode words leads to better achievement than a later or more haphazard approach (Adams, 1990; Chall, 1989, 1996). Further, being able to decode words is necessary for children to become independent word learners and thus be able to develop as readers without teacher assistance (Share, 1995). This much seems clear. But such instruction can occur in a variety of settings, including traditional classes and whole language classes (Church, 1994; Dahl & Freppon, 1995; Mills et al., 1992). What is important is that phonics instruction is done well. Research (and common sense) suggest the following principles of good phonics instruction.

- *Good phonics instruction should develop the alphabetic principle*

The key to learning to decode words is the principle that letters can represent sounds. Many languages such as Chinese use logographs, or stylized pictures, to represent meanings. Others use symbols to represent whole syllables. English, like many other languages, uses letters to represent individual sounds in words. Although English is not entirely regular—that is, there is not always a one-to-one correspondence between letters and sounds—understanding that letters do have a relationship with the sounds in words is a hallmark of successful beginning readers (Adams, 1990).

At its most basic level, the *alphabetic principle* is the notion that letters in words may stand for specific sounds. Initially, children developing this principle understand that words have initial sounds. As this awareness develops, children learn more about letters and sounds, analyzing each word fully, and including more complex orthographic elements such as consonant blends (*bl*, *st*, *nd*), consonant digraphs (*th*, *sh*, *ch*, and *wh*), vowel digraphs (*ea*, *oa*, *oo*), diphthongs (*aw*, *au*, *ou*, *ow*), and phonograms (*ight* and *ough*).

One can observe children's growth in knowledge of the alphabetic principle through both their reading and invented spelling. Ehri (1992) described children's growth in accurate word reading as going through three stages. At first, children use a visual cue to recognize words. Cues can be simple, such as the two eyes in *look*, or more complex. This is a *pre-alphabetic* stage (Ehri, 1995), since children are not using letters and sounds but are instead using the look of each word.

As children develop phonological awareness, they begin to use some partial sound information in the word, such as an initial or final sound (see Stahl & Murray, 1998). Ehri

(1995) called this stage *phonetic cue reading*. In this stage, a child might substitute a word that begins with the same letter, such as *bird* for *bear*, when reading words in text or in lists.

As children learn more words, phonetic cue reading becomes less efficient, and children analyze the word more deeply. In the *cipher* or *full alphabetic* stage (Ehri, 1995), children use all the letters and sounds. At this stage, children's reading can still be labored, relying on sounding out or other, less efficient strategies. With greater practice, children will develop automatic word recognition so that they do not have to think about the words in a text and can concentrate fully on the meaning of the text (Chall, 1996; Ehri, 1995).

Another way of observing children's growth of the alphabetic principle is to look at their invented spellings. Children go through a similar set of stages in how they invent spellings for words (see Bear & Barone, 1989; Gillet & Temple, 1990; Zutell & Rasinski, 1989). Initially, a child may spell a word by drawing a picture or scribbling something that looks like writing (Harste, Burke, & Woodward, 1982). As children learn that words need letters, they may use random letters to represent a word. Gillet and Temple (1990) called this the *prephonemic* stage. At this point, the writers themselves are the only ones who can read what they have written.

As children begin to think about sounds in words, their spelling may represent only one sound in a word, usually an initial sound, and occasionally a final sound. Sometimes they represent a word with a single letter, or pair of letters, but often they represent a word with the correct initial letter followed by some random letters. For example, one child in our reading clinic wrote *fish* with an initial *f* and continued by adding an additional six letters, stating that "words that begin with *f* have a lot of letters in them."

As children analyze words further, they go to a *letter name* stage, where they use the names of letters to represent sounds. Here they represent at least all of the consonants in a word, often not using vowels. For example, they might spell *girl* as GRL or *ten* as TN. Gillet and Temple (1990) called the next stage *transitional*. In this stage, children use vowels, and the words they write resemble the actual word, like DRAGUN for *dragon*. However, children in this stage may not always use conventional spellings.

- *Good phonics instruction should develop phonological awareness*

The key to the development of the alphabetic principle, word recognition, and invented spelling is phonological awareness. Phonological awareness is one of the most important concepts to arise out of the past 20 years of research in reading (Stanovich, 1991). Phoneme awareness is the awareness of sounds in *spoken* words. As words are spoken, most sounds cannot be said by themselves. For example, the spoken word /cat/ has one continuous sound and is not pronounced "kuh-a-tuh." Children ordinarily concentrate on the meaning and do not think of the sounds in the word. But, since letters represent sounds, a child must learn to think of words as having *both* meaning and sound in order to understand the alphabetic principle (Stahl & Murray, 1998).

As children grow in their recognition of words, from nonalphabetic to phonetic cues to full alphabetic reading, and as they grow in their invented spelling from prealphabetic to early phonemic to letter name and transitional spelling, they are also growing in their ability to analyze spoken words. In the beginning, children are able to analyze the initial sound in words, since this sound can be perceived easily when they say a word (see Stahl & Murray, 1994; 1998). As they analyze more of the word, often by stretching a word out, they are able to include more letters in their word recognition and spelling. They also develop a sense of phoneme identity (Byrne & Fielding-Barnsley, 1991; Murray, 1995), or an understanding that the /s/ in *sun* is the same sound as the /s/ in *bus*.

Many tasks have been used to teach children to become aware of sounds in spoken words. Among these tasks are:

- *Rhyming,* either by recognizing rhymes or rhyme production,
- *Word-to-word matching tasks,* which involve having a child determine whether a series of words begins or ends the same, or which word in a group is the odd man out (e.g., determining which word does not belong in a group of words such as *man, move,* and *pit*),
- *Sound-to-word matching tasks,* which involve having a child determine whether a particular sound can be found in a word (e.g., determining whether there is an /m/ in *man*),
- *Initial (or final) sounds,* in which the child gives the first (or last) sound in a spoken word (e.g., the first sound in *fish*),
- *Segmentation,* which involves breaking a word up into sounds, a very difficult task for children to do orally. This task usually requires some sort of concrete aid such as Elkonin boxes (Clay, 1993; Elkonin, 1973) or boxes set up like this (☐☐☐) in which a child puts a counter or letter in the box when he or she hears a new sound in a word, wooden blocks (Calfee, Lindamood, & Lindamood, 1973), or letters (Hohn & Ehri, 1983),
- *Blending,* the flip side of segmentation, which involves putting spoken sounds together into a word (e.g., recognizing that /k/a/t/ is *cat*), and
- *Deletion and manipulation,* in which a child is told to mentally remove a portion of a word to make another word (e.g., the child is asked to say *coat,* and then to say it again without the /k/). In more complex manipulation tasks, children are asked to remove a phonemic segment and put it elsewhere in the word to make a new word, or to perform other complex manipulations, such as in Pig Latin.

A good phonics program should contain at least one of these tasks. Although phoneme awareness is often conceived as manipulating *spoken* words, often this awareness is taught as an introduction to teaching letter sounds. Thus, a program that begins by having a child listen to a word and say the first sound as a way of introducing a letter sound is giving some attention to phoneme awareness, but probably not enough to help a child with difficulty in this area.

There are other ways of developing phoneme awareness that should be part of a beginning reading program. One way is to read alphabet books to children. We found that 4-year-old children who were read one alphabet book per day significantly improved in their awareness of phonemes (Murray, Stahl, & Ivey, 1996). To understand why *b* is for *bear,* for example, the child needs to understand that the first sound of *bear* is /b/ (Yaden, Smolkin, & MacGillivray, 1993). This understanding is the beginning of phonological awareness.

Another way to develop this awareness is to encourage children to use invented spellings, because children need to think about sounds in words and usually do some form of segmentation in order to invent a spelling. Tangel and Blachman (1992) found that phonemic awareness training increased children's growth in invented spelling. It would make equal sense that practice in invented spelling would similarly increase phonological awareness.

How much attention to phoneme awareness is necessary depends on the child. A child with a history of reading problems may need a variety of activities and many repetitions. Other children may not need as much.

- *Good phonics instruction should provide a thorough grounding in the letters*

The other part of learning letter-sound relationships is learning the forms of letters. Efficient word recognition is dependent on children's thorough familiarity with letters. They should not have to think, for example, that the letter *t* is the one with the up and down line and the cross thingy. Instead, children should recognize *t* immediately. Adams (1990) suggested that children need to recognize the forms of the letters automatically, without conscious effort, to be able to recognize words fluently.

There is some uncertainty about whether knowing the names of letters is absolutely necessary. On one hand, children can learn to recognize words without knowing the names of letters, and some reading programs do not require that children learn the names of the letters (Adams, 1990). On the other hand, knowing the names of letters is one of the best predictors of success in reading (Chall, 1996). Knowing the names of letters also helps children talk about letters. All in all, it is preferable to teach the names of letters, although children can begin to learn to read without knowing *all* the names of the letters. Thus, children should be reading and listening to connected texts before they know, and as they are learning, the names of all of the letters of the alphabet.

Children often learn the names of letters first through an alphabet song. As many parents can attest, memorizing the song often leads to confusion, most notably the notion that there is a letter called "elemenope." But nearly all children recover from that confusion and eventually learn to identify the letters individually. Some programs begin with the alphabet song and teach the letters in order. Other programs begin with letters with easily pronounced sounds such as *m, n,* and *s* and proceed to teach the consonants, then the vowels. We know of no research to determine the best order for introducing letters. When teaching the alphabet, a good phonics program will make sure that children can identify both capital and lowercase letters individually, in any order.

- *Good phonics instruction should not teach rules, need not use worksheets, should not dominate instruction, and does not have to be boring*

There are a number of misconceptions about phonics instruction. Although traditional phonics instruction did teach rules, used worksheets, and was, frankly, often boring, it does not have to be.

Clymer (1963, reprinted 1996) reviewed commonly taught phonics rules and compared them to the words that primary children were likely to encounter in their reading. He found that commonly taught rules were rarely applicable to any more than 75% of the words children encounter in their reading. For example, the rule *when two vowels go walking, the first one does the talking*, is applicable to about 45% of words children encounter. The rule applies for the words *boat, fail,* and *meet*, but does not apply for *does, would,* or *bread.* The lack of applicability does not mean that teachers should never state a rule. Often a rule is useful for clarifying the aspect of the word that is under study. But it does mean that students should not be required to memorize rules, nor should a teacher give students words and have them tell which phonics rule applies. Further, as Adams (1990) pointed out, vowel sounds are more consistent in phonograms. This research suggests that vowels might be taught through phonograms, at least as part of an effective phonics program.

What seems to work in phonics instruction is direct teacher instruction, not practice on worksheets. Two observational studies by Haynes and Jenkins (1986) and Leinhardt, Zigmond, and Cooley (1981) found that the amount of time students spent on worksheets did not relate to gains in reading achievement. This may be because completing worksheets takes students' time away from reading stories or content material, and because instructional aspects of worksheets are often poorly designed (Osborn, 1984). What appeared to be most relevant was time spent reading connected text (Leinhardt et al., 1981).

In the 1970s and 1980s, much instructional time was devoted to having students complete workbooks. A typical lesson might consist of a teacher providing a brief introduction to a skill, what Durkin (1978/1979) called *mentioning,* followed by student practice using worksheets. In a typical lesson there was not only a phonics skill taught, but another phonics skill reviewed, a comprehension skill taught or reviewed, and another worksheet used to review the story. At that time, one of the authors was working for a school district as an observer of reading instruction and noted that only 40% of the time allocated for reading instruction was used for reading connected text. The additional 60% was spent on doing worksheets or supplemental work, such as *Weekly Reader.* Gambrell, Wilson, and Gantt (1981) observed that average readers spent about 6 minutes per day reading connected text. Children with reading problems spent considerably less, about 1 minute per day on average.

Currently, children spend considerably more time reading connected texts. This is as it should be. Effective phonics instruction should not take a great deal of classroom time. Programs such as those of Eldredge and Butterfield (1986; Eldredge, 1995) and the Benchmark School Word Identification program (Gaskins et al., 1988; Gaskins, Ehri, Cress, O'Hara, & Donnelly, 1996/1997) are designed to be taught in no more than 15–20 minutes per day.

Brisk lessons, such as those of Eldredge and Butterfield (1986) and Gaskins et al. (1988, 1996/1997), need not be boring. Of course, boring is in the eye of the beholder, but we have observed high rates of engagement and interest in direct instruction lessons (Stahl, Osborn, & Pearson, 1994). A survey of exemplary primary-grade teachers found that these teachers were highly effective in teaching decoding and also maintained high levels of class engagement (Pressley et al., 1996). Our point is that phonics instruction need not be boring, especially if the instruction is kept brisk, to the point, and does not take an excessive amount of time each day.

- *Good phonics instruction provides sufficient practice in reading words*

There are three types of practice that might be provided in a phonics program—reading words in isolation, reading words in stories (i.e., expository and narrative texts), and writing words. The ultimate purpose of phonics instruction is for children to learn to read words. Many researchers (see Adams, 1990, for a review) conclude that people identify words by using spelling patterns. These patterns are learned through continued practice in reading words containing those patterns. In addition, all successful phonics programs provide a great deal of practice in reading words containing the letter-sound relationships that are taught. Therefore, the practice given in reading words is extremely important.

Reading Words in Isolation.   Phonics programs differ in how much practice they provide in reading words in isolation. Some programs will provide only two or three words as examples of each letter-sound relationship. Others will provide 50 or more examples. Although we do not know what is an optimal number of examples, the more practice that children have in reading words with various patterns, such as silent *e* or short *o* pattern words, the better they will be at reading words with those patterns. It is important for children to look at words in isolation at times so that they can examine the patterns in words without the distractions of context. (Of course, such practice should be minimal and never should dominate instruction.) Good phonics instruction might contain a moderate amount of word practice in isolation, enough to get children to recognize words automatically but not enough to drive them to boredom.

Reading Words in Stories.   It is important that children read words in stories or short pieces of expository text. The purpose of reading is comprehension. Reading words in stories may allow children to apply their phonics knowledge to tasks that allow for comprehension of a message as well as to sounding out words. One study found that children who read stories with a high percentage of words that contained letter-sound correspondences that they were taught had significantly higher word recognition than children who read texts that did not contain words that matched their phonics lessons (Juel & Roper/ Schneider, 1985). Our informal analyses of texts suggest that many texts do not match what is being taught. We suggest that children read at least some texts that contain a high percentage of words with patterns taught in phonics lessons.

These texts may be contrived, such as *Nat the Rat,* but need not be. There are interesting texts that contain a reasonable percentage of regular words that can be used to reinforce phonics instruction. For example, the classic books *Angus and the Cat* (Flack, 1931) or *The Cat in the Hat* (Seuss, 1957) could be used to reinforce the short *a* sound. (Trachtenburg, 1990, has a list of books that contain high percentages of various vowel patterns.) These texts should not be all that children read. Instead, we recommend that children read a mixture of books containing a high percentage of taught patterns and books ranging more widely in vocabulary. One study found that having children read widely seemed to enhance the performance of a successful phonics-oriented beginning reading program (Meyer, 1983).

Therefore, teachers should have stories for children to read in which they can practice using phonics knowledge in reading for comprehension. Stories (and other prose) should be comprehensible, that is, they should not just be a series of unrelated sentences, although these stories do not have to be elaborate (and cannot be in the beginning of instruction). These stories should be discussed for comprehension, as part of the reading lesson, so that the child will remember that the purpose of reading is getting meaning. We recommend that children read these stories as well as other material at an appropriate, instructional level.

Writing Words.   Practice in writing words is usually of two types—either writing words from dictation or using invented spellings. Both of these approaches have their place in beginning reading instruction, and both are valuable ways of practicing letter-sound correspondences.

Dictation is used in many successful phonics programs. In these programs, after a letter-sound correspondence is taught, children practice that correspondence by writing words from dictation. For example, for the short *a* sound, children may write words such as *pat, hand,* and *cap.* This seems to be a reasonably useful practice, one that could be easily added to any program that does not provide for it.

Invented spelling is more controversial. Invented spelling refers to the practice of having children invent their own spellings in their writings, using what they know about letters and sounds. At the early stages of learning to read, a teacher encouraging students to use invented spellings need not correct these spellings, as invented spelling allows children to focus on their developing knowledge of letters and sounds. This development seems to mirror a child's development in both phoneme awareness and letter-sound knowledge (Bear & Barone, 1989; Stahl & Murray, 1998). One study found that having children write using invented spelling greatly improved their phonics knowledge and other word recognition skills (Clarke, 1989).

As children develop letter-sound knowledge, teachers should expect greater control of conventional spelling, at least in final drafts. Invented spelling, as discussed above, has its greatest effect on children's phoneme awareness and knowledge of letter-sound correspondences. Too often teachers have let children continue inventing spellings beyond the point where the practice is useful to fulfill these instructional goals. The result is that some children do not learn to spell conventionally, and the practice of invented spelling in the early grades, where it is particularly useful, has come under attack.

• *Good phonics instruction leads to automatic word recognition*

In order to read books, children need to be able to read words quickly and automatically. If a child stumbles over or has to decode slowly too many words, comprehension will suffer (Samuels, Schermer, & Reinking, 1992). Although we want children to have a strategy for decoding words they do not know, we also want children to recognize many words automatically and be able to read them in context.

The practice activities discussed above—reading words in isolation, reading words in stories, and practicing words through writing—are intended to teach children to recognize the large numbers of words that have a regular pattern. Children learn to read automatically through the reading of stories (Fleisher, Jenkins, & Pany, 1979/1980; Rasinski, 1991; Samuels et al., 1992). Sometimes this practice can use repeated reading or the reading of the same story over and over until the child is able to read it fluently (Herman, 1985; Samuels et al., 1992; Stahl, Heubach, & Cramond, 1997). At other times, it may involve applying phonics lessons to reading books that contain taught letters. It is, however, important to see phonics instruction not as an end but as a means to help children read words automatically.

• *Good phonics instruction is one part of reading instruction*

It is necessary to remember that phonics instruction is only one part of a total reading program. Reading instruction has many different goals. We want children to enjoy reading and be motivated to read. We want children to comprehend what they read. We want children to be able to recognize words quickly and automatically. We know that children do not enjoy reading if they cannot comprehend or if they have to struggle sounding out each and every word. Therefore, we want children to have a good background in letter-sound correspondences and be able to apply this knowledge to recognizing words quickly and automatically. But at the same time, children will not enjoy reading if the only reading they do is sounding out words. Good reading instruction contains a balance of activities around these different goals. For enjoyment, children should be able to choose at least some of the books that they read (Morrow & Tracey, 1998; Turner, 1995) and should be read aloud to from a variety of books from different genres (Feitelson, Kita, & Goldstein, 1986). For comprehension, children should engage in discussions and questioning about the content of what they read. Although phonics instruction is an extremely important part of beginning reading, it is only one part.

Specific Approaches to Phonics Instruction

The conditions under which these principles can be met occur in a variety of reading programs. Reviews of research in this area suggest that it is the emphasis on early and systematic phonics instruction that makes a program effective and that differences between approaches are relatively small (Chall, 1996; Dahl & Freppon, 1995). In this section, we will discuss and review phonics instruction, both traditional and contemporary, from a variety of instructional philosophies. What we call traditional approaches are approaches that were in vogue during the 1960s and 1970s but seem to be returning as teachers grapple with how to teach phonics. Contemporary phonics approaches are those that have been used frequently in the past decade.

Traditional Phonics Approaches

Research on traditional phonics approaches includes mammoth federally funded studies (Abt Associates, 1977; Bond & Dykstra, 1967; Dykstra, 1968), large-scale district evaluations (Kean, Summers, Raivetz, & Farber, 1979), and reviews of research such as that of Adams (1990) and Chall (1996). These reviews consistently find that early and systematic phonics instruction is more effective than later and less systematic instruction.

The differences in quality between phonics approaches are small. Generally, reviews have found a slight advantage for synthetic approaches over analytic approaches (e.g., Chall, 1996), but these differences may be due not to differences in method but instead to differences in coverage, practice, or other factors.

Analytic Phonics Approaches
Analytic approaches begin with a word that a child already knows and breaks this word down into its component parts. For example, a teacher might begin an analytic phonics lesson by writing the word *bed* on the board and saying something like "the sound in the middle of the word *bed* makes an /e/ sound, which we call the short *e*." The teacher might then say some other words aloud, such as *hen, met, bat, run,* and *rest,* and ask students to raise their hands if the middle sound of the word was a short *e* sound. This instruction might be followed by having students read a series of words on the board, each containing a short *e* sound, and then having students complete a worksheet or two. This analytic approach might be typical of a basal reading lesson in the 1970s. Such lessons tend to be confusing to follow, especially since they seem to have largely been used as an introduction to the worksheets, rather than as lessons in themselves (Durkin, 1988).

Linguistic Approaches.   Another variety of phonics instruction that might be called ana-lytic is the so-called linguistic method. This method is based on the theories of linguist Leonard Bloomfield (Bloomfield & Barnhart, 1961) who reasoned that one cannot pro-nounce many of the sounds that consonants make in isolation (that is, the first sound of *cat* is not /kuh/ but the unpronounceable /k/). Because children cannot sound words out, they should learn words in patterns (such as *cat, rat,* and *fat*) and induce the pronunciations of unknown words from known patterns.

The results of this method were easily lampooned texts such as: "Dan is a man. /Nat is a cat./ Nat is fat./ Nat sat on a mat." Adams (1990) called linguistic texts *visual tongue-twisters,* explaining that these texts made little sense and were so loaded with similar words that they were a challenge for anyone, even a proficient reader or a learner, to read aloud. Although texts like these have gone on to well-deserved oblivion, we have seen the demand for decodable texts (e.g., California Department of Education, 1995) lead to the use of some poorly written texts. It is a challenge to write texts that are both decodable and coherent, but it can be done.

Synthetic Phonics Approaches

The other major division of traditional phonics approaches are the synthetic phonics approaches. Such phonics approaches begin with teaching students individual letters or groups of letters and then showing students how to blend these letters together to form words. A synthetic phonics lesson may begin with the teacher writing a letter on the board, such as *a,* and then saying, "This is the letter *a,* and it makes the sound /a/." The teacher might write a word containing that letter, such as *rat,* and pointing at the letters from left to right have the class blend the word together in unison. This might be followed by some group instruction in reading words with the short *a,* such as *bat, ham, fan, and,* and *ran.* Then the students might read a story containing a high percentage of words with the short *a* sound.

When one of the authors reviewed supplemental phonics programs (Osborn, Stahl, & Stein, 1997), we found many of the programs we reviewed for home or supplemental use in schools were synthetic phonics programs. These supplemental programs are usually locally produced and appear to be used only in certain regions of the U.S. Many are based on Orton-Gillingham principles but without the extensive training that such programs entail (Gillingham, 1956). In addition, Direct Instruction approaches seem to be undergoing a resurgence. These two synthetic phonics approaches will be reviewed below.

Orton-Gillingham Approaches.   Approaches based on Orton-Gillingham methods begin with direct teaching of individual letters paired with their sounds through a VAKT (i.e., visual, auditory, kinesthetic, and tactile) procedure that involves tracing the letter while saying its name and sound, blending letters together to read words and sentences, and finally reading short stories constructed to contain only taught sounds. Among those approaches based on Orton and Gillingham's work are the Slingerland approach (Lovitt & DeMier, 1984), the Spaulding approach (Spaulding & Spaulding, 1962), Recipe for Read-ing (Traub, 1977), and Alphabetic Phonics (Ogden, Hindman, & Turner, 1989). There are differences among these approaches, largely in sequencing or materials, but these approaches all have the general characteristics discussed. Spelling the words from dictation is also part of an Orton-Gillingham lesson. Each letter sound is learned to mastery through repetition. More advanced lessons involve teaching learners to blend syllables together and read more complex texts. Teachers are specially trained to use Orton-Gillingham methods.

An Orton-Gillingham lesson might begin with the teacher showing the child a card with a letter such as *m*. The teacher might say, "This is the letter *m*, and it says /m/." Then the teacher might take the child's finger and trace the letter, saying, "*M* (letter name), /m/ (sound)." This sequence is repeated until the child has mastered the letter and its sound. The child writes the letter in the air and then on paper, while repeating its name and sound. When a group of letters is mastered, the teacher presents some words containing those sounds. Each of the sounds is identified sequentially. The teacher models blending the sounds together to make a word. This process is repeated, with the child increasingly being held responsible for blending the sounds together. Also in the lesson is spelling from dictation. The same words used in reading are dictated, and the child is supposed to write the sounds that he or she hears. If the child cannot spell the word, the teacher stretches the word when pronouncing it so that each sound can be heard individually, and the child then writes those sounds down. In addition, there are simple books containing words with the taught sounds that the child and teacher read for practice.

In spite of the longevity of use of the Orton-Gillingham approach, there is relatively little research on it. There have been numerous case studies attesting to the approach's effectiveness, beginning with Monroe (1932). These case studies do not, however, meet the criteria for rigorous qualitative research. Other studies of the Orton-Gillingham approach have not included control groups (Ogden et al., 1989; Vickery, Reynolds, & Cochran, 1987). Without a control group, it is hard to tell whether the program worked better than any other.

Kline and Kline (1975) reported a clinical retrospective, comparing the reading abilities of children who were diagnosed as dyslexic in their clinic and given either Orton-Gillingham–based instruction or whatever instruction was given in the child's school. They found that nearly all of the Orton-Gillingham–trained subjects made significant progress while only half of the school-treated subjects did. Again, since the study did not employ typical controls, the differences could have related to reasons the different subjects got different treatments or some other extraneous variables.

Other studies have used single-subject designs, with replications. Lovitt and Hurlburt (1974) and Lovitt and DeMier (1984) compared the Slingerland approach with a linguistic approach that did not include direct instruction in letter-sound correspondences. They found both approaches equally effective. Silberberg, Iversen, and Goins (1973) found that a conventional phonics approach produced the strongest results, significantly greater than those from the Orton-Gillingham approach on 6 of the 10 measures employed.

Given that the Orton-Gillingham approach and its variations have been in use for more than 60 years, this is a disappointing amount of research. When Orton-Gillingham was compared to conventional instruction for children with reading problems (Kline & Kline, 1975), it seemed to be more effective. When compared to with other approaches that were new to the student, the Orton-Gillingham approach did not seem any more effective than any other approach. Given the small number of studies, however, it is difficult to draw any conclusions.

Direct Instruction Approaches. The Direct Instruction approach of Englemann was first published under the name of Distar (Englemann & Bruner, 1969), later Reading Mastery. The Distar approach is a synthetic phonics approach, based on a behavioral analysis of decoding (Kameenui, Simmons, Chard, & Dickson, 1997). Students are taught letter sounds (not letter names, at least in the beginning stages of the program) through highly structured instruction using cuing and reinforcement procedures derived from behavioral analyses of instruction. The task of decoding is broken down into its component parts, and each of these parts is taught carefully and deliberately (see Kameenui et al., 1997).

Instruction proceeds from letter sounds to blending to reading words in context. Instruction is scripted, with the teacher using a flip book containing both the stimuli for children's responses and a script of what the teacher is to say. The lessons are fast-paced, with high student involvement. The text for the first-year program is written in a script that, although it preserves English spelling, cues the reader to silent letters (by making the letters relatively small) and different vowel sounds (placing a macron over long vowels). Children practice in specially constructed books containing taught sounds, although children may be encouraged to read widely in children's literature as well (e.g., Meyer, 1983).

Early research with Distar found strong effects (Adams & Englemann, 1996), but in this research Direct Instruction programs have been compared to programs that differed from it on many dimensions. The major study of the effects of Distar is the study of Project Follow Through classes (Abt Associates, 1977). This was a national project, involving hundreds of classes. Distar was the only program that produced achievement in poor students that was near the national average. In this study, and in many of the early studies, Distar was compared to approaches that had radically different goals than Distar and did not stress phonics as strongly as it did.

Adams and Englemann (1996) performed a meta-analysis on the effects of Direct Instruction (in areas including comprehension and mathematics) on student achievement and found that Direct Instruction approaches produced large effect sizes on achievement measures. Although these results are impressive, they need to be viewed critically. First, both Adams and Englemann are associated with Reading Mastery, and their review has not been peer reviewed, so this is not an independent review. Second, we have, in a cursory survey using ERIC, found a number of relevant studies not included in the Adams and Englemann review, including some studies that did not find salutary effects for Distar in beginning reading. Thus, further research investigating the success of Reading Mastery seems warranted.

Contemporary Phonics Approaches

In this section, we discuss three contemporary phonics approaches: (a) spelling-based approaches, (b) analogy-based approaches, and (c) embedded phonics approaches. All of these approaches are usually described in the literature as components of larger reading instruction programs. For example, spelling-based approaches are implemented in programs such as the Multimethod, Multilevel Instruction Program (e.g., Cunningham & Hall, 1997), the Charlottesville Volunteer Tutorial or Book Buddies Project (e.g., Invernizzi, Juel, & Rosemary, 1996/1997; Johnston, Juel, & Invernizzi, 1995), and the Howard Street Tutoring Program (e.g., Morris, 1992). Analogy-based approaches are one aspect of the

Benchmark Word Identification Program (e.g., Gaskins et al., 1996/1997), and embedded phonics approaches are utilized in programs such as Reading Recovery (Clay, 1993) or in whole language classrooms (e.g., Dahl & Freppon, 1995; Freppon & Headings, 1996). Thus, it is important to consider the instructional context in which these contemporary phonics approaches often occur.

Spelling-Based Approaches

Three contemporary approaches to phonics instruction, Word Study (e.g., Bear, Invernizzi, Templeton, & Johnston, 1996), Making Words (e.g., Cunningham & Cunningham, 1992; Cunningham & Hall, 1994), and Meta-Phonics (Calfee, 1998; Calfee & Henry, 1996), are based on spelling principles.

Word Study.   In Word Study, students examine words and word patterns through strategies such as sorting, in which students categorize words and pictures according to their common orthographic features. Word Study instruction is based on students' developmental levels of orthographic knowledge and is an approach to teaching phonics, vocabulary, spelling, and word recognition. In Word Study, the teacher bases instruction on word features that students are writing but are confusing (e.g., Bear et al., 1996). For example, when a child spells *rane* for *rain* and makes similar errors in other aspects of his or her writing, the teacher may begin instruction with the child on long *a* word patterns.

Word Study is based on research on how orthographic knowledge develops (e.g., Templeton & Bear, 1992) and is included in this section on contemporary approaches to phonics instruction because of recent, published descriptions of Word Study in widely read texts and journals. For example, Word Study has been described in teacher resources (e.g., Bear et al., 1996) and in journal articles (e.g., Barnes, 1989; Bloodgood, 1991; Gill, 1992; Invernizzi, Abouzeid, & Gill, 1994; Invernizzi et al., 1996/1997; Morris, Ervin, & Conrad, 1996; Schlagal & Schlagal, 1992; Templeton, 1989, 1991, 1992).

Much of the Word Study research is described in the contexts in which this approach occurs. For example, Invernizzi et al. (1996/1997) described the use of Word Study in the Charlottesville Volunteer Tutorial program over a 3-year time period. In this program, low-achieving first- and second-grade students are tutored in reading by trained community volunteers. During the third year of program implementation, tutored students' pre- to posttest gain scores increased statistically significantly on measures of alphabet knowledge, phonemic awareness, and word recognition, and 86% of all students read with 90% accuracy a benchmark first-grade level trade book during the third year of the implementation of the tutoring program.

Additionally, Morris et al. (1996) provided a case study of a sixth-grade student with severe reading difficulties in a university-based reading clinic. A reading tutor worked with this student once a week for 2 years in a clinic tutoring program in which Word Study was included, and the student made 2 years' growth in reading and spelling as measured by informal reading assessments.

The effectiveness of the Word Study approach to phonics instruction has been documented in conjunction with other aspects of teaching and supporting reading; for example, writing, reading of instructional level texts, and rereading independent texts. Thus, it is difficult to document in an empirical sense the effects of word study instruction per se, although this type of phonics instruction seems to be effective as one component in reading interventions and programs.

Making Words.   In Making Words (e.g., Cunningham & Cunningham, 1992; Cunningham & Hall, 1994), students are given six to eight different letters on letter cards. Then, the teacher calls out words with two, three, four, and more letters that can be formed using the students' letters, with the teacher and students first making the words and then sorting words based on their common spelling patterns or other orthographic features. At the end of this activity, the teacher challenges the students to use all of their letters to make a big word. The big word is related to something the children are reading.

Making Words is one component of the Working With Words block in the Multimethod, Multilevel Instruction Program (e.g., Cunningham & Hall, 1997). As was the case with Word Study, the effectiveness of this approach to phonics instruction is described in the context of overall reading program effects. In a recent description of program results, Hall and Cunningham (1996) documented that 85% of students in the Multimethod, Multilevel Instruction Program were reading at or above grade level by the end of their first-grade year, and 94% of students were reading on grade level by the end of their second-grade year as measured by informal reading inventory data.

Objectively, it is not as easy to determine the success of Word Study and Making Words in isolation in improving students' word identification abilities as compared to some of the described traditional phonics approaches. However, both of these approaches seem to be effective as part of overall approaches to teaching reading.

Meta-Phonics.   In this approach, reading and spelling are taught simultaneously through social interaction and group problem solving. Sounds are introduced through phonemic awareness instruction. This instruction stresses articulation as a key to learning sounds (Calfee, 1998; Calfee et al., 1973). Thus, /p/ /t/ and /k/ are *popping sounds*. Vowels are taught as *glue letters*. After these are established, students are given letters and sounds and asked to make a make a word, through adding consonants to vowels. Students begin with short consonant-vowel-consonant words but progress to longer words such as *discombobulate* or *sassafras*.

This component has been embedded in a larger program, Project READ (Calfee, 1998). Preliminary results suggest that the program has been successful in three school settings. Students who have used this program were at or above district or national averages in reading comprehension, fluency, word recognition, spelling, and writing. These evaluations were informal, without a true control group, and also were conducted as part of a redesign of reading instruction, making it difficult to ascertain how important this component was to overall achievement gains. This approach awaits a fuller, more controlled evaluation.

Analogy-Based Approaches

In analogy-based approaches to phonics instruction, students learn how to decode words they do not know by using words or word parts they do know. For example, students learn that if they can read the words *he, send,* and *table,* they can compare and contrast these words with the word parts in the unknown word *de/pend/able* to help them decode this word. Decades ago, the research of Patricia Cunningham (e.g., Cunningham, 1975/1976, 1978, 1979, 1980) focused on using analogy-based approaches to help students decode unknown words.

Analogy-based approaches are currently used as one instructional component in the Benchmark Word Identification Program (e.g., Gaskins, Gaskins, & Gaskins, 1991; 1992). Current versions of this decoding program include phonics approaches other than analogy-based approaches (see Gaskins et al., 1996/1997), such as teaching students ways to analyze all sounds in a word. In the analogy-based phonics component, students learn 120 key words with common phonogram patterns and word parts. Five to six new words are introduced to students every week, with the teacher providing explicit instruction to students on how to use these key words to decode other words.

There are three different types of research support for analogy-based approaches, all of which suggest using some caution in implementing those approaches. First are basic research studies. Goswami's work (1993, 1998) suggests that young children can use analogies before they can use other phonological information to read words. Bruck and Treiman (1992) and Ehri and Robbins (1992), however, found that children need to be able to use phonetic cue reading, or initial letter-sound relationships, in order to take advantage of analogies in reading. The differences between Goswami's work and Bruck and Treiman's and Ehri and Robbins's studies lie in experimental design. (In Goswami's studies, the analogue word is always available for the child; in the other studies, the child has to rely on memory.) In practice, analogies should be used after children can recognize initial sound cues, which is how they are used in Cunningham's (1995) and Gaskins et al.'s (1996/1997) approaches.

The second line of research on analogies comes from directed studies. Haskell, Foorman, and Swank (1992) and Sullivan, Okada, and Niedermeyer (1971) found that an analogy approach and a synthetic approach performed equally well, and both were more effective than whole-word approaches. Fayne and Bryant (1981) found that a rime-based strategy was not as effective as teaching children initial bigrams (e.g., *co-g*). These were short-term studies. White and Cunningham (1990), in a yearlong study, found that analogy training produced statistically significant effects on measures of both word recognition and comprehension.

Finally, analogy approaches are part of successful reading programs, including the approach used at the Benchmark School (Gaskins et al., 1988; see also Cunningham, 1995). The experience at Benchmark is illustrative of both the strengths and limits of an analogy-based approach. The program began as a direct adaptation of analogies with metacognitive strategy training to help children transfer the use of analogy-based decoding in their reading (Gaskins et al., 1992). This program seemed to be successful with many of the children with reading problems at Benchmark, but there were a number of children who did not succeed. In an attempt to reach more children, the program was modified to include a more thorough analysis of the words taught as anchor words (Gaskins et al., 1996/1997), thus teaching more phonological information along with the analogy words. Our conclusion is that analogies can be a very powerful teaching approach but need to be taught after a child has reached the phonetic cue level and in conjunction with other decoding approaches.

Embedded Phonics Approaches

In embedded phonics approaches, phonics instruction occurs in the context of authentic reading and writing experiences. The phonics instruction in Reading Recovery and in many whole language classrooms are examples of embedded approaches to phonics instruction.

Phonics in Reading Recovery.   Reading Recovery (Clay, 1993) is a one-on-one tutorial program intended for the lowest 20% of first-grade children in a school. Although lessons are based on daily individual diagnosis of children's needs, there is a common lesson structure (Clay, 1993). First, lessons begin with a rereading of two or more books of the student's choice. The purpose of this rereading is to develop fluency. Next, the student rereads the book that was introduced the previous day. The teacher makes a running record of this reading and addresses one or two teaching points immediately following the running record. Following the running record, there is *making and breaking* with magnetic letters. Next, the child writes a sentence-length story with the help of the teacher. This help may include hearing and recording sounds in words using Elkonin boxes (Elkonin, 1973). After that, the story is cut up and reassembled. Finally, the teacher introduces a new book, using Clay's (1991) procedures, and the child attempts an independent first reading of the book.

Lessons are based on Goodman's (1976) model, suggesting that readers use three cuing systems to recognize words in context. Clay (1993) called these systems visual, structural, and meaning cues. One study found that most of the children referred to Reading Recovery needed work on the visual system (Center, Wheldall, Freeman, Outhred, & McNaught, 1995), especially phonological processes (Iversen & Tunmer, 1993). Within the lesson structure, the teacher has a number of options to teach children to better use visual cues. The individual nature of a Reading Recovery lesson enables the teacher to direct the child's attention to aspects of words relevant to their development. Work with magnetic letters, cut-up sentences, and carefully selected gradient texts gently nudge the Reading Recovery student to the next level of visual sensitivity, balancing the child's reading work through the utilization of and reliance on multiple cuing systems. Thus, phonics instruction is woven throughout the lessons.

Letter sprees are activities that involve the direct teaching of letter names, learned to the point of automaticity (Adams, 1990; Clay, 1993). In their writing, children use invented spellings to approximate words, although the final product always is spelled conventionally. Also, teachers integrate work with Elkonin boxes into spelling work, having children use the boxes to reflect on each sound in a word.

In making and breaking words, the teacher uses magnetic letters to give children practice in reading phonetically controlled words. This component has been part of Reading Recovery from the beginning, but recently it has received more emphasis. Iversen and Tunmer (1993) found that they were able to help children discontinue the program earlier by adding a phonological recoding component to the Reading Recovery lesson.

Reading Recovery teachers can also choose texts that reflect children's increasing mastery of phonics. A teacher might choose a text that requires the child to direct attention to particular visual features of words. If a child is, for example, noticing initial-sound relationships, the teacher would choose a book in which the child must use these relationships to read the book successfully. In the beginning Reading Recovery lessons, texts are highly predictable, and the pattern provides a scaffold for children's reading. As texts become less predictable over the course of the lessons, teachers decrease the amount of scaffolding they provide, encouraging children to use more visual features of words. The result of these cumulative decisions, in text reading and through other aspects of the lessons, is that children advance in their word recognition abilities and phonological awareness (Stahl, Stahl, & McKenna, 1997).

Reading Recovery has been cited by Adams (1990) as an excellent example of what good phonics instruction can be. Although children do receive a great deal of work with letters and sounds, the instruction is always integrated into the reading and writing of texts. Teachers keep track of students' increasing mastery of the visual cuing system in conjunction with the other two systems. Children spend the majority of their lesson time reading and writing connected text, with very little time spent on phonics.

Reading Recovery has been found to be effective, at least for the children in the program (Center et al., 1995; Shanahan & Barr, 1995, Wasik & Slavin, 1993). In their conservative analysis, Center et al. (1995) found that Reading Recovery was able to accelerate the reading progress of 35% of the children who would not, under other programs, reach the level of their successful peers. Although there is some controversy about the cost effectiveness of Reading Recovery, the instruction given seems to be highly effective. Reading Recovery has been adapted to programs in group settings, and these programs seem to be effective in increasing children's reading achievement as well (e.g., Fountas & Pinnell, 1996; Hiebert, 1994; Taylor, Short, & Shearer, 1990).

Phonics in Whole Language Classrooms.   As we noted at the beginning of this article, whole language teachers do teach phonics. However, this instruction is often embedded in the context of teaching reading and is sensitive to the child's needs. Letter-sound instruction can occur as one of the cuing systems that children use to recognize words in reading (e.g., Weaver, 1994) and can also occur as part of writing instruction.

Whole language instruction varies considerably from teacher to teacher and from class to class (Watson, 1989). It may resemble the instruction in the Reading Recovery lessons described previously (although Reading Recovery is not a whole language approach; see Church, 1996). Some whole language teachers may provide less organized phonics instruction than occurs in Reading Recovery. An example of whole language phonics instruction comes from first-grade teacher Linda Headings's class:

> *I focus on using children's names a lot, especially in the beginning months, because of the significance of names in their lives. Names carry power in giving us identity, and I can gather information by doing this, too. I can see who is unsure and who is not, who is trying to figure out not only his or her own name but also the names of others. Over the next month, I use names to do language play, poetry, games and songs, and to engage with environmental print. That name immersion will be pulled back out and used when children have questions about invented spelling. "It starts like Bobby," I'll say. "Go find his name tag and see what letter his name starts with." I can use this with children who are poor risktakers or*

developmentally lagging. It also gives them the avenue to monitor their own learn-
ing. I teach and guide, and the child acts on his [sic] own and completes the pro-
cess by finding Bobby's name and writing the letter B. (Freppon & Headings,
1996, p. 71)

The instruction is embedded within the classroom framework, as names and name cards are used in a variety of classroom activities. Also, the name instruction is extended to other language activities, and the teacher strives to make the student an independent learner by not giving the child an answer, but instead providing the child a strategy for finding the answer (e.g., "It starts like Bobby").

In the accounts of phonics instruction from the projects of Dahl and Freppon (1995), Freppon and Dahl (1991), and Freppon and Headings (1996), who discuss observations of the same first-grade teacher, and from the work of Mills et al. (1992), we are given no examples of first-grade whole language teachers who teach something other than conso-nants. The lesson above is typical of what is presented in illustrative vignettes within these studies. Of course, just because lessons involving vowels or lessons involving the full examination of words were not present in vignettes does not mean that these teachers did not teach vowels. But it is still surprising that vowel lessons were not described, since one would expect that instruction in vowels occurs during the first-grade year (Anderson, Hie-bert, Scott, & Wilkinson, 1985).

The lack of phonics instruction beyond consonants may be indicative of whole lan-guage teachers' reticence to challenge their students. This may be symptomatic of a general lack of challenge in many whole language classes. One study found that children in whole language classrooms did not read as challenging materials as children in traditional classes and that the amount of challenge determined children's achievement at the end of the year (Stahl, Suttles, & Pagnucco, 1996). Church (1994, 1996), a whole language teacher in Nova Scotia, was also concerned that whole language teachers do not sufficiently challenge their students. In short, some reading programs based on the whole language philosophy may not encourage students to read more challenging texts and may not expose children to the types of phonics instruction they need to improve as readers and writers.

Research on Contemporary Approaches to Phonics
Although there are indications that the contemporary approaches discussed in this section were effective, there is a notable lack of controlled research to validate the effectiveness of these approaches. Part of the reason for the lack of research is the newness of these approaches. Another possible reason is the general trend of the field away from compara-tive research and toward descriptive research (McKenna et al., 1994). Although descriptive research can give us insights, without some sort of comparison it is difficult to tell whether these new approaches are more effective than traditional approaches. Such comparative research need not be a horse race in which different approaches are saddled up to see which one produces the highest scores on a standardized achievement test. Instead, such compar-isons may include qualitative aspects, such as in Dahl and Freppon's (1995) study, and should be directed toward what each approach might be effective at rather than toward choosing the most effective.

Constructions of Knowledge about Words

The principles discussed in the beginning of this article all relate to a teacher guiding students' constructions of knowledge about words. From a constructivist perspective, learners are thought to be actively constructing knowledge through their interactions with the world. This, of course, includes interactions with teachers and reading materials. Ordinarily, researchers have used a constructivist perspective to talk about comprehension, especially in conjunction with schema theory (e.g., Anderson & Pearson, 1984). Researchers in decoding rely on other psychological models, such as connectionism (Adams, 1990) and behaviorist models (Carnine, Silbert, & Kameenui, 1990). Neither of these models explicitly views the learner as actively constructing information about words.

Our observations of children show them very actively trying to make sense of words, in both their writing and their reading. A child who makes two or three attempts at a word in a text before coming up with one that makes sense and accommodates the letter-sound relationships that he or she knows is actively constructing word knowledge, as is the child who stretches out the letters in the word *camel* and produces *caml*.

Viewing decoding through a constructivist lens may be a whole language perspective (e.g., Weaver, 1994), but one need not adopt teaching techniques commonly associated with the whole language philosophy if one takes this perspective. A constructivist perspective is consistent with any of the methods discussed in the second section of this paper. Constructivism is not synonymous with discovery learning, since children can be guided in their constructions more or less explicitly. What constructivism implies is that the child is an active learner.

What children construct is a network of information about letters. They know, for example that *t* is more likely to be followed by *r* or *h* than by *q* or *p*, that *ck* never starts a word, that *q* is nearly always followed by *u* (with the exception of some Arabic and Chinese words) (see Adams, 1990; Venezky, 1970). Much of this information could be directly taught or learned from repeated experiences with print. Children do differ in their need for guidance. Some children will learn much of what they need to know about words from exposure (e.g., Durkin, 1966), but most children need some explicit support. This support might be provided in context, as in the embedded phonics instruction approaches, through analogy- or spelling-based approaches, or through more direct instruction. It could be that some children with reading problems require more direct instruction (Carnine et al., 1990).

The notion that children construct knowledge about words may explain why the differences among programs are small. As long as one provides early and systematic information about the code (Chall, 1996), it may not matter very much how one does it. If each of the programs discussed previously provides similar amounts of coverage with similar amounts of practice reading words in isolation and in context, they might all have similar effects. From a constructivist perspective, children learn by acting upon information; if the information is similar, the learning should be as well. The principles discussed in the first part of this article suggest the information that should be taught in a phonics program. If this information is made available to children, then it may not matter exactly how the instruction occurs.

An effective first-grade reading program, for example, might involve some systematic and direct instruction in decoding, with associated practice in decodable texts (Juel &

Roper/Schneider, 1985). These may include some contrived texts, if they are artfully and interestingly done. They also might include authentic literature chosen for repetition of taught patterns (Trachtenburg, 1990). Children also need a variety of engaging but easy texts, both for interest and for practice in reading a variety of materials. Some of these texts might be predictable where the context supports word recognition, at least until the child develops more independent word recognition strategies (Clay, 1993; Fountas & Pinnell, 1996). Predictable texts by themselves, however, may limit children's word learning (Duffy, McKenna, Vancil, Stratton, & Stahl, 1996), unless the teacher draws specific attention to words in those texts (Johnston, 1995). Writing, using invented spelling, is useful for developing word knowledge (Clarke, 1989). As they invent spellings, children need to integrate their developing phoneme awareness with their knowledge of sound-symbol correspondences (Stahl & Murray, 1998).

Because first-grade children are focused on decoding in their text reading (Chall, 1996), children's comprehension growth might best be accommodated by the teacher reading aloud to the children. Studies have found that children can learn new vocabulary words from hearing stories (e.g., Elley, 1989). In addition, teachers can model more advanced comprehension strategies with stories they read out loud to children since these stories are likely to have richer contexts than stories a child can read independently. This is not to say that comprehension should be ignored during children's reading. Basic strategies such as recall (Koskinen et al., 1988) or story grammars (Beck & McKeown, 1981) can be profitably taught to children at this age. An extensive reading program would likely improve first graders' motivation toward reading, as would a daily period of choice reading (Morrow & Tracey, 1998).

Thus, an effective first-grade program might involve elements associated with whole language (teacher reading aloud, invented spelling, free reading, extensive use of literature) as well as more direct instructional approaches (direct sound-symbol instruction, limited use of decodable or contrived texts). How these elements might be managed might also depend on the needs of the children. Children who enter first grade with a low literacy background may need more direct instruction to develop concepts that other children may have learned through print-based home experiences with literacy. Children with print-based literacy backgrounds may benefit from more time to choose their reading, with teacher support to read more and more complex materials.

Effective reading instruction requires that a teacher recognize multiple goals for reading instruction, and that different means are required to reach these multiple goals. Juggling these goals will always be a challenge. We are not sure, however, that the alleged balance we are seeing in some classroom reading programs is based on a forward-looking examination of what is needed for effective reading instruction; rather, it may be based, at least in part, on false allegations popularized by the media and accepted by some legislators and administrators describing the limited success of past reading programs.

The balance in some of today's reading programs appears to be an attempt to lay phonics instruction on top of a literature-based curriculum. This is easy. Good reading instruction, however, is difficult. It involves all teachers asking themselves what skills their students have, what their goals are, and how reading instruction can be directed toward all of their goals.

References

Abt Associates. (1977). *Education as experimentation: A planned variation model. Volume IV-B, Effects of follow-through models.* Cambridge, MA: Author.

Adams, G. L., & Englemann, S. (1996). *Research on direct instruction: 25 years beyond DISTAR.* Seattle, WA: Educational Achievement Systems.

Adams, M. J. (1990). *Beginning to read: Thinking and learning about print.* Cambridge, MA: MIT Press.

Anderson, R. C., Hiebert, E. F., Scott, J. A., & Wilkinson, I. A. G. (1985). *Becoming a nation of readers.* Champaign, IL: National Academy of Education and Center for the Study of Reading.

Anderson, R. C., & Pearson, P. D. (1984). A schema-theoretic view of basic processes in reading. In P. D. Pearson (Ed.), *Handbook of reading research* (pp. 255–292). White Plains, NY: Longman.

Barnes, G. W. (1989). Word sorting: The cultivation of rules for spelling in English. *Reading Psychology, 10,* 293–307.

Baumann, J. F., Hoffman, J. V., Moon, J., & Duffy-Hester, A. M. (1998). Where are teachers' voices in the phonics/whole language debate? Results from a survey of U.S. elementary classroom teachers. *The Reading Teacher,* 636–650.

Bear, D. R., & Barone, D. (1989). Using children's spellings to group for word study and directed reading in the primary classroom. *Reading Psychology, 10,* 275–292.

Bear, D. R., Invernizzi, M., Templeton, S., & Johnston, F. (1996). *Words their way: Word study for phonics, vocabulary, and spelling instruction.* Upper Saddle River, NJ: Merrill.

Beck, I. L., & Mckeown, M. G. (1981). Developing questions that promote comprehension: The story map. *Language Arts, 58,* 913–918.

Bloodgood, J. (1991). A new approach to spelling in language arts programs. *Elementary School Journal, 92,* 203–211.

Bloomfield, L., & Barnhart, C. L. (1961). *Let's read: A linguistic approach.* Detroit, MI: Wayne State University Press.

Bond, G., & Dykstra, R. (1967). The cooperative research program in first grade reading. *Reading Research Quarterly, 2,* 5–142.

Bruck, M., & Treiman, R. (1992). Learning to pronounce words: The limitations of analogies. *Reading Research Quarterly, 27,* 374–388.

Byrne, B., & Fielding-Barnsley, R. (1991). Evaluation of a program to teach phonemic awareness in young children. *Journal of Educational Psychology, 83,* 451–455.

Calfee, R. (1998). Phonics and phonemes: Learning to decode in a literature-based program. In J. Metsala & L. Ehri (Eds.), *Word recognition in beginning literacy.* Mahwah, NJ: Erlbaum.

Calfee, R., & Henry, M. (1996). Strategy and skill in early reading acquisition. In J. Shimon (Ed.), *Literacy and education: Essays in memory of Dina Feitelson* (pp. 97–118). Cresskill, NJ: Hampton Press.

Calfee, R. C., Lindamood, P., & Lindamood, C. (1973). Acoustic-phonetic skills and reading: Kindergarten through twelfth grade. *Journal of Educational Psychology, 64,* 293–298.

California Department of Education. (1995). *Every child a reader: The report of the California Reading Task Force.* Sacramento: Author. (http://www.cde.ca.gov/cilbranch/eltdiv/rdg_init.htm).

Carnine, D., Silbert, J., & Kameenui, E. (1990). *Direct instruction reading* (2nd ed.). Columbus, OH: Merrill.

Center, Y., Wheldall, K., Freeman, L., Outhred, L., & McNaught, M. (1995). An evaluation of Reading Recovery. *Reading Research Quarterly, 30,* 240–263.

Chall, J. S. (1989). Learning to read: The great debate twenty years later. A response to "Debunking the great phonics myth." *Phi Delta Kappan, 71,* 521–538.

Chall, J. S. (1996). *Learning to read: The great debate* (revised, with a new foreword). New York: McGraw-Hill.

Church, S. M. (1994). Is whole language really warm and fuzzy? *The Reading Teacher, 47,* 362–371.

Church, S. M. (1996). *The future of whole language: Reconstruction or self-destruction.* Portsmouth, NH: Heinemann.

Clarke, L. K. (1989). Encouraging invented spelling in first graders' writing: Effects on learning to spell and read. *Research in the Teaching of English, 22,* 281–309.

Clay, M. M. (1991). Introducing a new storybook to young readers. *The Reading Teacher, 45,* 264–273.

Clay, M. M. (1993). *Reading Recovery: A guidebook for teachers in training.* Portsmouth, NH: Heinemann.

Clymer, T. (1963). The utility of phonic generalizations in the primary grades. *The Reading Teacher, 16,* 252–258.

Clymer, T. (1996). The utility of phonic generalizations in the primary grades. *The Reading Teacher, 50,* 182–187.

Collins, J. (1997, October 27). How Johnny should read. *Time Magazine, 150*(17), 78–81.

Cunningham, P. M. (1975/1976). Investigating a synthesized theory of mediated word identification. *Reading Research Quarterly, 11,* 127–143.

Cunningham, P. M. (1978). Decoding polysyllabic words: An alternative strategy. *Journal of Reading, 21,* 608–614.

Cunningham, P. M. (1979). A compare/contrast theory of mediated word identification. *The Reading Teacher, 32,* 774–778.

Cunningham, P. M. (1980). Applying a compare/contrast process to identifying polysyllabic words. *Journal of Reading Behavior, 12,* 213–223.

Cunningham, P. M. (1995). *Phonics they use* (2nd ed.). New York: HarperCollins.

Cunningham, P. M., & Cunningham, J. W. (1992). Making words: Enhancing the invented spelling-decoding connection. *The Reading Teacher, 46,* 106–115.

Cunningham, P. M., & Hall, D. P. (1994). *Making words.* Carthage, IL: Good Apple.

Cunningham, P. M., & Hall, D. P. (1997, May). *A framework for literacy in primary classrooms that work.* Paper presented at the 42nd annual convention of the International Reading Association, Atlanta, GA.

Dahl, K. L., & Freppon, P. A. (1995). A comparison of inner-city children's interpretations of reading and writing instruction in the early grades in skills-based and whole language classrooms. *Reading Research Quarterly, 30,* 50–74.

Deford, D. E. (1985). Validating the construct of theoretical orientation in reading instruction. *Reading Research Quarterly, 20,* 351–367.

Duffy, A. M., Mckenna, M., Vancil, S., Stratton, B., & Stahl, S. A. (1996, December). *Tales of Ms. Wishy-Washy: The effects of predictable books on learning to recognize words.* Paper presented at the annual meeting of the National Reading Conference, Charleston, SC.

Durkin, D. (1966). *Children who read early.* New York: Teachers College Press.

Durkin, D. (1978/1979). What classroom observations reveal about reading comprehension instruction. *Reading Research Quarterly, 14,* 481–533.

Durkin, D. (1988). *A classroom observation study of reading instruction in kindergarten* (Tech. Rep. No. 422). Champaign, IL: Center for the Study of Reading, University of Illinois at Urbana-Champaign.

Dykstra, R. (1968). The effectiveness of code- and meaning-emphasis beginning reading programs. *The Reading Teacher, 22,* 17–23.

Ehri, L. C. (1992). Reconceptualizing the development of sight word reading and its relationship to recoding. In P. Gough, L. C. Ehri, & R. Treiman (Eds.), *Reading acquisition* (pp. 107–143). Mahwah, NJ: Erlbaum.

Ehri, L. C. (1995). Phases of development in learning to read words by sight. *Journal of Research in Reading, 18,* 116–125.

Ehri, L. C., & Robbins, C. (1992). Beginners need some decoding skill to read words by analogy. *Reading Research Quarterly, 27,* 12–26.

Eldredge, J. L. (1995). *Teaching decoding in holistic classrooms.* Englewood Cliffs, NJ: Merrill.

Eldredge, J. L., & Butterfield, D. (1986). Alternatives to traditional reading instruction. *The Reading Teacher, 48,* 32–37.

Elkonin, D. B. (1973). U.S.S.R. In J. Downing (Ed.), *Comparative reading* (pp. 551–579). New York: Macmillan.

Elley, W. B. (1989). Vocabulary acquisition from listening to stories. *Reading Research Quarterly, 24,* 174–187.

Englemann, S., & Bruner, E. (1969). *Distar reading program.* Chicago: SRA.

Fayne, H. R., & Bryant, N. D. (1981). Relative effects of various word synthesis strategies on the phonics achievement of learning disabled youngsters. *Journal of Educational Psychology, 73,* 616–623.

Feitelson, D., Kita, R., & Goldstein, Z. (1986). Effects of listening to series stories on first graders' comprehension and the use of language. *Research in the Teaching of English, 20,* 339–356.

Flack, M. (1931). *Angus and the cat.* Garden City, NY: Doubleday.

Fleisher, L. S., Jenkins, J. R., & Pany, D. (1979/1980). Effects on poor readers' comprehension of training in rapid decoding. *Reading Research Quarterly, 15,* 30–48.

Fountas, I. C., & Pinnell, G. S. (1996). *Guided reading: Good first teaching for all children.* Portsmouth, NH: Heinemann.

Freppon, P. A., & Dahl, K. L. (1991). Learning about phonics in a whole language classroom. *Language Arts, 68,* 190–197.

Freppon, P. A., & Headings, L. (1996). Keeping it whole in whole language: A first grade teacher's instruction in an urban whole language classroom. In E. McIntyre & M. Pressley (Eds.), *Balanced instruction: Strategies and skills in whole language* (pp. 65–82). Norwood, MA: Christopher-Gordon.

Gambrell, L. B., Wilson, R. M., & Gantt, W. N. (1981). Classroom observations of task-attending behaviors of good and poor readers. *Journal of Educational Research, 74,* 400–404.

Gaskins, I. W., Downer, M. A., Anderson, R. C., Cunningham, P. M., Gaskins, R. W., Schommer, M., & The Teachers of the Benchmark School. (1988). A metacognitive approach to phonics: Using what you know to decode what you don't know. *Remedial and Special Education, 9,* 36–41.

Gaskins, I. W., Ehri, L. C., Cress, C., O'Hara, C., & Donnelly, K. (1996/1997). Procedures for word learning: Making discoveries about words. *The Reading Teacher, 50,* 312–327.

Gaskins, R. W., Gaskins, J. C., & Gaskins, I. (1991). A decoding program for poor readers—and the rest of the class, too! *Language Arts, 68,* 213–225.

Gaskins, R. W., Gaskins, J. C., & Gaskins, I. (1992). Using what you know to figure our what you don't know: An analogy approach to decoding. *Reading and Writing Quarterly: Overcoming Learning Disabilities, 8,* 197–221.

Gill, J. T. (1992). Development of word knowledge as it relates to reading, spelling, and instruction. *Language Arts, 69,* 444–453.

Gillet, J. W., & Temple, C. (1990). *Understanding reading problems* (3rd ed.). Glenview, IL: Scott Foresman.

Gillingham, A. (1956). *Remedial training for children with specific disability in reading, spelling, and penmanship.* Cambridge, MA: Educators Publishing Service.

Goodman, K. S. (1976). Reading: A psycholinguistic guessing game. In H. Singer & R. B. Ruddell (Eds.), *Theoretical models and processes of reading* (2nd ed., pp. 497–508). Newark, DE: International Reading Association.

Goodman, K. S. (1986). *What's whole in whole language? A parent/teacher guide to children's learning.* Portsmouth, NH: Heinemann.

Goodman, K. S. (1993). *Phonics phacts.* Portsmouth, NH: Heinemann.

Goodman, K. S., & Goodman, Y. M. (1977). Learning about psycholinguistic processes by analyzing oral reading. *Harvard Educational Review, 47,* 317–333.

Goswami, U. (1993). Toward an interactive analogy model of reading development: Decoding vowel graphemes in beginning reading. *Journal of Experimental Child Psychology, 56,* 443–475.

Goswami, U. (1998). The role of analogies in the development of word recognition. In J. Metsala & L. Ehri (Eds.), *Word recognition in beginning literacy.* Mahwah, NJ: Erlbaum.

Gough, P. B., & Hillinger, M. L. (1980). Learning to read: An unnatural act. *Bulletin of the Orton Society, 30,* 179–196.

Hall, D. P., & Cunningham, P. M. (1996). Becoming literate in first and second grades: Six years of multimethod, multilevel instruction. In D. J. Leu, C. K. Kinzer, & K. A. Hinchman (Eds.), *Literacies for the 21st century,* 45th yearbook of the National Reading Conference (pp. 195–204). Chicago: National Reading Conference.

Harste, J. C., Burke, C. L., & Woodward, V. A. (1982). Children's language and world: Initial encounters with print. In J. A. Langer & M. T. Smith-Burke (Eds.), *Reader meets author/Bridging the gap* (pp. 105–131). Newark, DE: International Reading Association.

Haskell, D. W., Foorman, B. R., & Swank, P. A. (1992). Effects of three orthographic/phonological units on first grade reading. *Remedial and Special Education, 13,* 40–49.

Haynes, M. C., & Jenkins, J. R. (1986). Reading instruction in special education resource rooms. *American Educational Research Journal, 23,* 161–190.

Herman, P. A. (1985). The effect of repeated readings on reading rate, speech pauses, and word recognition accuracy. *Reading Research Quarterly, 20,* 553–565.

Hiebert, E. H. (1994). A small group literacy intervention with Chapter I students. In E. H. Hiebert & B. M. Taylor (Eds.), *Getting reading right from the start* (pp. 85–106). Boston: Allyn & Bacon.

Hoffman, J. V., Mccarthey, S. J., Abbott, J., Christian, C., Corman, L., Curry, C., Dressman, M., Elliott, B., Matherne, D., & Stahle, D. (1994). So what's new in the new basals? A focus on first grade. *Journal of Reading Behavior, 26,* 47–73.

Hohn, W. E., & Ehri, L. C. (1983). Do alphabet letters help prereaders acquire phonemic segmentation skill? *Journal of Educational Psychology, 75,* 752–762.

Invernizzi, M., Abouzeid, M., & Gill, T. (1994). Using students' invented spellings as a guide for spelling instruction that emphasizes word study. *Elementary School Journal, 95,* 155–167.

Invernizzi, M., Juel, C., & Rosemary, C. A. (1996/1997). A community volunteer tutorial that works. *The Reading Teacher, 50,* 304–311.

Iversen, S., & Tunmer, W. E. (1993). Phonological processing skills and the Reading Recovery program. *Journal of Educational Psychology, 85,* 112–126.

Johnston, F. R. (1995, December). *Learning to read with predictable text: What kinds of words do beginning readers remember?* Paper presented at the annual meeting of the National Reading Conference, New Orleans, LA.

Johnston, F., Juel, C., & Invernizzi, M. (1995). *Guidelines for volunteer tutors of emergent and early readers.* Charlottesville, VA: University of Virginia McGuffey Reading Center.

Juel, C., & Roper/Schneider, D. (1985). The influence of basal readers on first grade reading. *Reading Research Quarterly, 20,* 134–152.

Kameenui, E. J., Simmons, D. C., Chard, D., & Dickson, S. (1997). Direct instruction reading. In S. A. Stahl & D. A. Hayes (Eds.), *Instructional models in reading* (pp. 59–84). Mahwah, NJ: Erlbaum.

Kean, M. H., Summers, A. A., Raivetz, M. J., & Farber, I. J. (1979). *What works in reading? Summary and results of a joint school district/Federal Reserve Bank empirical study in Philadelphia.* Philadelphia: Office of Research and Evaluation. (ERIC Document Reproduction Service ED 176 216)

Kline, C. L., & Kline, C. L. (1975). Follow-up study of 216 dyslexic children. *Bulletin of the Orton Society, 25,* 127–144.

Koskinen, P. S., Gambrell, L. B., Kapinus, B. A., & Heathington, B. S. (1988). Retelling: A strategy for enhancing students' reading comprehension. *The Reading Teacher, 41,* 892–896.

Leinhardt, G., Zigmond, N., & Cooley, W. (1981). Reading instruction and its effects. *American Educational Research Journal, 18,* 343–361.

Levine, A. (1994, December). Education: The great debate revisited. *Atlantic Monthly, 274*(6), 38–44.

Lovitt, T. C., & Demier, D. M. (1984). An evaluation of the Slingerland method with LD youngsters. *Journal of Learning Disabilities, 17,* 267–272.

Lovitt, T. C., & Hurlburt, M. (1974). Using behavior-analysis techniques to assess the relationship between phonics instruction and oral reading. *Journal of Special Education, 8,* 57–72.

Mcintyre, E., & Pressley, M. (1996). *Balanced instruction: Strategies and skills in whole language.* Norwood, MA: Christopher-Gordon.

Mckenna, M. C., Stahl, S. A., & Reinking, D. (1994). A critical commentary on research, politics, and whole language. *Journal of Reading Behavior, 26,* 211–233.

Meyer, L. A. (1983). Increased student achievement in reading: One district's strategies. *Research in Rural Education, 1,* 47–51.

Mills, H., O'Keefe, T., & Stephens, D. (1992). *Looking closely: Exploring the role of phonics in one whole language classroom.* Urbana, IL: National Council of Teachers of English.

Monroe, M. (1932). *Children who cannot read.* Chicago: University of Chicago Press.

Moorman, G. B., Blanton, W. E., & Mclaughlin, T. (1994). The rhetoric of whole language. *Reading Research Quarterly, 29,* 308–329.

Morris, D. (1992). *Case studies in teaching beginning readers: The Howard Street tutoring manual.* Boone, NC: Fieldstream Publications.

Morris, D., Ervin, C., & Conrad, K. (1996). A case study of middle school reading disability. *The Reading Teacher, 49,* 368–377.

Morrow, L. M., & Tracey, D. (1998). Motivating contexts for young children's literacy development: Implications for word recognition development. In J. Metsala & L. Ehri (Eds.), *Word recognition in beginning literacy.* Mahwah, NJ: Erlbaum.

Murray, B. A. (1995). *Which better defines phoneme awareness: Segmentation skill or identity knowledge?* Unpublished doctoral dissertation, University of Georgia, Athens.

Murray, B. A., Stahl, S. A., & Ivey, M. G. (1996). Developing phoneme awareness through alphabet books. *Reading and Writing: An Interdisciplinary Journal, 8,* 307–322.

Ogden, S., Hindman, S., & Turner, S. D. (1989). Multisensory programs in the public schools: A brighter future for LD children. *Annals of Dyslexia, 39,* 247–267.

Osborn, J. (1984). The purposes, uses, and contents of workbooks and some guidelines for publishers. In R. C. Anderson, J. Osborn, & R. J. Tierney (Eds.), *Learning to read in American schools: Basal readers and content texts* (pp. 45–112). Hillsdale, NJ: Erlbaum.

Osborn, J., Stahl, S. A., & Stein, M. (1997). *Teachers' guidelines for evaluating commercial phonics packages.* Newark, DE: International Reading Association.

Pearson, P. D. (1989). Reading the whole language movement. *Elementary School Journal, 90,* 231–241.

Pressley, M., Rankin, J., & Yakoi, L. (1996). A survey of instructional practices of primary teachers nominated as effective in promoting literacy. *Elementary School Journal, 96,* 363–384.

Rasinski, T. V. (1991). Fluency for everyone: Incorporating fluency instruction in the classroom. *The Reading Teacher, 43,* 690–692.

Routman, R. (1996). *Literacy at the crossroads.* Portsmouth, NH: Heinemann.

Samuels, S. J., Schermer, N., & Reinking, D. (1992). Reading fluency: Techniques for making decoding automatic. In S. J. Samuels & A. E. Farstrup (Eds.), *What research says about reading instruction* (2nd ed., pp. 124–144). Newark, DE: International Reading Association.

Schlagal, R. C., & Schlagal, J. H. (1992). The integral character of spelling: Teaching strategies for multiple purposes. *Language Arts, 69,* 418–424.

Seuss, Dr. (1957). *The cat in the hat.* Boston: Houghton Mifflin.

Shanahan, T., & Barr, R. (1995). Reading Recovery: An independent evaluation of the effects of an early instructional intervention for at-risk learners. *Reading Research Quarterly, 30,* 958–996.

Share, D. L. (1995). Phonological recoding and self-teaching: Sine qua non of reading acquisition. *Cognition, 55,* 151–218.

Silberberg, N. E., Iversen, I. A., & Goins, J. T. (1973). Which remedial reading method works best? *Journal of Learning Disabilities, 6,* 547–556.

Spaulding, R., & Spaulding, W. T. (1962). *The writing road to reading.* New York: Morrow.

Stahl, K. A. D., Stahl, S. A., & Mckenna, M. (1997). *The development of phonological awareness and orthographic processing in Reading Recovery.* Unpublished manuscript, University of Georgia, Athens.

Stahl, S. A. (1997). Models of reading instruction: An introduction. In S. A. Stahl & D. A. Hayes (Eds.), *Instructional models in reading* (pp. 1–29). Hillsdale, NJ: Erlbaum.

Stahl, S. A., Heubach, K., & Cramond, B. (1997). *Fluency oriented reading instruction* (Research Report). Athens, GA: National Reading Research Center.

Stahl, S. A., & Murray, B. A. (1994). Defining phonological awareness and its relationship to early reading. *Journal of Educational Psychology, 86,* 221–234.

Stahl, S. A., & Murray, B. A. (1998). Issues involved in defining phonological awareness and its relation to early reading. In J. Metsala & L. C. Ehri (Eds.), *Word recognition in beginning literacy* (pp. 65–87). Mahwah, NJ: Erlbaum.

Stahl, S. A., Osborn, J., & Pearson, P. D. (1994). *Six teachers in their classrooms: Looking closely at beginning read-*

ing (Tech. Rep. No. 606). Champaign, IL: Center for the Study of Reading, University of Illinois at Urbana-Champaign.

Stahl, S. A., Suttles, C. W., & Pagnucco, J. R. (1996). The effects of traditional and process literacy instruction on first graders' reading and writing achievement and orientation toward reading. *Journal of Educational Research, 89,* 131–144.

Stanovich, K. E. (1991). The psychology of reading: Evolutionary and revolutionary developments. *Annual Review of Applied Linguistics, 12,* 3–30.

Sullivan, H. J., Okada, M., & Niedermeyer, F. C. (1971). Learning and transfer under two methods of word-attack instruction. *American Educational Research Journal, 8,* 227–240.

Tangel, D. M., & Blachman, B. A. (1992). Effect of phoneme awareness instruction on kindergarten children's invented spellings. *Journal of Reading Behavior, 24,* 233–262.

Taylor, B. M., Short, R., & Shearer, B. (1990, December). *Early intervention in reading: Prevention of reading failure by first grade classroom teachers.* Paper presented at the annual meeting of the National Reading Conference, Miami, FL.

Templeton, S. (1989). Tacit and explicit knowledge of derivational morphology: Foundations for a unified approach to spelling and vocabulary development in the intermediate grades and beyond. *Reading Psychology, 10,* 233–253.

Templeton, S. (1991). Teaching and learning the English spelling system: Reconceptualizing method and purpose. *Elementary School Journal, 92,* 185–201.

Templeton, S. (1992). New trends in an historical perspective: Old story, new resolution—Sound and meaning in spelling. *Language Arts, 69,* 454–463.

Templeton, S., & Bear, D. R. (Eds.). (1992). *Development of orthographic knowledge and the foundations of liter-acy: A memorial Festschrift for Edmund H. Henderson.* Hillsdale, NJ: Erlbaum.

Trachtenburg, P. (1990). Using children's literature to enhance phonics instruction. *The Reading Teacher, 43,* 648–653.

Traub, N. (1977). *Recipe for reading* (2nd ed.). New York: Walker.

Turner, J. C. (1995). The influence of classroom contexts on young children's motivation for literacy. *Reading Research Quarterly, 30,* 410–441.

Venezky, R. L. (1970). *The structure of English orthography.* The Hague, The Netherlands: Mouton.

Vickery, K. S., Reynolds, V. A., & Cochran, S. W. (1987). Multisensory training approach for reading, spelling and handwriting: Orton-Gillingham based curriculum in a public school setting. *Annals of Dyslexia, 37,* 189–200.

Wasik, B. A., & Slavin, R. E. (1993). Preventing early reading failure with one-to-one tutoring: A review of five programs. *Reading Research Quarterly, 28,* 178–200.

Watson, D. J. (1989). Defining and describing whole language. *Elementary School Journal, 90,* 129–142.

Weaver, C. (1994). *Reading process and practice: From socio-psycholinguistics to whole language.* Portsmouth, NH: Heinemann.

White, T. G., & Cunningham, P. M. (1990, April). *Teaching disadvantaged students to decode and spell by analogy.* Paper presented at the annual meeting of the American Educational Research Association, Boston.

Yaden, D. B., Smolkin, L. B., & Macgillivray, L. (1993). A psychogenetic perspective on children's understanding about letter associations during alphabet book readings. *Journal of Reading Behavior, 25,* 43–68.

Zutell, J., & Rasinski, T. (1989). Reading and spelling connections in third and fifth grade students. *Reading Psychology, 10,* 137–155.

Phonemic Awareness and the Teaching of Reading

A Position Statement from the Board of Directors of the International Reading Association

INTERNATIONAL READING ASSOCIATION

Much has been written regarding phonemic awareness, phonics, and the failure of schools to teach the basic skills of reading. The Board of Directors offers this position paper in the hope of clarifying some of these issues as they relate to research, policy, and practice.

We view research and theory as a resource for educators to make informed instructional decisions. We must use research wisely and be mindful of its limitations and its potential to inform instruction.

What Is Phonemic Awareness?

There is no single definition of phonemic awareness. The term has gained popularity in the 1990s as researchers have attempted to study early literacy development and reading disability. Phonemic awareness is typically described as an insight about oral language and in particular about the segmentation of sounds that are used in speech communication. Phonemic awareness is characterized in terms of the facility of the language learner to manipulate the sounds of oral speech. A child who possesses phonemic awareness can segment sounds in words (for example, pronounce just the first sound heard in the word top) and blend strings of isolated sounds together to form recognizable word forms.

Often, the term *phonemic awareness* is used interchangeably with the term *phonological awareness*. To be precise, phonemic awareness refers to an understanding about the smallest units of sound that make up the speech stream: phonemes. Phonological awareness encompasses larger units of sound as well, such as syllables, onsets, and rimes. We use the term phonemic awareness in this document because much of the theoretical and empirical literature focuses specifically on phonemes. We also choose to use this term because of its more common use in the professional literature and in professional discussions.

Why the Sudden Interest in Phonemic Awareness?

The findings regarding phonemic awareness are not as new to the field of literacy as some may think, although it is only in recent years that they have gained wide attention. For over

Source: Phonemic Awareness and the Teaching of Reading (1998). A Position Statement from the Board of Directors of the International Reading Association. *Reading Online* [Online]. Available http:// www.readingonline.org. May 1999. Copyright 1998 by the International Reading Association. All rights reserved.

50 years discussions have continued regarding the relation between a child's awareness of the sounds of spoken words and his or her ability to read. In the 1940s some psychologists noted that children with reading disabilities were unable to differentiate the spoken word into its sounds and put together the sounds of a word. Psychological research intensified during the 1960s and 1970s. Within the reading educational community there was research (for example, the "First-Grade Studies" in 1967) hinting at the important relation between sound awareness and learning to read.

Recent longitudinal studies of reading acquisition have demonstrated that the acquisition of phonemic awareness is highly predictive of success in learning to read-in particular in predicting success in learning to decode. In fact, phonemic awareness abilities in kindergarten (or in that age range) appear to be the best single predictor of successful reading acquisition. There is converging research evidence to document this relation, and few scholars would dispute this finding. However, there is considerable disagreement about what the relation means in terms of understanding reading acquisition and what the relation implies for reading instruction.

Isn't Phonemic Awareness Just a 1990s Word for Phonics?

Phonemic awareness is not phonics. Phonemic awareness is an understanding about spoken language. Children who are phonemically aware can tell the teacher that *bat* is the word the teacher is representing by saying the three separate sounds in the word. They can tell you all the sounds in the spoken word *dog*. They can tell you that, if you take the last sound off *cart* you would have *car*. Phonics, on the other hand, is knowing the relation between specific, printed letters (including combinations of letters) and specific, spoken sounds. You are asking children to show their phonics knowledge when you ask them which letter makes the first sound in *bat* or *dog* or the last sound in *car* or *cart*. The phonemic awareness tasks that have predicted successful reading are tasks that demand that children attend to spoken language, not tasks that simply ask students to name letters or tell which letters make which sounds. In fact, if phonemic awareness just meant knowledge of letter-sound relations, there would have been no need to coin a new term for it.

How Does Phonemic Awareness Work to Facilitate Reading Acquisition?

That phonemic awareness predicts reading success is a fact. We can only speculate on why the strong relation exists. One likely explanation is that phonemic awareness supports understanding of the alphabetic principle—an insight that is crucial in reading an alphabetic orthography. The logic of alphabetic print is apparent to learners if they know that speech is made up of a sequence of sounds (that is, if they are phonemically aware). In learning to read, they discover that it is those units of sound that are represented by the symbols on a page. Printed symbols may appear arbitrary to learners who lack phonemic awareness.

If phonemic awareness is the best predictor of success in beginning reading, shouldn't we put all our time and effort in kindergarten and early reading into developing it?

Most researchers in this area advocate that we consciously and purposefully attend to the development of phonemic awareness as a part of a broad instructional program in reading and writing. Certainly, kindergarten children should have many opportunities to engage in activities that teach them about rhyme, beginning sounds, and syllables. How much time is needed for this kind of focused instruction is something only the teacher can determine, based on a good understanding of the research on phonemic awareness and of his or her students' needs and abilities. Research suggests that different children may need different amounts and forms of phonemic awareness instruction and experiences. The research findings related to phonemic awareness suggest that although it might be necessary, it is certainly not sufficient for producing good readers. One thing is certain: We cannot give so much attention to phonemic awareness instruction that other important aspects of a balanced literacy curriculum are left out or abandoned.

Is Phonemic Awareness a Single, Momentary Insight? Or, Is It Best Described as a Skill That Develops Gradually Over Time?

Phonemic awareness has been measured using a variety of tasks that appear to tap into an individual's ability to manipulate the sounds of oral language. However, some tasks may require a more sophisticated understanding of sound structures than others. For example, rhyming appears much earlier than segmentation abilities for most children. Also, it seems to matter that children can hear the sounds of a spoken word in order, but it is not clear how early or late this ability does or should develop. Researchers are still working to identify the kinds of tasks and what aspects of phonemic awareness they might tap. It appears from the research that the acquisition of phonemic awareness occurs over time and develops gradually into more and more sophisticated levels of control. Some research suggests that there is a diversity of developmental paths among children. How much control is necessary for the child to discover the alphabetic principle is still unclear. There is no research evidence to suggest that there is any exact sequence of acquisition of specific sounds in the development of phonemic awareness, only that there is increasing control over sounds in general.

It Has Been Stressed That Phonemic Awareness Is an Oral Language Skill and That It Has Nothing to Do with Print, Letters, or Phonics. Is This True?

It is true that phonemic awareness is an insight about oral language, and that you can assess phonemic awareness through tasks that offer no reference to print. However, to suggest that there is no relation between the development of phonemic awareness and print is misleading. There is evidence to suggest that the relation between phonemic awareness and learning to read is reciprocal: phonemic awareness supports reading acquisition, and reading instruction and experiences with print facilitate phonemic awareness development. The question remains as to the amount and forms of phonemic awareness one must have in order to profit from reading instruction that is focused on decoding. For instance, some research suggests that the abilities to blend and isolate sounds in the speech stream support reading acquisition while the ability to delete sounds from spoken words is a consequence of learning to read. The precise relation between phonemic awareness abilities and reading acquisition remains under investigation.

How Can Phonemic Awareness Be Taught?

The answer to this question has both theoretical and practical implications. Theorists interested in determining the causal contribution of phonemic awareness to learning to read have conducted experimental studies in which some students are explicitly taught phonemic awareness and some are not. Many of the early studies in this genre focused on treatments that emphasize oral language work only. The findings from these studies suggest phonemic awareness can be taught successfully.

More recently, there have been studies of phonemic awareness training that combine and contrast purely oral language approaches to the nurturing of phonemic awareness abilities, with approaches that include interaction with print during the training. These studies suggest that programs that encourage high levels of student engagement and interaction with print (for example, through read-alouds, shared reading, and invented spelling) yield as much growth in phonemic awareness abilities as programs that offer only a focus on oral language teaching. These studies also suggest that the greatest impact on phonemic awareness is achieved when there is both interaction with print and explicit attention to phonemic awareness abilities. In other words, interaction with print combined with explicit attention to sound structure in spoken words is the best vehicle toward growth.

Some research suggests that student engagement in writing activities that encourage invented spelling of words can promote the development of phonemic awareness. These findings also are consistent with continuing research into the sources of influence on phonemic awareness abilities before students enter school. It is clear that high levels of phonemic awareness among very young children are related to home experiences that are filled with interactions with print (such as being read to at home, playing letter games and language play, and having early writing experiences).

Do All Children Eventually Develop Phonemic Awareness? Shouldn't We Just Let Them Develop This Understanding Naturally?

Naturally is a word that causes many people difficulty in describing language development and literacy acquisition. Insofar as it is natural for parents to read to their children and engage them with print and language, then phonemic awareness may develop naturally in some children. But if we accept that these kinds of interactions are not the norm, then we have a great deal of work to do in encouraging parents to engage their young children with print. We need to provide the information, the tools, and the strategies that will help them ensure that their young children will be successful in learning to read.

In schooling, the same advice holds true. Most children—estimated at more than 80%—develop phonemic awareness by the middle of first grade. Is this natural? Yes, if the natural model of classroom life includes opportunities to engage with print in a variety of ways and to explore language. However, we know that there are many classrooms where such engagement and explicit attention to sounds and print are not natural. We must equip teachers with the information, tools, and strategies they need to provide these kinds of learning opportunities in their classrooms.

The problem is most severe in terms of consequences when the students from economically disadvantaged homes, where the resources and parent education levels are lowest, enter schools that have limited resources and experience in promoting engagement with print. The students who need the most attention may be those who receive the least. We have a responsibility in these situations not to rely on the "natural" and to promote action that is direct, explicit, and meaningful.

What Does This Mean for Classroom Practice?

First, it is critical that teachers are familiar with the concept of phonemic awareness and that they know that there is a body of evidence pointing to a significant relation between phonemic awareness and reading acquisition. This cannot be ignored.

Many researchers suggest that the logical translation of the research to practice is for teachers of young children to provide an environment that encourages play with spoken language as part of the broader literacy program. Nursery rhymes, riddles, songs, poems, and read-aloud books that manipulate sounds may be used purposefully to draw young learners' attention to the sounds of spoken language. Guessing games and riddles in which sounds are manipulated may help children become more sensitive to the sound structure of their language. Many activities already used by preschool and primary-grade teachers can be drawn from and will become particularly effective if teachers bring to them an understanding about the role these activities can play in stimulating phonemic awareness.

What about the 20% of Children Who Have Not Achieved Phonemic Awareness by the Middle of First Grade?

The research on this statistic is as clear as it is alarming. The likelihood of these students becoming successful readers is slim under current instructional plans.

We feel we can reduce this 20% figure by more systematic instruction and engagement with language early in students' home, preschool, and kindergarten classes.

We feel we can reduce this figure even further through early identification of students who are outside the norms of progress in phonemic awareness development, and through the offering of intensive programs of instruction.

Finally, there may be a small percentage of these students who may have some underlying disability that inhibits the development of phonemic awareness. Several scholars speculate that this disability may be at the root of dyslexia. More research is needed in this area, however. There is some promise here in the sense that we may have located a causal factor toward which remedial assistance can be tailored.

Some people advocate that primary teachers allocate large amounts of time to teaching students how to perform better on phonemic awareness tasks. There are no longitudinal studies that support the effectiveness of this practice in increasing the reading achievement of the children when they reach the intermediate grades.

What Position Does the International Reading Association Take Regarding Phonemic Awareness and the Teaching of Reading?

The International Reading Association already has issued a position paper on the role of phonics in the teaching of reading. That paper stresses the importance of phonics in a comprehensive reading program.

In this position statement we have attempted to elaborate on the complex relation between phonemic awareness and reading. We do so without taking away from our commitment to balance in a comprehensive reading program.

On the positive side, research on phonemic awareness has caused us to reconceptualize some of our notions about reading development. Certainly, this research is helping us understand some of the underlying factors that are associated with some forms of reading disability. Through the research on phonemic awareness, we now have a clearer theoretical framework for understanding why some of the things we have been doing all along support development (for example, work with invented spelling). Additionally, the research has led us to new ideas that we should continue to study.

On the negative side, we are concerned that the research findings about phonemic awareness might be misused or overgeneralized. We are very concerned with policy initiatives that require teachers to dedicate specific amounts of time to phonemic awareness instruction for all students, or to policy initiatives that require the use of particular training programs for all students. Such initiatives interfere with the important instructional decisions that professional teachers must make regarding the needs of their students. We feel the following suggestions for good reading instruction will lead to the development of phonemic awareness and success in learning to read:

- Offer students a print-rich environment within which to interact;
- Engage students with surrounding print as both readers and writers;
- Engage children in language activities that focus on both the form and the content of spoken and written language;
- Provide explicit explanations in support of students' discovery of the alphabetic principle; and
- Provide opportunities for students to practice reading and writing for real reasons in a variety of contexts to promote fluency and independence.

We must keep in mind, though, that it is success in learning to read that is our goal. For students who require special assistance in developing phonemic awareness, we should be prepared to offer the best possible instruction and support.

Suggested Readings

1. What is phonemic awareness?

Adams, M. J. (1990). *Beginning to read: Thinking and learning about print.* Cambridge, MA: Massachusetts Institute of Technology Press.

Calfee, R. C., & Norman, K. A. (in press). Psychological perspectives on the early reading wars: The case of phonological awareness. *Teachers College Record.*

Share, D. L. (1995). Phonological recoding and self-teaching: Sine qua non of reading acquisition. *Cognition, 55,* 151–218.

Stahl, S. A., & Murray, B. (1998). Issues involved in defining phonological awareness and its relation to early reading. In J. L. Metsala & L. C. Ehri (Eds.), *Word recognition in beginning literacy.* Hillsdale, NJ: Erlbaum.

Yopp, H. K. (1988). The validity and reliability of phonemic awareness tests. *Reading Research Quarterly, 23,* 159–177.

2. Why the sudden interest in phonemic awareness?

Bradley, L., & Bryant, P. E. (1983). Categorizing sounds and learning to read: A causal connection. *Nature, 301,* 419–421.

Goswami, U., & Bryant, P. (1990). *Phonological skills and learning to read.* Hove, UK: Erlbaum.

MacDonald, G. W., & Cornwall, A. (1995). The relationship between phonological awareness and reading and spelling achievement eleven years later. *Journal of Learning Disabilities, 28,* 523–527.

Share, D., Jorm, A., Maclean, R., & Matthews, R. (1984). Sources of individual differences in reading achievement. *Journal of Educational Psychology, 76,* 1309–1324.

Stanovich, K. E. (1986). Matthew effects in reading: Some consequences of individual differences in the acquisition of literacy. *Reading Research Quarterly, 21,* 360–407.

Stanovich, K. E. (1995). Romance and reality. *The Reading Teacher, 47,* 280–291.

Stuart, M., & Coltheart, M. (1988). Does reading develop in a sequence of stages? *Cognition, 30,* 139–181.

Sulzby, E. (1983). A commentary on Ehri's critique of five studies related to letter-name knowledge and learning to read: Broadening the question. In L. M. Gentile, M. L. Kamil, & J. S. Blanchard (Eds.), *Reading research revisited.* Columbus, OH: Merrill.

Wagner, R. K., & Torgesen, J. K. (1987). The nature of phonological processing and its causal role in the acquisition of reading skills. *Psychological Bulletin, 101,* 192–212.

Yopp, H. K. (1995). A test for assessing phonemic awareness in young children. *The Reading Teacher, 49,* 20–29.

3. Isn't phonemic awareness just a 1990s word for phonics?

Ehri, L. C. (1997). Grapheme-phoneme knowledge is essential for learning to read words in English. In J. L. Metsala & L. C. Ehri (Eds.), *Word recognition in beginning literacy.* Hillsdale, NJ: Erlbaum.

Stahl, S. A., & Murray, B. (1997). Issues involved in defining phonological awareness and its relation to early reading. In J. L. Metsala & L. C. Ehri (Eds.), *Word recognition in beginning literacy.* Hillsdale, NJ: Erlbaum.

4. How does phonemic awareness work to facilitate reading acquisition?

Ehri, L. C. (1991). Development of the ability to read words. In R. Barr, M. L. Kamil, P. B. Mosenthal, & P. D. Pearson (Eds.), *Handbook of reading research: Volume 2* (pp. 383–417). White Plains, NY: Longman.

Goswami, U., & Bryant, P. (1990). *Phonological skills and learning to read.* Hove, UK: Erlbaum.

Gough, P., & Hillinger, M. (1980). Learning to read: An unnatural act. *Bulletin of the Orton Society, 30,* 180–196.

Hoover, W., & Gough, P. (1990). The simple view of reading. *Reading and Writing: An Interdisciplinary Journal, 2,* 127–160.

5. Is phonemic awareness a single, momentary insight? Or, is it best described as a skill that develops gradually over time?

Christensen, C. A. (1997). Onset, rhymes, and phonemes in learning to read. *Scientific Studies of Reading, 1,* 341–358.

Nation, K., & Hulme, C. (1997). Phonemic segmentation, not onset-rime segmentation skills, predicts early reading and spelling skills. *Reading Research Quarterly, 32,* 154–167.

Stahl, S. A., & Murray, B. A. (1994). Defining phonological awareness and its relationship to early reading. *Journal of Educational Psychology, 86,* 221–234.

Stanovich, K. E., Cunningham, A. E., & Cramer, B. B. (1984). Assessing phonological awareness in kindergarten children: Issues of task comparability. *Journal of Experimental Child Psychology, 38,* 175–190.

Yopp, H. K. (1988). The validity and reliability of phonemic awareness tests. *Reading Research Quarterly, 23,* 159–177.

6. It has been stressed that phonemic awareness is an oral language skill and that it has nothing to do with print, letters, or phonics. Is this true?

Ehri, L. (1979). Linguistic insight: Threshold of reading acquisition. In T. Waller & G. E. MacKinnon (Eds.), *Reading research: Advances in theory and practice* (Vol. *1,* pp. 63–114). New York: Academic Press.

Huang, H. S., & Hanley, R. J. (1995). Phonological awareness and visual skills in learning to read Chinese and English. *Cognition, 54,* 73–98.

Huang, H. S., & Hanley, R. J. (1997). A longitudinal study of phonological skills, and Chinese reading acquisition among first-graders in Taiwan. *International Journal of Behavioral Development, 20* (2), 249–268.

Liberman, I., Shankweiler, D., Fischer, F., & Carter, B. (1974). Explicit syllable and phoneme segmentation in the young child. *Journal of Experimental Child Psychology, 18,* 201–212.

Mann, V. (1986). Phonological awareness: The role of reading experience. *Cognition, 24,* 65–92.

Perfetti, C., Beck, I., Bell, L., & Hughes, C. (1987). Phonemic knowledge and learning to read are reciprocal: A longitudinal study of first grade children. *Merrill-Palmer Quarterly, 33,* 283–319.

Read, C., Zhang, Y., Nie, H., & Ding, B. (1986). The ability to manipulate speech sounds depends on knowing alphabetic writing. *Cognition, 24,* 31–45.

Wagner, R. K., Torgesen, J. K., & Rashotte, C. A. (1994). Development of reading-related phonological processing abilities: New evidence of bidirectional causality from a latent variable longitudinal study. *Developmental Psychology, 30,* 73–87.

7. How can phonemic awareness be taught?

Baker, L., Sonnenschein, S., Serpell, R., Scher, D., Fernandez-Fein, S., Munsterman, K., Hill, S., Goddard-Truitt, V., & Danseco, E. (1996). Early literacy at home: Children's experiences and parents' perspectives. *The Reading Teacher, 50,* 70–72.

Ball, E. W., & Blachman, B. A. (1991). Does phoneme awareness training in kindergarten make a difference in early word recognition and developmental spelling? *Reading Research Quarterly, 26* (1), 49–66.

Cunningham, A. E. (1990). Explicit versus implicit instruction in phonological awareness. *Journal of Experimental Child Psychology, 50,* 429–444.

Ehri, L. C. (1984). How orthography alters spoken language competencies in children learning to read and spell. In J. Downing & R. Valtin (Eds.), *Language awareness and learning to read* (pp. 119–147). New York: Springer-Verlag.

Lundberg, I., Frost, J., & Peterson, O. P. (1988). Effects of an extensive program for stimulating phonological awareness in preschool children. *Reading Research Quarterly, 23,* 264–284.

McGuinness, D., McGuinness, C., & Donohue, J. (1995). Phonological training and the alphabetic principle: Evidence for reciprocal causality. *Reading Research Quarterly, 30,* 830–853.

Scanlon, D. M., & Vellutino, F. R. (1997). A comparison of the instructional backgrounds and cognitive profiles of poor, average, and good readers who were initially identified as at risk for reading failure. *Scientific Studies of Reading, 1,* 191–216.

Torgesen, J. K., Morgan, S. T., & Davis, C. (1992). Effects of two types of phonological awareness training on word learning in kindergarten children. *Journal of Educational Psychology, 84,* 364–370.

Wagner, R. K., & Roshotte, C. A. (1993). *Does phonological awareness training really work? A meta-analysis.* Paper presented at the annual meeting of the American Educational Research Association, Atlanta, GA.

Winsor, P., & Pearson, P. D. (1992). *Children at risk: Their phonemic awareness development in holistic instruction* (Tech. Rep. No. 556). Champaign, IL: Center for the Study of Reading.

8. Do all children eventually develop phonemic awareness? Shouldn't we just let them develop this understanding naturally?

Fletcher, J., Shaywitz, S., Shankweiler, D., Kayz, L., Liberman, I., Stuebing, K., Francis, D., Fowler, A., & Shaywitz, B. (1994). Cognitive profiles of reading disability: Comparisons of discrepancy and low achievement definitions. *Journal of Educational Psychology, 86* (1), 6–23.

9. What does this mean for classroom practice?

Adams, M. J., & Bruck, M. (1995). Resolving the "Great Debate." *American Educator, 8,* 7–20.

Beck, I., & Juel, C. (1995). The role of decoding in learning to read. *American Educator, 8,* 21–25, 39-42.

Griffith, P. L., & Olson, M. W. (1992). Phonemic awareness helps beginning readers break the code. *The Reading Teacher, 45,* 516–523.

Murray, B. A., Stahl, S. A., & Ivey, M. G. (1996). Developing phoneme awareness through alphabet books. *Reading and Writing: An Interdisciplinary Journal, 8,* 307–322.

Richgels, D., Poremba, K. J., & McGee, L. M. (1996). Kindergartners talk about print: Phonemic awareness in meaningful contexts. *The Reading Teacher, 49,* 632–642.

Yopp, H. K. (1992). Developing phonemic awareness in young children. *The Reading Teacher, 45,* 696–703.

Yopp, H. K. (1995). Read-aloud books for developing phonemic awareness: An annotated bibliography. *The Reading Teacher, 48,* 538–543.

10. What about the 20% of children who are not getting phonemic awareness by the middle of first grade?

Juel, C. (1994). *Learning to read and write in one elementary school.* New York: Springer-Verlag.

Liberman, I. Y., Shankweiler, D., & Liberman, A. M. (1991). The alphabetic principle and learning to read. In *Phonology and reading disability: Solving the reading puzzle.* Washington, DC: International Academy for Research in Learning Disabilities, U.S. Department of Health and Human Services, Public Health Service; National Institutes of Health.

Snow, C. E., Barnes, W. S., Chandler, J., Goodman, I. F., & Hemphill, L. (1991). *Unfulfilled expectations: Home and school influences on literacy.* Cambridge, MA: Harvard University Press.

Stanovich, K. E. (1986). Matthew effects in reading: Some consequences of individual differences in the acquisition of literacy. *Reading Research Quarterly, 21,* 360–407.

Torgesen, J. K., Wagner, R. K., & Rashotte, C. A. (1997). Prevention and remediation of severe reading disabilities: Keeping the end in mind. *Scientific Studies of Reading, 1,* 217–234.

Draft prepared for the International Reading Association Board of Directors by James W. Cunningham, University of North Carolina at Chapel Hill, Chapel Hill, North Carolina, USA; Patricia M. Cunningham, Wake Forest University, Winston-Salem, North Carolina, USA; James V. Hoffman, University of Texas-Austin, Austin, Texas, USA; Hallie Kay Yopp, California State University, Fullerton, California, USA

Adopted by the Board of Directors, April 1998 Board of Directors at time of adoption: John J. Pikulski, President; Kathryn A. Ransom, President-Elect; Carol Minnick Santa, Vice President; Alan E. Farstrup, Executive Director; Richard L. Allington; Betsy M. Baker; James F. Baumann; James V. Hoffman; Kathleen Stumpf Jongsma; Adria F. Klein; Diane L. Larson; John W. Logan; Lesley M. Morrow.

A print version of this statement is available in brochure form from the International Reading Association in quantities of 10, prepaid only. Please contact the Association for pricing information. Single copies are free upon request by sending a self-addressed, stamped envelope. Requests from outside the U.S. should include an envelope, but postage is not required.

Integrating Sources

1. Locate and contrast key statements made by Stahl, Duffy-Hester, and Stahl and the IRA Position Statement regarding the role of phonics in an effective reading program. Do you agree or disagree with these conclusions? Defend your choice.

2. Which article has the most realistic plan for contending with problem readers? Again, defend your choice.

Classroom Implications

1. In what ways do you find the recommendations of these authors (a) feasible in real classroom settings and (b) impractical and idealistic?

    a. Stahl, Duffy-Hester, and Stahl

    b. IRA Position Paper

2. Describe an eclectic approach to beginning reading instruction that draws on both of these writers. Try it!

Annotated Bibliography

Historical References

Clymer, T. (1963). The utility of phonics generalizations in the primary grades. *The Reading Teacher, 16,* 252–258.

This is an often quoted study in which Clymer showed that most phonics generalizations were applicable in only very limited situations and thus the extensive teaching of these rules was open to question.

Flesch, R. (1955). *Why Johnny can't read and what you can do about it.* New York: Harper and Row.

This book was widely read by the general public and received extensive coverage in the mass media. Flesch, a noted linguist, emphasized the fact that the ultimate answer to most reading problems, in his opinion, was simply to base all reading instruction on the heavy use of phonics. This book was criticized by many in the professional education community as being an overly simplified answer to a very complex problem.

Gray, W. S. (1948). *On their own in reading.* Chicago: Scott, Foresman.

This is a classic discussion of the role of word analysis in the teaching of reading. It is an excellent reference for those needing background information on how classroom teachers can use the different aspects of word analysis in an effective reading program.

Current References

Adams, M. J. (1990). *Beginning to read: Thinking and learning about print.* Cambridge, MA: MIT Press.

This is a foundation book in the current thinking about the role of word analysis as being a part of effective reading instruction. It reviews the past history of the debate concerning word analysis, noting that many of the current arguments about this topic have been debated in the past as well. A strong case is presented for the appropriateness of word analysis instruction in beginning reading. This book contains an excellent bibliography of related references on this topic.

Ball, E. W. (1997). Phonological awareness: Implications for whole language and emergent literacy programs. *Topics in Language Disorders, 17,* 14–26.

This article reviews the important relationship between phonological awareness and early success in reading. The results of this research indicated that those kindergarten students who received direct letter-sound instruction did significantly better in first grade then did those students who had not had this instruction.

Busink, R. (1997). Reading and phonological awareness: What we have learned and how we can use it. *Reading Research and Instruction, 36,* 199–215.

This article illustrates both research and classroom experiences that decoding skills are strongly associated with phonological awareness. Suggests this lack of phonological awareness as being particularly important when working with the problem reader.

Erickson, L., & Juliebo, M. F. (1998). *The phonological awareness handbook for kindergarten and primary teachers.* Newark, DE: International Reading Association.

This reference presents classroom activities which teachers can use to enhance phonological awareness in their students. Of particular importance is the authors' defense of phonological awareness as a basis for successful reading and spelling.

Gaskins, I., Ehri, L., Cress, C., O'Hara, C., & Donnelly, K. (1996–1997). Procedures for word learning: Making discoveries about words. *The Reading Teacher, 50,* 312–327.

Places the role of the effective sound/symbol relationship in the context of a total classroom language arts program. A particularly strong article on specific techniques teachers can use to enhance all aspects of the reading process through knowledge of phonics.

Hull, M. A., & Fox, B. J. (1998). *Phonics for the teacher of reading: Programmed for self-instruction.* Upper Saddle River, NJ: Merrill.

This self-programmed book is designed to help classroom teachers learn the fundamentals of phonics and its application to the classroom reading program.

Lapp, D., & Flood, J. (1997). Where's the phonics? Making the case (again) for integrated code instruction. *The Reading Teacher, 50,* 696–700.

Describes a classroom reading program in which phonics is taught both explicitly as well as in the content of written text. A number of specific classroom applications of word analysis are discussed in relation to a balanced reading philosophy. Contains an excellent bibliography of related references.

Morrow, L. M., & Tracey, D. H. (1997). Strategies used for phonics instruction in early childhood classrooms. *The Reading Teacher, 50,* 644–651.

This article is based on an extensive study of the early use of phonics in a classroom setting. Results indicated that as children progressed in school, particularly in kindergarten and the primary grades, there was a dramatic change from contextual to explicit instruction. Included with this article is a very helpful review of the past history of phonics instruction and the effects these developments of the past have had on the current teaching of phonics.

Strickland, D. S. (1998). *Teaching phonics today: A primer for educators.* Newark, DE: International Reading Association.

This book is designed to help classroom teachers incorporate phonics instruction in the effective literacy classroom. Contents include a discussion of why the public feels so strongly about phonics as well as specific phonics strategies for the classroom teacher. Each of these techniques is clearly described, including the rationale for its use in reading instruction.

You Become Involved

Phonics

The value of phonics knowledge and phonics instruction is clear in research. From the reading, writing, and discussion opportunities provided during this chapter, you should have expanded your schema structures related to the phonics topic. To help you further organize those pieces of information, complete the following synthesis activities.

1. Use one- or two-word phrases to list the concepts or ideas you remember about phonics or phonics instruction. You should look back into the articles if you need to. Use a separate sheet of paper to construct your list.
2. Cut the phrases apart and arrange them in categories. Label the categories. Feel free to rearrange the phrases until you are satisfied with the categories.
3. Number the categories in some order. For example, you could number by importance, sequence for instruction, and so on.
4. Use your numbered categories and phrases to write a summary paper that explains what you have learned about phonics and phonics instruction.

3

MULTICULTURAL DIVERSITY

To diffuse a uniformity and purity of language in America—to destroy
the provincial prejudices that originate in the triffling differences of dialect,
and produce reciprocal ridicule—to promote the interest of literature and
harmony of the United States—is the most ardent wish of the Author.
—*NOAH WEBSTER (1798)*

Perhaps language makes its greatest contribution
as a social instrument in welding together a group
through community of purpose and of understanding.
—*DORA SMITH (1944)*

All children who are becoming literate, whether blind,
sighted, second language, first language, average, gifted, slow,
at risk, or disabled, need to feel that the process is meaningful.
—*FRANK MAY (1998)*

The schools today are truly a multicultural community. Students in the typical classroom represent a wide variety of countries and cultures. Many bring with them a
rich and varied background, most notably in their first languages. It is the role of the
classroom teacher, while encouraging this diversity in all students, to be an effective language and reading teacher as well (Hansen-Krening & Mizokawa, 1997).

Questions abound on how to most effectively meet the educational needs of
this diverse community of students. Answers to these many problems are, in
today's society, often answered according to political, social, or economic factors
as opposed to educational needs. For instance, note the following questions:

1. What language should be used for primary instruction, especially in the area of
reading and the language arts?
2. For those students who use English as a second language, what are the most
appropriate teaching techniques and materials?

3. What materials work best to encourage multicultural knowledge in all students?

4. How can a sense of community be created in the classroom which encourages respect by all for the various cultures represented in a classroom?

Reasons to Encourage Multicultural Education

There are many reasons for teachers to encourage students to read widely about other cultures and peoples. We live in a world community today which is dramatically impacted by events from many differing locations throughout this group of nations. Where at one time we could feel comfortable in our isolation, this is not true today and will be even less so in the future. Not only is there better communication between nations and culture groups, but there is also a dramatic increase in the numbers of international students we now have in our classrooms. It thus becomes the responsibility of the teacher to encourage a wider knowledge of diversity in each student.

The readings in this section were selected to help you carefully consider the many challenges as well as the many rewards in the effective teaching of multicultural education, especially through the use of reading and writing.

As You Read

The following selections provide an overlook of the growing field of multicultural education with particular emphasis on reading and writing. Anderson and Gunderson (1997) note how the learning process changes when both the teachers and the students see this process from a multicultural prespective. Kaser and Short (1998) discuss the important role of the students in a classroom as they become more aware of other cultures in their learning activities. Consider the following questions as you read:

1. How is multiculturalism defined?

2. What are the current multicultural issues that educators should work to incorporate into instruction? Classrooms? Schools?

3. How does education change when viewed through multicultural lenses?

References

Anderson, J., & Gunderson, L. (1997). Literacy learning outside the classroom. *The Reading Teacher, 50,* 514–516.

Franquiz, M. E., & Reyes, M. (1998). Creating inclusive learning communities through English language arts: From Chanclas to Canicas. *Language Arts, 75,* 211–220.

Hansen-Krening, N., & Mizokawa, D. T. (1997). Exploring ethnic-specific literature: A unity of parents, families, and educators. *Journal of Adolescent & Adult Literacy, 41,* 180–189.

Kaser, S., & Short, K. G. (1998). Exploring culture through children's connections. *Language Arts, 75,* 185–192.

May, F. B. (1998). *Reading as communication.* Upper Saddle River, NJ: Merrill/Prentice-Hall.

Smith, D. (1944). Growth in language power as related to child development. In N. B. Nenry (Ed.), *Teaching Language in the Elementary School. Forty-Third Yearbook of the National Society for the Study of Education, Part II* (pp. 52–97). Chicago: The Department of Education, the University of Chicago.

Webster, N. (1798). *The American Spelling Book.* Boston: Isaiah Thomas and Ebenzer Andrews, p. 10.

Literacy Learning from a Multicultural Perspective

JIM ANDERSON
University of British Columbia,
Vancouver, Canada

LEE GUNDERSON
University of British Columbia,
Vancouver, Canada

Alice was an extraordinary third grader. She was an immigrant who in 2 years had become fluent in English; her intelligence had qualified her as an intellectually gifted student. Alice was most content at school when she was filling out pages in a workbook. She and her family believed that answering questions and filling in "bubbles" in multiple-choice workbook items were essential learning activities that represented the basic goal of literacy learning: to master a set of discrete skills.

Indeed, Alice's parents, like many other Asian immigrants, generally believed that learning should focus on skills, that it should involve memorizing the important pieces of language with a focus on grammar, and that academic knowledge is a set of facts to be memorized.

North American teachers, however, often support an emergent literacy learning model that views learning as exploration in which children construct their own meanings in an environment where risk taking is encouraged. It is important that teachers understand their developmental perspective as a cultural view that is not universally shared.

Heath and Mangiola (1991) remind us, "All cultural groups have some unique ways of transmitting background knowledge about the world and of asking their children to display what they know" (p. 14). That is, different cultural groups have different ways of teaching and learning and different views of what it means to teach and to learn. Gunderson (in press) notes,

> *What seems true across cultures and political affiliations is that parents, teachers, and other interested adults seek "the best" for students. However, what is true both within and between cultures and groups is that there are fundamental disagreements as to what constitutes "the best."*

When we first read Shirley Brice Heath's (1983) *Ways With Words,* we saw it through the lens of a deficit model. We now read this work as a call for schools to accept different ways of knowing and different ways of becoming literate.

During the last several years, we have interviewed about 60 Chinese Canadian, Iranian Canadian, and Indo-Canadian parents and approximately 100 students from three school districts (Anderson, 1995; Gunderson, in press). We have found that most of the Chinese, Iranian, and Indian parents and many of their children oppose diametrically many aspects

Source: From Anderson, J., & Gunderson, L., (1997, March). Literacy learning from a multicultural perspective. *The Reading Teacher, 50*(6), 514–516. Reprinted with permission of Jim Anderson and the International Reading Association. All rights reserved.

of emergent literacy. Furthermore, some of the literacy activities that parents consider important for their children are antithetical to an emergent literacy perspective. Our analyses have revealed major differences in beliefs about teaching and learning related to accuracy/precision, locus of control, assessment/accountability, expectations, and rote memorization.

Accuracy/Precision

A key assumption undergirding emergent literacy is that learning to read and write are imprecise processes involving approximation and invention on the part of young learners and that adult standards of correctness and convention will not be met in the initial stages of learning. This view was not shared by many of the parents, who tended to believe that accuracy and precision are important from the beginning. Many of these parents were quite critical of invented spelling, suggesting as one parent did that "Yes, I'll correct him as well as telling him that it's not good!" or as another said, "It's important to learn correct spelling [before attempting to write stories, notes and so forth]."

Many parents saw little value in children's early attempts at reading. One parent for example suggested that "It's not real reading." Parents also spoke of the need for neatness in printing and handwriting. "It's important for children to learn to print neatly; if not, [they] will never improve."

Locus of Control

Within an emergent literacy perspective, children are seen as constructing their own literacy. Teachers are sometimes seen as facilitators of learning, and the importance of direct instruction is downplayed. Many parents had quite different views. They tended to believe that teachers should impart information, and students should learn and retain it. For example, one parent reported, "I saw my son's classroom and everyone was talking. I couldn't find the teacher; she was sitting down reading."

Similarly, while storybook reading is often portrayed by mainstream educators as a highly interactive event in which the participants "negotiate" meaning, many parents in our studies believed the child's role is to listen and remember. One parent stated, "I like my son to retell the story for me after I finish reading it. It would be too disturbing if he interrupted."

Assessment/Accountability

Several parents indicated the need to check children's understanding through a series of questions about stories they had heard or read themselves. As one parent said, "I like to ask [my] child questions at the end of each story and explain to her if she doesn't understand"; another remarked "That way [by asking questions] I'll know if he has grasped what he has read." Commenting on her child's report card, one parent lamented "My Grade 3 son doesn't get any grades." Their views of assessment and evaluation were related to their views concerning memorization and learning.

Expectations

As we listened to the parents in our studies, it became clear to us that fundamental differences existed between parental expectations and the expectations they believed North American schools held. For example, many decried the lack of homework, complaining that "The teachers don't give enough homework" and "They let the students talk too much." Others stated, "The way they teach is different from Hong Kong."

Rote Memorization

An often repeated criticism of school learning practices related to memorization. Both students and parents found the lack of memorization difficult to understand, suggesting "Canadian schools are too easy; you don't have to work hard." The preferred method of learning was rote memorization and lots of it: "In Hong Kong we spent all day in class memorizing, memorizing, memorizing, and then when we go home at night we do some more." Memorization meant that students were learning; they were acquiring knowledge.

Discussion

Parents and children who come to North America from other countries have differing views about teaching and learning, views that are different both across and between groups. Many arrive with the cultural belief reinforced by their own school experiences that the teacher is the source of knowledge, which she/he should communicate to students. Our studies indicated this belief in the transmission model crosses both cultural and socioeconomic boundaries. For many immigrants, learning represents the acquisition of a large number of facts through rote memorization.

Some of the Asian parents believed passionately that an emergent literacy approach violated their children's right to learn the knowledge they needed to succeed. The view that teaching should involve a focus on facts is shared by parents in immigrant and nonimmigrant groups across North America and by some teachers as well (Anderson, 1994).

It is simply not enough to dismiss divergent views about young children's literacy learning as wrong. Although we believe these differences between parental beliefs and expectations about literacy learning/teaching and school-based literacy practices are problematic, we do not see them as insurmountable. We believe that we can honor and respect parents' beliefs while at the same time help them understand the reasons behind our literacy programs. However, educators must recognize the incongruences we have described and take steps to address them.

Parents must be informed about the nature and expectations of the school's reading and writing programs on a regular and systematic basis. For example, regular ongoing sessions for parents of primary-grade children, in which such things as the developmental stages of invented spelling are explained through the use of portfolios of children's work from previous years, are essential.

Because many parents will equate learning with rote memory and isolated drill and practice, we think it is important to help parents envision learning more broadly. We must make our classrooms inviting spaces for parents so that we can demonstrate this broader view to them. Parental involvement in the classroom is a marvelous way to allow them to view and understand the teaching and learning that takes place there.

We also believe it is important for teachers to recognize that there are many ways for children to learn to read and write and that emergent literacy reflects a particular perspective of literacy acquisition. Teachers should encourage parents to support their children's literacy learning in ways familiar to them, even though the practices might not reflect the teachers' beliefs. Indeed, teachers can provide a range of literacy activities, including some considered more traditional, which build on what parents do at home. Many parents and students have deeply ingrained beliefs about what teaching and learning should be; some of these beliefs may be antithetical to the tenets of emergent literacy. The most difficult problem for teachers is to examine critically parental beliefs and to design programs that will allow for diversity without compromising well established principles of language and literacy teaching and learning.

Our research has raised questions that have no simple answers. We resist the temptation to trivialize the complexity of the problems by offering simplistic solutions. Instead, we suggest that teachers consider a range of possible ways to address diverse beliefs and expectations. For example, to address parental concerns about rote memorization, teachers may have children self-select rhymes, poetry, raps, songs, and stories to memorize as homework assignments. These activities promote phonemic awareness and are valued by parents.

Parents can learn how to support their children's developing knowledge of spelling in ways that do not belittle invented spelling. For example, the teacher can show parents that instead of responding negatively to a child's spelling of *was* as *wuz* by saying "That's wrong!" they can say something like "That's a good try. You spelled it like it sounds, but I spell it w-a-s."

Teachers, like parents, want to provide the best learning environments for their students. In our zeal to provide what we are convinced are the best literacy programs, we must take caution not to ignore children's out-of-school literacy experiences. Even though they may be entirely different from those valued by teachers, students' experiences need to be acknowledged, valued, and built upon.

References

Anderson, J. (1994). Parents' perceptions of emergent literacy. *Reading Psychology, 15,* 165–187.

Anderson, J. (1995). Listening to parents' voices: Cross cultural perceptions of learning to read and to write. *Reading Horizons, 35,* 394–413.

Gunderson, L. (in press). Different cultural views of whole language. In S. Cakmak & B. Comber (Eds.), *Inquiry into what? Empowering today's youngsters, tomorrow's citizens.* Urbana, IL: National Council of Teachers of English.

Heath, S. B. (1983). *Ways with words: Ethnography of communication, communities, and classrooms.* Cambridge, MA: Cambridge University Press.

Heath, S. B., & Mangiola, L. (1991). *Children of promise: Literate activity in linguistically and culturally diverse classrooms.* Washington, DC: National Education Association.

Exploring Culture through Children's Connections

SANDY KASER   *KATHY G. SHORT*

Miguel: I think that corn dancers are like our folklorico dancing.

Joe: No, they are not the same. When an Indian dances, it is a kind of prayer. We pray by dancing.

Brad: But, why do you still do that? You pray to the sun and stuff, and you are supposed to pray to God. I am Christian and I pray to God.

Class: (Murmurs) We are Catholic and we pray to God.

Joe: I am Catholic and I am Indian also. We pray to one God, but we believe his spirit is in all of nature. There is like a spirit for each thing in nature. Indians dance all their lives, like from age three. The whole tribe goes to dances. It's not like you can choose.

This dialogue grew out of children's connections to literature within a classroom context where they were encouraged to bring their lives and cultural identities into school. Through their literature discussions, children considered diverse perspectives in how they viewed themselves, each other, and the world. We believe that this type of dialogue is one means of supporting a broader view of culture and that this might lead to a greater possibility for social change.

When we entered the classroom as children, we were expected to be "ready" for school—we either adjusted to school or were left behind. When we entered the classroom as teachers, school has begun to change, most notably in recognizing the differing experiences that children bring from home. Our initial experiences with multicultural education were characterized by a superficial focus on ethnicity, where each ethnic group was studied in isolation as a theme study, a learning center, a set of books, or a special monthly focus. We soon grew dissatisfied with this approach because it set people apart with the assumption that more information would lead to more understanding which would, in turn, bring about mutual valuing and a change in behavior (Banks, 1994). The approach narrowly defined culture and eliminated important characteristics that shape each of us as people. It also implied that ethnicity was static and uniform, rather than dynamic.

Our dissatisfaction led us to explore approaches which build on children's home experiences (Moll, 1992; Taylor & Dorsey-Gaines, 1988) and the diverse ways in which children learn (Leland & Harste, 1994). However, our thinking about diversity was restricted because, while schools continued to value diversity; they did so *only* as long as students could meet society's narrow standards for excellence—as long as they turned out to be the same.

We believe that difference is still not respected or acted upon. Schools continue to focus on the same end points for all students despite the fact that it is difference, not sameness, that make a democracy strong and creates powerful learning environments (Edelsky, 1994). Through building on the different ways of living that students and teachers bring to the classroom, new possibilities are created in everyone's lives. We wanted to explore classroom settings that valued everyone's strengths.

In this article, we will share Sandy's attempts as a teacher to highlight diversity and children's cultures in more authentic ways. The "I" voice is Sandy's to indicate her role as a teacher researcher. The "we" voice reflects the thinking we did together.

Examining Children's Connections to Culture

I teach in a Tuscon school that serves a diverse multiethnic working-class community. Despite my best efforts, my "multicultural" lessons had never led to powerful classroom sharing about children's own connections. I searched for a vehicle that would connect home and school and signal to children that who they are is of value in school. I devised a cross-curricular, literature-based Family Studies Inquiry to encourage students to explore their own experiences and roots and therefore to understand themselves (Kaser, 1995). The students themselves became the curriculum, with the study of family as a framework and literature discussion as a vehicle for response. The flowchart [in Figure 1] shows how the curriculum actually developed over the year.

I saw one of my responsibilities as providing students with access to books that might contextualize their diverse perspectives. Books were chosen to encourage students to explore their own cultures and those of others inside and outside the classroom. Although I collected the books, students were given choice in selecting books to examine more closely. They also had the freedom to explore issues within those books that were of greatest importance to learn to them at that moment. In their literature circles, we hoped that students would share issues related to the literature in an authentic way through collaboration, reflection, and dialogue—"How does my family compare to the family in the story?" "How do my traditions compare to your traditions?" "What would I like to know more about?"

The literature circles consisted of small groups of four to five students who engaged in conversation and dialogue about a book (Short & Pierce, 1990). Sometimes students used discussion strategies, such as creating a web of their connections, sketching the meaning of the story using "Sketch to Stretch," or sharing significant quotes through "Save the Last Word for Me" (Short & Harste, 1996) to facilitate their thinking.

Throughout these experiences, I collected student artifacts, took field notes, kept a teaching journal, and tape recorded literature discussions. To make sense of the data, I constructed profiles of three students to document individual responses across the year. Throughout this process, Kathy and I talked frequently about a wide range of curricular and research issues. While issues of culture pervaded the entire curriculum, we decided to focus on literature discussions in order to examine children's talk and thinking about culture. From previous experiences, we knew that these discussions were particularly generative for this type of talk. Focusing my data collection on these discussions within the broader classroom context was an important strategy for me as a teacher researcher.

FIGURE 1   Curriculum Flowchart of Family Studies Inquiry

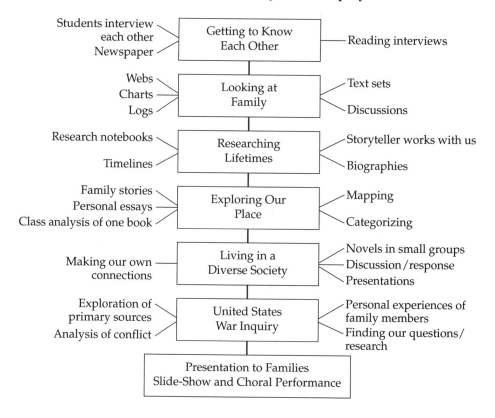

As students shared issues that were significant to them, I realize I was still operating under a restricted view of culture. I has assumed that, because the students came from diverse ethnic backgrounds, issues of ethnicity would be the most important aspect of culture that they would want to explore. I searched for books that reflected many different ethnic perspectives. What the students taught us, however, was that culture can never be defined that narrowly for *any* person. While ethnicity mattered to them, other aspects of their own cultures, such as gender, religion, family, community, and social class were sometimes of greater importance to them or were interwoven with issues of ethnicity and race.

Examining Children's Own Cultural Identities

To understand the cultural identities that were most significant to children, I examined three students closely to see what issues occurred repeatedly in their conservations and writing across the year (Kaser, 1994).

Rosanna's Connections to Family

Rosanna connected with the Family Studies Inquiry immediately and talked with her family all year long about their history and traditions. As she shared her stories, the whole class gained a rich sense of her values as a Mexican American. The children saw her stories as authentic knowledge, based on the experiences of a member of the classroom community, rather than mandated learning.

Yet, from the beginning, Rosanna was most interested in issues of family structure. While her focus on family was obviously interwined with her ethnic heritage, family-structures-as-culture was her most significant area of inquiry that year. She examined a text set on families and listed issues that concerned her, such as "the possibility of dad being laid off, kids with two families, favorite belongings of families, expectations for boys and girls, families of different races, and foster families." She was particularly interested in foster families and researched this topic throughout the year.

It was Rosanna's self-directed research and discussion of family structures that moved the class to consider situations different from their own—an essential move if they were to understand and respect difference. Students began to see family structure as part of their cultural heritage rather than valuing one kind of family over another.

Brad's Connections to Family and Religion

Brad began the year with a strong focus on family and generational cultures as he pursued books and conversations about grandparents. The first text set Brad explored dealt with grandfathers and led to the following discussion about his connections:

Brad: My grandpa used to take us fishing in Pinetop. We did a lot of stuff like that with him. He died and we don't do that stuff . . . well, sometimes we do things like that and fish, but I miss him.

Joe: I just wish I could have done things with my grandfather. I wish I knew stories that my grandfather would have told me.

Dan: Me, too, Brad, you were lucky. I will have to wait and see if my grandfather will tell me stories in heaven. But it is still sad for you.

Brad later chose to read *Racing the Sun* (Pitts, 1988) which deals with a grandfather/ grandson relationship. He continued to work through the death of his grandfather in the group and made a web in his log about his connections [see Figure 2].

The Family Studies focus gave Brad the opportunity to revisit his experience through literature, talk, and writing. Within his discussion group, he found a friend in Joe who shared stories of his own grandfather. Discussions of grandparents led naturally to discussions of heritage, and, although Brad had a strong Mexican American and European American heritage, the cultural aspect that seemed of greatest importance to him throughout that year was religion. Midway through *Racing the Sun,* Brad made this log entry:

I connect with the book in a religious way. People say that the point of time we're in now is the new age. My family and I have to keep our Christian ways as does the grandfather in *Racing the Sun* who has to keep his Indian ways. Next time, we may want to talk a little about people in our families who do and don't keep up with the family's background.

FIGURE 2   Brad's Conection to *Racing the Sun* (Pitts, 1988)

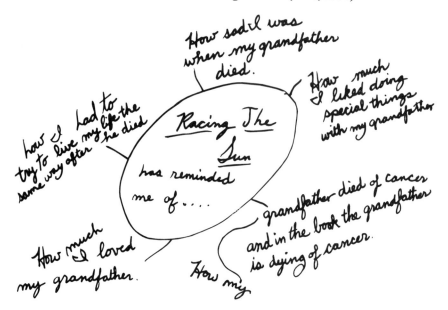

Brad did a considerable amount of writing on religion, and contributed to a class discussion comparing his view of God to his perceptions of American Indian views of God. His interest in these views grew out of his friendship with Joe, a Pima Indian.

The family inquiry also allowed Brad to explore his family's religious belief system and what it might mean to him in the future. He spoke thoughtfully about religious traditions within the lager class community. Brad contributed in an authentic way to the class' understandings of cultural diversity and encouraged others to share and ask questions. In the past, he had always taken a leadership role in group situations and often ignored others' perspectives. Perhaps through the personal nature of his inquiry into his grandfather's death and religion, he became more respectful of others' viewpoints and contributed to the group instead of feeling he had to be the group leader.

Joe's Connections to Ethnicity

Joe became eagerly involved in the Family Studies focus and quickly chose the "grandfathers" text set to discuss. Joe enjoyed the format of literature circles and wrote in his log after the first session. "It went really well. Everybody just jumped right in."

Joe "jumped in" during his first session by talking about his favorite book in the set, *Knots on a Counting Rope* (Martin 1987). He explained that his grandfather had been a Pima dancer and talked about attending gatherings where the old people tell stories. He referred to the illustrations to help his classmates imagine what his grandfather looked like as he danced.

The second book Joe read was *Racing the Sun* (Pitts, 1988). While Brad chose this book because it was about grandparents, Joe was drawn to the fact that the main characters were Navajo. He made the following observations in the group discussion about the grandfather's desire to return to the reservation to die:

Joe: In the city, he was home alone with the family working. He wanted to go to people who were more into their culture, like he was.

Brad: The father did not want to go, it says on page 117. For the same reasons—each one wanted to stay in his own culture.

Joe: Brandon [the grandson] wanted to go because he was getting interested in his culture. He was getting closer to the grandfather. The grandfather shared stories, chants and jogging, and growing plants. Besides, the father did go back.

After the group spent a few minutes discussing what happened when the family went to the reservation, Joe raised an issue that was important to him:

Brad: Well, anyway, I think the book is about how to take on the new ways without having to give up the old.

Joe: You shouldn't give up on your heritage.

Brad: Yeah, but, sometimes people aren't proud of heritage because traditions seem silly.

Randy: It doesn't seem up-to-date. He even calls it "the old ways."

Brad: I think the father was just trying to get away from the stereotyping of Indians—riding horses, shooting arrows.

Joe: Yeah, well, I still think people should stay in their heritage, but no one in my family is into it. Like that guy in the story, they want to go on with life and pretend they are not Indian. I feel more like Brandon. I'm interested.

Marcus: I'm like Brandon, too. I want to remember.

In this discussion, Joe took on the stance of an authority as the only American Indian in the group and drew upon his connections to his own ethnicity. It was apparent throughout the year that Joe was thinking through what being Indian meant to him. He developed an awareness of how people around him viewed their own ethnic heritage and how they in turn, are viewed by the broader society. Joe clearly saw the Family Studies focus as a place where he could articulate his concerns and understandings. He felt a sense of identity with the Indian characters in the books he read, and was more participatory in discussions about these books. Joe expressed disappointment that his family seemed to place more importance on becoming part of mainstream society than on developing their own ethnic uniqueness. I introduced Joe to a resource teacher who supported him in finding people and materials to further his inquiry. His focus on ethnicity contributed to and was interwoven throughout class discussions of culture. As a result, the Family Studies focus helped draw him closer to rather than set him apart from his peers.

Because Kathy and I had not decided ahead of time which issues students needed to study or how they should respond to what they read, students were able to create meaning for themselves. Although I created the instructional framework, learning took place because students could make connections to their knowledge and experiences, searching out new information based on the interests and needs.

The use of quality children's literature that was enjoyable and culturally diverse was crucial to the Family Studies focus. The literature selections enabled a range of issues related to culture to surface, and students knew they could do their own thinking and could enter into dialogue to make sense of the literature and their own lives.

Expanding Our Definition of Culture

As we examined children's talk and how they chose which aspects of their cultures were most significant that year, we realized the importance of defining culture as all the ways in which people live and think in the world. Geertz (1973) defines culture as "the shared patterns that set the tone, character and quality of people's lives" (p. 216). These patterns include language, religion, gender, relationships, socioeconomic status, ethnicity, race, family structures, region, and rural, suburban, and urban communities.

According to Fleck (1935), thought collectives are groups of people who learn to think in similar ways because they share a common interest, exchange ideas, maintain interaction over time, and create a history that affects how they think and live. Since most individuals think and act within several thought collectives at a time, this view captures the dynamic, evolving nature of culture as each person interacts with, and is changed through, transactions with other cultures.

These understandings about culture were important to us for several reasons. One was that they allowed us to see the diversity of children's own interconnected talk and issues of culture. Another was that they removed the "other" within the classroom. When culture is defined only as ethnicity and race, many people view culture as a characteristic of particular groups and as outside of the experience of everyone else. From this perspective, multicultural curriculum remains a separate unit or book, not a characteristic of the learning environment. We realized that, when students and teachers recognize the cultures that influence their own lives and thinking, each becomes more aware of how and why culture is important to everyone else. These understandings do not devalue culture or promote cultural "sameness," rather, they highlight differences across cultures as important and valued in creating community and pushing everyone's learning.

In examining children's talk, we also noted that it was important that children choose the aspects of culture they did and did not want to discuss. Based on what I knew about the children's lives, we noticed that some students chose not to talk about particular issues of their cultural identities. We respected their right to make these decisions. On occasion, we observed that students were able to discuss some of their concerns by talking about a character from a book rather than about themselves.

Understanding "Kid Culture"

As we examined the transcripts, Kathy and I noticed that there was one aspect of culture which we had consistently overlooked. Students often discussed how a book related to the culture they shared with members of their age group, an identity we came to think of as "kid culture." These issues went beyond differences in their personal histories and cultural identities to a set of shared kid values.

Students' Views of Kid Culture

One day, I read aloud *Angel Child, Dragon Child* (Surat, 1983), the story of a Vietnamese girl who is ridiculed because of her ethnic dress. I hoped the book would spark a discussion about accepting differences. Instead, the class was incensed that someone had not told the girl how kids dress in school. It was clear that students read people by the way they dress and that they knew how to dress to give the right message to peers.

Rosanna: It was sad in the book when they teased her because she was different. They said she wore pajamas.

Manny: Yeah, that was pretty dumb. Somebody should have told her to dress like all the other kids. She has to fit in more. How you dress in school is important.

Rosanna: It's important because people look at you and judge you by what you are wearing on the outside.

Joe: Most people dress according to their personality. Like some people are all laid-back and some come to school like fashion plates.

Brad: And you can tell gang members by how they dress. And the gang wanna-be's dress like gang members and act all cool, but everyone knows they are not in the gangs.

Rosanna: Like if you are a nature person who goes hiking and stuff, you wear khaki clothes and hiking boots, even if you are not hiking that day.

Manny: And she just walked in and communicated. "Hey look at me. I'm different." She was different enough.

Brad: If it was us in Vietnam, then *we* would be the different ones.

The next day, Dan brought the book up again. He said he felt sorry for the girl because "when you go to a new school you don't always know the rules." From his conversation, it was clear that he meant the implied rules known only by students, not the school rules. He shared his experience of moving to a new school and soon many of the students were telling their own stories about moving. They agreed that moving to a new school was one of the hardest things a kid has to do and adults didn't understand how hard it was. "They just walk in the door and tell you, boom! 'You have to go live with your Dad' and boom, your whole life is different," said Dan. The discussion then moved into the lack of power kids feel around adults. The class felt that kids made up "rules" for each other because it gave them power for a change.

In later literature discussions, students talked about other issues such as the importance of parents considering how names will affect children and realizing that certain names can be embarrassing. They talked about the difficulty of making decisions because of divided loyalties between family, peers, and their desires as a child. They felt especially strong about situations where parents disagree and the child's decision can be seen as siding with one parent over the other.

We realized that students were connecting cultural diversity with the expectations and 5 culture of their own age level. The struggle to figure out who they were as individuals was a struggle they shared, irrespective of differences in their family cultural characteristics. This is consistent with Bullivant's definition of culture as "a social group's design for surviving in and adapting to its environment" (1989. p. 27).

Even as early as elementary school, children view each other through their shared definitions of "kid culture"—the underground peer culture of how children at a certain age think about themselves. Lurie (1990) points out, "Anyone who has spent time around children and observed them carefully, or really remembers what it was like to be a child, knows that childhood is also a separate culture, with its own rituals, beliefs, games, and customs, and its own, largely oral, literature" (p. 194).

Children often use peer talk to judge and to control the behaviors of classmates. These kid culture issues of acceptance and rejection touch all aspect of their lives—music, talk, appearance, behavior, values and priorities, as well as ways of maintaining and achieving status.

Adults' Views of Kid Culture

As adults, teachers are excluded from kid culture and we had to work hard to understand and value the ways in which this culture entered into children's talk. Newkirk (1992) found that first- and second-grade children brought a discourse into literature groups which he initially found annoying and believed was "off task." In reexamining this talk, he became convinced that it was a valid form of discourse from childrens' own culture. Children came to groups "not as total novices but as members of a rich oral culture that has its own repertoire of responses" (p. 9).

While we wanted to encourage children to accept and value differences, significant changes in their attitudes often could not occur because children had another more powerful agenda that we were not taking into account. Kid culture has a tremendous influence on children and frequently involves values that conflict with other aspects of their cultures and with teachers' values. Yet, this culture is left out of curriculum designed to explore cultural diversity. Either we are unaware of it as adults or we assume that children will grow out of it. Other times, we find this culture in conflict with the values of cultural diversity which we are trying to promote, and so we ignore or judge it. For example, we talk about celebrating differences and yet sameness and acceptance are foundational in the world of kids. Children respond by taking their culture underground and not examining it critically. We also knew that, as adults, we couldn't force children to discuss kid culture issues. We could, however, create an environment in which they felt free to discuss this aspect of their identities.

Students talk about literature allowed us to identify what was missing in other situations. One day, a School Resource Officer talked to students and had them perform skits about "saying no to drugs" and walking away from those who offer drugs. They were given strategies that incorporated adult language that would be viewed negatively or ignored within their kid culture. Some students had family members who used drugs and belonged to gangs and they knew that life on the streets among their peers just wasn't that simple. They needed language and strategies to avoid drugs that fit their own culture of peers and the street. Because the officer's comments did not connect to their world, they simply rejected his comments as irrelevant and repeated what she wanted them to say without engaging with the issues.

make connections across all aspects of their cultural identities. One of our goals is to help students bring together the cultures of home, school, and peers, and explore the connections and the dysjunctions across those cultures. In order for this to occur, they need space for sharing issues of kid culture through peer talk in "kid-friendly" schools.

Implications for Schools and Classrooms

In thinking about the children's responses to the Family Studies Inquiry, we identified what seemed to be key characteristics of the curriculum which provided room for valuing differences in experiences, ways of learning, and outcomes in the classroom. The first was the importance of setting up engagements that allow teachers to really *listen* to students. We found that ways of listening needed to be planned into the day, or we missed hearing what children were saying because of the hectic nature of classroom life. Teachers need a sense of students' thinking in order to support them in making connections and building from their own experiences to engage with new ideas. In addition, both dialogue and storying are essential for children in making connections and considering new ideas. Children need to be constantly encouraged to share oral, written, and visual stories from their lives so that they can explore their own connections. Through this sharing of stories, they develop a sense of community which allows them to enter into dialogue with each other. Dialogue involves thinking out loud with others so that their ideas and connections are considered reflectively and critically. Dialogue focuses on inquiry and critique and so takes learners beyond their own ideas to consider new perspectives and ways of viewing the world (Peterson, 1992).

Dialogue in literature circles provides children with multiple perspectives as they enter the story world of the book and share their interpretations with each other. They make connections to their lives and cultural identities and examine other possible worlds through the characters in books and the talk of their peers.

In encouraging dialogue, we are aware that disclosure of self through dialogue or writing is not culturally appropriate for some children. Our belief in the importance of literature and dialogue is the result of our own cultural values. While we remain committed to their role in children's learning, we also believe that we have no right to force children to make personal disclosures outside their family contexts. However, should students choose not to discuss these issues, they can still benefit from hearing others' perspectives and are better able to make thoughtful decisions about what they read.

Another essential characteristic is that the curriculum is focused on inquiry, on children searching for the questions that are significant for them, instead of on "covering" a particular topic through activities. Even when the topic is mandated by the school, children can still find their own questions within that topic. American history was part of the mandated school curriculum for fifth grade, but as a teacher, I waited to see where it would fit with children's questions. Their interest in time lines and family histories led them to the realization that their own family members had participated in significant events in American and Mexican history. Once the class moved into this study, I did not decide on the topics of study. Instead, students spent time reading and talking so they could determine their questions and form groups based on those questions.

Research that involved children's own families and communities was integral to their inquiries. Children collected oral family stories, researched their family time lines, and

Our experiences convinced us that children feel that the discourse of kid cultur
place in the classroom. When they do not talk like adults, they are judged to be not j
ferent, but deficient. Nodelman (1992) asserts that adults attempt to speak for cl
even through children's literature, because adults believe children are incapable of
ing for themselves. They see children as different from, and presumably inferior to,
as thinkers and speakers. He suggests that some adults view children as innocent rath
lacking in intelligence, but this assumption still allows adults to have "power over chi
(p. 30).

Providing Space in the Classroom for Kid Culture

We found that, instead of urging children to get back on task when they engaged i
from kid culture, they needed structures to support them in exploring this talk openl
critically) with each other. When presented with an alternative perspective, students
to find where it might fit with what they already know, understand, or have experie
Time and opportunity for this talk is essential for children if we really believe that they
to bring their lives into the classroom.

Nodelman (1992) points out that as adults, we will never completely escape the "i
rialist" tendencies which are at the heart of our discourses with children. We also can r
completely understand kid culture because that culture changes with each generation
by its very definition, excludes us as adults. However, adults can become aware of the
in which we oppress and deny kid culture, and we can move beyond thinking childre
"like us" or seeing them as "the other."

During the Family Studies Inquiry, I learned to listen to children's comments an
questions when I didn't understand or value what they were saying. In the past, I w
have rejected or ignored their discussions of the importance of dressing in particular
in favor of what I saw as more direct connections to the book. Instead of judging stud
I tried to reply to their comments out of a sincere desire to understand what they were
ing (Barnes, 1976). As they expanded on their comments, the class could explore kid
ture and social attitudes within their own contexts. However, if my comments or quest
communicated judgmental questioning, they immediately stopped sharing any connect
to, or reflection on their kid culture.

Kathy and I also found that children needed to talk in small groups where teachers
not present. No matter how carefully I tried to listen empathetically, I was an "outsider"
there were certain aspects of kid culture that were not discussed when I was present. 1
humor, for example, was rarely shared with me because they presumed I wouldn't ur
stand or like it. We respected their need to keep some of their discussions of issues pr
from us as adults.

"If the only talk that matters is that which is patterned off adult conversation, stud
can conclude that what matters most to them, their culture, has little place in the classro
(Newkirk, 1992, p. 10). Educators have known for years that when children feel their
tural identities have no place in the classroom, they often reject the curriculum, resist le
ing, and may eventually drop out of school. We believe that these same findings app
children who feel that adults deny or devalue their kid culture. Children have learned t
silent about that culture around adults and, in so doing, that culture becomes even r
powerful in their lives. There is no opportunity to explore or critique their kid culture

interviewed family members. Their experiences in school led them to ask questions and gather data from their families. Sharing this data with each other led them to new questions and research which then led them back again to their families.

All of these characteristics of curriculum are based on our belief that cultural diversity is a *strength* for building powerful learning contexts, *not a problem to be solved.* Difference, not sameness, makes a classroom and society strong. Along with Sleeter and Grant (1987), we believe that our goal is not to develop multicultural education as an additive to the curriculum, but to create an education that *is* multicultural.

The goal of schools in our modern global society is to create productive citizens who have marketable skills. The goal of education in traditional oral societies is for children to learn how to become human beings—to figure out who they are and where they fit in the broader scheme of things (Oleska, 1995). We believe that both goals are essential in schools today. To become a citizen but lose yourself as a person is not acceptable within school contexts. Indeed, schools should be places to explore *both* the common goals that connect us as citizens and the differences that make us human. A strong democracy depends on differences in perspectives and ways of knowing to create new possibilities. If schools truly respect and build on difference, diversity can become a strength for creating powerful classroom learning environments *and* a stronger democratic society.

References

Banks, J. (1994). *Multiethnic education: Theory and practice.* Needham Heights, MA: Allyn & Bacon.

Barnes, D. (1976). *From communication to curriculum.* Portsmouth, NH: Heinemann.

Bullivant, B. M. (1989). Culture: Its nature and meaning for educators. In J. Banks & C. Banks (Eds.), *Multicultural education: Issues and perspectives* (pp. 27–48). Needham Heights, MA: Allyn & Bacon.

Edelsky, C. (1994). Education for democracy. *Language Arts, 71,* 252–257.

Fleck, L. (1935). *The genesis and development of a scientific fact.* Chicago: University of Chicago Press.

Geertz. C. (1973). *The interpretation of cultures.* New York: Basic Books.

Kaser, S. (1994). *Exploring cultural diversity.* Unpublished Ed.S. thesis. University of Arizona, Tuscon.

Kaser, S. (1995). Creating a learning environment that invites connections. In S. Steffy & W. Hood (Eds.), *If this is social studies, why isn't it boring?* (pp. 57–71). York, ME: Stenouse.

Leland, C., & Harste, J. (1994). Multiple ways of knowing: Curriculum in a new key. *Language Arts, 71,* 337–345.

Lurie, A. (1990). *Don't tell the grown-ups: Subversive children's literature.* Boston: Little, Brown.

Martin, B. (1987). *Knots on a counting rope.* New York: Holt.

Moll, L. (1992). Bilingual classroom studies and community

analysis: Some recent trends. *Educational Researcher, 21*(2), 21–24.

Newkirk, T. (1992). *Listening in.* Portsmouth, NH: Heinemann.

Nodelman, P. (1992). The other: Orientalism, colonialism, and children's literature. *Children's Literature Association Quarterly, 17*(1), 29–35.

Oleska, M. (1995). *Communicating across cultures.* [Videotape series.] Juneau, AK: University of Southeastern Alaska.

Peterson, R. (1992). *Life in a crowded place.* Portsmouth, NH: Heinemann.

Pitts, P. (1988). *Racing the sun.* New York: Avon.

Short, K., & Harste, J. (1996). *Creating classrooms for authors and inquirers.* Portsmouth, NH: Heinemann.

Short, K., & Pierce, K. M. (Eds.). (1990). *Talking about books.* Portsmouth, NH: Heinemann.

Sleeter, C., & Grant, C. (1987). An analysis of multicultural education in the United States. *Harvard Education Review, 57,* 421–444.

Surat, M. (1983). *Angel child, dragon child.* New York: Scholastic.

Taylor, D., & Dorsey-Gaines, C. (1988). *Growing up literate: Learning from inner-city families.* Portsmouth, NH: Heinemann.

Integrating Sources

1. If Anderson and Gunderson were invited to make suggestions for improving the multicultural climate in the classroom scenarios described by Kaser and Short, what might those suggestions be?

2. Work with a group to identify the themes common to both of these articles. What themes are unique to each article? Which themes are currently evident in your school and school district? Which themes are not evident in your school and school district? Why?

Classroom Implications

1. What are the multicultural representations in your school district? Your school?

2. Interview the ESL teacher in your district to determine how bilingual children are helped to speak English. What is the philosophy of the ESL program?

3. Examine your classroom to determine whether it is a multicultural community. Make a plan for improvement.

4. To what extent are you preparing your students for life in the new millennium? What will the consequences be for your students future?

Annotated Bibliography

Beaty, J. (1997). *Building Bridges with Multicultural Picture Books for Children 3–5.* Des Moines, IA: Merrill Prentice-Hall.

A book that shows teachers how to choose appropriate multicultural picture books, incorporate extension activities, and build curriculum using picture boks. Each chapter concludes with learning activities, references, and additional readings.

Cruz, M., & Duff, O. (1997). Celebrating heritage through literature. *English Journal, 86,*(5), 78–79.

An article that describes ways to promote cultural literacy by focusing on the literary contributions of authors of color. Identifies favorite selections by various authors.

Hopkins, D., & Tastad, S. A. (1997). Censoring by omission: Has the United States progressed in promoting diversity through children's books? *Journal of Youth Services in Libraries, 10,*(4), 399–404.

An article that discusses the scarcity of Multicultural children's books. Specifically identifies racial bias in older books, new stereotypes in children's literature, political correctness, and ways that quality Multicultural literature may be accessed.

MacPhee, J. S. (1997). "That's not fair!": A white teacher reports on white first graders' responses to multicultural literature. *Language Arts, 74,*(1), 33–40.

A study of white, affluent first-grader's responses to four books that cast African Americans as major characters. Students show sensitivity to others feelings and addressed issues of racial prejudice.

McKinney, L. J. (1997). The road not taken: Assessing rural teachers' knowledge of Multicultural children's literature. *Rural Educator, 18,*(3), 7–11.

A study indicating that while tradebooks may address cultural diversity better than textbooks, they are less available to rural teachers. Five textbooks surveyed contained 28 percent multicultural stories; however, of 148 teachers surveyed, only 4 percent of the books used in their classrooms addressed cultural diversity.

Rogers, T., & Soter, A. (Eds.). (1997). *Reading across cultures: Teaching Literature in a Diverse Society.* New York: Teachers College Press.

Stories of teachers use of literature to engage students in critical discussions, and elicit various perspectives in pursuit of understanding.

You Become Involved

1. Work with a group to create a concept map (web) of the issues identified in the articles.
2. As a group, decide which issue and related details are the most critical for schools to address.
3. Present your concept map to the class for discussion.

4

READING ASSESSMENT

Let him now take liberty to exercise himself in any English
book till he can perfectly read in any place of a book that
is offered him; and when he can do this, I adjudge him
fit to enter into a *Grammar* Schoole, but not before.
—*C. H. (1659)*

... that the teacher's evaluation of the pupil's
progress in learning to read should not be limited to
appraising specific skills but should also be concerned
about the influence of instruction on the development
of interest in reading, a taste for good literature, and
in general should be directed to determining the effects of
reading and learning to read on the pupil's development.
—*I. H. ANDERSON AND W. F. DEARBORN (1952)*

The manner in which we teachers assess children's
growth toward literacy can have a major impact on their
concept of reading and writing.... If we use only multiple-
choice tests to check on students' retention of what they have
read, they will learn that reading is basically a process
of memorizing information for pleasing someone else.
—*FRANK MAY (1998)*

The issue of reading assessment is today one of the most vigorously debated topics among teachers as well as the general public (Miller, Hayes, & Atkinson, 1997;
Valencia & Au, 1997). Questions such as who should develop tests, what is the role
of testing in our schools, and how should these test results be used effectively are
critical and, in many cases, still unresolved issues.

Historically, students' assessment data have been used for making instructional decisions, such as student placement, class grouping, materials selection,
and so on. In addition, assessment procedures have been used to measure literacy
program effectiveness and to track student achievement over time. More recently,

school districts and government leaders have utilized assessment results to support various types of school reform, most notably in the areas of teacher accountability and curricular change.

State and National Reading Assessment Initiatives

Perhaps the most dramatic recent development in assessment is the increasingly wide use of state and national testing programs. While the intent of these assessment initiatives is to measure large groups of students on specific skills, such as ability levels in reading comprehension for all third graders in a state, this ideal has not consistently been met. Often the results of state tests have been used to compare and contrast the academic achievements of school districts, specific schools, as well as the teaching expertise of individual teachers.

The various uses of state and national assessment results are both an educational as well as political issue: educational, in that these measures give a general picture of the achievement level of large groups of students and thus provide guidance for the planning of statewide curriculum evaluation and suggested changes in current practices; political, in that many decisions are being made based on these test results, which most would agree are clearly inappropriate. For instance, as noted above, to measure individual teacher practices related to a state test is clearly inappropriate, and yet major decisions are being made on the basis of these results, for example, teachers' salaries, continued approval of teachers' licenses, and even faculty salaries.

Closely related to the issue of state and national assessment is the establishment of standards for many academic areas. For instance, in reading, a set of standards for evaluating teacher knowledge and practice in reading has been developed (*Standards,* 1994, 1999). The roles and responsibilities of various literacy providers are defined in these *Standards* with regard to professional training as well as instructional practices. With the development of standards comes concern over how they will be used, once established. The basic dilemma is simply: Should these standards be used only to measure existing practices, or are they designed to drive the curriculum through the establishment of goals and objectives which must be met by all school districts? Currently this is still an open and unresolved issue.

Administrative versus Instructional Uses of Assessment Results

The need for accurate, current, and essential information about students' academic progress is a critical need for both classroom teachers and school administrators. Traditionally, this information has been provided by various types of standardized assessment measures. The results from these tests have increasingly been subject to criticism from many who say these conclusions do not accurately measure actual student performance or knowledge of a specific academic area.

The uses of this test data are fundamentally different for administrators and teachers. Whereas the former group is interested in assessment results as a way of measuring total curriculum development and the effectiveness of large groups of students, <u>teachers are most concerned with the academic growth of their classes as well as individual student growth</u>. This is an example of one of the dichotomies related to reading assessment.

Process versus Product Assessment

Any test designed to measure a child's ability in a given area at a given time is primarily concerned with the *product* of learning. On the other hand, measures such as observation and miscue analysis, designed to provide information about the processes of reading, tend to be more qualitative in nature. Quantitative product measures include standardized tests but also tests devised to measure the mastery of specific skills. Whether a teacher's practice is better informed by specific-skill product tests or by continuously compiled process measures will depend largely on the teacher's instructional philosophy. Much of the controversy in this area is a direct result of conflicting literacy philosophies concerning the role of the teacher, the effective use of literacy materials, and the type of assessment being used.

Traditional versus Progressive Standardized Comprehension Formats

Traditionally, standardized tests of reading comprehension have relied on short passages followed by a combination of literal and inferential comprehension questions. Sometimes, the troublesome task of composing good questions has been circumvented by using a multiple-choice cloze format, which requires the reader to choose the best word for completing sentences. These approaches have been challenged in recent years on several grounds. First, they fail to assess a student's ability to integrate information across large samples of text. Second, they fail to account for prior knowledge. Present-day initiatives to bring comprehension test formats into line with reading theory have led to longer selections (for example, entire short stories or textbooks change), to prior knowledge tests administered before the students begin to read, and to the use of questions that draw on information located at more than one point in the selection. Whether such test reforms can satisfy critics is inevitably related to a question that is essentially political: What should be expected of students in terms of comprehension?

Constructive versus Reconstructed Assessment of Reading

If you believe that comprehension is largely a matter of discerning what an author has intended to convey, then you have taken a reconstructive view. That is, you probably see the goal of the reader to be "reconstructing" the author's meaning that has been encoded in print. If so, you probably have little objection to using traditional assessment formats to determine the extent to which students have been successful in their effort to reconstruct meaning. On the other hand, you may view the reading process as a "transaction" between what a reader *wishes* to derive from a text and what the text offers the reader. A reader's personal desires, cultural background, language distinctions, and so forth will all determine what is actually "constructed" from a given reading experience. If you take this view, then a traditional comprehension assessment format will have serious shortcomings in that it will have been constructed by someone removed from the immediate learning environment, who has specific ideas about what meaning a reader should derive, which answers to questions are "correct," and so on.

Situated versus Decontextualized Assessment

Standardized tests, and for that matter other types of paper-and-pencil tests, may produce misleading results because they requires students to apply skills in artificial, contrived settings. Critics of such measures have argued that it is more valid to observe how students perform "authentic" tasks undertaken for reasons the students value. That is to say, the assessment should be situated within the learning context (Farr & Greene, 1993). This view has great appeal but poses serious logistical problems. It might prove especially difficult to use truly situated assessment for administrative purposes given the lack of uniformity among the techniques used by various teachers. One of the outcomes of the drive toward situated assessment has been the development of portfolios. These provide collections of records of performance during authentic tasks. Whether the benefits of portfolios outweigh their inherent disadvantages (e.g., size, subjectivity, lack of uniformity, etc.) is a decision that individual teachers must ultimately make.

As You Read

Tierney (1998) delineates 12 principles for assessment that shift assessment from outside the classroom to inside the classroom. Neill (1997) outlines a new assessment system in which student learning becomes central to this reform. Here are some concerns related to literacy assessment you might consider as you read:

1. How are a district's need to monitor literacy growth best accomplished in the classroom?
2. To what extent have assessment reforms made assessment practices more valid measures?
3. Are performance or standardized measures better suited to the ongoing assessment needs of classroom teachers? Students? Parents? School districts?
4. What should be the purposes of classroom assessment? District-wide assessment? Statewide assessment?

References

Anderson, I. H., & Dearborn, W. F. (1952). *The psychology of teaching reading*. New York: Roland Press.

C. H. (1659). *The Petty-Schoole shewing a way to teach little children to read English with delight and profit. (Especially according to the New Primer.)* London: Printed by J. T. for Andrew Crook, at the Green Dragon in Pauls Church Yard.

May, F. B. (1998). *Reading as communication* (5th ed.). Upper Saddle River, NJ: Merrill/Prentice-Hall.

Miller, S. D., Hayes, C. T., & Atkinson, T. S. (1997). State efforts to improve students' reading and language arts achievement: Does the left hand know what the right is doing? *Reading Research and Instruction, 36,* 267–286.

Neill, D. M. (1997). Transforming student assessment. *Phi Delta Kappan, 78,* 34–58.

Standards for the assessment of reading and writing. (1994). Newark, DE: International Reading Association.

Standards for literacy professionals and paraprofessionals. (1999). Newark, DE: International Reading Association.

Tierney, R. J. (1998). Literary assessment reform: Shifting beliefs, principled possibilities, emerging practices. *The Reading Teacher, 51,* 374–390.

Valencia, S. W., & Au, K. (1997). *Portfolios across educational contexts: Issues of evaluation, teacher development, and system validity. Reading Research Report #73.* Athens, GA: University of Georgia and College Park, MD: University of Maryland. (ERIC Document Reproduction Service No. ED 402 558).

Literacy Assessment Reform

Shifting Beliefs, Principled Possibilities, and Emerging Practices

ROBERT J. TIERNEY

Developing better assessment practices requires more than simply choosing a new test or adopting a packaged informal assessment procedure. Indeed, it is difficult to imagine "plastic wrapped" versions of what these new assessment systems intend. Unfortunately, some assessment practices may be repackaged versions of old tests rather than new ways of doing assessment. And some assessment practices, regardless of the label (authentic assessment, alternative assessment, student-centered assessment, responsive evaluation, classroom-based assessment, or constructive assessment), may be compromised as they are made to fit tenets or principles out of character or inconsistent with the aspirations of these possibilities. Contributing to the confusion may be reverence for certain technical attributes espoused by some pyschometricians and a predilection or political climate that tends to perpetuate top-down assessment and curriculum reform. Not surprising, professionals may differ in whether or not new forms of assessment live up to their promise.

In hopes of helping to sort out some of these dilemmas—the oxymorons, compromises or, at the very least, different views of assessment, learners and learning, I have tried to make the ramifications of my definition of assessment more explicit with the articulation of a number of principles, which I describe in this article.

These principles for assessment emanate from personal ideals and practice as much as theory and research—a mix of child-centered views of teaching, pluralistic and developmental views of children, constructivist views of knowing, and critical theoretical views of empowerment. The view that I espouse strives to be in harmony with Bruner's (1990) notion that a democratic society "demands that we be conscious of how we come to our knowledge and be as conscious as we can be about the values that lead us to our perspectives. It asks us to be accountable for how and what we know" (p. 31). Likewise, my goal is aligned with constructivists' ways of knowing and the notion of responsive evaluation that Guba and Lincoln (1989) as well as others (e.g., Lather, 1986; Stake, 1983) have espoused:

> *Responsive evaluation is not only responsive for the reason that it seeks out different stakeholder views but also since it responds to those items in the subsequent collection of information. It is quite likely that different stakeholders will hold very different constructions with respect to any particular claim, concern, or issue. As we shall see, one of the major tasks of the evaluator is to conduct the evaluation in such a way that each group must confront and deal with the constructions of all*

Source: From Tierney, R. J. (1998, February). Literacy assessment reform: Shifting beliefs, principled possibilities, and emerging practices. *The Reading Teacher, 51*(5), 374–390. Reprinted with permission of Robert J. Tierney and the International Reading Association. All rights reserved.

the others, a process we shall refer to as a hermeneutic dialectic. (Guba & Lincoln, 1989, p. 41)

I also find my views aligning with critical theorists (e.g., Baker & Luke, 1991; Freire & Macedo, 1987; Gee, 1990; hooks, 1989, 1994) who suggest that the point of literacy is to reflect upon, and be empowered by, text rather than to be subjugated by it—that literacy contributes to social transformation as we connect with what we read and write, not in acquiescence, but in reaction, reflection, and response.

In accordance with these notions, I contend that to be both accountable and empowered, readers and writers need to be both reflective and pragmatic. To do so, readers and writers need to be inquirers—researching their own selves, considering the consequences of their efforts, and evaluating the implications, worth, and ongoing usefulness of what they are doing or have done. Teachers can facilitate such reflection by encouraging students to keep traces of what they do, by suggesting they pursue ways to depict their journey (e.g., webs or a narrative or listing of steps) and by setting aside time to contemplate their progress and efforts. These reflections can serve as conversation starters—conversations about what they are doing and planning to do and what they did and have learned. I suggest moving toward conversations and notes rather than checklists, rubrics, and more formal evaluations, which seem to distance the student from what she/he is doing, has done, or might do.

These principles stem from a concern that new assessment efforts need to be principled and thoughtful rather than faddish. They reflect a need for a major paradigm shift as regard to how we assess, why we assess, and the ways these assessments are manifest in the classroom. Some ramifications include a new type of professionalism on the part of teachers, a shift in the relationship between testing and teaching and between teacher, students, and parents. In general, these principles call for a willingness to recognize complexity and diversity and an approach to assessment that begins from inside rather than outside the classroom. Are we succeeding in terms of shifting such values? Currently, there are several efforts occurring that are simultaneously studying and supporting such shifts (see, for instance, Tierney, Clark, Fenner, Wiser, Herter, & Simpson, in press). I am optimistic enough to think we have the makings of a movement that is beginning to establish its own identity—one that is aligned with contemporary views of learning, and more consistent with pluralistic and constructivist ethics (see especially Moss, 1996).

The Principles

- *Principle 1:   Assessments should emerge from the classroom rather than be imposed upon it.*

Classrooms are places where wonderful ideas are encountered every day; where children engage with one another in a myriad of social interactions; where learning can occur as the culmination of a unit of work, in conjunction with an experiment, or as students work with others or watch others work. Learnings may be fleeting, emerging, reinforced, and challenged. Oftentimes teachers expect certain learnings; at other times, teachers are surprised at what is learned.

The learnings that occur in classrooms are difficult to predict. Children are different not only in their interests and backgrounds, but also in terms of their literacies. While most teachers may begin the year with a sense of what they want to cover, generally they do not consider their plans to be cast in stone. Indeed, they are quick to adjust to their assessment of their students' needs and even to discard and begin afresh. They are more apt to begin with a menu of possibilities and an open-ended agenda, which allows for learning that is opportunistic and individualized.

With the movement to more child-centered approaches, teaching and learning have become less prescriptive and predetermined and have given way to notions of emergent literacy and negotiated curriculums. Most teachers espouse following the lead of the child. Unfortunately, testing practices tend to abide by a different orientation. Many forms of traditional tests do not measure what is valued and what is occurring in classrooms. Changes in testing have not kept pace with shifts in our understanding of learning and literacy development. Moreover, they often perpetuate an approach to assessment that is from the outside in rather than from the inside out. Indeed, I often argue that one of the reasons for emergent assessment is to ensure that assessment practices keep up with teaching and learning rather than stagnate them by perpetuating the status quo or outdated views of literacy learning.

Compare, if you will, these two scenarios: Students in one classroom are engaged in a wide array of reading and writing experiences, projects, book talks, conferences, and workshops. In conjunction with these activities the students keep journals in which they discuss their reflections, including their goals and self-assessment of their achievements. In addition, each student maintains a log of his or her reading and writing activities, as well as a folder that contains almost everything. Portfolios, in turn, are used to keep track of the key aspects of their work over time. During teacher conferences with the students, the teacher encourages the students to note what they have achieved and want to pursue further. The teacher keeps her/his own informal notes on what is occurring—focusing on a menu of different aspects drawn from a menu of possibilities that the teacher and some colleagues developed. The menu supports but does not constrain the notes that the teacher keeps on the students. As part of the process, these notes are shared with the students, who are encouraged to add their own comments to them. At parent-teacher conferences and student-led parent conferences both the teacher and the student refer back to these notes, portfolios, etc. to remind themselves of and share what has occurred.

The students in another classroom are engaged in a wide array of activities but are not encouraged to monitor themselves. Periodically the teacher distributes a checklist to each student with a preset listing of skills that the child has to check. Likewise the teacher may interrupt the flow of activities and check the students in terms of these preset listing of skills. The skills on the list bear some relationship to some things that are done, but there are a host of things that are not included and some other things that are included that do not seem to apply. The listing of skills was not developed by the teacher nor is it open ended. Instead, the list was developed by a curriculum committee for the district. In some ways the list reflects a philosophy and approach that do not match the current situation. Nonetheless, the teacher is expected to keep the checklist and file it. After the checklist is completed and filed it is not reexamined or revised.

The first example is representative of an inside-out approach—that is, what is assessed and the manner in which the assessment of various learnings is carried out and originates from within the classroom. An inside-out approach does not involve overly rigid a priori determinations of what should be looked for nor does it restrict the types of learning to be examined. In addition, assessment is negotiated among the parties that are involved.

Our second example may give the illusion of being inside out, but it actually perpetuates the outside-in approach. In this classroom the teacher uses informal assessment procedures, but they do not fit with or emerge from the classroom, and there is no negotiation between teacher and student. While the second type of classroom may represent an improvement over classrooms that depend upon standardized assessments and periodic checks, it has some major shortcomings in terms of what is being done and how these things are negotiated. Such a classroom does not invest in or trust the professionalism and problem-solving abilities of teachers, as well as the need for student involvement.

- *Principle 2:   Effective testing requires teacher professionalism with teachers as learners.*

Many of the assessment practices in schools (especially standardized tests) have a dysfunctional relationship with teachers and learners. Whereas in most relationships you expect a give and take, actual testing practices in schools seem more estranged than reciprocal, more detached than intimate. This should come as no surprise for oftentimes testing personnel have separated themselves and their instruments from teachers and students. Testing divisions in school districts generally have detached themselves from teachers and students or have forced teachers and students to work on their terms. In some districts, the testing division may use tenets tied to notions of objectivity and reliability to leverage control of what is tested as well as how, when, and why testing occurs.

If teachers become involved in making assessment decisions, the complexity of dealing with individual differences and differences across classes and schools is apt to surface. It may become problematic to assume that different students can be assessed with the same test, that comparisons across students' are straightforward, or that students' performance and progress can be adequately represented with scores derived by periodical administrations of tests.

Quite often teachers will make reference to the tests that they are required to use, principals will allude to the district and state policy, and the district and state lay the responsibility on the public. Some systems seem to be either resistant to change or entrenched in their commitments.

But, teachers relinquishing control of assessment leads to a loss of self-determinacy and professionalism, which is problematic for a number of reasons. It seems to accept and reinforce the view that teachers cannot be trusted. It removes responsibility for instructional decisions from the hands of those who need to be making them. As a result, it decreases the likelihood that assessment will be aligned with teaching and learning and increases the separation between how learning is occurring in classrooms and how it is tested and reported. It depersonalizes the experience and serves as an excuse for relinquishing responsibility. Essentially, the external control of testing and standardization of testing procedures tend to perpetuate teacher and student disenfranchisement.

Teachers are in a better position to know and learn about an individual's development than outsiders. They are with the student over time across a variety of learning situations. As a result they become aware of the subtle changes and nuances of learning within and across individuals. They are sensitive to student engagement, student interests, student personalities, and the idiosyncrasies of students across learning activities. They are less likely to overstate or ascribe too much significance to results on a single test that may have an alienating impact upon a student. They are in a better position to track and assess learning in the context of teaching and child watching, and therefore to help students assess themselves. Effective teachers are effective learners themselves; they are members of a community of learners in a classroom.

So how might assessment be changed? Teachers, in partnership with their students, need to devise their own classroom assessment systems. These systems should have goals for assessment tied to teaching and learning. These goals should be tied to the types of learning and experiences deemed desirable and, therefore, should be established by those most directly invested in the student's education—the teachers and the students themselves. These standards/features should be open ended and flexible enough to adjust to the nuances of classroom life. Tied to these goals might be an array of assessment activities from formalized procedures to very informal, from student self-assessment activities to teacher observations to periodical assessments via portfolios or other ways of checking progress.

Teachers and students need to be willing to change and recognize that there exists no quick fix or prepackaged way to do assessment. Indeed, prepackaged assessments are apt to be the antithesis of what should be developed. Unfortunately, teachers, students, and caregivers may have been enculturated to view assessment as predetermined rather than emergent and as having a look and feel quite different from more direct and classroom-derived assessments.

More direct forms of assessment might involve ongoing monitoring of students by sampling reading and writing behaviors, maintaining portfolios and journals, holding periodic conferences, and keeping anecdotal records. Several teachers and state efforts suggest that the community will support, if not embrace, such changes. We have numerous affidavits from teachers to that effect, which are corroborated by published reports of others such as Shepard and Bliem (1995), who found community support for performance assessments or more direct methods of assessment over traditional assessments was forthcoming and considerable when caregivers were presented with examples of the options.

- *Principle 3:   Assessment practices should be client centered and reciprocal.*

The notion that assessment should empower students and caregivers suggests an approach consistent with a more client-centered approach to learning. A client-centered approach to assessment is not novel. In areas such as psychotherapy and medicine, client-centered orientations are more the rule than the exception. In a court of law the judicial process hinges upon the notion of advocacy for a client. In attempts at being client centered, teachers are apt to consider what students take away from tests or teacher-student conferences. A shift to client-centered approaches addresses how assessment practices are helping students assess themselves—i.e., the extent to which students might know how they can check their own progress. Indeed, the development of assessment practices with such provisions may have far-reaching consequences. It suggests that we should shift the whole orientation of assessment from developing better methods of assessing students toward better methods of helping students assess themselves.

So how might client-centered assessment look? It would look like child-centered learning. Teachers would strive to help students assess themselves. Their orientation would shift from subjecting students to assessment practices to respecting students for their self-assessment initiatives. This entails a shift from something you *do to* students to something you *do with* them or help them *do for themselves*—a form of leading from behind.

A number of classrooms have in place the beginnings of student self-assessment vehicles via the use of journals, logs, and portfolios. But this is just a beginning; self-assessment should extend to every aspect of the classroom, from helping students formulate their own learning goals, to helping students make decisions on what they can handle and need, to having them collaborate in the development of report cards and parent-teacher conferences. Too, the involvement of students in their own assessment helps with the management of such activities. This might entail having students set their own goals at the beginning of a unit (not unlike what is proposed with K-W-L); hold conferences with teachers, parents, or peers as they progress or wrestle with issues; look at their efforts and study their progress; and set future goals at the end of a unit in conjunction with parent conferences, or as alternatives to report cards.

There are numerous ways to start these conversations. I ground my conversations about assessment for and with students in the actual portfolio without the intrusion of a grade or score. Scores and grades only give the illusion of accuracy and authority; conversations connected to portfolios or other forms of more direct assessment unmask the bases for decision making and spur the conversation toward a consideration of the evidence, an appreciation of assumptions and the negotiations of goals. "Let's look," "I can show you," "It's like this," "I see what you mean," and "Do you think" displace more general and removed conversations, which tend to be categorical rather than contributory.

Various forms of self-analysis can complement portfolios and be wonderful springboards for such conversations. For example, sometimes I will have students represent their progress and goals with bar graphs or other visual representations (e.g., Venn diagrams, landscapes) in a fashion akin to "then," "now," and "future" and use these graphs as conversation starters. In turn, the visuals serve as the basis for having students delve into their portfolios and examine evidence about what they have achieved and what they might focus upon or set their sights on.

- *Principle 4:   Assessment should be done judiciously, with teachers as advocates for students and ensuring their due process.*

A useful metaphor, if not rule, for rethinking assessment can be derived from aligning assessment with judicial processes. In a court of law, an individual on trial is given an advocate who presents evidence, including testimony, to present a case on behalf of the client. The client and the lawyer work in tandem. The trial is judged upon whether or not the client was given a just hearing and whether or nor her or his representation was adequate. The client has the right to see the evidence presented for and against her or him, the right to reports developed, the right to present his or her own evidence and arguments, and the right to appeal. Also, in the event the client is not satisfied with his or her representation, the client has the right to request someone else to support his or her making a case or, if concerned about procedure, to request a retrial.

Now consider how students are put on trial in our school systems. They may or may not have an advocate, they may or may not be given adequate representation, and the evidence that is presented may or may not best represent their cases. They may not see the reports that are developed. Indirect indicators such as standardized tests, of questionable (if not circumstantial) quality, serve as the basis for decisions that restrict opportunities. In a host of ways assessment activities appear less judicious than they should be. Indeed, students are rarely given the right to appeal or to provide their own evidence—it is as if the students' right to due process is violated.

An examination of the law governing public schools raises some interesting concerns regarding schooling. Over the last 30 years, some key U.S. Supreme Court decisions have been offered that should direct our thinking. In Tinker v. Des Moines Independent School District, 393 U.S. 503 (1969), a case involving freedom of speech, the Court established some key principles undergirding students' rights. The Court wrote: "In our system, state operated schools may not be enclaves for totalitarianism....Students in schools, as well as out of school are possessed of fundamental rights which the State must respect." This position was reaffirmed in the case of Goss v. Lopez, 419 U.S. 565 (1975). As Justice White stated, "young people do not 'shed their constitutional rights' at the schoolhouse door"—the right to due process is of particular importance when the impact of an event "may interfere with later opportunities."

I would hope that legislators pursue practices that place students' rights at a premium rather than displace such a goal with practices that serve first to protect themselves against legal challenges. At a minimum, I would hope that any assessments afford students better due process, including the right of disclosure and presentation of evidence on behalf of the student, as well as the right to appeal the use of indirect or circumstantial evidence. Moreover, I would hope my appeal for judicious assessment shifts the pursuit of such to being both a goal and a right.

Unfortunately, some U.S. state legislators may be more intent on protecting themselves against possible litigation than ensuring that students' rights have been fully supported. For example, they might consider that the spirit of due process has been satisfied when students have been given advance notice of tests and what these tests will entail—that is, in lieu of opportunities to appeal or students providing their own "alternative" evidence of progress or proficiencies. Also, an insipid development occurs when teaching to the test is used to maximize the legal defensibility of tests. In particular, states will often try to finesse the possibility of legal challenges of test bias by ensuring that students have had the opportunity to learn the content covered on tests. To avoid litigation and appear to address local needs, they will establish programs to prepare students for the tests and therefore "make" their tests unbiased by definition. The attitude of most institutions and states is to emphasize legal defensibility ahead of protection for and advocacy on behalf of students.

- *Principle 5: Assessment extends beyond improving our tests to the purposes of assessment and how results from assessment are used, reported, contextualized, and perceived.*

Any consideration of assessment needs to be broadly defined to encompass an exploration of the relationship between assessment and teaching, as well as facets such as report cards, parent-teacher-student conferences, and the student's ongoing record. These facets should not be viewed as exempt from scrutiny in terms of the principles described herein. They should be subjected to the same guidelines.

Just as the goals for developing better classroom-based assessment procedures are tied to the principles discussed herein, so report cards, records, and other elements must be examined in terms of whether they adequately serve the ends for which they are intended. Take, if you will, report cards. Do report cards serve the needs of the student, teacher, and parent? Do they represent a vehicle for ongoing communication and goal setting? Are they done judiciously? If not, how might the method of reporting be changed to afford such possibilities? Or, take, if you will, the student's records. For what purposes are the records used? Are the records adequate for these purposes?

Changes in assessment should be viewed systemically. When teachers contemplate a shift in classroom assessment, it is rarely a matter of simply making selected adjustments or additions. What a teacher does with one facet should and will affect another. For example, a teacher who incorporates a portfolio approach is likely to become dissatisfied with traditional forms of reporting progress. The solution is not to shy away from such changes, but to realize that they will need to occur and, if they do not, to realize that the failure to make such changes may undermine the changes already made. Teachers start to feel as if their new assessment initiatives are being compromised. Students may begin to sense mixed messages if teachers advocate student decision-making and then reassert their singular authority via the determination of a grade without any student input or negotiation. That is, teachers move in and out of assessment practices tied to very different underlying principles. I feel as if the worth of assessment efforts such as portfolios may be diminished if the portfolios are graded or graded inappropriately either without any student input or without consideration for diversity and richness—especially, what the portfolio might mean to the student. We need to keep an eye on achieving students' engagement in their own learning as we negotiate future goals and possibilities against the type of judgments that are made and reported by whom and how.

We should not underestimate the importance of parent or caregiver involvement in such efforts. Rather than keep the parent or caregiver at arm's length in the negotiations over reform, we need to embrace the concerns that parents have and the contributions that they can make. In those situations where teachers pursue alternatives to report cards, parent contributions may be crucial. Parents need to be informed of the goals and engaged in contributing to the efforts. Because not all parents might see the advantages, they may need choices. And, there are ways to avoid holding all parents hostage to what one parent or a small number express as concerns. For example, in pursuit of student-led conferences as an alternative to report cards, Steve Bober (1995) presented parents in Massachusetts with a description of two alternatives and offered them a choice—student-led conferences or more traditional report cards. Parents choosing student-led conferences were also expected to write letters to their children after each conference. Apart from the distinctiveness of the practice, what is notable is how Bober engaged parents as informed partners in the practice.

- *Principle 6: Diversity should be embraced, not slighted.*

Oftentimes those assessing students want to remove any cultural biases rather than recognize diversity and support individual empowerment. They often pursue culture-free items and analysis procedures as a way of neatening and comparing. In pursuit of straightforward comparisons they assume that to be fair more items are needed, and therefore, the use of authentic assessment procedures will create problems, especially since the "time-consuming nature of the problems limits the number" (Linn, Baker, & Dunbar, 1991, p. 18). In addition, they seem to support as a given the use of the same analysis systems for the responses of all students. They expect a respondent to interpret a task in a certain way and respond in a set manner and may not tolerate variation in response, even if such variation might be justified. Whereas they might allude to the context-specific nature of any assessment, they tend to retreat from considering individuals on their own merits or in their own ways.

The term *culture-free tests* seems an oxymoron. I suspect that it is well nigh impossible, and certainly questionable, to extract cultural influences from any test or measure of someone's literacy. Literacy, your own and my own, is inextricably connected to cultural background and life experiences. Culture-free assessments afford, at best, a partial and perhaps distorted understanding of the student. In other words, assessments that do not build upon the nature and nuances of each individual's experiences should be viewed as limited and perhaps flawed. Just as teachers attempt to engage students by building from their background of experiences, so assessment should pursue a goal of culture sensitivity. Classroom teaching does not occur by ignoring or removing diversities. Nor should such a view of assessment be dismissed because of its ideological or sociopolitical considerations: Recognition or validation of one's own experience would seem a basic human right.

We need to aspire to culturally based assessment practices. In some ways I see this pursuit consistent with John Ogbu's (1988, 1991) notions about beginning to meet the needs of African American students—namely, an approach to educational reform that has a cultural ecological orientation. I envision cultural ecological assessments that build upon, recognize, and value rather than displace what students have experienced in their worlds.

For a number of years literacy educators have been willing to sidestep complex issues of culturally sensitive assessments by appealing to the need to make straightforward comparisons. For years standardized test developers and the National Assessment of Educational Progress have retreated from dealing with issues of nonuniformity and diversity as they have pursued the development of scales for straight-forward comparisons across individuals. In conjunction with doing this, they have often revised their assessment instruments to ensure that results fit their models or views of literacy. For example, they are apt to exclude items on topics tied to specific cultural interests and to remove items that show an advantage for one group over another. Even recent attempts espousing guidelines for new approaches to performance assessment (e.g., Linn et al., 1991) or exploring bias in testing minorities (Haney, 1993) may have fallen prey to the same view of the world.

- *Principle 7:   Assessment procedures may need to be nonstandardized to be fair to the individual.*

As teachers try to avail students of every opportunity within their control, they are constantly making adjustments as they "read" the students—their dispositions, verbal abilities, familiarities, needs, and so on. We look for ways to maximize the learning for different students, and we know that different students may need different amounts of encouragement and very different kinds of support. If we standardized our teaching, we know what would apt to be the end result—some students with wonderful potential would reveal only certain sides of themselves and might not achieve their potential or even reveal who they are and what they might contribute and learn.

Allowing for individual or even group differences creates havoc with the desire to standardize assessment. Standardization approaches each individual and group in the same way—that is, students perform the same tasks at the same time, and then their responses are assessed using the same criteria. But if different students' learning repertoires are different and different students enlist different strategies and have different values, etc., and different approaches to testing, then what may be standard for one student may be unique for another.

Studies across cultures, across classrooms, and within classrooms suggest that different students respond in different ways to different forms of assessment depending upon their histories—cultural, classroom, or personal. As my previous principle suggested, how students respond should be looked at as different across situations and against a "comparative canvas, one that takes into account the nature of the community that students inhabit, both the community of the classroom and the community of society with all of its past and present conditions and hopes for the future" (Purves, 1982, p. 345). Green and Dixon (1994) have emphasized that students construct "situated repertoires associated with particular models for being a student...not generic ones" (p. 237). We have ample demonstrations as to how the responsiveness of various groups and individuals in testing situations depends on their view of the social dynamics of the situation (Basso, 1970; Crumpler, 1996; Ogbu, 1988; Philips, 1983).

Indeed, there is always a tension between a need for uniformity across individuals and groups and the use of procedures that are sensitive to the different literacy developments of students, as well as the students' own predispositions to respond differently to different people in different ways at different times. On numerous occasions my assessment of some students has been revised as a result of pursuing more than one mode of response, as well as establishing different kinds of partnership with them or watching them interact over time in different situations with different individuals or groups. In turn, what may serve as a vehicle for uncovering the literacies of one student may not be a satisfactory method for uncovering those of another student or those of the same student at another time. Teachers need to be willing to use different means with different students whether they are assessing or teaching.

The decision-making process may also be complicated by certain of our own predilections. In conjunction with my work on portfolios, I am always surprised at the analyses that learners have done of their progress and the types of goals that they choose to pursue. They ascribe to elements in their portfolios significance that I may have overlooked or not have been able to see. And, their decisions to proceed are often at variance with what I would have suggested.

- *Principle 8: Simple-minded summaries, scores, and comparisons should be displaced with approaches that acknowledge the complex and idiosyncratic nature of literacy development. Straightforward comparisons across individuals are usually arbitrary, biased, and narrow.*

Assuming an approach to assessment with a new openness to complexity, respect for diversity, and interest in acquiring a rich picture of each student, then how might decisions be made about students? Those decisions that require reflection upon the individual's progress and prospects will likely be bountiful. Teachers who pursue an open-ended and diverse view of students will find little difficulty negotiating new areas of pursuit with and for individual students. Decisions that demand comparisons from one individual to the next will be problematic, but these difficulties are not insurmountable. They require a willingness to deal with uncertainties, to entertain possibilities, and to negotiate decisions, including the possibility that there will be lack of agreement. The problems with comparisons are confounded when people assume that straightforward continuums or single scores can adequately describe students.

Comparisons based upon scores are so problematic for a host of reasons: (a) Each student's development is unique; (b) the literacies of one student will be different from another, and even the same literacies will involve differing arrays of facets; and (c) some of these facets will be unique to a certain situation. Literacy development is sufficiently different from one student to the next that the types of comparisons that might be made are quite complex and multifaceted. The term *literact abilities* rather than *literacy ability* seems in order. If you were trying to portray the character of these developments, you might find yourself gravitating to describing individuals on their own terms. Unfortunately, the terms of comparison in place with standardized tests and NAEP assessments and implicit in many of the attempts to score portfolios and other classroom-based data are often insensitive to such complexity. Looking at different individuals in terms of a single score masks variability and individuality. Again, test makers err on the side of a level of simplification not unlike a massive "conspiracy of convenience" (Spiro, Vispoel, Schmitz, Samarapungavan, & Boerger, 1987, p. 180).

The drive for uniformity is quite pervasive. Our assessment and instructional programs oftentimes include long lists of skills as outcomes to be assessed, taught, and mastered. It is assumed that skills are neatly packaged and discrete and that each makes a uniform contribution to literacy development. It is assumed that students acquire these skills to mastery and that their ability to use them is uniform across literacy situations. In authentic reading and writing situations within which genuine purposes are being pursued, this is unlikely. Across literacy situations certain attributes may be more likely to be enlisted than others, and they are apt to be enlisted as clusters rather than one by one or discretely.

Too often literacy educators have ignored the complexities of the issues and have fallen back on convenience rather than exploring possibilities. Take, if you will, the attempts to wed some of the data emerging from performance assessment (e.g., portfolios) with rubrics. The data generated from a portfolio might involve a rich array of samples or observations of the students' work across situations and time. These samples are apt to represent the students' pursuit of different goals, utilizing different resources, including content, under varying conditions. In some ways student classroom samples may vary as much as the works of art from an artist's portfolio. Each sample may represent very different achievements and processes. When you hold them, examine them, and discuss their significance you are in touch with the actual artifact and not some distant derivative.

It is at this point, some would argue, that we can use a rubric to affix a score or scores or a sum total score to the student's work. But we need to examine a question that is the reverse of what is often asked. Instead of asking how we rate the portfolio, we should be asking whether the rubric measures up to the portfolio or to the assessment of complex performance. Moreover, in classrooms do we need a measure that is a distant derivative when we have the primary sources—the actual samples—to examine and reexamine using an array of lenses or perspectives? Whereas I argue for the context-specific nature of any assessment, advocates of rubrics seem to want to dismiss idiosyncrasies and variation— that is, they would retreat from being willing to consider individuals on their own merits or in their own ways. Unless rubrics are used to prompt a consideration of possible ways to analyze work or as conversation starters in conjunction with revisiting the students' work samples, I see few advantages to their use in classrooms.

Sometimes assessment of reading and writing becomes more far-fetched by adding together a set of subscores. A key assumption often undergirding the use of such scores— especially the suggestion that they can be added and used as the basis of comparative decision making—is that the full and detailed portrait of an individual's literacies has been afforded. Unfortunately, these dimensions are not exhaustive, these determinations of degree are not accurate, and they should not be added. To be able to do so, we would have to do the following:

1. include all of the attributes or be assured that the partial listing that was developed is representative;
2. determine how these attributes are configured across situations;
3. assume that ample evidence will be provided for assessing these attributes;
4. develop scales for assessing attributes; and
5. generate an algorithm that works across individuals by which we might combine the elements and their dimensions.

I would posit that we do not have such samples, sampling procedures, ways of procuring evidence, adequate scales, or algorithm. And it is problematic to assume that an algorithm that simply represents sums would ever be adequate. The complexity of literacy is such that we cannot assume a basis for generating or combining scores.

Literacy assessments cannot and should not be so rigid. Perhaps there are some benchmarks that are appropriate across all students. Perhaps there are benchmarks appropriate to some readers and not others. But such benchmarks are likely to represent a partial view of any student's literacies. The use of scores and continua as ways of affording simplification and comparability has a tendency to camouflage the subjectivity of assessment and give test developers the allusion of objectivity. The use of scores and continua is not more objective; it is arbitrary. Guba and Lincoln (1989) have suggested the shift toward accepting the inevitability of relativism and the complexities across different settings may require the ongoing, ecumenical, and recursive pursuit of shared possibilities rather than a single set of absolute truths.

- *Principle 9:   Some things that can be assessed reliably across raters are not worth assessing; some things that are worth assessing may be difficult to assess reliably except by the same rater.*

Oftentimes, test makers and researchers will perseverate on whether or not they can consistently measure certain abilities. They tout reliability as the major criteria for whether or not a test is valid. The end result is that some things that are worth measuring are discarded and some things that are not worth measuring or valuing achieve an elevated level of importance. Typically, complex and individualistic learning tends to be shortchanged whereas the currency of learnings that are easier to define may be inflated. For example, in writing assessment, constructs such as style or voice may be shortchanged, while spelling and punctuation may be inflated. In reading, constructs such as self-questioning, engagement, and interpretation may be shortchanged, while speed, factual recall, and vocabulary may be elevated.

Unfortunately, reliability is translated to mean that two different scorers or raters will be able to assess the same thing in the same way. Unless a high degree of agreement across raters is achieved, test makers will deem a measure unreliable and therefore question its worth. In so doing, they may be making the mistake of assuming that reliability equates to agreement when verifiability may be a better approach.

We should be willing to accept differences of opinion in terms of how certain abilities are rated or discerned. Some abilities and strategies are difficult to pin down in terms of clear operational definitions. Different raters or even the same raters at different times are apt to develop different constructions of the same phenomena. Sometimes these shifts arise as a result of the different predispositions of the raters. Sometimes they arise as different facets of the phenomena are taken into account either by different raters or the same rater. Sometimes they arise as a result of differences in how students enlisted certain abilities. Such differences should not be viewed as surprising, for they coincide with two key tenets of most current views of learning: the notion of an ongoing constructive nature of knowing; and the situation-specific nature of learning. Differences are apt to exist across and within an individual's literacies (e.g., reading a newspaper for purposes of locating an advertisement versus reading a romance novel for pleasure) and from one individual to the next. In other words, some features may or may not apply to some students' literacy, and some facets may apply uniquely to individuals.

One should not be seduced into thinking that variables that are easy to define should be looked at to the exclusion of those that are difficult to assess. It may be foolish to exclude some facets because they are difficult to assess or because they look different either across students or situations or by the raters. Likewise, one should not be seduced into thinking that every reading and writing act is the same and involves the same variables. If the only literacy facets scored are those common across students and those that can be scored with high reliability across different students' responses, then certain facets will be given more weight than they deserve, and some important facets may be excluded.

- *Principle 10:   Assessment should be more developmental and sustained than piecemeal and shortsighted.*

To assess how well a student is doing, our vision or vistas need to change. If assessment goals are tied to development, then we need to look at patterns and long-term goals. What we see or look for in a single selection or case may not be helpful in looking for patterns across cases, selections, or circumstances. For example, as a reader or writer reads and writes a single selection, we might look for engagement and active involvement. Across situations we might want to consider the extent to which the interest and engagement are maintained across a range of material for different purposes. We also might be interested in the extent to which the student has developed a value for reading and writing that is reflected in how he or she uses reading and writing inside and outside the class. This may be apparent in her or his self-selection of books or self-initiated writing to serve different purposes.

Within areas such as the students' abilities to read with understanding, our goal for a single selection might be the extent to which a reader understands the main idea or theme or can draw conclusions using selected details, etc. Across selections or in the long term, we might be interested in how the students use different books to contribute overall understandings tied to units or projects or their own developing understandings of the world. Or, we might be interested in self-assessment. With a single selection we could focus on the reader's or writer's ability to monitor reading and writing, to set goals for a specific selection, and to problem-solve and wrestle with meaning-making. Across selections we might be interested in the reader's or writer's ability to set goals and assess progress across several selections. In looking across selections, you should not expect that students will always appear to reveal the same level of sophistication with skills and strategies or necessarily use the same skills and strategies. See Table 1 for other short-term, long-term contrasts.

TABLE 1 Short- and Long-Term Contrasts in Assessment	
Short-Term/Single Instance	Long-Term/Multiple Situations
Affect	
Engaged	Value
Active	Self-seeking ongoing
Thoughtful	Habit
Strategies	
Planning	Flexible, reflective, coordinated,
Fixing up and troubleshooting	selective, customized
Making connections	
Looking back, forward, and beyond	
Collaborating	Community building
Outcomes	
Main idea	Overall understandings, intertextual
	connections
Details	Projects
Conclusions	Applications
Implications	Range of problems and activities
	Overall understandings and themes
Self-Assessment	
Self-monitoring	Self-scrutiny, goal setting, self-
Online problem solving	determinations
	Overall goals, progress, patterns

A shift toward assessment that examines students over time aligns assessment with classroom practices that pursue sustained engagement and aim to help students derive an understanding of patterns. It shifts our teaching and learning to long-term possibilities rather than the specific and short-term objectives of a lesson.

- *Principle 11:   Most interpretations of results are not straightforward. Assessment should be viewed as ongoing and suggestive, rather than fixed or definitive.*

In many ways teaching involves constant redevelopment or continuous experimentation and adjustments to plans, directions, and future goals. To appreciate the complexities and sophistication of teaching, consider the image one conjures up for a sportsperson. In certain sports (e.g., baseball, tennis) involving eye-hand coordination with racquets or bats, players will begin their swing and constantly be making subtle adjustments as balls with different velocities, rotations, and angles are thrown at them. But sporting events pale in comparison with the dynamics of teacher-student interactions—the adjustments, just in time decision making, and ebb and flow of activities that occur. Teachers deal with students whom they may be trying to respond to, motivate, mobilize, develop, and coach while understanding their needs, beliefs, strategies, and possible ways of responding as they are interacting with one another and dealing with the rest of their lives. Not surprising, teachers have to be a mix of ecologist, developer, advocate, coach, player, actor-director, stage manager, mayor, and sometimes counselor. Teachers are always planning and recognizing the need to make constant adjustments to what they are doing and what they might do next.

For these purposes, the typical assessment data (e.g., scouting reports of students provided by school records, premeasures of abilities, standardized or even informal assessments) may provide limited guidance to teachers in terms of the moment-by-moment decision making and even planning for the next day or week or even month. Too often typical student records seem as limited as a mug shot taken of the learner; you may be able to identify the learner (depending upon your ability to see likenesses) but may not. Certainly, the mug shot will not afford you an appreciation of the character of the student, nor will it help you understand the range of things that the student can do, nor will it support your ability to negotiate either long-term or short-term learning goals.

Most classroom-based assessments offer more promise but are still limited. Classroom-based assessment procedures may give teachers a better sense of how students will proceed in like circumstances and may also afford a fuller picture of the student across time. Portfolios, for example, are equivalent to scrapbooks involving multiple snapshots of the learner in a variety of contexts. Such assessments might afford a fuller and richer depiction of the learner and his or her pattern of development, but judgments—especially prescriptions—are never as straightforward as they might appear. The possibility of obtaining a complete vision of a learner is complicated by our inability to constantly monitor a learner, delve into and interpret his or her innermost thoughts, and achieve more than one perspective on the learner. It is also tied to the ever-changing nature of learning. Apart from the fact that our snapshots of classroom learning tend to be still shots of the learner, these images are tied to a place and time that has become more historical than current. Such limitations might be viewed as a problem if we were to perseverate on wanting to pin down what to do next with a student and be sure to stick to a set course. Instead, they should be anticipated and viewed as tentative bases for where and when one might begin. While we can develop short- and long-term goals and plans, we should not approach our teaching as if our prescriptions should not be altered, assessment fixed, nor directions more than suggestive.

Likewise, we should not approach assessment as if our results need be final or base our subsequent actions as if we have derived a decision that is any better than a hunch. We should avoid assuming that our assessments do anything more than afford us information that we might consider. No assessment should be used as restrictively or rigidly as decisions made in courts of law, yet I fear that many are. Instead we should reinforce what needs to occur in classrooms—constant adjustments, shifts, and ongoing decision making by teachers who are constantly watching, learning, coaching, and responding to students, peers, and others.

- *Principle 12:   Learning possibilities should be negotiated with the students and stakeholders rather than imposed via standards and assessment that are preset, prescribed, or mandated.*

The state within which I reside (along with many other states) has been seduced into thinking that standard setting may be the answer to improving education by ensuring that teachers teach and students learn certain basic skills. I find myself quite discouraged that our professional associations have aligned with similar efforts. Historically, standard setting (and the proficiency testing that it spurs) has tended to restrict access and experimentation at the same time as it has tended to support agendas tied to gatekeeping and exclusion.

The standard-setting enterprise and the proficiency-testing industry have the potential to perpetuate the view that we can set targets that we can easily reach. Unfortunately, it is problematic to assume that development is simply setting a course for the student from A to B—especially when A is not taken into account and B is tied to views of outcomes looking for expertise rather than individual assessment of development. Without ample consideration being given for where students are and how and why they develop and their aspirations, we are apt to have our targets misplaced and our learning routes poorly aligned. I was in attendance at one of the many sessions on standards sponsored by the International Reading Association and the National Council for Teachers of English, when a speaker talked about standards using the analogy of a basketball player of the caliber of Michael Jordan as the "standard." As the speaker discussed the worth of setting standards based upon what we view as aspirations, I mulled over my height and my skill and what I might do to improve. Then I reminded myself of my reasons for playing basketball and where I am insofar as my background in basketball. I play basketball for fun, to be with my sons, and for exercise. We need to realize that we should be asking who is deciding? Whose standards are being represented? In some ways the quest for educational improvement via standards and in turn proficiency testing places a premium on uniformity rather than diversity and favors prepackaged learning over emerging possibilities.

In a similar vein, advocates of standards emphasize the importance of the role of making judgments by comparisons to Olympic skating and other activities where success is measured by the trophies one achieves or the graded measures that are applied. I think we need to challenge this metaphor and question the emphasis on judgment rather than support. I prefer to think of a teacher as a coach rather than a judge—a supporter and counselor versus a judge and award- or grade-giver. I would like to see teachers view their role as providing guidance, handholding, and comments rather than As, Bs, and Cs or some score. In my view of a more ideal world, I see teachers, students, and caregivers operating in a kind of public sphere where they are part of the team negotiating for a better self. In this regard, I find myself fascinated with several classroom projects: with the kind of self-reflection and analysis occurring amidst the community-based preschool efforts of Reggio Emilia (Forman, 1993, 1994) where teachers, students, and community work together developing and implementing curriculum plans, ponder the right questions to ask to spur students' reflections, develop insights, and learn; with the work of Short, Harste, and Burke (1996) on developing inquiry in Indianapolis schools (as they engage students and teachers in considering the anomalies, patterns, and ways of looking at themselves); with the work of the Santa Barbara Classroom Discourse Group (1992a, 1992b), a community of teachers, researchers, and students interested in understanding how life in classrooms is constructed and how expectations and practices influence opportunities to access, accomplish, and learn in school; and with the work of Fenner (1995) who uses a general form of Toulmin's (1958) analysis of argumentation to examine classroom conversations and student self-assessments with portfolios and looks for ways to help students look at themselves in terms of evidence, assumptions, claims, and goals. Fenner's approach to self-assessment moves us away from the typical checklist that asks students to detail in rather vague and unsubstantiated fashion their strengths and goals in a kind of "hit and miss" fashion.

Unfortunately, rather than language that suggests a view of classrooms as developmental and nurturing, oftentimes the metaphors adopted by those involved in the testing, proficiency, and standards enterprises seem more appropriate to developing consumer products connected to prescribed guidelines and uniform inspection procedures. That is, they seem to fit with our views of industry rather than nurturing human potential (Wile & Tierney, 1996). With this in mind, I would suggest that we should assess assessment based on whether it is parsimonious with a society's bill of rights and our views of individual rights, opportunities, and freedoms.

I fear that standards will perpetuate the effects uncovered when Ellwein, Glass, and Smith (1988) surveyed the history of the effects of various statewide proficiency testing—gatekeeping and the removal rather than enhancement of opportunities. Indeed, in Ohio and I would suspect other states, Ellwein et al.'s (1988) findings are being replicated. With the introduction of proficiency testing more students are dropping out. Ironically, the tests were intended to improve instruction, but fewer students are taking them, which in turn suggests that more students are passing them. So by keeping these dropouts invisible, advocates of proficiency testing and legislators claim the reform is having positive effects—that is, as more students leave or drop out, abhorring or deterred by the situation, legislators and advocates (including the media) erroneously suggest or advertise falsely that more students are passing.

Closing Remarks

My principles for assessment emanate from a mix of child-centered views of teaching, developmental views of children, constructivist views of knowing, critical theoretical views of empowerment, and pluralistic views of society. I view them as suggesting directions and guidelines for thinking about the why, how, where and when, who, and what of assessment.

Why?

To develop culturally sensitive versus culturally free assessments

To connect assessment to teaching and learning

To connect assessment to students' ongoing goal setting, decision making, and development

To become better informed and make better decisions

To develop assessment that keeps up with teaching and learning

How?

Collaborative, participatory, client centered

Coach-like, supportive and ongoing rather than judgmental, hard-nosed, and final

Supplemental and complementary versus grade-like and summative

Individually, diversely, not prepackaged

Judiciously

Developmentally

Reasoned

Where and When?

Amidst students' lives

Across everyday events and programs

In and out of school

Opportunistically, periodically, continuously

Who?

Students, teachers, and stakeholders

What?

Ongoing learning: development, resources, and needs

Complexities

Individuals and groups

Evidence of progress and decision making

Programs, groups, individuals

In describing the essence of my proposition, I would like to return to where I began. I believe an overriding principle, which is perhaps my 13th or more of a penumbra, is *assess-*

ment should be assessed in terms of its relationship with teaching and learning, including
the opportunities learners are offered and the rights and respect they are accorded.

Shifts in my own thinking about assessment began occurring when I asked myself this question: If I were to assess assessment, what criteria might I use? My answer to this question was that assessment practices should empower teachers, students, and their caregivers. In other words, assessment practices should enrich teaching and learning. As I explored how tests might be used as tools of empowerment for teachers and learners, I became interested in whether this type of assessment actually helped teachers and students (as well as the student's caregiver, resource teachers, principal, and others) achieve a more expanded view of the student's learning. I also wanted to know whether testing contributed to developing goals and formulating plans of action, which would suggest that assessment practices were empowering. My view of empowerment includes:

Teachers having a fuller sense (expanded, refined, different) of the students' abilities, needs, and instructional possibilities;

Students having a fuller sense of their own abilities, needs, and instructional possibilities;

Teachers integrating assessment with teaching and learning (this would entail the dynamic/ongoing use of assessment practices, as well as assessment tailored to classroom life); accommodating, adapting, adjusting, customizing—shifting assessment practices to fit with students and their learning and adjusting teaching in accordance with feedback from assessments;

Students engaging in their own self-assessments as they set, pursue, and monitor their own goals for learning in collaboration with others, including peers, teachers, and caregivers.

Communities of teachers, students, and parents forming and supporting one another around this assessment process.

The use of standardized tests, tests accompanying the published reading programs, and even teacher-made tests do not expand teachers' views of their students' learning over time, nor suggest ways the teacher might help them. Nor are such tests integrated into classroom life. They tend to displace teaching and learning activities rather than enhance them.

Likewise, students rarely seem to be engaged in learning how to assess themselves. When my colleagues and I interviewed teachers with whom we began working in assessment 10 years ago, most teachers did not conceptualize the goal of testing to be helping students reflect or obtain feedback on their progress, nor did they envision tests as helping students establish, refine, or achieve learning goals. When we interviewed students, we found that students in these classes tended to have a limited and rather negative view of themselves, and they had set few learning goals. Attempts to examine the impact of more learner-based assessments yielded quite contrasting results. In classrooms in which portfolios were becoming an integral part of classroom life, teachers and students had developed a fuller sense of their own abilities (Carter, 1992; Carter & Tierney, 1988; Fenner, 1995; Stowell & Tierney, 1995; Tierney, Carter, & Desai, 1991).

A study by Shavelson, Baxter, and Pine (1992) provides other confirmation of the worth of aligning assessment to the teaching and learning in classrooms. In their attempts to examine variations in instructional programs, they concluded that direct observations and more emergent procedures captured the shifts in learning while traditional methods (multiple choice, short answer) did not. Such findings should come as no surprise to those of us who have been involved in research on the effects of teaching upon learning; that is, very few literacy researchers would rely upon a standardized test to measure the effectiveness of particular teaching strategies with different students. Instead, we are apt to pursue a range of measures, and some of us would not develop our measures a priori. In fact, several efforts have demonstrated the power of new assessment approaches to evaluate and guide program development and teacher change effectively (see Tierney et al., 1993).

Designing these new assessment approaches has to do with a way of teaching, testing, and knowing that is aligned with a set of values different than what has been and still is espoused by most educational reformers. Unfortunately, the power of some of the psychometricians and their entrenched values related to testing make the emergence of alternative assessment procedures difficult. Indeed, I see the shift as involving a cultural transformation—a shift away from what I view as a somewhat totalitarian practice tied to "old science" and metaphors that equate student learning to quality control.

Mike Rose (1995) suggests in *Possible Lives* that classrooms are created spaces, and the successful ones create spaces where students feel safe and secure; they are the classrooms in which students are willing to stretch, take risks, and pursue their interpretive authority for themselves and with others. In a similar vein, Kris Gutierrez and her colleagues (Gutierrez, Rymes, & Larson, 1995), in discussing teacher-student discourse, assert the need for spaces where students and teachers can connect or transact with each other, rather than pass by one another. The key is finding ways to effect involvement and transaction rather than detachment and monolithic responses.

Assessment must address making futures possible and pursuable rather than impossible or improbable. We must create spaces where students, teachers, and others can achieve futures and spaces wherein the dynamics and practices are such that they challenge but do not undermine the ecology of who students are and might become.

References

Baker, A., & Luke, A. (1991). *Toward a critical sociology of reading pedagogy.* Philadelphia: John Benjamin's.

Basso, K. (1970). "To give up on words": Silence in Western Apache culture. *Southwest Journal of Anthropology, 26,* 213–230.

Bober, S. (1995, July). *Portfolio conferences.* Presentation at Lesley College Literacy Institute, Cambridge, MA.

Bruner, J. (1990). *Acts of meaning.* Cambridge, MA: Harvard University Press.

Carter, M. (1992). *Self-assessment using writing portfolios.* Unpublished doctoral dissertation, The Ohio State University, Columbus.

Carter, M., & Tierney, R. J. (1988, December). *Writing growth: Using portfolios in assessment.* Paper presented at the National Reading Conference, Tucson, AZ.

Ellwein, M. C., Glass, G. V., & Smith, M. L. (1988). Standards of competence: Propositions on the nature of testing reforms. *Educational Researcher, 17*(8), 4–9.

Fenner, L. (1995). *Student portfolios: A view from inside the classroom.* Unpublished doctoral dissertation, The Ohio State University, Columbus.

Forman, G. (1993). Multiple symbolizations in the long jump project. In C. Edward, L. Gandini, & G. Forman (Eds.), *The hundred languages of children* (pp. 171–188). Norwood, NJ: Ablex.

Forman, G. (1994). Different media, different languages. In L. Katz & B. Cesarone (Eds.), *Reflections on the Reggio Emilia approach* (pp. 41–54). Urbana, IL: ERIC/EECE.

Freire, P., & Macedo, D. (1987). *Literacy: Reading the word and the world.* South Hadley, MA: Bergin & Garvey.

Transforming Student Assessment

D. MONTY NEILL

Imagine an assessment system in which teachers had a wide repertoire of classroom-based, culturally sensitive assessment practices and tools to use in helping each and every child learn to high standards; in which educators collaboratively used assessment information to continuously improve schools; in which important decisions about a student, such as readiness to graduate from high school, were based on the work done over the years by the student; in which schools in networks held one another accountable for student learning; and in which public evidence of student achievement consisted primarily of samples from students' actual schoolwork rather than just reports of results from one-shot examinations.

Many would probably dismiss this vision as the product of an overactive imagination. However, these ideas are at the core of *Principles and Indicators for Student Assessment Systems,* developed by the National Forum on Assessment and signed by more than 80 national and local education and civil rights organizations.[1] The widespread support for this document indicates a deep desire for a radical reconstruction of assessment practices, with student learning made central to assessment reform. In this article I draw on *Principles* to outline what a new assessment system could look like and to suggest some actions that can be taken to further assessment reform.

The seven principles endorsed by the Forum are:

1. The primary purpose of assessment is to improve student learning.
2. Assessment for other purposes supports student learning.
3. Assessment systems are fair to all students.
4. Professional collaboration and development support assessment.
5. The broad community participates in assessment development.
6. Communication about assessment is regular and clear.
7. Assessment systems are regularly reviewed and improved.

Classroom Assessment

Assessment for the primary purpose of improving student learning must rest on what the Forum calls "foundations" of high-quality schooling: an understanding of how student learning takes place, clear statements of desired learning (goals or standards) for all students, adequate learning resources (particularly high-quality teachers), and school structures and practices that support the learning needs of all students.

Assessment to enhance student learning must be integrated with, not separate from, curriculum and instruction.[2] Thus assessment reform is necessarily integrated with reform

Source: From "Transforming Student Assessment" by D. Monty Neill, 1997, *Phi Delta Kappan, 79,* pp. 34–40, 58. Reprinted by permission.

Gee, J. (1990). *Social linguistics and literacies: Ideologies in discourse.* New York: Falmer Press.

Green, J., & Dixon, C. (1994). Talking knowledge into being: Discursive and social practices in classrooms. *Linguistics and Education, 5,* 231–239.

Guba, E. G., & Lincoln, Y. S. (1989). *Fourth generation evaluation.* Newbury Park, CA: Sage.

Gutierrez, K., Rymes, B., & Larson, J. (1995). Script, counterscript, and underlife in the classroom: James Brown versus *Brown v. Board of Education. Harvard Educational Review, 65,* 445–471.

Haney, W. (1993). Testing and minorities. In L. Weis & M. Fine (Eds.), *Beyond silenced voices* (pp. 45–74). Albany, NY: State University of New York Press.

hooks, b. (1989). *Talking back.* Boston: South End Press.

hooks, b. (1994). *Teaching to transgress: Education as the practice of freedom.* New York: Routledge.

Lather, P. (1986). Research as praxis. *Harvard Educational Review, 56,* 257–277.

Linn, R. L., Baker, E. L., & Dunbar, S. B. (1991). Complex performance assessment: Expectations and validation criteria. *Educational Researcher, 20*(8), 15–21.

Moss, P. (1996). Enlarging the dialogue in educational measurement: Voices from interpretive research traditions. *Educational Researcher, 25*(1), 20–28.

Ogbu, J. (1988). Literacy and schooling in subordinate cultures: The case of Black Americans. In E. Kintgen, B. Kroll, & M. Rose (Eds.), *Perspectives on literacy* (pp. 227–242). Carbondale, IL: Southern Illinois University Press.

Ogbu, J. (1991). Cultural perspective and school experience. In C. Walsh (Ed.), *Literacy as praxis: Culture, language and pedagogy* (pp. 25–50). Norwood, NJ: Ablex.

Phillips, S. (1983). *The invisible culture: Communication and community on the Warm Springs Indian reservation.* New York: Longman.

Purves, A. (1982). Conclusion to an international perspective to the evaluation of written composition. In B. H. Choppin & T. N. Postlethwaite (Eds.), *Evaluation in education: An international review series* (Vol. 5, pp. 343–345). Oxford, England: Pergamon Press.

Rose, M. (1995). *Possible lives.* Boston: Houghton Mifflin.

Santa Barbara Classroom Discourse Group. (1992a). Co structing literacy in classrooms; literate action as socia accomplishment. In H. Marshall (Ed.), *Redefining student learning: Roots of educational change* (pp. 119–150). Norwood, NJ: Ablex.

Santa Barbara Classroom Discourse Group. (1992b). The referential and intertextual nature of classroom life. *Journal of Classroom Interaction, 27*(2), 29–36.

Shavelson, R., Baxter, G. P., & Pine, J. (1992). Performance assessment: Political rhetoric and measurement reality. *Educational Researcher, 21*(4), 22–27.

Short, K. G., Harste, J. C., & Burke, C. (1996). *Creating classrooms for authors and inquirers.* Portsmouth, NH: Heinemann.

Spiro, R. J., Vispoel, W. L., Schmitz, J., Samarapungavan, A., & Boerger, A. (1987). Knowledge acquisition for application: Cognitive flexibility and transfer in complex content domains. In B. C. Britton & S. Glynn (Eds.), *Executive control processes* (pp. 177–200). Hillsdale, NJ: Erlbaum.

Stake, R. (1983). The case study method in social inquiry. In G. Madaus, M. Scriven, & D. Stufflebeam (Eds.), *Evaluation models* (pp. 279–286). Boston: Kluwer-Nijhoff.

Tierney, R. J., Carter, M., & Desai, L. (1991). *Portfolio assessment in the reading-writing classroom.* Norwood, MA: Christopher Gordon.

Tierney, R. J., Clark, C., Fenner, L., Wiser, B., Herter, R. J., & Simpson, C. (in press). A portfolio discussion: Assumptions, tensions and possibilities. *Reading Research Quarterly.*

Tierney, R. J., Wile, J., Moss, A. G., Reed, E. W., Ribar, J. P., & Zilversmit, A. (1993). *Portfolio evaluation as history: Evaluation of the history academy for Ohio teachers* (occasional paper). National Council of History Education, Inc.

Toulmin, S. (1958). *The uses of argument.* Cambridge, England: Cambridge University Press.

Wile, J., & Tierney, R. J. (1996). Tensions in assessment: The battle over portfolios, curriculum and control. In R. Calfee & P. Perfumo (Eds.), *Writing portfolios in the classrooms: Policy and practice, process and peril* (pp. 203–218). Hillsdale, NJ: Erlbaum.

in other areas of schooling. In particular, schools need to ensure the development of "authentic instruction," which involves modes of teaching that foster understanding of rich content and encourage students' positive engagement with the world.

Both individual and societal interests come together in classroom instruction and assessment. Assessment works on a continuum. Helping the student with his or her individual interests and ways of thinking lies at one end. At the other are the more standard ways of knowing and doing things that society has deemed important. In the middle are individualized ways of learning, understanding, and expressing socially important things. There are, for example, many ways for a student to present an understanding of the causes of the U.S. Civil War.

For all these purposes, teachers must gather information. Teachers must keep track of student learning, check up on what students have learned, and find out what's going on with them. Keeping track means observing and documenting what students do. Checking up involves various kinds of testing and quizzing. Finding out is the heart of classroom assessment: What does the child mean? What did the child get from the experience? Why did the child do what he or she did? To find out, teachers must ask questions for which they do not already know the answers.[3]

To gather all this information, teachers can rely on a range of assessment activities. These include structured and spur-of-the-moment observations that are recorded and filed; formal and informal interviews; collections of work samples; use of extended projects, performances, and exhibitions; performance exams; and various forms of short-answer testing. In this context, teachers could use multiple-choice questions, but, as the Forum recommends, they would have a very limited role.

The evidence of learning can be kept in portfolios, which in turn can be used by students and teachers to reflect on, summarize, and evaluate student progress. Documentation systems, such as the *Primary Language Record,* the *Primary Learning Record,* the *California Learning Record,* and the *Work Sampling System,* can be used to organize assessment information and to guide evaluation of student learning.[4]

Following the continuum from individual to societal interests, evaluation should be both "self-referenced" and "standards-referenced."[5] The former evaluates the learner in light of her own goals, desires, and previous attainments and thus helps the student understand and further her own learning. In this way standards for the student's learning emerge from her work, not just from external sources. Standards-referenced evaluation is by now commonly understood. For example, students can be evaluated against the *Curriculum and Evaluation Standards for School Mathematics* of the National Council of Teachers of Mathematics.[6] Standards-based assessment has been mandated in the new federal Title I legislation. Whether standards are established by the school, district, or state, the Forum recommends wide participation in the standards-setting process. However, as the slogan "standards without standardization" suggests, excellence can take many forms. Thus, according to the ideals of *Principles,* "Assessment systems allow students multiple ways to demonstrate their learning."

When students are allowed multiple ways to show what they have learned and can do, evaluation becomes more complex. It becomes essential for educators to define "high quality" in a lucid way and to let students, parents, and the community know what variations on such quality look like. Clear scoring guides and examples of student work of varying kinds and degrees of quality are needed.

An additional objective of classroom performance assessment, supportive of both self-referenced and standards-referenced evaluation, is that students learn to reflect on and evaluate their own work. After all, an important goal of school is for students to be able to learn without relying on teachers. As students become engaged in developing scoring guides and evaluating work, they learn more deeply what good work looks like, and they more clearly understand their own learning processes.

The process of assessment, however, is not just focused on evaluating student accomplishment. Rather, the heart of assessment is a continuing flow in which the teacher (in collaboration with the student) uses information to guide the next steps in learning. The educator must ask, What should I do to help the student progress? This can be a very immediate issue (How can I help him get past a misunderstanding in multiplying fractions?) and thus should be an integrated part of the daily process of instruction. The question can be asked after any significant moment of assessment, such as completion of a project. It can also be asked periodically during the year and at the end of the year, at moments designed for summing up and planning.

The assessment practices outlined above are not common, even though these kinds of approaches are now widely promoted in the professional literature. Substantial professional development for teachers and restructuring of school practices are needed if this kind of assessment is to flourish.

Schools are not likely to make the effort to change merely so that they can use performance assessment. Rather, they will attempt to transform curriculum, instruction, school structures (such as school size and the length of class periods), and assessment, as well as to institute the requisite professional development, as it becomes clear that the changes produce improved learning and more interested and engaged students. Thus this vision of assessment reform flows from a broader vision of what it means to educate young people—what they should learn and be able to do, how they should act, what kinds of people they should become. Assessment, in other words, cannot be divorced from consideration of the purposes of schooling.

Implications for Equity

A powerful concern for equity should underlie all efforts to reform assessment. Traditional tests have presumed that assessing all students in the same format creates a fair situation. However, the process of test construction, the determination of content, and the use of only one method—usually multiple-choice—all build in cultural and educational biases that favor some ways of understanding and demonstrating knowledge over others.[7] Testing's power has, in turn, helped shape curriculum, instruction, and classroom assessment to advantage certain groups. Thus the uniformity and formal equity of the tests contribute to real-world educational inequity.

The solution is to allow diversity to flourish and to do so in ways that neither unfairly privilege some methods of demonstrating knowledge nor excuse some students from learning what society has deemed important. Too often, however, "different" has meant "lesser." For example, to meet the supposed needs of students in vocational education, the curriculum may be watered down. Students of color and those from low-income backgrounds have been most damaged by low expectations and low-level curricula. With regard to assessment, as Norman Frederiksen noted over a decade ago, the "real test bias" is that "multiple-choice tests tend not to measure the more complex cognitive abilities,"[8] which in turn are not taught, especially to low-income students.[9] This double bias must be overcome.

Students come from many cultures and languages. Instruction and assessment should connect to the local and the culturally particular and not presume uniformity of experience, culture, language, and ways of knowing.

In the context of classroom assessment, perhaps the thorniest issue is whether teachers will be able to assess all their students fairly, accurately, and comprehensively. Such evaluation requires more than that teachers be unbiased; they must also understand their students. Classroom performance assessments can provide a powerful vehicle for getting to know students. For example, the learning records noted above all ask teachers to interview students and their parents at the start of the year, to inquire about the child's learning experiences and interests. Classroom performance assessment requires thinking about the child and about the contexts in which the child is or is not successfully learning. Teachers who do not know their students cannot do self-referenced evaluation.

The hope is that, as teachers make use of instructional and assessment practices that give them more powerful insights into each student's learning processes and styles, they will be more likely to hold high expectations and provide strong support for learning for all their students. At least some evidence is beginning to show that this can happen. The use of clear, strong standards can also help—though standards should be flexible enough to accommodate student diversity. For example, a standard stating that students should understand various interpretations of the separation of powers spelled out in the U.S. Constitution could be met in a variety of ways, such as an essay, an exhibition, a performance by a group of students, or a short story.

Teachers must also help all their students learn the ins and outs of the assessment methods being used. For example, when students select materials for a portfolio, teachers must ensure that all students know what the portfolio is used for, how to construct it, and how it will be evaluated. Students may need help in thinking about choosing work for projects or portfolios so that they will be able to select activities that best show their accomplishments.

Finally, equity requires meeting the needs of all students, including those who are learning English and those with disabilities or other special needs. Teachers must be able to assess their students in ways that allow them to demonstrate their learning and that provide the information teachers need to guide their future learning. Assessors need to know how to make accommodations and adaptations that are congruent with classroom instructional practices.

Back to Basics?

Some critics have argued that, while performance assessments are useful for assessing more advanced learning, multiple-choice tests are fine for the "basics." Others have even maintained that using performance assessment will undermine teaching of the "basics."[10] These misconceptions are dangerous.

What is meant by the "basics"? Presumably, the term encompasses reading well across a range of subject areas, writing fluently for a variety of purposes, and knowing and understanding math well enough to use it as needed in common educational, social, and employment settings. Rather than opposing such basics, it was largely because so many students were not attaining them that many educators became advocates of performance assessment.

Effective writing, for example, requires feedback on one's actual writing—that is, performance assessment. Writing assessment cannot be reduced to multiple-choice tests. But writing a few paragraphs on a topic about which students may know little and care less provides only minimally useful information. Good writing involves using knowledge and understanding and takes time for reflection and revision. High-quality performance assessment encourages just such practices and is therefore a needed element of learning the "basic" of clear writing.

Another troublesome notion is that first one learns the "basics"—usually defined as being able to do sufficiently well on a low-level multiple-choice test—and then, almost as a reward, one gets to read something interesting or apply math to a real problem. However, denying many students the opportunity to engage in real thinking while they learn some impoverished version of the "basics" only guarantees that the "later" for thinking will never arrive for them.

A somewhat more subtle variant of this idea is that first one learns content and then one learns to apply it. This approach, though discredited by cognitive psychology,[11] now appears to be making a comeback. It is wrong for several reasons. First, humans learn by thinking and doing. The content one thinks about and the thinking itself can and should get more complex as one learns, but one does not learn without thinking.[12] Schooling, however, can narrow and dull the range and intensity of thought by a focus on drill and repetition with decontextualized bits of information or skills. Such narrowed schooling is inflicted most often on children from low-income backgrounds and on students of color. It also reduces the likelihood of connecting schoolwork to the local and cultural contexts of the students.

In the "first know, then do" approach, it could be argued that math has a content knowledge that can be "learned" and then "applied." However, if one does not know how to go about solving the problem (application), knowing the math procedures does not help. More fundamentally, "the distinction between acquiring knowledge and applying it is inappropriate for education."[13] Separating knowing from doing for testing purposes reinforces instruction that isolates these elements, usually with the result that students don't grasp deep structures of knowledge and can't use the procedures and information they supposedly know.[14]

This separation of knowing and doing is used to justify calls, by test publishers and others, for multiple measures—using multiple-choice tests for basic facts and performance assessments for the ability to use knowledge. While it may be true that teachers can separately and efficiently test for declarative knowledge using multiple-choice or short-answer questions, it is critical that educators not allow the occasional use of such tools to reinforce an artificial separation that has had substantially harmful effects on schooling.

These separations also lead to complete confusion in some subjects. For example, multiple-choice reading tests are not described and used as measuring a few limited aspects of "reading skills"; they are erroneously described as measuring "reading."[15] The pervasiveness of these tests makes separating the test from its use a misleading exercise that only serves to disguise the difficulty of using these dangerous products safely.

This version of "basics first" also implies that whether one is excited about or engaged in learning has nothing to do with the results of learning. But if students don't get engaged, they won't think very much or very seriously about their schoolwork, and their learning will suffer.[16] A curriculum organized on "drill and kill" to raise test scores is no way to foster a desire to learn.

This does not mean that attention to particular bits (e.g., phonics) or that repetition in instruction is never acceptable. However, these practices must be subordinate elements of curriculum and instruction, to be used as needed and appropriate for a particular student or group. To determine need, a teacher must understand the particular student or group—which is to say, the teacher must assess students' actual strengths and learning needs, which requires classroom-based performance assessment.

Outside the Classroom

Assessment is, of course, used outside the classroom. Indeed, tests made for such purposes as comparing students to national norms, certifying their accomplishments (or lack thereof), and providing public accountability have come to dominate both public conceptions of assessment and classroom assessment practices. Teachers do use a range of methods, though not often enough and not well enough, but the underlying conceptions of what it means to assess and how to do it are dominated by the model of the external, multiple-choice, norm-referenced test. This domination tends to reduce curriculum and instruction to endless drill on decontextualized bits modeled on multiple-choice questions.[17] Thus assessment beyond the classroom must be changed for two fundamental reasons: to provide richer and fairer means of assessment for these purposes and to remove the control the tests exert over classroom instruction and assessment.

School Improvement

If classroom-based assessment is essential for student learning, it is equally essential for school improvement. If teachers talk with one another about student learning, then they will reflect on how to help particular children learn and how to improve the school as a whole.

The Prospect School in Vermont pioneered the use of such a collaborative process. Teachers met regularly to discuss student work.[18] A similar process has been adopted at the Bronx New School, an elementary school in New York City.[19] In a powerfully moving section of *Authentic Assessment in Action,* a teacher describes working with Akeem, a child who seemed destined for school failure, if not worse. The rich information provided by the Bronx New School's assessment practices enabled his teacher to improve her work with Akeem. But only the process of collaboration among the staff gave her the insights and help she needed to keep struggling to find a way to work successfully with him. Akeem remains in school, is progressing well, and can envision a solid future for himself.

As the examples in this book and a growing body of work on professional development show,[20] talking with one another helps teachers improve their practice and simultaneously work on improving their schools. As with individuals, knowing what works and what does not, figuring out why, and then deciding how to make improvements are essential parts of school progress.

Certification and Making Decisions

Principles and Indicators states that decisions about individuals and schools should be made "on the basis of cumulative evidence of learning, using a variety of assessment information, not on the basis of any single assessment." Neither important individual decisions, such as high school graduation or special placement, nor collective sanctions or rewards for a school should be made on the basis of a test used as a single, required hurdle. The work students actually do should be used to make these decisions.

In many ways this approach is the same one that was used historically: if a student passed his or her courses, that student graduated, perhaps with honors if he or she did well. The problem was that this approach became divorced from high expectations and serious standards, so that some students could graduate knowing very little. The solution often imposed has been the high school exit test, which appears to be enjoying an unfortunate comeback after a decline in the first half of the 1990s. High-stakes exit tests are now used in 17 states,[21] with still more states planning to adopt them. The use of such tests means that some deserving students do not obtain diplomas, in some instances the dropout rates increase, and often schooling is ever more intensively reduced to a test-coaching program.

There is a better way: hold schools, in collaboration with the community, responsible for establishing clear and public criteria for graduation. That way, the community knows what students who graduate actually must know and be able to do. Such requirements can be flexible, with student strengths in one area allowed to balance weaknesses in another.

In this better way, each student compiles a record of achievement through portfolios, culminating projects or exhibitions, or simply doing a good job in a serious course. The record becomes the evidence used for determining readiness for graduation. Independent evaluations of the graduation requirements and of the work students are actually doing can be used to determine the quality of student accomplishments.

It is simply unconscionable—and even violates the quite conservative *Standards for Educational and Psychological Testing*[22]—to allow major decisions to be made on the basis of one-time exams. The testing profession should unite with reformers to educate and pressure policy makers to stop this practice.

Accountability

Key areas of school accountability include student achievement, equity, the proper use of funds, and whether the school provides a supportive environment for its children. My focus here is on student achievement.

Students, their parents or guardians, and their teachers need to know how individual students are doing in terms of the school's curriculum, relevant standards, and the student's previous achievement and interests. This individualized accountability information comes mostly from in-school work: various forms of performance assessment provide substantial information for reporting, through conferences and report cards, on individual student learning.

How should information about schools and districts—evidence of accountability for learning by groups of students—be obtained and presented? Usually, this is done with standardized test results from commercial norm-referenced tests or statewide criterion-referenced tests.[23] Most items on both types are multiple-choice questions. Individual scores are aggregated to provide school and district scores. Unfortunately, aggregation can produce results that are misleading or simply wrong.[24] Extensive evidence also shows that these tests often do not measure much of the curriculum, and scores on them are apt to be inflated by teaching to the tests, thereby invalidating the results.[25] This combination of limited measures and coaching has truly damaging effects on the curriculum. Thus the effort to attain accountability effectively undermines the quality of education. This perverse result needs to be changed.

Principles and Indicators suggests that, for evidence of accountability, states and districts rely on a combination of sampling from classroom-based assessment information (e.g., portfolios or learning records) and from performance exams. In essence, the process could work along the following lines.

Each teacher, using scoring guides or rubrics, indicates where on a developmental scale or a performance standard each student should be placed and attaches evidence (records and portfolio material) to back up the decision. A random sample of the portfolios or learning records is selected from each classroom. Independent readers (educators from other schools, members of the community, and so on) review the records as evidence of student learning and place students on the scale. The scores of teachers and readers are then compared to see whether the judgments correspond. If they do not, various actions, beginning with another independent reading, can be used to identify the discrepancy. A larger sample from the classroom can be rescored. In addition, several procedures can be used to adjust the scores to account for teacher variation in scoring ("moderation"). Initial agreement among readers is usually low to moderate, but it can rise quickly if (1) the readers are welltrained and (2) the guides to what is in the records and how to score them are very clear.[26] Professional development can be targeted to help teachers improve their scoring.

This procedure validates teacher judgments and makes teachers central to the accountability process. It enables independent reviews of teachers' evaluations to check for equitable treatment of the students.

Another advantage of this approach is that it is not necessary to ask all students to enter the same kinds of work. Substantial diversity can be allowed in the records and portfolios, provided that they demonstrate student learning in the domain.

Such models have been used fairly extensively in Britain (and were proposed as the basis for a national assessment system there) and in pilot projects in the U.S.[27] This process is similar to what Vermont does with its portfolios. Developers of the *Primary Language Record,* the *Primary Learning Record,* the *California Learning Record,* and the *Work Sampling System* have begun to explore methods of rescoring. A project in the California Learning Assessment System included the development of an "organic portfolio" for the purposes of accountability; readers scored portfolios for evidence of learning in math and language arts domains derived from the California curriculum frameworks.

Using classroom-based information for accountability involves selecting from a wide range of data rather than trying to generalize from a narrow set of information, as is done in most testing programs. There may be a danger that, in trying to choose from wide data, the requirements for selection of material come to dominate instructional practice. However, allowing diversity in the components of the record or portfolio and rescoring only a sample might prevent such a harmful consequence. In any event, this concern must be considered in any effort to use a valuable classroom assessment for accountability purposes.

As an additional means of checking on the overall accuracy of the portfolio process, the Forum suggests that primarily performance exams can be administered. Using a matrix sample, as is done by the National Assessment of Educational Progress (NAEP), every student in a sample of students is administered one part of the entire exam. The parts are then assembled to provide district or state scores. The results of the exam can be compared at the school level to scores on the sample of portfolios. If a discrepancy exists, further work can be done to find the cause of the difference.

Time and money constraints limit what can be administered in one or a few performance exam sittings, making it difficult to include enough tasks to be able to generalize about student learning in the area being tested. Through sampling, much more can be assessed for the same cost than if every student took an entire test.

Performance exams are often used by states to direct and then measure reforms in curriculum and instruction. These efforts seem to have had mixed results. However, on-demand assessments are limited in their classroom utility, even as a model for classroom assessment practices, because they do not help teachers learn to do continuous classroom assessment. That is, most assessment reform at the state level has involved attempting to find formative, classroom uses for summative, on-demand exams. It is a nearly impossible task, though exam items can be the basis for interesting classroom projects if adapted to involve formative aspects of assessment as well. The on-demand exam approach to overcoming the limitations and dangers of traditional multiple-choice tests will probably prove to be a limited success. These exams make much more sense when used on a sampling basis for assessing achievement at the school or district level and as a complement to classroom-based information. In time, they may prove to be unnecessary.

Beyond Scores

A new approach to accountability should involve more than changing the measures of student learning. It should involve alternative ways of using information both to improve schools and to inform the public.

For example, groups of schools in New York City are beginning to form networks in which they share the development of standards for student learning and of means to assess students and faculty.[28] In this way, they work together to improve the schools and to hold one another accountable for, among other things, enhanced student learning. Evidence of learning exists at the school level through portfolios, exhibitions, and other presentations of student work, and one purpose of the networks is to help schools refine these assessment processes. One network has printed a portfolio describing the schools, their procedures, and their accomplishments. Its next step will be to have a group of outsiders evaluate and publicly report on the network. This effort somewhat resembles the school quality review process that has begun in New York State, in which teams of educators and members of the public spend a week closely exploring a school and making a report to that school.

These processes are based on the understanding that improvement and accountability should not be separated, any more than instruction and assessment should be. This approach also proposes to move accountability largely to the communities served by the school. It accepts that real accountability is a human and social process and therefore asks for human engagement in looking at schools and striving to make them better.

Accountability reform can thus take several complementary approaches. One is to revise how assessment is done, shifting from testing every student with a simplistic exam to using a combination of classroom-based information and on-demand performance exams. Both methods should use sampling procedures to report on student achievement in light of agreed-upon standards. This can be done at district or state levels. The second approaches is to ask schools to work together in networks to hold one another accountable and to bring the community back into the process of evaluating the schools and networks. These complementary processes can help improve school practices and ultimately improve student learning.

However, parents, the public, and other social institutions have become conditioned to seeing test scores. Indeed, test scores have become nearly synonymous with accountability. But in order to avoid paying the price of forever narrowing schooling to what can be easily and cheaply measured, parents will have to exchange these narrow statistics for richer local information. They can rely on school-based data about their child's performance in light of standards and then use school-level information, also in relation to standards, to compare schools and districts. Through this procedure, parents can determine how well their child is learning.

What Next?

We are in reactionary times. While far more states include some form of performance testing today than at the start of the decade and more have such assessments in the planning or development stage, California and Arizona have dropped performance exams, and such exams are under attack in Kentucky and elsewhere. A right-wing ideological offensive has been mounted against performance assessment in many locales.[29] The calls for "basics" are often trumpeted together with calls for "basic skills tests." In a "get tough" environment in which we are seeing an increase in the use of graduation and even grade-promotion tests, more testing seems to be on the agenda. This includes President Clinton's proposed mostly multiple-choice exam in reading and math.

Yet the problems with traditional testing have not gone away. Those tests offer no solution to the educational needs of our children. Assessment is thus at a crisis point: the old model is incapable of meeting real needs, and a new approach is not yet clear. In this situation, most states have done little more than tinker at the edge of reform, adding some constructed-response items to mostly multiple-choice tests.[30] Whatever forms of exams are eventually used, they cannot provide much help for teachers in learning to integrate assessment with instruction in a continuous flow—and that is the heart of assessment in the service of learning.

Far better, then, to build an assessment system from the bottom up, relying on teachers and seeking to improve the quality of curriculum and instruction as well as assessment. Construction of this sort of accountability system will require time and effort, but it is a road worth following. Those who seek to reconstruct assessment should consider uniting around the Forum's *Principles and Indicators for Student Assessment Systems* and taking a number of actions.

First, reform advocates, educators, and researchers must continuously point out the limits of and the harm done by traditional testing. Comparing multiple-choice items to real work in portfolios or even to performance exam tasks and asking parents or community members which option represents the kind of work children should be doing is one powerful educational tool. When shown the alternatives, parents typically prefer performance tasks to multiple-choice items.[31] If parents could consistently get the richer information provided by such assessments, they might be willing to give up their desire for simplistic test scores. We should also expose the limitations of the tests. Few parents, not even many teachers, understand the underpinnings and structures of norm-referenced, multiple-choice standardized tests and therefore understand how narrow and biased they are. In 1994 a slight majority of the public thought that essays would be preferable to multiple-choice tests.[32] This indicates a solid base on which to build public understanding of the need to transform assessment.

Second, educators who understand the harm done by the tests should take all possible steps to block their use. Teachers in Japan boycotted exams for elementary students, forcing the government to drop them.[33]

Third, researchers should shift their emphasis away from a one-sided focus on new exams and toward classroom-based approaches. Foundations and government agencies must be persuaded to apply resources to such approaches.

Fourth, school systems should expand and focus professional development on creating schools as communities of learners that integrate curriculum, instruction, and assessment in ways that are helpful to all students. This approach often requires restructuring the school. Parents and the community must be involved in and educated about the process, as they must be about new assessment practices. Networks of such schools can be a basis for redesigning accountability and explaining it to the public.

Finally, educators can do a lot in their schools and districts, even when faced with external "basic skills" multiple-choice tests. They can implement high-quality classroom assessments and share them with parents and the community. Widespread use of such assessments can form a base for a renewed effort to curtail traditional standardized tests and to construct assessment systems that support learning.

Endnotes

1. National Forum on Assessment, *Principles and Indicators for Student Assessment Systems* (Cambridge, Mass.: FairTest, 1995). *Principles* can be purchased for $10 from FairTest, 342 Broadway, Cambridge, MA 02139. Note that the idea of "schools in networks" is not included in the Forum document. All references to the Forum are from this document.

2. The discussion on performance assessment draws heavily on D. Monty Neill et al., *Implementing Performance Assessment: A Guide to Classroom, School, and System Reform* (Cambridge, Mass.: FairTest, 1995). See also National Forum on Assessment, op. cit.; and *Selected Annotated Bibliography on Performance Assessment,* 2nd ed. (Cambridge, Mass.: FairTest, 1995).

3. Edward Chittenden, "Authentic Assessment: Evaluation and Documentation of Student Performance," in Vito Perrone, ed., *Expanding Student Assessment* (Alexandria, Va.: Association for Supervision and Curriculum Development, 1991), pp. 22–31.

4. Myra Barrs et al., *Primary Language Record* (Portsmouth, N.H.: Heinemann, 1988); Hillary Hester, *Guide to the Primary Learning Record* (London: Centre for Language in Primary Education, 1993); Mary Barr, *California Learning Record* (El Cajon, Calif.: Center for Language in Learning, 1994); and Samuel J. Meisels

et al., "The Work Sampling System: Reliability and Validity of a Performance Assessment for Young Children," *Early Childhood Research Quarterly,* vol. 10, 1995, pp. 277–96.

5. Peter H. Johnston, *Constructive Evaluation of Literate Activity* (New York: Longman, 1992); and Patricia F. Carini, "Dear Sister Bess: An Essay on Standards, Judgment, and Writing," *Assessing Writing,* vol. 1, 1994, pp. 29–65.

6. *Curriculum and Evaluation Standards for School Mathematics* (Reston, Va.: National Council of Teachers of Mathematics, 1989).

7. D. Monty Neill, and Noe J. Medina, "Standardized Testing: Harmful to Educational Health," *Phi Delta Kappan,* May 1989, pp. 688–97.

8. Norman Frederiksen, "The Real Test Bias: Influence of Testing on Teaching and Learning," *American Psychologist,* March 1984, p. 193.

9. George F. Madaus et al., *The Influence of Testing on Teaching Math and Science in Grades 4–12* (Chestnut Hill, Mass.: Center for the Study of Testing, Evaluation, and Educational Policy, Boston College, 1992).

10. "KERA: What Works, What Doesn't," *Daily Report Card,* 22 May 1996 (on-line); and Fran Spielman, "Schools Try New Tests, Curriculum," *Chicago Sun-Times,* 22 September 1995.

11. Lauren B. Resnick, *Education and Learning to Think* (Washington, D.C.: National Academy Press, 1987); and Lauren B. Resnick and Daniel P. Resnick, "Assessing the Thinking Curriculum: New Tools for Educational Reform," in Bernard R. Gifford and Mary C. O'Connor, eds., *Future Assessments: Changing Views of Aptitude, Achievement, and Instruction* (Boston: Kluwer, 1992), pp. 37–76.

12. James Hiebert et al., "Problem Solving as a Basis for Reform in Curriculum and Instruction: The Case of Mathematics," *Educational Researcher,* May 1996, pp. 12–21; and Scott G. Paris et al., "The Development of Strategic Readers," in P. David Pearson, ed., *Handbook of Reading Research, Vol. 2* (New York: Longman, 1991), pp. 609–40.

13. Hiebert et al., p. 14.

14. Howard Gardner, *The Unschooled Mind* (New York: Basic Books, 1991); and Resnick and Resnick, op. cit.

15. Deborah Meier, "Why the Reading Tests Don't Measure Reading," *Dissent,* Winter 1982–83, pp. 457–66.

16. John Raven, "A Model of Competence, Motivation, and Behavior and a Paradigm for Assessment," in Harold Berlak et al., eds., *Toward a New Science of Educational Testing and Assessment* (Albany: State University of New York Press, 1992), pp. 85–116; and Thomas Kellaghan, George F. Madaus, and Anastasia Raczek, *The Use of External Examinations to Improve Student Motivation* (Washington, D.C.: American Educational Research Association, 1996).

17. Joan L. Herman and Shari Golan, "The Effects of Standardized Testing on Teaching and Schools," *Educational Measurement: Issues and Practice,* Winter 1993, pp. 20–25, 41; George F. Madaus, "The Influence of Testing on the Curriculum," in Laura N. Tanner, ed., *Critical Issues in the Curriculum: 87th NSSE Yearbook, Part I* (Chicago: National Society for the Study of Education, University of Chicago Press, 1988), pp. 83–121; Thomas A. Romberg et al., "Curriculum and Test Alignment," in Thomas A. Romberg, ed., *Mathematics Assessment and Evaluation* (Albany: State University of New York Press, 1992), pp. 61–74; and Mary Lee Smith, "Put to the Test: The Effects of External Testing on Teachers," *Educational Researcher,* June/July 1991, pp. 8–11.

18. Walter Haney, "Making Tests More Educational," *Educational Leadership,* October 1985, pp. 4–13.

19. Linda Darling-Hammond, Jacqueline Ancess, and Beverly Falk, *Authentic Assessment in Action: Studies of Schools and Students at Work* (New York: Teachers College Press, 1995).

20. See especially Judith Warren Little, "Teachers' Professional Development in a Climate of Educational Reform," *Educational Evaluation and Policy Analysis,* Summer 1993, pp. 129–51.

21. Linda Ann Bond et al., *State Student Assessment Programs Database, School Year 1994–1995* (Washington, D.C., and Oak Brook, Ill.: Council of Chief State School Officers and North Central Regional Educational Laboratory, 1996).

22. American Educational Research Association, American Psychological Association, and National Council on Measurement in Education, *Standards for Educational and Psychological Testing* (Washington, D.C.: American Psychological Association, 1985).

23. Bond et al., op. cit.

24. Walter Haney and Anastasia Raczek, "Surmounting Outcomes Accountability in Education," in *Issues in Educational Accountability* (Washington, D.C.: Office of Technology Assessment, 1994).

25. Thomas M. Haladyna, Susan Bobbit Nolen, and Nancy S. Haas, "Raising Standardized Achievement Test Scores and the Origins of Test Score Pollution," *Educational Researcher,* June/July 1991, pp. 2–7; Robert M. Linn, M. Elizabeth Graue, and Nancy M. Sanders, "Comparing State and District Results to National Norms: The Validity of the Claims That 'Everyone Is Above Average,'" *Educational Measurement: Issues and Practice,* Fall 1990, pp 5–14; and Lorrie A. Shepard, "Inflated Test Score Gains: Is the Problem Old Norms or Teaching the Test?," *Educa-*

tional Measurement: Issues and Practice, Fall 1990, pp. 15–22.

26. Suzanne Lane et al., "Generalizability and Validity of Mathematics Performance Assessment," *Journal of Educational Measurement,* Spring 1996, pp. 71–92; Robert Linn, "Educational Assessment: Expanded Expectations and Challenges," *Educational Evaluation and Policy Analysis,* Spring 1993, pp. 1–16; William Thomas et al., *The CLAS Portfolio Assessment Research and Development Project Final Report* (Princeton, N.J.: Educational Testing Service, 1996); and "Using Language Records (PLR/CLR) as Large-Scale Assessments," *FairTest Examiner,* Summer 1995, pp. 8–9.

27. Myra Barrs, "The Road Not Taken," *Forum,* vol. 36, 1994, pp. 36–39.

28. Deborah Meir and Jacqueline Ancess, "Accountability by Bloated Bureaucracy and Regulation: Is There an Alternative?," interactive symposium at the annual meeting of the American Educational Research Association, New York, April 1996.

29. "Right Wing Attacks Performance Assessment," *FairTest Examiner,* Summer 1994, pp. 1, 10–11.

30. D. Monty Neill, *State of State Assessment Systems* (Cambridge, Mass.: FairTest, 1997).

31. Lorrie A. Shepard and Carribeth L. Bliem, *Parent Opinions About Standardized Tests, Teacher's Information, and Performance Assessments* (Los Angeles: Center for Research on Evaluation, Standards, and Student Testing, CSE Technical Report 367, 1993); and John Poggio, "The Politics of Test Validity: Performance Assessment as a State-Sponsored Educational Reform," interactive symposium at the annual meeting of the American Educational Research Association, New York, April 1996.

32. Jean Johnson and John Immerwahr, *First Things First: What Americans Expect from the Public Schools* (New York: Public Agenda Foundation, 1994).

33. "Japanese Teachers Block Tests," *FairTest Examiner,* Spring 1996, p. 9.

Integrating Sources

1. Compare and contrast Tierney's views with Neill's of reading assessment according to the following topics:

   a. Teacher's use of the results of both standardized and informal reading tests to help improve student performance

   b. How reading test results are being used to measure teacher performance in the classroom, curriculum decision in reading education, and evaluation of district literacy goals

2. If you were to design an effective classroom reading assessment program based on the material you have read in the section, what would be the major components of this testing effort?

Classroom Implications

1. How can classroom teachers effectively use literacy assessment results in their teaching? Suggest some specific problems that must be overcome in this area as well as appropriate solutions.

    a.

    b.

    c.

2. Describe what you believe is an effective classroom program of literacy assessment. What types of tests would you use, including both formal and informal tests? How would you use the results of these assessment procedures both in terms of designing the total literacy curriculum as well as teaching individual students?

Annotated Bibliography

Dudely, M. (1997). The rise and fall of a statewide assessment system. *English Journal, 86,* 15–20.

Describes the development of a statewide writing assessment program in which students wrote essays based on literary-based prompts. Addresses the publics' concerns and how test developers worked to achieve the desired outcomes.

Greder, G. R. (1997). Issues in early childhood screening and assessment. *Psychology in the Schools, 34,* 99–106.

Raises serious questions about the interpretation and efficacy of the results of commonly used early childhood assessment procedures. Concludes that for most of these tests as they are now constructed and used, there are major questions as to their current results.

Miller, S. D., Hayes, C. T., & Atkinson, T. S. (1997). State efforts to improve students' reading and language arts achievement: Does the left hand know what the right is doing? *Reading Research and Instruction, 36,* 267–286.

A research project that resulted in discrepent perceptions of state officials, school principals, curriculum directors, and classroom teachers regarding a change in statewide assessment. Of particular note was the fact that state officials assumed the new state tests would automatically change classroom instruction where for most teachers they were uninformed of these new expectations.

Paulsen, K. J. (1997). Curriculum-based measurement: Translating research into school-based practice. *Intervention in School and Clinic, 32,* 162–167.

Describes an evaluation instrument teachers can use to develop interventions for children with learning difficulties prior to the formal evaluations for special services.

Shepard, L. A. (1997). Children not ready to learn? The invalidity of school readiness testing. *Psychology in the Schools, 34,* 85–97.

Describes a professional development project for teachers in learning instructional practices and performance procedures that support assessment reform.

Shepard, L. A., Kagan, S. L., & Wurtz, E. (1998). Goal 1 early childhood assessments resource group recommendations. *Young Children, 53,* 52–54.

Describes a year-long study that examined student learning as evidenced by performance assessment measures. Conclusions emphasized the importance of sustained professional development for teachers as a vital part of instructional reform.

Taylor, K., & Walton, S. (1997). Co-opting standardized tests in the service of learning. *Phi Delta Kappan, 79,* 66–70.

Discusses the affect of taking standardized norm-referenced tests on children's motivation, attitudes, and strategies. Describes an intervention that details a workshop agenda designed to help children learn to cope with standardized tests.

Valencia, S. W. (1997). Authentic classroom assessment of early reading: Alternatives to standardized tests. *Preventing School Failure, 41,* 63–70.

Argues for and provides examples of children's work in relation to performance assessment.

Vukelich, C. (1997). Assessing young children's literacy: Documenting growth and informing practice. *The Reading Teacher, 50,* 430–434.

Describes effective methods and procedures for measuring literacy growth in young children. Of particular note is the Checklist suggested for classifying current reading skills in beginning readers.

You Become Involved

Assessment

Prior to the 1980s and 1990s, assessment and evaluation practices had not undergone extensive reevaluation in schools. Students' learning was generally evaluated using standardized achievement tests and alternative-choice classroom tests. Since that time, educators, government leaders, and communities have begun to question and seek alternative measures for examining individual student's progress, making program and instructional decisions, and evaluating school effectiveness from a global perspective. Using your reading, experience, and discussion with others, complete the following activities.

1. How do assessment and evaluation differ? Who should have a role in assessment practices and what should that role be? Who should have a role in evaluation? What should that role be?
2. Make three concentric time lines of factors and events that relate to assessment/evaluation. Time line 1 should reflect *school* issues and trends, time line 2 should reflect *societal* issues and trends, and time line 3 should reflect *global* issues and trends. Use the chart provided to complete the time line. When you have completed the time lines, analyze for the following purposes:

   a. What story does each time line tell about our history?
   b. Look at each time line in relation to the other two. What patterns and connections do you see?
   c. How have the assessment issues dealt with by schools, communities, and states addressed societal and national issues?

Assessment/Evaluation Time Lines

	1970	1980	1990	2000...
Schools				
Societal				
Global				

5

LITERACY MATERIALS

If three or four persons agree to read the same book, and each bring
his own remarks upon it, at some set hours appointed for conversation,
and they communicate mutually their sentiments on the subject, and
debate about it in a friendly manner, this practice will render the reading
of any author more abundantly beneficial to everyone of them.
—*ISAAC WATTS (1811)*

One of the primary reasons for learning to read is the pleasure one gets
from contact with good books. Long before a child can read for himself,
he may have a preview of joys to come if his parents and teachers create
a stimulating environment in which they share picture storybooks with
him, tell stories for him, and say poems and verses with him.
—*W. S. GRAY ET AL. (1953)*

The [good reading teacher] . . . believes that the goal of reading
instruction is to develop readers who are skillful, strategic,
motivated, independent, knowledgeable, and appreciative
of literature. This teacher embraces a literature-
based perspective, combining trade book reading
with the reading of basal anthology selections.
—*JAMES BAUMANN ET AL. (1998)*

The controversy surrounding the effective use of materials for reading instruction
has been a long-standing one. Historically, the major disagreement in this discussion of literacy materials was the effective use of the basal reader. While the dialogue on use of the basal reader has by no means ended, the discussion of literacy
materials has today expanded to include the selection of appropriate types of literature, censorship, and the teachers' role in the use of literacy materials. Each of
these topics evoke a wide range of opinions, which represent a wide spectrum of
belief and practice. For some, the use of literacy materials represents the most
important aspect of their classroom reading instruction while for other teachers,
materials are of a secondary nature.

Basal Readers

The use of the basal reader is still very common in many classrooms. While at one time these materials were often the primary tool of reading instruction, this situation has dramatically changed in the last few years. Today, teachers use the basal reader in a wide variety of ways. For instance, some use the basal reader, but tend not to rely on the various suggestions taken from the teacher's manual; others see the basal as being primarily a supplement to their literature-based instruction; and still others chose not to use the basal reader at all. Each of these uses of the basal reader present the classroom teacher a wide variety of decisions which must be solved. Rather than take a firm stand on the basal, the effective reading teacher should investigate each of these options and then make a personal decision as to the role of the basal reader in his or her classroom reading instruction.

Literature-Based Instruction

There are very few literacy programs today that do not have a large literature component of some type. While few would object to this emphasis on the wide use of literature as a foundation for effective reading, there are various viewpoints, and differences of opinion on this goal can be met. For instance, questions as to how you select books—especially for individual students, appropriate organizational plans for instruction using literature-based materials, and how you effectively measure growth and progress in classrooms of this type are frequently asked by teachers.

Other questions related to a literature-based reading program involve the availability of literature materials and the related dilemma of new money to use for the purchase of multiple copies of individual books.

Censorship

The concern over the censoring of school materials is not a recent phenomenon (Donelson, 1997; Trent, 1997; West, 1997). For many years various pressure groups have tried to influence the selection and use of almost all literacy materials. What has changed today is the fact that groups opposed to certain types of reading materials tend to be more organized and politically active. Teachers need to be aware of potential problems and know how to effectively deal with the many issues related to the censorship of classroom literacy materials.

The Teacher's Role in the Use of Literacy Materials

When using the basal reader, the role of the teacher is often clearly defined in terms of teaching responsibilities. The extended use of literature is much less obvious. For instance, during a literature experience, is the teacher the leader of the discussion, a participant in the literature group, or just an observer? Perhaps the teacher assumes just one of these roles, or on other occasions all three, or even none at all. A related question is the role of the classroom teacher in the selection of materials to be read, both in terms of classroom reading as well as individual reading experiences.

As You Read

The articles that follow develop many issues related to basal or literature-based instruction. Weaver (1989) and Groff (1989) take opposing sides in their reactions to *The Report Card on Basal Readers* (Goodman et al., 1988), a highly critical report on the basal reader. In line with Weaver's negative stance is the call to action developed by the National Council of Teachers of English (1989).

The issues surrounding basal readers and their literature-based alternatives are political as well as instructional. You will need to come to terms with both the politics and the pedagogy of reading instruction in order to answer the following questions.

1. How are basals or literature-based programs compatible with your own literacy philosophy?
2. Are teachers necessarily "deskilled" by using basals?
3. How are basals and literature-based programs aligned with current perspectives on how children acquire literacy knowledge?
4. What changes would you make in either basals or literature-based programs that would make them compatible with your teaching beliefs?

References

Baumann, J. E., Hoffman, J. V., Moon, J., & Duffy-Hester, A. D. (1998). Where are teachers' voices in the phonics/whole language debate? Results from a survey of U.S. elementary classroom teachers. *The Reading Teacher, 51,* 636–650.

Crawford, P. A. (1997). Looking for love (and literature and pedagogy) in all the wrong places: Hopeful teachers and the illusion of change in basal readers. *Teaching and Learning Literature with Children and Young Adults, 7,* 5–14.

Donelson, K. (1997). "Filth" and "pure filth" in our schools—Censorship of classroom books in the last ten years. *English Journal, 86,* 21–25.

Goodman, K. S., et al. (1988). *Report card on basal readers.* Katonah, NY: Richard C. Owen.

Gray, W. S., et al. (1953). *Guidebook to accompany the new Our New Friends.* Chicago: Scott, Foresman and Company, p. 26.

Groff, P. (1989). An attack on basal readers for the wrong reasons. In C. B. Smith (Ed.), *Two reactions to the report card on basal readers in print* (pp. 8–13). Bloomington, IN: ERIC/REC (Educational Resources Information Center/Clearinghouse on Reading, English, and Communication).

National Council of Teachers of English. (1989). Basal readers and the state of American reading instruction. *Language Arts, 66,* 896–898.

Trent, C. (1997). Censorship and the Internet: A stand for school libraries. *School Library Media Quarterly, 25,* 223–227.

Watts, I. (1811). *The improvement of the mind.* London: F. C. and J. Rivington.

West, M. (1997). *Trust your children: Voices against censorship in children's literature.* New York: Neal-Schuman.

Weaver, C. (1989). The basalization of America: A cause for concern. In C. B. Smith (Ed.), *Two reactions to the report card on basal readers in print* (pp. 4–7). Bloomington, IN: ERIC/REC (Educational Resources Information Center/Clearinghouse on Reading, English, and Communication).

Basal Readers and the State of American Reading Instruction

A Call for Action

THE COMMISSION ON READING,
NATIONAL COUNCIL OF TEACHERS OF ENGLISH

The Problem

As various national studies suggest, the problem of illiteracy, semi-literacy, and aliteracy in the United States appears to be growing, due at least in part to escalating standards of literacy in the workplace and in the civic area. And at a time when our information-age society demands increased literacy from all citizens, reading instruction is locked into a technology that is more than half a century out-of-date.

Basals: Part of the Problem

There is a significant gap between how reading is learned and how it is taught and assessed in the vast majority of our classrooms today. This gap is perpetuated by the basal reading series that dominate reading instruction in roughly 90 percent of the elementary classrooms in the United States. Such textbook series are often viewed as complete systems for teaching reading, for they include not only a graded series of books for the students to read but teachers' manuals telling teachers what and how to teach, workbooks and dittos for the students to complete, sets of tests to assess reading skills, and often various supplementary aids. Because of their comprehensiveness, basal reading systems leave very little room for other kinds of reading activities in the schools where they have been adopted. This is all the more unfortunate because current theory and research strongly support such conclusions as the following:

- Basal reading series typically reflect and promote the misconception that reading is necessarily learned from smaller to larger parts.
- The sequencing of skills in a basal reading series exists not because this is how children learn to read but simply because of the logistics of developing a series of lessons that can be taught sequentially, day after day, week after week, year after year.
- Students are typically tested for ability to master the bits and pieces of reading, such as phonics and other word-identification skills, and even comprehension skills. How-

Source: From "Basal Readers and the State of American Reading Instruction: A Call for Action" by The Commission on Reading, National Council of Teachers of English, 1989, *Language Arts, 66.* Copyright 1989 by the National Council of Teachers of English. Reprinted with permission.

ever, there is no evidence that mastering such skills in isolation guarantees the ability to comprehend connected text, or that students who cannot give evidence of such skills in isolation are necessarily unable to comprehend connected text.

- Thus for many if not most children, the typical basal reading series may actually make learning to read more difficult than it needs to be.
- So much time is typically taken up by "instructional" activities (including activities with workbooks and skill sheets) that only a very slight amount of time is spent in actual reading—despite the overwhelming evidence that extensive reading and writing are crucial to the development of literacy.
- Basal reading series typically reflect and promote the widespread misconception that the ability to verbalize an answer, orally or in writing, is evidence of understanding and learning. Thus even students who appear to be learning from a basal reading series are being severely shortchanged, for they are being systematically encouraged not to think.
- Basal reading series typically tell teachers exactly what they should do and say while teaching a lesson, thus depriving teachers of the responsibility and authority to make informed professional judgments.
- "Going through the paces" thus becomes the measure of both teaching and learning. The teachers are assumed to have taught well if and only if they have taught the lesson. Students are assumed to have learned if and only if they have given "right" answers.
- *The result of such misconceptions about learning and such rigid control of teacher and student activities is to discourage both teachers and students from thinking, and particularly to discourage students from developing and exercising critical literacy and thinking skills needed to participate fully in a technologically advanced democratic society.*

Recommended Actions for Local Administrators and for Policymakers

For Local Administrators

- Provide continual district inservice for teachers to help them develop a solid understanding of how people read and how children learn to read and how reading is related to writing and learning to write.
- Provide time and opportunities for teachers to mentor with peers who are trying innovative materials and strategies.
- Support teachers in attending local, regional, state, and national conferences to improve their knowledge base, and support continued college coursework for teachers in reading and writing.
- Allow/encourage teachers to use alternatives to basal readers or to use basal readers flexibly, eliminating whatever their professional judgment deems unnecessary or inappropriate: for example,

   — encourage innovation at a school level, offering teachers a choice of basals, portions of basals, or no basal, using assessment measures that match their choice

— discuss at a school level which portions of the basal need not be used, and use the time saved for reading and discussion of real literature
— provide time for teachers to work with one another to set innovative programs.

- Give teachers the opportunity to demonstrate that standardized test scores will generally not be adversely affected by using alternatives to basal readers, and may in fact be enhanced.
- Provide incentives for teachers to develop and use alternative methods of reading assessment, based upon their understanding of reading and learning to read.
- Allow/encourage teachers to take charge of their own reading instruction, according to their informed professional judgment.

For Policymakers

- Change laws and regulations that favor or require use of basals, so that

  — state funds may be used for non-basal materials
  — schools may use programs that do not have traditional basal components
  — teachers cannot be forced to use material they find professionally objectionable.

- Provide incentives to local districts to experiment with alternatives to basals, by

  — developing state-level policies that permit districts to use alternatives to basals
  — changing teacher education and certification requirements so as to require teachers to demonstrate an understanding of how people read, of how children learn to read, and of ways of developing a reading curriculum without as well as with basals
  — mandating periodic curriculum review and revision based upon current theory and research as to how people read and how children learn to read
  — developing, or encouraging local districts to develop, alternative means of testing and assessment that are supported by current theory and research in how people read and how children learn to read
  — funding experimental programs, research, and methods of assessment based upon current theory and research on reading and learning to read.

The Basalization of America

A Cause for Concern

CONSTANCE WEAVER

In 1985 when the Commission on Reading of the National Council of Teachers of English (NCTE) asked Kenneth Goodman to undertake a study of basal reading programs, we were motivated not so much by the national reports on the nation's literacy as by personal observation during our day-to-day interactions with teachers and children. In traditional classrooms, most children were learning to read at least minimally, even though some were not succeeding very well in their reading programs.

We also saw, however, what others have documented: that even the "good" readers typically read for surface accuracy and details rather than for thoughtful response, and that, all too often, they read just to answer questions rather than for enjoyment or to gain information or understanding (Applebee et al., 1988). In short, we noticed that in the typical curriculum-oriented classroom, children were more likely to go mechanically through the paces of their lessons (Bloome, 1987) than to engage meaningfully in reading, writing, and thinking.

The National Assessment of Educational Progress (NAEP) studies further document what we have observed: that although the majority of our young people are learning to read at a surface level, they are not learning to reason effectively about what they read and write. Few, in fact, are able to analyze, evaluate, and extend the ideas that they encounter in print (Applebee et al., 1987; Venezky et al., 1987). As business and industry repeatedly tell us, such superficial literacy is no longer enough in our increasingly complex and technological society.

Knowing that basal reading systems are used in more than 90 percent of the nation's classrooms (Anderson et al., 1985), we on the NCTE's Commission on Reading naturally asked ourselves a question that others too have asked (e.g., Venezky et al., 1987; Anderson et al., 1985): Is there something about today's basal reading programs, or about basal programs as a genre, that might contribute to such passive and superficial reading as that documented by the NAEP reports?

This and other questions were explored for the Commission by Kenneth Goodman, Patrick Shannon, Yvonne Freeman, and Sharon Murphy. In addition to examining previous research on basals and the use of basals, they also undertook detailed analyses of several current basal reading programs (mostly with 1986 or 1985 copyright dates), including the six series that together account for about 80 percent of the money spent on basals (Goodman et al., 1988, p. 46). This research and analysis culminated in the *Report Card on Basal Readers* (Goodman et al., 1988).

Source: From "The Basalization of America: A Cause for Concern" by Constance Weaver, in C. B. Smith (Ed.), *Two Reactions to the Report Card on Basal Readers in Print* (No. 1, pp. 4–7). Bloomington, IN: ERIC. Copyright 1989, ERIC/REC (Educational Resources Information Center/Clearinghouse on Reading, English, and Communication) at Indiana University (Bloomington). Reprinted by permission.

The authors of the *Report Card* freely admit that "While we have tried to be fair in this report we have not tried to be neutral. We are concerned for what is good or bad for learners and the teachers trying to help them become literate" (Goodman et al., 1988, p. v).

Hence the authors made scant mention of recent improvements in basal reading programs, but focused instead on problems and concerns that remain. I shall do the same, for now focusing only upon the philosophy implicit in basal series, its ramifications, and its out-of-date research base.

The Basic Premise, Promise, and Principle of the Basal Program

"The central *premise* of the basal reader is that a sequential, all-inclusive set of instructional materials can teach all children to read" (Goodman et al., 1988, p. 1). The implicit *promise* to administrators and teachers is that if the program is followed in detail, then they are not to blame if pupils fail to read easily and well; any problems must lie with the learners themselves (p. 103). Naturally, in order to deliver on this promise, the basal reading programs must *control* teaching and learning; thus control becomes the guiding *principle* of the basal programs (p. 97).

What is controlled? Virtually everything, at least in theory. For example:

1. The basals control the reading curriculum. The various instructional, practice and assessment activities associated with basals demand so much time that there is very little, if any, for other reading and writing.

2. The basals control teachers through the language used in the teachers' manuals. Instead of offering suggestions, the TMs give directions: "Do this." "Do that." While teachers can of course ignore the directions, they typically buy into the implicit promise of the basal, perhaps in part because they are intimidated by the imperative language of the teachers' manuals as well as by the fact that the basal programs appear to be "scientific" (Goodman et al., 1988, pp. 40–43). In any case, the language of the TMs suggests to both teachers and administrators that teachers are not competent to make instructional decisions, even on minutiae. Such an implication undermines the professionalism of teachers instead of enhancing it.

3. The basals control students in a variety of ways, one of the most insidious being through the use of questions to which a single "right" answer is expected, usually an answer based upon the text itself (p. 81). Often, "Even when the question is intended to draw on 'background knowledge' and require 'critical thinking,' a simple conformist answer is suggested as a model" (p. 77).

4. The basals control the sequence in which reading "skills" (and now sometimes "strategies") will be taught, if not learned. The bulk of a basal reading program consists of materials for teaching, practicing, and testing isolated reading "skills," reflecting an implicit assumption that reading is learned "a word, or sound, or a skill at a time" (p. 70). The implication is that this broad *scope* of skills is both necessary and sufficient for learning to read. The *sequence* of skills is derived by moving from smaller parts toward larger wholes, beginning with and emphasizing skills for identifying words, and moving toward skills for comprehending sentences and paragraphs.

5. The basals control the language of the reading selections, particularly at the earliest levels, on the assumption that simplifying the vocabulary, sentence structure, and/or the letter/sound patterns in beginning materials will make them easier to read. Thus the basals include "simple" selections like "I can go. Can you go?" "I will help you. You can go." "Help! Help! I can not go" (p. 67; from Houghton Mifflin Reading, 1986, Level B—but the selection is typical of most basals).

6. Perhaps most damaging of all, the basal programs control—along with standardized and state-mandated testing—what counts as "reading." The essence of the basal program is not the pupil anthologies and their reading selections, but rather the ancillary materials for teaching, practicing, and testing reading skills. In sheer bulk, these materials far outweigh the reading selections. Examination of these materials led the authors of the *Report Card* to estimate that a basal reading program engages children in reading literary and other texts only about 10 percent to 15 percent of the time that is ostensibly devoted to "reading" (p. 73). The ultimate reduction is in the basal tests, which reduce reading to the skills which can be easily measured with paper and pencil (p. 83). So "reading is not making sense of print anymore. It is doing well on the basal tests" (p. 108).

Are Basal Readers Scientific?

Such strict control of reading makes perfectly good sense according to the science of the 1920s, when basal reading programs were first being developed. Today's basals are still solidly rooted in those principles from business, industry, and science—particularly behavioral psychology—that motivated the development of the earliest basal series. These principles are reflected in the "laws of learning" articulated by Edward Thorndike (Goodman et al., 1988, pp. 12–13). The *Report Card* illustrates throughout its discussion of the contemporary basal how today's programs reflect the view of teaching and learning rooted in Thorndike's "laws." To summarize: "The *Law of Readiness* results in the readiness materials and in the tight sequence in which skill is built upon skill. The *Law of Exercise* produces drills and exercises in pupil books, workbooks, and supplemental materials. The *Law of Effect* supports the sequence of first learning words and skills and then using them in reading selections; and the *Law of Identical Elements* results in the focus on isolated skills in testing for development of reading ability and for the close match between the items in the exercises and the tests" (p. 98). Thus, from the viewpoint of the science upon which basal programs are based, strict control of teaching and learning and of what counts as "reading" is not only justifiable, but necessary.

But is this science the best that the late twentieth century has to offer? Both the authors of the *Report Card* and the members of NCTE's Commission on Reading would respond with a resounding "No!"

The Newer Science: A Multidisciplinary Consensus

Within the past twenty or so years, a multidisciplinary consensus has developed regarding the nature of learning, the relationship between teaching and learning, the nature of the reading process, and the acquisition of literacy. (Space precludes listing most primary sources, but see such references as the following: Goodman et al., 1988, pp. 137–139; Weaver, 1988; Lindfors, 1987; Raphael and Reynolds, 1986; Smith, 1986; Teale and Sulzby, 1986; Crismore, 1985; Harste et al., 1984; Newman, 1985; Pearson, 1984; Shuy, 1981; and Holdaway, 1979.) Converging research from cognitive psychology and schema theory and language acquisition, from linguistics and psycholinguistics and sociolinguistics, and from reading and emergent literacy leads to conclusions such as the following:

1. From infancy, children actively develop, test, and refine hypotheses about their world. As preschoolers, for example, virtually all children learn to use their native language according to its basic rules, with feedback from the adults with whom they communicate but with almost no direct instruction whatsoever.
2. Reading is a highly complex and active process of meaning-seeking. Readers actively construct meaning as they interact with a text, and the meaning so constructed depends as much upon the prior knowledge and strategies of the reader as upon the words of the text.
3. Texts consisting of only a few simple words repeated in equally simple and stilted sentence patterns are typically less predictable and thus more difficult to read than texts consisting of a greater variety of words that occur in more natural sentence patterns resembling normal speech.
4. Both language and literacy develop best in the context of their use—that is, in situations which are functional and intrinsically motivational for learners. Children develop literacy best in an environment enriched with literature and "littered with literacy."
5. Learning to read is a process that develops over time, but in complex ways—not a skill or a strategy at a time, even when it is taught that way.

Such well-documented observations as these suggest that reading is not best learned when taught as if it involved mastering a sequence of skills and strategies, from simple to increasingly complex. For many and perhaps most of our youth, teaching reading one skill at a time may in fact mitigate against their developing the ability to analyze, evaluate, and extend what they read, or to read well enough to solve everyday problems in adult life (e.g., Venezky et al., 1987, pp. 28, 44–46; Applebee et al., 1987).

Although pupils may well benefit from the modeling and guided practice of certain skills and strategies, particularly strategies for getting meaning and for monitoring comprehension, they nevertheless do not need or necessarily benefit from an elaborate program that teaches isolated skills and strategies lesson-by-lesson, day-by-day, week-by-week, for seven or nine years. There is ample evidence that independent reading does considerably more to develop reading ability than all the workbooks and practice sheets children typically complete in a basal reading program (e.g., Anderson et al., 1985, pp. 75–76).

I shall risk going further than the *Report Card* and admit that I think it questionable whether basal reading systems as a genre can go very far towards meeting this basic objection to teaching reading as a long, drawn-out process of mastering a sequence of skills and strategies. After all, basals are a product of the American economy, in which profit is the bottom line. One way for basal publishers to increase profit is by enlarging their share of the market, but another and perhaps more practical way is to increase the sheer volume of materials in a basal reading program, especially the consumable materials that have to be replaced every year.

This is not to say that the authors and editors of basals are either ignorant of the newer knowledge base, or unscrupulous; typically they are neither, and in fact there is considerable truth to the argument that publishers are only providing the kinds of materials that the market demands. Furthermore, the latest series often do reflect some aspects of the newer understanding in philosophy statements in the teachers' manuals, as well as in certain other aspects of instruction. Nevertheless, it seems clear that it is in the *publishers'* best interests to *increase* the volume of materials for teaching, practicing, and assessing reading skills and strategies, not to decrease them. However, scientific evidence from a convergence of disciplines in the last two decades or more suggests that increasing the use of such materials is certainly *not* in the best interests of *children.*

An Attack on Basal Readers
for the Wrong Reasons

PATRICK GROFF

The *Report Card on Basal Readers* (RC) was prepared by the National Council of Teachers of English's Commission on Reading in response to its obvious dislike of what it calls "the absolute dominance of basal readers" (BRs) in today's reading instruction programs (p. iv). The report admits in its preface that it takes an "advocate's position" against the use of basal readers in our nation's classrooms. The *Report Card* thus gives an early warning that the document is not the report of a neutral-minded study of the effectiveness of BRs. To the contrary, the *Report Card* appears to be the result of comparison by its authors of their peculiar convictions about reading instruction with the methods for this purpose recommended by the BRs.

It is rightly judged by the *Report Card* that these two points of view on the teaching of reading are incompatible. The BR system stands in the way of the implementation of their conceptions about reading teaching, the authors of the RC appear to have concluded. The report was written, then, to persuade teachers, reading experts, or anyone else with influence over how reading is taught in schools, to join in the effort to eliminate basal readers from the schools.

False Charges against Basal Readers

Expectations given readers early on by the RC that it will be a passionate endorsement of certain articles of faith about reading instruction, rather than an open-minded examination of the effectiveness of BRs, are quickly fulfilled by the document. It argues in its first chapter that the "central premise of the basal reader" is that even teachers who are otherwise incompetent will be able to teach all children to read well if they use the basal reader (p. 1). The RC maintains that BRs say that "everything" a child needs to read in order to perfect this skill is found in the readers. So students' and teachers' performances are judged entirely by basal tests, the report concludes.

None of these allegations against the typical basal reader is accurate, however. It would be patiently absurd, of course, for BRs to be so outlandishly boastful about their capabilities and influence. BRs do claim, it is true, that they can teach children at large to read better than can any other system of instruction that is presently available. This presumption is a far cry, however, from what the *Report Card* avers that BRs profess in their own behalf.

Source: From "An Attack on Basal Readers for the Wrong Reasons" by Patrick Groff, in C. B. Smith (Ed.), *Two Reactions to the Report Card on Basal Readers in Print* (No. 1, pp. 8–13). Bloomington, IN: ERIC. Copyright 1989, ERIC/REC (Educational Resources Information Center/Clearinghouse on Reading, English, and Communication) at Indiana University (Bloomington). Reprinted by permission.

The exaggerated charges made against basals by the report in its first chapter are useful warnings for critical readers of this document, nonetheless, since they alert the critic in yet another way that the RC was conceived and written as a piece of special pleading for a peculiar opinion of how reading ability should be developed. The overstatements made about BRs in chapter one of the report thus caution anyone to read the document with his or her guard up.

The Central Issue about the RC

The RC is correct, nonetheless, in protesting the BR's claim that everything it presents in its various books and manuals is there "for scientific reasons" (p. 1). There is other reasonable doubt, which I share, that "findings from research have not been the most compelling force behind changes that have occurred in basal reader programs" (Durkin, 1987, p. 335). Implicit in the report's statement that BRs "have not reflected the best and most up-to-date knowledge of science" (p. 31), is the claim that everything in the reading instruction program it favors is based on a preponderance of scientific evidence, however.

A more pertinent and manageable question is: Given the likelihood that basal readers can and should be improved, are their shortcomings less or more significant than are those found in the reading program, the *Report Card* advocates? This question will become the crux of my critique of the report. The vital issue for any critical reader of the RC thus is: Is it more or less likely that the reading program that it proposes will bring on greater achievement in reading for children than can the typical basal system?

Why the RC Objects to Basal Readers

Before moving to a direct confrontation of this issue, however, it seems proper first to comment on the major reasons, other than the supposed ineffectiveness of BRs, why the RC denounces their use. The report dislikes how the ethos of business, science, and psychology of the day is reflected in the manner in which the BR is written, how in effect the basals try to maintain scientific management in the teaching of reading. As to the effectiveness of this relationship, the RC admits that "basal reading materials met the expectations of a public and profession enthralled with business, science, and psychology as they tried to find a remedy for the apparent crisis in reading instruction" (p. 19). Nonetheless, the RC castigates even the fine-turning of basal programs over the years that has been done in accordance with changes in the ethos of business, science, and psychology.

On the other hand, the continuous reformations in the content of basals have much impressed teachers—so much so, that in popularity referendums teachers are found to approve wholeheartedly of the series' self-proclaimed values (Shannon, 1983). It is clear, then, that most of today's teachers simply do not believe the senior author of the RC's contention that the use of basals results in "detrimental effects on students' desire and ability to read" (p. 24). Whether teachers truly should have such faith in the RC plan will be discussed in due course.

The RC strenuously disapproves of this kind of teaching, however. It goes so far as to concur with Smith (1973) that one of the easy ways to make learning to read hard is to ensure that phonics skills are learned and used by children. But not so, say the many reviews of the experimental research on the value of phonics teaching. In my identification of 120 such reviews, I found they all agree that the acquisition of phonics skills by learners makes a vital contribution to their reading development (Groff, 1987). "The research is clear," says the recent *Handbook on Reading Research,* "if you want to improve word-identification ability, teach phonics" (Johnson and Baumann, 1984, p. 595). A key factor found commonly in schools with extraordinarily successful reading programs is that they all teach phonics "to a much greater degree than most" (Weber, 1983, p. 545).

Neither does the *Report Card's* proposition that children cannot be "active learners" of reading if they carry out assignments overtly directed by their teachers (p. 126) have significant corroboration from the experimental research. Typically the empirical findings about teaching support Berliner and Rosenshine's (1977, p. 393) conclusion that "the classroom behavior of the successful teacher is characterized by direct instruction, whereby students are brought into contact with the curriculum materials and are kept in contact with them until the requisite knowledge is acquired." An acceptance of the RC's notion that children learn only under their own initiatives thus cannot be a necessary condition of professionalism in teaching.

It is not altogether clear from the RC how teachers who become liberated from the BRs might express their newly acquired authority. Apparently, teachers with freshly gained dominion over reading programs firmly in hand would not be expected to do any direct instruction, teach any given set of reading skills or vocabulary, provide any individual pupil practice materials like worksheets, follow any common methodology or procedures from class to class, externally control to any significant extent the strategies children have found it useful to become consciously aware of when learning to read (metacognition), or regularly test children using normative measures. If children are given "the opportunity to learn for themselves" (p. 130), they would have teachers who "respond to what the child is trying to do" (p. 129), by encouraging him or her "to take risks in reading," that is, to guess at the identity of words by using context cues (p. 130).

The Unsoundness of Context Cues

It may be, however, that the most potentially hazardous item in the list of practices that research has failed to corroborate is maintaining children at the guessing-at-words or context cue stage of word recognition. The RC makes clear its approval of the idea that "it makes sense to have children behaving like skilled readers to the fullest extent possible from the beginning" (p. 130). With this belief in focus, it is puzzling, then, why the RC persists in its denunciations of the BR's view "that learning to read is, more than anything else, learning words and skills for identifying words" (p. 66) rather than learning to use context cues.

I have surveyed the research on the facilitating effect of context cues on word recognition and comprehension (Groff and Seymour, 1987). The research findings on these topics suggest that it remains an open question (at the very best) whether context has any effect

Having failed to document that there is any widespread lack of confidence an
teachers as to the relative effectiveness of BRs versus the RC plan for teaching reading
report maintains, nonetheless, that the favorable judgments of basals by teachers are
result of teachers' general unawareness that in so doing they are acting unprofessionall
teachers became professional-minded, the RC bluntly contends, they would reject the
of BRs. The RC argues, then, that teachers who accept its heterodoxical point of view ab
reading instruction are professionals. Those who do otherwise, are not. It must be noted t
this remarkable denunciation of teachers who disagree with it is made by the RC befor
presents any evidence that the plan its authors recommend for teaching is actually super
to that which the BRs offer. This RC criticism of teachers also overlooks the evidence tl
in fact they may not be slavish adherents of basals (Durkin, 1984; Russavage et al., 198.

It is reasonable at this point to refer to descriptions of highly successful reading pr
grams to determine if the teachers involved in them are professional by the RC standard
It is clear that even the most eminently accomplished reading teachers in such program
(Hoffman and Rutherford, 1984) do not meet the criteria set by the RC for professionalism
Hoffman and Rutherford analyzed reports on eight reading programs that had attained rel
atively high pupil achievement to identify the key elements of teacher practices, instruc
tional programming, and school environment that they had in common. The teachers in
these outstanding reading programs did not conform to several of the recommendatior
made for instruction by the RC. Who is truly out of step in this regard, then, America's o
standing teachers or the authors of the RC? The RC cannot say it respects these teache
"exercise of professional judgment" (p. 153), and at the same time accuse them of unj
fessional practices because their teaching does not confirm the RC proposal for rea
instruction. This would be a grossly inconsistent judgment.

BRs and Teacher Effectiveness

The first part of the *Report Card* proposes, then, what it assumes is a logical syl
about teacher effectiveness. This deduction goes like this: a) BRs persuade instruc
teach reading in a relatively ineffectual manner; b) teachers internalize the seducti
oric about the capacities of BRs; and c) teachers then use and defend an inferior i
reading instruction. In this supposedly wrongful instruction, speech sounds, lett
words are isolated. Children are taught to recognize words out of context. The F
mently opposes such "fracturing and narrowing" of the language (p. 82).

Is such teaching at odds with the research findings, as the RC insists? It ap
Reviews of the research (e.g., Chall, 1967 and 1983; Johnson and Baumann, 198
son et al., 1985; Perfetti, 1985; Groff, 1987) suggest that reading programs that te
fashion—and which teach a controlled, carefully sequenced, hierarchical order o
words—produce the greatest amount of reading achievement that is possible
practice with words is carried on in such programs to the point of overlearn
pupils learn to decode words effortlessly and accurately (automatically). Teac
superior reading programs expect that pupils' learning will be a direct result o
ing, and they are not disappointed.

on mature reading behavior. Henderson (1982, p. 345) believes the research reveals that "there are good grounds for disputing whether any facilitatory effect of sentence context obtains if the task closely resembles normal reading." Studies show that there is no greater difference between good and poor readers' abilities to recognize words in sentence contexts than in isolation. By the time they are third graders, children do not make significantly fewer errors when reading words in contexts than as isolated items. Eye movement studies indicate that good readers normally fixate their eyes on three or four words per second. When individual words can be recognized so automatically, it is unlikely that the able reader needs to spend time guessing at their identity in context.

Teaching children to continue to use context cues runs the risk of maintaining young readers at this crude level of word recognition and thus of hindering their overall reading growth. As Gough (1981, p. 95) correctly depicts the issue: "Goodman [senior author of the RC] is dead wrong about what separates the skilled adult from the beginning reader, and hence what must be accomplished in reading acquisition. The most conspicuous difference between good and poor readers is found in the swift and accurate recognition of individual words, in decoding, and the mastery of this skill is at the heart of reading acquisition." The research, as Gough notes, devastates a main plank of the RC reading program—that it is vital to teach numerous context cues to children learning to read. With this main section of its proposed methodology reduced to shambles, the RC's goal of settling "what is good or bad for learners" (p. v) is notably frustrated.

Summary

The *Report Card on Basal Readers* is a legitimate document in the sense that its main purpose is to create dissatisfactions on the part of teachers toward the methods of instruction they commonly use. That is, it would be foolhardy to argue that BRs now teach reading totally in accordance with what the empirical research says about this instruction. Moreover, there doubtless never will be a point in time when teachers will be able to say with confidence that a faultless or irreproachable stage in the evolution toward perfection in instruction has been reached.

Large numbers of reading professionals have devoted their efforts over the years to promoting reading reform under the assumption that the state of the art in reading instruction can be steadily improved. Change and progress in the manner in which reading instruction is customarily given, including teacher dissatisfaction with it, thus should be nourished, not suppressed. One cannot find fault, therefore, with the apparent basic motives of the authors of the RC. It should be conceded that their goal in producing this document was to improve the manner in which reading is taught in school and, through this means, reduce the degree of illiteracy in the nation. Nonetheless, as noted in the body of this discussion, serious questions can be raised about the recommendations the RC makes for teaching reading, inquiries that go beyond the fundamental objectives of its authors in writing the book.

As is admitted by its authors, the RC was conceived and written as a means of popularizing the particular approach to reading instruction that was favored, at the time of the publication of the RC, by the Commission on Reading of the National Council of Teachers of English. The analysis I have made of the contents of the RC reveals, however, that the radical plan for teaching reading that the RC advocates has basic shortcomings. By attempting to defend a predetermined point of view about reading instruction, rather than to examine, in a disinterested way, both sides of the debate over this teaching that continues to boil over, the authors of the RC also show more commitment to ideology than to the scientific method.

The prime fault of the special pleading for a particular approach to the teaching of reading found in the RC is that the document fails to provide any convincing evidence that an implementation of the RC plan for reading development will result in greater reading achievement for children than is possible with BR systems. From most accounts of research (Chall, 1967 and 1983; Johnson and Baumann, 1984; Anderson et al., 1985; Perfetti, 1985; Groff, 1987), it can be inferred that a use of the RC approach in fact would eventuate in less reading development for children than is attainable with BRs.

This is not to say that the RC has not accurately exposed some essential weaknesses of the BR system. It is true, for example, that the basal readers' claim that they scrupulously follow the research evidence when these books are written is not altogether accurate. It is also correct to charge, as the RC does, that BRs spend too much time on activities other than having children read independently. One can find basal lessons and tests that do not accomplish all their teachers' manuals claim they do. BRs do exemplify the difficulty of creating stories with high literary quality that are easy enough for beginners to read.

I recently examined how phonics is taught in grades 1 and 2 in five leading BRs. I found that pupils who used these books would not be fully prepared to decode about 60 percent of the new words presented in BR lessons (Groff, 1988). The BRs thus are also guilty of not teaching phonics intensively enough, and of using the analytic, implicit approach to word recognition which teaches about sight words and context cues. BRs present a less than desirable sequence of phonics skills, a discredited syllabication procedure, and too little practice on vowel phoneme-grapheme correspondences. They also tend to ignore the evidence that multisyllabic words are significantly more difficult to recognize than are monosyllabic ones. It was striking to realize that the errors the BRs make in teaching doubtless cause some unfortunate side effects. With BRs, children's acquisition of automatic decoding skills are delayed. Their ability, in turn, to read independently from a wide variety of sources is handicapped.

By its own admission, the RC thinks few of these faults of the BR have any consequential importance. It holds that any straightforward kind of phonics instruction will handicap the attainment by children of independent reading skills, and thus that "exercises designed to teach phonics and vocabulary directly are likely to be unnecessary and even counterproductive" (Goodman, NCTE, 1986, p. 359). The loyalty of the authors of the RC to such immoderate and unreasonable views of reading development drastically reduces the chances that the type of reading instruction it espouses will find widespread acceptance by reading teachers. In the final analysis, therefore, the RC tends to be self-defeating. It frequently battles against the BRs for wrong reasons, and thus blunts the thrust of the accurate exposé it makes of many of their shortcomings.

Integrating Sources

1. Contrast Groff's quote from Berliner and Rosenshine with Weaver's statement about independent reading. Are these statements really at odds?

2. Reexamine the five conclusions Weaver reaches from research. Does she deal with Groff's concern about the role of context?

3. Both Weaver and the NCTE Call for Action deal in some detail with the issue of the control basals exercise. Contrast Groff's view of this issue.

Classroom Implications

1. In what ways have these sources changed or reinforced your own views on reading instruction?

2. Can you suggest ways that basals might be modified to appeal to both Groff and Weaver, or at least to take a step in that direction?

3. What experiences have you had with basal instruction that tends to confirm or refute points made by Weaver, Groff, or the NCTE Call for Action?

Annotated Bibliography

Duffy, A. M. (1997). *Using children's literature in the literacy classroom: Research from the National Reading Research Center*. Athens, GA: National Reading Research Center.

This report details various classrooms which use a variety of instructional practices including both a literature-based as well as a basal reader approach.

Gardner, J. (1997). New fashioned book burning. *English Journal, 86,* 63–64.

This article reports on the results of a classroom experimental lesson in book burning. The purpose and justification for this lesson are explained in relationship to censorship.

McMahon, S. I., & Raphael, T. (Eds.). (1997). *The book club connection*. Newark, DE: International Reading Association.

This book of collected papers discusses the role of the book club concept as an important avenue for the encouragement of wide reading in various types of literature. The contents include both the theoretical as well as practical classroom applications of the book club format. There is also an extensive bibliography included in this volume.

Payne, B., & Manning, B. H. (1997). Basal reader instruction: Effects of comprehension monitoring training on reading comprehension, strategy use, and attitude. *Reading Research and Instruction, 32,* 29–38.

This report of research reports the effectiveness of metacognition instruction as an aid to comprehension, strategy use, and reader's attitude. The results of this work indicate that students can effectively be taught to use metacognition in their classroom reading, especially through the use of the basal reader.

Robinson, L. S. (1997). The development of basal reader teacher's manuals. *Reading Horizons, 32,* 209–224.

This article reports on the historical development of the teacher's manuals, which are an important part of most basal reading series. Concludes that while no manual is intended to replace the professional judgement of the teacher, they still can be a valuable asset to the effective classroom reading program.

Short, K. G. (Ed.). (1995). *Research & professional resources in children's literature: Piecing a patchwork quilt*. Newark, DE: International Reading Association.

This annotated bibliography of resources related to literature materials is a very useful volume for the classroom teacher. Sections include thematic units, a literature-based curriculum, and reader response research and practice. There is also a very complete annotated listing of professional literature related to professional resources in children's literacy materials.

Thelen, J. N. (1995). A new look at the journey from basal to whole language. *Teaching PreK–8, 26,* 86–87.

This article reports on the pros and cons of whole language, basal readers, and literature-based reading instruction. It compares and contrasts these language philosophies, especially in terms of the use of literacy materials.

You Become Involved

1. Contrast one of the current manuals of a basal series with an older version from the same publisher. What kinds of changes have been made? Do you detect trends that may be present across time? If so, list them.

2. Is it possible for a basal series to meet the objections of critics? Try your hand at outlining the characteristics a series would need to have in order to satisfy the objections you have read about in this chapter. Which, if any, of those characteristics would be so alien to the philosophy of basals that they might be impossible to implement within a series?

6

SPELLING

To divide syllables into a word [is] called spelling.
—*WILLIAM BULLOCK (1580)*

The reading ability required in spelling is the
ability to recognize words in isolation without
any contextual aid whatsoever; many of the
words are undoubtedly unknown to the child.
—*GUY AND EVA BOND (1943)*

We know that children's spelling is an extension of their overall
language development and follows a natural progression from
nonstandard [invented spelling] to conventional spelling.
—*JOAN P. GIPE (1998)*

The teaching of spelling has in recent years become one of the "hot buttons" in literacy education. Parents, as well as many teachers, have increasingly become alarmed at the apparent larger numbers of students who are having great difficulty in spelling correctly. Perhaps the only commonality in this debate is the universal belief that the ability to spell correctly is a fundamental attribute of literate people and thus must be taught in an effective and useful manner to all students.

Tradition suggests that the best way to teach spelling was to introduce a carefully controlled curriculum of words on a regular basis. Word lists were most often taken from spelling textbooks which arranged or clustered spelling words, often according to some common characteristic such as letter arrangement (e.g., words beginning with the *ph* sound at the beginning, compound words, etc.).

Each of these words were to be learned to the point of mastery, primarily through memorization. Historically, teachers seldomly tended to deviate from these prescribed lists, other than to infrequently add specific words of particular student interest or need. Spelling was considered a separate subject from the other language arts and thus, little integration was done with the various subject matter areas in terms of the selection of appropriate words to include on student's spelling lists.

In recent years, a number of these traditionally-followed ideas and practices have been challenged by new thinking and approaches to spelling instruction. For instance, in many language classrooms the use of a predetermined set of spelling words, such as that based on a spelling textbook, has been exchanged for those groupings of words students have encountered in either their individual reading or personal writing experiences. The emphasis on mastery of a selected number of words as being the mark of excellence in spelling has also become a topic of debate. While there is no question among educators as to the importance of being able to use spelling in an effective manner, how this goal is reached is certainly open to serious debate today.

Invented versus Formal Spelling

There is probably no more contentious issue today in spelling education than that which is commonly called by educators, "developmental, temporary, constructed, or invented spelling." In this approach to spelling instruction, students are encouraged on initial writing drafts to simply spell words as they think they sound phonetically without undo effort at having each word spelled correctly. Revision and editing of these first drafts are encouraged so that with each new writing sample misspelled words are identified and corrected. Children's efforts at invented spelling have been carefully studied (Bissex, 1980; Graves, 1983; Invernizzi et al., 1997; Read, 1971, 1975; Templeton, 1992) and tend to progress through a series of identifiable stages from little knowledge of the written alphabet and letter-sound correspondences through the formal standardized spelling of words. Teachers who advocate invented spelling believe their students are encouraged to become more fluent writers without the burden of correctness in their initial spelling efforts. Other educators seriously disagree with the use of invented spelling, saying that all this philosophy of spelling has done is to encourage a generation of students who have little knowledge or willingness to spell correctly, at even the most elementary levels.

Embedded versus Leveled Approaches

Traditional approaches to spelling instruction are most frequently based on the careful selection of a small number of words that are taught until students are able to spell each correctly. Teachers who follow this paradigm believe that until a selected group of words are mastered, it is unproductive to proceed on to the study of additional words.

For many teachers, the opportunity to use spelling in the natural context of the reading/writing process seems to make the most sense. Called *embedded* or *contextualized* spelling, students learn to spell as they find a need to use specific words. Thus, rather than a prescribed list of words which all of the members of a class must learn to a mastery level, spelling becomes a much more personalized experience with language. Often the words selected are related to the integration of the curriculum, especially as this process relates to content reading.

As might be expected, there is a body of research which supports all of these various approaches to the teaching of spelling. Advocates of any one position argue for their view of spelling and decry others as being less than effective. We have tried in the following readings to present the various opinions on the very volatile issue. In the final analysis, it will be you, the classroom teacher, who must decide on how you develop, plan, and teach spelling to your students.

As You Read

The selections that follow develop the above issues in detail. Miller (1996) notes how the use and misuse of invented spelling has given opponents ammunition to criticize this view of spelling. He asks some compelling questions as to why misconceptions of invented spelling have developed and what might be done to correct the situation.

Invernizzi, Abouzeid, and Bloodgood's article (1997) presents an overview of classroom word study, especially as it includes spelling, grammar, and meaning. Consider the following questions before you read:

1. Why has invented spelling been criticized?
2. How do literacy researchers suggest that spelling be taught?
3. When should children spell correctly?

References

Bissex, G. (1980). *GNYS AT WRK: A child learns to read and write.* Cambridge, MA: Harvard University Press.

Bond, G. L., & Bond, E. (1943). *Developmental reading in high school.* New York: Macmillan.

Bullock, W. (1580). *Booke at large, for the amendment of orthographie for English speech.* Oxford: Christ Church.

Gipe, J. A. (1998). *Multiple paths to literacy.* Upper Saddle River, NJ: Prentice-Hall.

Graves, D. H. (1983). *Writing: Teachers and children at work.* Portsmouth, NH: Heinemann.

Invernizzi, M. A., Abouzeid, M. P., & Gill, J. T. (1997). Using students' invented spelling as a guide for spelling instruction that emphasizes word study. *The Elementary School Journal, 95,* 155–167.

Miller, E. (1996). The case of invented spelling: How theory becomes target practice. *The Harvard Education Letter, 12,* (March/April), 5–7.

Read, C. (1971). Pre-school children's knowledge of English phonology. *Harvard Educational Review, 41,* 1–34.

Read, C. (1975). *Children's categorization of speech sounds in English.* Urbana, IL: National Council of Teachers of English.

Templeton, S. (1992). Old story, new resolution: Sound and meaning in spelling. *Language Arts, 69,* 454–463.

The Case of Invented Spelling

How Theory Becomes Target Practice

EDWARD MILLER

Of all the developments in reading research during the past 30 years, few have provided as much fodder for the wars over whole language a "invented spelling." Starting in the late 1960s and early 1970s, Charles Read and other researchers noticed that young children's writings revealed important information about how they make sense of spoken language and construct strategies to represent what they hear (see "Teaching Spelling," *HEL,* November 1985). Linguists like Carol Chomsky pointed out that early writing, with alphabet blocks and similar materials, was a powerful way to encourage reading.

"Children ought to learn how to read by creating their own spellings for familiar words as a beginning," Chomsky wrote in 1971 in *Childhood Education.* "What better way to *read* for the first time than to try to recognize the very word you have just carefully built up on the table in front of you?"

Chomsky emphasized the importance of "being attuned to the child's pronunciation" and not inhibiting preschoolers' first attempts to write by insisting on proper spelling. She told the story of three-year-old Harry, who had learned how to spell his name, which he pronounced "Hawwy." When he tried to write the word *wet* he chose the initial letter *r.*

"Now *r* is correct for him, as a matter of fact," wrote Chomsky. "In this child's pronunciation, *r* and *w* are alike when initial in the syllable. For him *wet* begins the same as the second syllable of his name."

She continued: "Had I said 'No!' when Harry chose the *r* and insisted on *w* (which corresponds to no reality for him), he would have gotten that sad message children so often get in school: 'Your judgments are not to be trusted. Do it my way whether it makes sense or not; forget about reality.' Far better to let him trust his own accurate judgments and progress according to them than to impose an arbitrariness that at this point would only interfere."

Research on invented spelling led to a developmental theory of how children experiment with phonemic rules and patterns, and scholars urged teachers to allow children to spell inventively in the earliest stages of learning. This view fit neatly with the emerging philosophy of whole language, which emphasized early writing and eschewed the repetitive drills and workbook exercises of strict phonics instruction.

Gone Haywire

To the critics of whole language and other "child-centered" learning theories, the very idea of "invented spelling" is ridiculous. The notion that teachers should ignore spelling errors—or actually encourage children to spell words wrong—confirms their view that the

Source: From "The Case of Invented Spelling: How Theory Becomes Target Practice" by Edward Miller, 1996, *The Harvard Educational Letter, 12,* pp. 5–7. Reprinted by permission.

liberal education establishment has abandoned traditional values and gone completely hay-wire. The most vocal critics pounce on invented spelling as a source of horror stories that illustrate just how mindless American education has become.

Charles Sykes relates one such story at the beginning of a chapter called "The New Illiteracy" in his 1995 book, *Dumbing Down Our Kids,* which received admiring reviews in the *Wall Street Journal,* the *New York Times,* and *USA Today:* "Mrs. Wittig couldn't fathom why her child's teacher would write 'Wow!' and award a check-plus (for above average work) to a paper that read: 'I'm goin to has majik skates. Im goin to go to disenelan. Im goin to bin my mom and dad and brusr and sisd. We r go to se mickey mouse.'"

Sykes explains that "many educationists [his term for trendy, liberal educators] in charge of teaching reading and writing no longer believe that it is necessary to teach or to correct spelling. Educationists noticed that many children misspelled words and realized that it would take a great deal of time, effort, and commitment to fix the problem. Instead, they discovered 'invented spelling.' Children weren't getting the words wrong, they were acting as 'independent spellers,' and any attempt to correct them would not only stifle their freedom, but smother their tender young creativity aborning. Such ideas have been widely seized upon by educationists who see the natural, unconscious, and effortless approach to spelling not only as progressive and child-centered, but a lot less work as well."

Advocates of whole language, Sykes continues, "believe that children learn 'naturally,' that children learn best when 'learning is kept whole, meaningful, interesting and functional,' and that this is more likely to happen when children make their own choices as part of a 'community of learners' in a noncompetitive environment. 'Whole language' advocates describe 'optimal literacy environments,' which they say 'promote risk taking and trust.'"

Sykes doesn't bother to explain the actual origins of "educationist" ideas about invented spelling in developmental psychology and linguistics. But he adroitly skewers the whole-language movement by making fun of its warm and fuzzy jargon while suggesting that the real reason why this philosophy has become so popular is that teachers are lazy.

Missing the Point

One-sided as Sykes's attack is, it is not entirely off-base. Some teachers have adopted practices associated with invented spelling inappropriate ways. Read, Chomsky, and other researchers wrote about the value of invented spelling in the context of very young children's first attempts to write and read. They encouraged teachers to pay attention to the systematic thinking revealed by kids' inventive spelling (rather than to see only errors to be corrected) and to use these insights to guide their teaching strategies. They never expected invented spelling to become a classroom activity in and of itself or to replace the organized teaching of proper spelling in elementary school.

Yet that is just what has happened in many classrooms. Marcia Invernizzi of the University of Virginia and colleagues argue that Read's findings have been misapplied. They say that his fundamental insight, "that invented spellings provide a direct clue to a child's current understanding of how written words work, and that direct instruction in spelling can be timed and targeted to this understanding, has, for the most part, been missed."

The theory of developmental word knowledge traces children's understanding across three overlapping levels of English spelling: sound, pattern, and meaning. In the first stage, children perceive the direct one-to-one correspondence between letters and sounds. At the second tier, they realize that the system is more complicated and begin to recognize letter combinations and patterns that have an indirect relation to sound—that a silent *e,* for example, can affect the pronunciation of the vowel preceding it. At the third level, they begin to observe the connections between spelling and meaning, as in polysyllabic Latin- and Greek-derived words. Thus, the second syllable in *competition* is spelled with an *e,* not because of its sound but because it is related to the word *compete.*

Invernizzi and her colleagues outline a system of organized spelling instruction that is guided by teachers' analysis of their students' invented spelling and their levels of development. They give examples such as the following writing sample from Tasha, a sixth-grader:

> If I could be the managor of the cafeteria at Linkhorne Middle School, I would make some awsome changes. The instalation of a sound system would by my first decesion. The kids could rotate bringing there own choice of musick. Then I would make radacle changes in the menu like we'd have hamburger and fries and no rootine school menues.

The researchers note that Tasha has a free-flowing style and uses polysyllabic words. They write that "the teacher needs to be able to see Tasha's spellings not as errors but as inventions that signal the next move toward correctness that Tasha needs to make." Tasha is poised, they argue, to enter the "meaning" tier in her word knowledge, but her spelling inventions "revolve around the pattern principle of the tier before."

The insights gained from such research are valuable, and many teachers will agree that it is important to recognize the spirit in Tasha's writing rather than to focus only on its flaws. It would be absurd to accuse Invernizzi of believing that it is not necessary to teach spelling. But we also see trouble brewing here: to say that Tasha's misspellings are "not errors" is to guarantee that some sixth-grade parents will panic. Thus the reasonable investigations of researchers become the inflammatory rhetoric of exposés and talk radio.

The Real Question

Even some teacher-friendly publications have obscured rather than illuminated the invented-spelling feud. *NEA Today* published a "debate" between two third-grade teachers on opposite sides of the issue. But the headline—"Can Kids 'Lrn tu Spel' by Misspelling?"—reveals a fundamental misconception about the role of invented spelling. Of course kids can't learn to spell by misspelling. The real question is, "Can teachers learn to teach better by seeing misspellings in a different way?" The defender of invented spelling in this debate, unfortunately, did nothing to clarify the point.

Advocates of whole language have been bludgeoned with the club of invented spelling abuses, but many experts who are convinced of the value of invented spelling actually favor a balanced approach to the teaching of reading that combines whole-language and direct phonics instruction.... "The process of invented spelling is essentially a process of phonics," writes Marilyn Jager Adams in her landmark study, *Beginning to Read.* "The evidence that invented spelling activity simultaneously develops phonemic awareness and promotes understanding of the alphabetic principle is extremely promising, especially in view of the difficulty with which children are found to acquire these insights through other methods of teaching."

Teachers need to be aware of the nuances of research in invented spelling and the larger controversies they relate to. Methods for teaching reading and writing are not all-or-nothing propositions: encouraging young children's experiments with language is not inconsistent with direct instruction in phonics or with a teacher's commitment to the importance of correct spelling.

For Further Information

M. J. Adams. *Beginning to Read: Thinking and Learning About Print.* Cambridge, MA: MIT Press, 1990.

M. Invernizzi, M. Abouzeid, and J. T. Gill. "Using Students' Invented Spellings as a Guide for Spelling Instruction That Emphasizes Word Study." *Elementary School Journal* 95, no. 2 (November 1994): 155–167.

L. Kelly and E. Sheridan-Regan. "Can Kids 'Lrn tu Spel' by Misspelling?" *NEA Today* 12, no. 4 (November 1993): 39.

C. Sykes. *Dumbing Down Our Kids: Why American Children Feel Good About Themselves But Can't Read, Write, or Add.* New York: St. Martin's Press, 1995.

Integrated Word Study

Spelling, Grammar, and Meaning in the Language Arts Classroom

MARCIA A. INVERNIZZI   JANET W. BLOODGOOD

MARY P. ABOUZEID

Much has been written about the importance of phonemic awareness in the early stages of literacy acquisition (see Adams, 1990; Beck & Juel, 1995). Certainly the weight of evidence underscores the importance of knowing how the alphabetic system represents language segments smaller than the word when learning to read. But is language awareness important beyond the beginning-to-read stages? Is there any value in learning how written language represents other aspects of language, such as grammar and meaning, through its orthography? For those students who have mastered phonics and sound-symbol relationships, how can orthographic awareness be used to further develop their reading and writing abilities?

Teaching students how spelling represents meaning and parts of speech strengthens language arts instruction in the upper elementary grades by helping students learn about and reflect on language use. This article explores the relationships of spelling to word meaning and grammar and how *word study* techniques enhance student understanding of these relationships. The techniques described provide a theoretical framework for the coordination of spelling, vocabulary, and grammar instruction through a range of reading and writing activities in a literature-based, integrated language arts program. The word study initiatives described in this article are still under development, but the techniques are currently being used for classroom instruction in several central Virginia schools.

What Is Word Study?

Word study involves students grouping words into categories of similarity and difference (Abouzeid, Invernizzi, Bear, & Ganske, 1995; Bear, Invernizzi, & Templeton, 1996; Morris, 1982). Students categorize words according to spelling, meaning, and use patterns in order to better understand how spelling represents a word's meaning and grammatical function. The content of word study at any particular grade is based on research in developmental spelling (Henderson, 1990; Templeton & Bear, 1992) that shows that children acquire specific features of words in a hierarchical order— from basic letter-to-sound correspondences, to patterns associated with long and short vowel sounds, to structures within words associated with syllables and affixation, and finally, to Greek and Latin roots and stems that appear in derivational families.

Central to word study is differentiating based on students' demonstrated levels of orthographic awareness (Bloodgood, 1991; Invernizzi, Abouzeid, & Gill, 1994). The word study activities discussed in this article are for students well beyond the beginning stages of reading and who are able to read independently, silently, and from books of considerable length. The students demonstrate consistent control of simple grapheme-phoneme correspondences in their writing; consonants, blends, digraphs, vowels, and high-frequency spelling patterns are all spelled correctly. For these students, also referred to as a Syllable Juncture students (Henderson, 1990; Henderson & Templeton, 1988; Schlagal, 1992), writing errors occur in unaccented final syllables (e.g., *circel* for *circle, nickle* for *nickel*) and syllable structures preserved through consonant doubling and *e*-drop (e.g., *stoping* for *stopping, gazzing* for *gazing*). Syllable Juncture students build awareness of spelling-meaning and spelling-grammar connections through the study of homophones of more than one syllable, homographs, and the role of unaccented syllables in signaling parts of speech.

Homophones are one example of how spelling patterns indicate differences in meaning, although sound does not change. Spelling-meaning connections are explicit in upper level word study of this kind. Note the distinctions in meaning in the following words, categorized by spelling pattern:

pail	pale	there	their
tail	tale	where	wear
mail	male	here	hear
sail	sale		

Word sorts and games that call attention to these homophones allow students to internalize spelling-meaning connections and to develop mnemonics for difficult words like *there* and *where*.

Homographs illustrate how syllable stress signals different grammatical roles. The following categories show how two different parts of speech are represented by syllable stress. The categories highlight a common relationship between syllable stress and word function for many homographs.

Stress in First Syllable	*Stress in Second Syllable*
subject (noun, adjective)	subject (verb)
conduct (noun, adjective)	conduct (verb)
rebel (noun, adjective)	rebel (verb)
console (noun, adjective)	console (verb)

After studying the connections reflected in spelling patterns and syllable stress, students embark on a combination of the two. Two-syllable homophones (e.g., *effect, affect; alter, altar*) provide interesting words for vocabulary and grammar study. For example, *alter* and *altar* differ in the spelling of the unaccented final syllables. As we will see later, unaccented final syllables provide a rich source of semantic and syntactic information; they signal parts of speech.

Word Study in an Integrated Language Arts Unit

The integration of social studies with language arts in the upper elementary grades is a common way to make history real and put students inside the heads and hearts of other generations. The Civil War, for example, may be studied by reading and discussing trade books along with traditional social studies texts. Children's literature about the war, including picturebooks and fiction and nonfiction chapter books, is available at many different reading levels. These books are read for both their literary value and historical content. Within a literature-based unit on the Civil War, words from such texts can be analyzed for their contributions to the author's craft as well as for their form and function. Word study techniques can enhance student understanding of the Civil War and of language arts. For example, since unaccented final syllables provide information about a word's grammatical function and meaning, teachers might scan the available texts for words ending in *-er, -ar,* and *-or,* making this spelling feature part of the study of the Civil War.

Concepts Sorts

The following /er/ words were taken from a variety of fiction and nonfiction trade books related to the Civil War in addition to a fifth-grade social studies text (Versteeg & Skinner, 1991). They are sorted by meaning, an activity commonly referred to as a *concept sort* (Gillet & Kita, 1980).

commander	traitor	tormentor	honor
officer	deserter	captor	favor
drummer	prisoner	victor	anger
soldier		marauder	horror
major		liberator	clamor
gunner			

Word-conscious teachers might play "Guess My Category" as a prereading vocabulary exercise, asking such questions as:

What do *commander, officer, drummer,* and so on have in common?

How are they related to military characters we have discussed?

How are a *traitor* and a *deserter* alike?

Are all deserters traitors?

How do the words *traitor* and *deserter* apply to Say Curtis in *Pink and Say* (Polacco, 1994) or Charley Skedaddle in *Charley Skedaddle* (Beatty, 1987)?

Why are *tormentor, captor,* and *victor* grouped together?

How are they different from the first category?

What about *honor, favor,* and *anger?*

Are these words you would place in another category?

What do all these classifications have to do with what we've learned so far about the Civil War?

After discussing words in this manner, students write the words in their notebooks as a beginning place and add to the lists as they read.

Spelling-Meaning Connections

After sorting a list of words by meaning, the same words can be reorganized into categories that reflect spelling patterns. Words that are spelled with *-ar* are added for additional contrast.

-er	*-or*	*-ar*
commander	major	cellar
officer	captor	peculiar
anger	victor	spectacular
soldier	honor	
deserter	favor	
prisoner	clamor	

This activity allows students to group words by the pattern of the unaccented final syllable. In so doing, they come to realize that *-er* is the most common spelling of /er/ and that *-ar* endings frequently indicate descriptive adjectives.

Spelling-Grammar Connections

As children scan the pages of their texts to find other words ending in *-er*, *-ar*, and *-or*, they might find additional classifications by parts of speech:

older	water	regular	color
taller	river	peculiar	honor
bolder	saber	spectacular	favor
longer	corner	particular	horror
bigger	paper		terror
sooner	silver		clamor
thinner			
smaller			

Other spelling-grammar connections become apparent. Comparative adjectives as well as many concrete nouns end in *-er;* while abstract nouns end in *-or.*

A final sort of nouns ending with /er/ gives students a glimpse of word origins and their connections to spelling. Nouns of agency (e.g., *teacher, farmer, actor, conductor*) usually have *-er* or *-or* endings. Those with more common Anglo-Saxon roots end in *-er,* while words with Latin origins end in *-or*. *Scholar* is an interesting exception that could be grouped with other *-ar* nouns (e.g., *collar, pillar*) and discussed.

Reading, Writing, Word Study, and Literary Analysis

Studying words of more than one syllable also offers opportunities to build awareness of how language is used in narrative writing. For example, many books about the Civil War use dialect in character dialogue. Dialect speech is often difficult for students to read and understand. As an extension of the word study described above, a look at words written in dialect helps students understand these words and how to decode them. Frequently, dialect speech collapses unaccented syllables into shorter pronunciations. Word like *figgerin'* for *figuring* and *tol'able* for *tolerable* (Hunt, 1964), challenge students to read alternate spellings of words they may already know.

Adding an /er/ dialect column to the *-er, -ar, -or* sort provides a structure for alerting students to alternate forms of English. Spelling gets more complicated when word forms change, such as *furriners* for *foreigners, 'tater* for *potato, purtier* for *prettier,* giving students a task akin to translation. Dialect study provides an opportunity to discuss the meaning element of English words, that is, the root of a word as a constant in understanding meaning.

Old-fashioned expressions, or words not commonly used today, like *stoked, cleaved, I allow,* and *dry goods,* may also be difficult for students to understand. When students investigate these dialect words and phrases, they become familiar with the language and customs of the period and focus attention on terms that might hinder comprehension.

Pink and Say (Polacco, 1994), an excellent picturebook for a read-aloud introduction to Civil War issues, uses dialect to develop the atmosphere of the story. By putting themselves in the place of a young black soldier fighting to end slavery or a wounded white deserter beginning to understand the personal conflicts of the war, students better understand the conditions and conflicts of this era. A running list of dialect words and phrases used in *Pink and Say* could be sorted structurally and used to extend the book in a variety of written responses (Bromley, 1992). One group of fifth-grade students organized their dialect list structurally, by the part of the word omitted, and grammatically, by unusual verb form:

beginning	*middle*	*end*	*verbs*
'spect	mess-o' -beans	sloggin'	git
'til	near 'nuff	flushin'	afeared
'cause	heap o' trouble	trustin'	brung
	so's	mornin'	smote

With greater understanding of the spelling and grammatical role of these dialect forms, the students created dialect of their own as they extended a section of *Pink and Say* for the readers' theater. The students also demonstrated their understanding of the characters' personality by using Pink's and Say's character traits and language to complete the scene.

Narrator: Moe Moe Bay sent Pink and Say to the root cellar when the marauders
came to ransack her home again.

Pink: She's *drawing'* them off.

Say: My heart's *beatin'* so loud, they'll hear it, *sure 'nuff.*

Pink: *Jest* settle down. *Ain't nothing* left for them raiders to take. We got *nothin'* to
fear.

Say: Sounds like they're *clearin'* out. (pause) What's that shot?

Pink: *They's tryin'* to scare Moe Moe Bay. She''ll call us up soon as they *git* out of
sight.

Narrator: The call never came.

The original concept sort of /er/ words and other word sorts that develop as books are
read provide a springboard for writing activities. One teacher modeled the use of word lists
to create simple poems (McCraken & McCraken, 1986). She used a list of nouns, then
embellished and extended their meaning with adjectives: "War is horror, terror, clamor, and
tragedy" became "War has peculiar honor, spectacular clamor, particular horror, and
unending death." By using adjectives to add descriptive power to simple word lists, students
are sensitized to the role of word choice in poetry or other types of writing.

One literature group chose to respond to *Charley Skedaddle* (Beatty, 1987) using
poetry. Inspired by the book and the song, "The Drummer Boy of Shiloh" (Schreiber,
Stepien, Patrick, Remy, Gay, & Hoffman, 1983). Terrence wrote a verse that incorporated
several of the /er/ words his word study group had previously classified.

Commander please have mercy.
A *drummer* I want to be.
I'll fix your *dinner* and shine your shoes.
If you will *favor* me.

Another group of fifth graders read *Who Comes with the Cannons?* (Beatty, 1992), a
novel about orphaned Quaker Truth Hopkins who left Indiana in 1861 to live with relatives
in North Carolina. Students responded to the novel at the point where Truth is heading north
with her uncle on the Underground Railroad in an attempt to rescue cousin Robert from
military prison. The students were challenged to include words introduced in the concept
sort and to embellish their writing with adjectives and abstract nouns from the grammar
sort. Previously, Alicia had developed the character web shown in Figure 1 for Truth and
her relatives, and she used this as she responded in Truth's voice to her fears about Robert's
fate:

The *conductor* just told me about the *prisoner* camps. There is much *hunger,* sickness,
and other *horrors* there. I am worried about my cousin getting sick because there are
no *doctors.* I have heard that many *prisioners* are dying of *fever.* Robert is one of the
younger, smaller boys, and he is likely to get sick. He was very *slender* the last time I
saw him. I hope his *captors* are treating him kindly.

FIGURE 1   Character Web from *Who Comes with Cannons?*

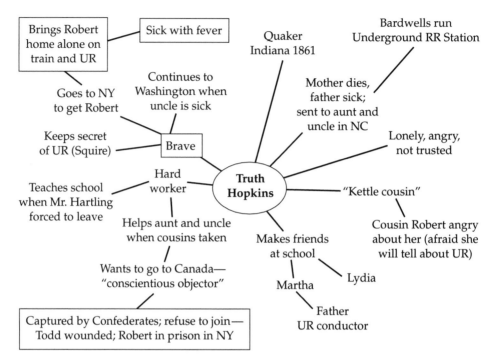

Word Study Extension Activities

As a wrap-up to the study of words ending in /er/, word study groups played "*AR ER OR Trivia*," a game of morphophonemic awareness that is shown in Figure 2 (McMullen, 1988). Choosing a category (*-er, -ar, -or*) and a question with a value of 100 to 500 points, students quizzed each other, giving clues such as: "In the category *-ar* for 200 points, name the following word: A two-syllable noun with the double letters *ll* in the middle; a short *e* in the first syllable; is used to refer to a room in an underground location" (*cellar*); and "From the category *-or* for 300 points, name this word: A two-syllable noun; short *i* in the first syllable; comes from the Latin word meaning conqueror" (*victor*). In this fashion, students tested their awareness of spelling-meaning and spelling-grammar connections and generalized to other words with the same patterns.

    The word study examples discussed in the Civil War unit primarily dealt with unaccented final syllables since these words are commonly misspelled by students in the Syllable Juncture stage of spelling development. Unaccented syllables provide a wealth of information about a word's meaning and function. In terms of the history of our language, unaccented final syllables are often vestiges of Old English, when English was an inflected language; hence, they signal grammatical class. Other word features appropriate for study by intermediate readers and writers include syllable structures and accomodations at the place where syllables meet. Such word study might include a comparison of base words with the inflected spellings (e.g., *slog, slogging*) as well as classifications by sound, pattern,

FIGURE 2 **Game Lay-Out for AR ER OR Trivia (Adapted from McMullen in Bear, Invernizzi, & Templeton, 1996)**

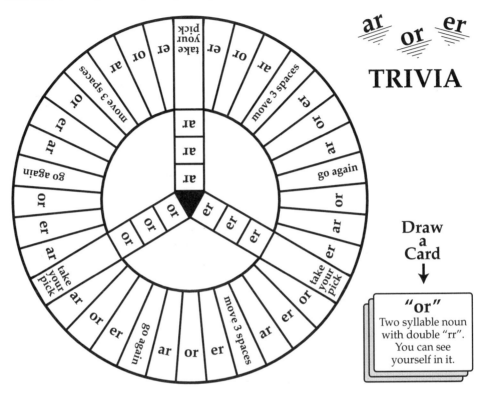

and part of speech. Words ending in *-y,* for example, provide a rich corpus for analysis. Sorting multi-syllable words ending in *-y* into two categories, by sound and grammatical class, leads to some interesting discoveries. For example, *apply, certify, occupy,* and *rely* all end in the /ai/ sound, and they are all verbs. *Butterfly* is memorable for its unique form (a compound word) and function (not a verb, although *fly* alone could be). In these words, either primary or secondary stress rests on the final syllable. Final *-y* also has the /i/ sound in words with unaccented final syllable (e.g., *hurry, family, angry*). *Country, silly,* and *certainly* all end in /i/ and form three different grammatical categories:

Noun	*Adjective*	*Adverb*
country	sorry	seriously
cemetery	silly	horribly
custody	starry	hurriedly
celery	happy	certainly
gypsy	pretty	happily

Interesting hypotheses about the doubling pattern evident in the second column (adjectives) can be tested by adding more examples from reading. Further analyses of the third column (adverbs) leads to learning about spelling changes necessitated by affixation (e.g., *happy* to *happily; horrible* to *horribly*).

Why Include Word Study in a Language Arts Program?

There are three reasons for adopting a word study approach to spelling, vocabulary, and grammar instruction in a language arts program: (1) Word study provides theoretical integrity for the integration of word-level skills within the context of reading and writing; (2) word study imitates the fundamental cognitive learning process of categorization and brings this process to conscious attention; and (3) word study is hands-on, student-centered, developmentally appropriate, and fun.

Theoretical Integrity

Word study is based on extensive research of children's development of word knowledge as they learn to read and write (cf. Templeton & Bear, 1992). Students must quickly and accurately perceive word patterns in order to recognize, produce, and understand written language (Perfetti, 1991). Accurate, rapid word recognition is facilitated by opportunities to engage in meaningful reading and to examine the same words, both in and out of context (Morris, 1989). Word-conscious teachers link word study to literature; provide a flexible sequence that includes instruction in grammar, literacy analysis, and writing; and provide hands-on, repeated practice. Word study makes explicit how spelling patterns and word structures reflect meaning and use.

Fundamental Cognitive Process

Word study imitates basic cognitive learning processes: comparing and contrasting categories of word features and discovering similarities and differences within and between categories. Students are asked to compare words within a category, to note patterns of consistency, and to look across categories to note contrasts. Repeated word sorting routines require students to discriminate and make critical judgments about spelling patterns, word structures, word meanings, and use. This simple but powerful approach toward knowledge can be used not only to learn about language form and function but to also foster comprehension. Words ending in *-er, -ar,* and *-or* may be sorted by concepts or by spelling patterns and grammar, as done in the Civil War unit above. Both activities entail classifying and categorizing the basic cognitive process of learning.

Student-Centered Learning

A word study approach to spelling-meaning and spelling-grammar connections is different from traditional instruction involving worksheets and grammar book exercises. Because the principles of word study are based on developmental research on how children learn to recognize (read), produce (write), and use (understand) written words, word study is developmentally appropriate. That is, word study differentiates word-level instruction according to students' demonstrated levels of orthographic awareness; it authentically integrates word-level skills with reading and writing vocabulary: and the activities are student-centered. Although teacher-taught rules seldom stick, hypotheses and conclusions that students develop themselves are more readily generalized to their reading and writing vocabulary.

Differentiation

The content of word study instruction differs based on what students are currently studying in spelling. Students' spelling errors are interpreted according to features spelled correctly, and instruction is targeted to features that are used but often confused (Invernizzi et al., 1994). For example, the students working on the Civil War unit correctly spelled the features in most one-syllable words and inconsistently used syllable conventions such as doubling, *e*-drop, *y*-to-*i* change, and the schwa (ə) sound in unaccented syllables. Word study addressed these issues within the context of a meaningful, reading-based vocabulary.

Authenticity

Word study in an integrated language arts program uses the words actually read and written by students. Instruction begins with words from texts, provides opportunities to manipulate the same words out of context, then returns to texts to find other words that exemplify the same spelling-meaning connections. Word categories can segue into related writing activities.

Developmentally Appropriate

The most appealing aspect of word study is the student-centered activities. Students manipulate and categorize the words they read. Teachers stack the deck, so to speak, to focus attention on a particular contrast. A discovery-oriented, systematic program of word study is a teacher-directed, student-centered method for learning about written language form and function. When students make decisions about whether *marauder* is more closely related to *traitor* or *captor,* or whether *doctor* is more like *soldier, instigator,* or *peculiar,* independent analysis and judgment are demanded. Students make decisions for themselves. The game-like format of the activities makes word study motivating and fun.

There is more to spelling than grapheme-phoneme correspondences. Word study that focuses on spelling-meaning and spelling-grammar connections helps students expand their vocabulary, develop sensitivity to word choice in reading and writing, and build explicit awareness of how English orthography functions in the integrated language arts program.

References

Abouzeid, M. P., Invernizzi, M. A., Bear, D., & Ganske, K. (1995, December). *Word sort: An alternative to phonics, spelling, and vocabulary.* Paper presented at the 44th Annual National Reading Conference, San Diego, CA.

Adams, M. J. (1990). *Beginning to read: Thinking and learning about print.* Cambridge, MA: MIT Press.

Bear D., Invernizzi, M. A., & Templeton, S. (1996). *Words their way: Word study for phonics, vocabulary, and spelling instruction.* Englewood Cliffs, NJ: Merrill.

Beatty, P. (1987). *Charley Skedaddle.* New York: Morrow Junior Books.

Beatty, P. (1992). *Who comes with cannons?* New York: William Morris.

Beck, I. L., & Juel, C. (1995). The role of decoding in learning to read. *American Educator, 19* (8) 21–25, 39–42.

Bloodgood, J. W. (1991). A new approach to spelling instruction in language arts programs. *The Elementary School Journal, 92,* 203–211.

Bromley, K. D. (1992). A response-based view of writing with literature. In K. Wood & A. Moss (Eds.), *Exploring literature in the classroom* (pp. 111–142). Norwood, MA: Christopher-Gordon.

Gillet, J. W., & Kita, M. J. (1980). Words, kids, and categories. In E. H. Henderson & J. Beers (Eds.), *Developmental and cognitive aspects of learning to spell* (pp. 120–126). Newark, DE: International Reading Association.

Henderson, E. H. (1990). *Teaching spelling.* Boston, MA: Houghton Mifflin.

Henderson, E. H., & Templeton, S. (1986). The development of spelling ability through alphabet, pattern, and meaning. *The Elementary School Journal, 86,* 305–316.

Hunt, I. (1964). *Across five Aprils.* Chicago: Follett.

Invernizzi, M. A., Abouzeid, M. P., & Gill, J. T. (1994). Using students' invented spellings as a guide for spelling instruction that emphasizes word study. *The Elementary School Journal, 95,* 155–167.

McCracken, R. A., & McCracken, M. J. (1986). *Stories, songs, and poetry to teach reading and writing.* Winnipeg, Manitoba, Canada: Peguis.

McMullen, H. (1988). ER AR OR trivia. In M. A. Invernizzi, E. H. Henderson, & W. Weber (Eds.), *Word study manual* (pp. 178–181). Unpublished manuscript.

Morris, D. (1982). "Word sort": A categorization strategy for improving word recognition ability. *Reading Psychology, 3,* 247–257.

Morris, D. (1989). Editorial comment: Developmental spelling theory revisited. *Reading Psychology, 10,* iii–x.

Perfetti, C. A. (1991). Representations and awareness in the acquisition of reading competence. In L. Rieben & C. A. Perfetti (Eds.), *Learning to read: Basic research and its implications* (pp. 33–44). Hillsdale, NJ: Erlbaum.

Polacco, P. (1992). *Pink and Say.* New York: Philomel.

Schlagal, R. (1992). Patterns of orthographic development into the intermediate grades. In S. Templeton & D. Bear (Eds.), *Development of orthographic knowledge and the foundation of literacy: A memorial Festschrift for Edmund H. Henderson* (pp. 31–52). Hillsdale, NJ: Erlbaum.

Schreiber, J., Stepien, W., Patrick, J., Remy, R., Gay, G., & Hoffman, A. J. (1983). *American past and present.* Glenview, IL: Scott, Foresman.

Templeton, S., & Bear, D. (Eds.). (1992). *Development of orthographic knowledge and the foundation of literacy: A memorial Festschrift for Edmund H. Henderson.* Hillsdale, NJ: Erlbaum.

Versteeg, C., & Skinner, C. (1991). *Exploring America's heritage.* Lexington, MA: Heath.

Integrating Sources

1. Locate and contrast the advice given by these sources for contending with the problem of delays in acquiring correct spelling.

2. With respect to spelling instruction, do the views of Miller align with those of Invernizzi, Abouzeid, and Bloodgood? Give your reasons.

Classroom Implications

1. Discuss invented spelling and word study in terms of practicality.

2. Do you think the case for invented spelling varies with grade level? Explain your answer.

3. Do you think the case for word study varies with grade level? Explain your answer.

Annotated Bibliography

Fresch, M. J. (1997). Sort, search, and discover: Spelling in the child-centered classroom. *The Reading Teacher, 51,* 20–31.

Details a spelling instruction strategy which can be used to help students become more proficient spellers through individualized language instruction.

Gentry, J. R. (1987). *Spel...Is a four letter word.* Portsmouth, NH: Heinemann.

Gentry, J. R. (1997). *My kid can't spell!* Portsmouth, NH: Heinemann.

Two excellent books describing practical guidelines for helping students become better at spelling. While written primarily for parents, each of these books contains excellent ideas for classroom teachers as well.

Invernizzi, M. A., Abouzeid, M. P., & Bloodgood, J. W. (1997). Spelling, grammar, and meaning in the language arts classroom. *Language Arts, 74,* 184–192.

Describes various approaches to word study for upper elementary-age children, noting reasons for the importance of this knowledge in an integrated language arts classroom.

Snowball, D. (1997). Spelling strategies. Make smart use of sounds and spelling patterns. *Instructor, 106,* 34–35.

Describes three strategies which can help students hear sounds in words through phonemic awareness, sound/symbol relationships, and various spelling patterns.

Wilde, S. (1991). *Your kan red this!* Portsmouth, NH: Heinemann.

A classic in the teaching of spelling in the elementary classroom. Of particular interest is the integration of spelling into a total language arts program.

You Become Involved

1. The following story was written by a six-year-old girl:

   Ounce ther was a lone lee fraf and all his frends did was make fasise at him but he onlee smild be kuos he was alive. But one he got home he notiste that they were all cwitt to hav a porte for him and he was so supriste that day they all had dringks to. And that was his brth day porte and he was six years old all of the livd haple ever aftr
   the end

   Translation:
   Once there was a lonely giraffe, and all his old friends did was make faces at him, but he only smiled because he was alive. But one day [when] he got home he noticed that they were quiet to have a party for him, and he was so surprised that day. They all had drinks too. And that was his birthday party and he was six years old. All of them lived happily ever after.
   The End

   Examine the invented and conventional spellings to determine appropriate actions a teacher might take with this child.

2. Compare your conclusions with the conditions identified by Miller.
3. In your school what are the prevailing attitudes among the teachers concerning spelling? Does there seem to be a major difference of opinion? If so, how is it being handled? Everyone do what they please? A general attempt to reconcile differences? Other solutions?

7

EMERGENT LITERACY

I observe that betwixt three and four years of age a child
hath great propensity to peep into a book, and then is
the most reasonable time for him to begin to learn to read.
—*C. HOOLE (1660)*

When a child can talk, 'tis time he should learn to read.
And when he reads, put into his hands some very pleasant
book suited to his capacity, wherein the entertainment he
finds may draw him on, and rewards his pains in reading.
—*J. WAUGHT (1753)*

Consequently, it seems safe to say that, by postponing
the teaching of reading until children reach a mental
level of six and a half years, teachers can greatly
decrease the chances of failure and discouragement
and can correspondingly increase their efficiency.
—*MABEL MORPHETT AND CARLETON WASHBURNE (1931)*

Beginning in the 1970s, early childhood educators began to question some notions such as (1) that literacy growth necessarily begins with formal schooling, (2) that reading instruction should begin in first grade, and (3) that kindergarten should be devoted largely to getting children ready for such instruction (Fields & Spangler, 1995). The realization that signs of literate behavior can be observed at much younger ages led to a new view of how children move toward literacy. The idea that reading readiness was the proper goal of any instruction received prior to first grade gave way to the view that literacy slowly develops, or emerges, if children grow up in environments where literate acts are modeled and where opportunities to use print for relevant purposes abound.

Emergent literacy is a highly complex concept (Lesaik, 1997). It suggests that children are developing simultaneously with respect to many dimensions crucial to

197

eventual literate behavior. For example, a preschooler who is read to frequently begins to acquire an awareness of print, a sense of story structure, and so forth, with little or no "instruction." The same child may also experiment with writing, proceeding from pictographic representations to letter-like scribbling, and finally to letters and words. At the same time, the child's world knowledge and oral language steadily grow, providing the basis for later text comprehension. Thus, literacy emerges along many paths at the same time.

Instructional Issues

This sophisticated view of children's growth toward literacy raises numerous instructional issues (Tompkins & Hoskisson, 1995). One is the proper role of direct instruction—whether it should have any place in preschool or kindergarten settings, or whether teachers should serve mainly as facilitators who help children "figure out" literacy on their own (Williams & Davis, 1994). Another issue is how long to encourage invented spelling as children use it to examine the alphabetic principle. Still another point is what to do about children whose out-of-school environment has not been conducive to the emergence of literacy (Anderson, 1994). Finally, there is the problem of efficiency, or how to balance the competing forces of limited time and the need of children to explore in a risk-free, unpressured setting.

As You Read

Strommen and Mates note the evolution of children's ideas about reading. Results indicated that while children express their ideas and feelings about reading in different ways, the researchers found there was a consistent evolution of these ideas. Lesiak continues the discussion of emergent literacy with particular emphasis on what current research says about many current questions/problems in this area.

1. What definition of *emergent literacy* is most defensible?
2. What instructional implications does emergent literacy have for early childhood programs?
3. Which instructional practices are best aligned with the concept of emergent literacy?
4. What can be done to assist children whose backgrounds are dissimilar (i.e., cultural, social, ethnic) in terms of emergent literacy?

References

Adams, M. J. (1990). *Beginning to read: Thinking and learning about print.* Cambridge, MA: MIT Press.

Fields, M. V., & Spangler, K. L. (1995). *Let's begin reading.* (ERIC Document Reproduction Service No. ED 375 381).

Hoole, C. (1660). *A new discovery of the old art of teaching school in four treatises.* London: Printed by F.T. for Andrew Crook at the Green Dragon in Pauls Churchyard.

Lesiak, J. L. (1997). Research based answers to questions about emergent literacy. *Psychology in the Schools, 34,* 143–160.

McGee, L. M., & Purcell-Gates, V. (1997). So what's going on in research on emergent literacy. *Reading Research Quarterly, 32,* 310–318.

Morphett, M. V., & Washburne, C. (1931). When should children begin to read? *Elementary School Journal, 31,* 496–503.

Strommen, L. T., & Mates, Barbara F. (1997). What readers do: Young children's ideas about the nature of reading. *The Reading Teacher, 51,* 98–107.

Tompkins, G. E., & Hoskisson, K. (1995). *Language arts: Content and teaching* (3rd ed.). New York: Merrill.

Waught, J. (1753). *Education of children and young students in all its branches.* London: J. Waugh.

Williams, R. P., & Davis, J. K. (1994). Lead sprightly into literacy. *Young Children, 49,* 37–41.

What Readers Do

Young Children's Ideas about the Nature of Reading

LINDA TERAN STROMMEN   *BARBARA FOWLES MATES*

In recent decades, increased understanding of the complex process by which young children acquire spoken language (e.g., Bloom, 1970, 1973; Bowerman, 1973; deVilliers & deVilliers, 1974; Tough, 1977) has come about through investigations of how children learn to read. Reading is no longer perceived "as simply a cognitive skill to be learned, but as a complex sociopsycholinguistic activity" (Teale & Sulzby, 1989, p. 2). We now recognize that even very young children engage in the process of accruing the information and skills needed to become readers and that reading behaviors are concept based (Teale & Sulzby, 1989) and evolve over time (Gibson, 1989; Schickedanz, 1986; Sulzby, 1985).

This view of literacy development as a multifaceted process that begins very early in life has led a growing number of researchers (Bissex, 1980; Clark, 1984; Schickedanz, 1986; Sulzby, 1985), including the present authors, to examine children's emerging literacy. The observations described in this article contribute to this "portrait of young children as literacy learners" (Teale & Sulzby, 1989, p. 3) by focusing on children's ideas about what it is that people do when they read and exploring the implications of these ideas for instruction.

Background: Insights from Studies of Emergent Literacy

Studies of toddlers and preschoolers have revealed that young children's reading behaviors often do not agree with conventional definitions of what it means to read (Bissex, 1980; Downing, 1986; Dyson, 1984; Ferriero, 1978), and these behaviors change over time as children have more opportunities to interact with reading material and get feedback from skilled readers (Forester, 1986).

In the late 1960s John Downing began exploring young children's understanding of reading-related terms such as *word* and *letter* and concluded that young children very often enter school in a state of "cognitive confusion" (Downing, 1972, p. 3) about reading. While children's eccentric definitions of such terms may demonstrate concepts based on incomplete data rather than confusion per se, Downing's emphasis on the cognitive, problem-solving nature of reading and on the child's "application of general cognitive abilities to the task" (p. 3) laid the groundwork for extending the widely accepted view of young children as active constructivists (e.g., Fischer, 1980) to the realm of literacy. Researchers (e.g., Cochran, Cochran, Scalena, & Buchanan, 1984; Dyson, 1984; Ferriero, 1978; Ferriero & Teberosky, 1982, 1984; Hall, 1987; Rozin, Bressman, & Taft, 1974; Snow & Ninio, 1984) have assessed young children's knowledge of literacy concepts using a variety of methodologies.

Source: From Strommen, L., & Mates, B. F. (1997, October). What readers do: Young children's ideas about the nature of reading. *The Reading Teacher, 51*(2), 98–107. Reprinted with permission of Linda Strommen and the International Reading Association. All rights reserved.

It has become increasingly clear that a wide variety of early language and literacy experience is most conducive to acquisition of reading (Clark, 1984; Morrow & Rand, 1991; Snow & Ninio, 1984). Early, usually informal, adult-child interactions are a powerful determinant of the degree to which the young child's reading behaviors will become elaborated and approach adult expectations for what it means to read (Bissex, 1980; Gotchall, 1995; Neuman, 1991; Smith, 1984; Taylor, 1983; Teale, 1984). Many investigators view the child as an apprentice (Forester, 1986) or collaborator (Gibson, 1989) who observes adults' literacy behaviors and "plays the role of the skill user before having any skill" (Holdaway, 1986, p. 43). Others have identified consistent stages in children's reading behavior (Schickedanz, 1986; Sulzby, 1985).

Our Observations

Most emerging literacy studies utilize participant observation in classroom or home settings (Durkin, 1966; Sulzby, 1985; Taylor, 1983) or analysis of children's performance on literacy tasks (Ferriero & Teberosky, 1982). Others have designed tasks focused on determining children's knowledge of reading-related concepts (Downing, 1986; Rossman, 1980).

Our own approach was to elicit children's current ideas about what it is that readers do by engaging them in an open-ended dialog. This approach assumes that even quite young children can and do reflect on and talk about abstract matters of this nature. Research methodology that relies on discussions with young children gained credence with Piaget's seminal work (e.g., Piaget, 1929). The recent work of Gareth Matthews (1994) in exploring children's philosophical thinking supports the idea that "children consistently and happily develop philosophical trains of thought, evaluate those of others and try to think things through" (Gottlieb, 1994, p. 13).

Our goal was to explore children's ideas about the nature of reading and to determine if these young children, whose home and school environments offered a similar range of informal and formal reading experiences, would develop a similar sequence of concepts about what readers do. We did not attempt to correlate specific literacy experiences with the emergence of these concepts, although that would certainly be an appropriate next step.

Eighteen 3-year-old preschoolers, living in a suburb outside a large eastern U.S. city, were followed from their school entry through the completion of their kindergarten year, at age 5 or 6.

The preschool curriculum focused on building social skills through informal, child-centered, play activities. Children moved freely among block, family life, and arts and crafts activity centers. Classroom materials to promote literacy included a selection of picture storybooks, concept books, information books, and paper and writing tools. Teachers frequently read aloud to small groups of children, usually at transition times, encouraged children to read and write their names (for example, on art work), and wrote down what children asked them to. There was no formal literacy-related activity or instruction.

Upon entering kindergarten, the children were scattered among nine classes in public and parochial schools. The kindergarten curricula were quite consistent across classes and emphasized building reading skills in an environment that promoted literacy learning as an integral part of classroom life. A wide variety of language and literacy activities including storytime, experience charts, and journal and story writing incorporated explicit instruction in phonics as well as other skills. Classroom materials to promote literacy included classroom libraries and an assortment of writing and publishing materials, all of which were organized so that children could work in groups or independently. In addition, all but two of the children (whose schools did not offer this option) participated in a twice-weekly extended-day program that focused on literacy activities.

We met with each child individually for approximately 15 minutes during school hours five times during each school year. All children participated in the sessions willingly. During each session children were invited to choose and read from among a variety of picture storybooks. In addition, children were often invited to read print materials other than the books: cards with letters or letter-like symbols, sequences of letters, words, or short phrases; picture cards with single-word labels; short written texts; product packaging; and storybooks without illustrations. Children were asked questions such as whether items offered to them were "something to read," what part of the display they were reading, how they knew how to read (or what they needed to know), as well as who they knew who could read and what readers do when they read. Additional questions were asked in order to clarify children's thinking and pursue their trains of thought. Because our goal was to explore children's ideas, we did not adhere to rigid question formats.

At the onset of this study and again at its conclusion, each child's parent(s) was asked to respond to a questionnaire designed to elicit information about family literacy practices, values, and expectations. Most parents responded that they read childrens' storybooks aloud to their child (usually at bedtime) on a daily basis and took their child to the library with varying degrees of regularity. Only two parents regularly did formal reading activities such as teaching letters and sounds.

Findings: Children's Ideas about What Readers Do

At the conclusion of our 3 years of close observation, we were able to map the evolution of the children's ideas about what readers do. Although there was only moderate consistency in the ages at which concepts emerged, and there was some overlap, the sequence of conceptual development was quite uniform across all children. We cannot, of course, generalize to children of different cultural backgrounds or to those with very limited reading experiences.

- *Reading is one aspect of an interpersonal routine.*

At first, several of the 3-year-olds in our study described reading as a social routine in which a book has meaning only as part of a social situation in which the interpersonal dimension dominates. Although we did not find this thinking in all the children, in those children who expressed this view it preceded all other ideas about reading.

Kristina (3 years 2 months) described reading as follows: "We take a bath in the shower, then we go to bed. We read the story, then, when my light is off, I call daddy." Similarly, James (3 years 7 months) told us that when mommy reads "She turns the pages, she looks at the pictures, then she does the dishes."

When invited to read, children with this idea typically told us "Mommy can read" and declined to do so. Asked by the interviewer to show, "What does Mommy do with a book?"

Kristina (3 years 4 months) explained, "Mommy looks at the pictures, not letters. They [the letters] are just for doing letters." Here Kristina demonstrated an awareness of letters and some obvious experiences with print activities ("doing letters"), which her mother confirmed doing at home. However, it is significant that she had drawn a distinction between what one does with letters and what readers do.

Ryan (3 years 5 months) agreed to show us what his mother did when she read and began by turning the pages in a picture storybook from back to front. He then turned them from front to back. He continued, once again turning pages from back to front, but stopped his page turning to label one illustration, "That's a dad," and another, "It's nighttime." For these children, who were well beyond infancy, the reading process was still an inextricable part of an interpersonal routine, and the book's role was minor.

- *Readers focus on the book.*

The idea that reading is the interaction between a person (a reader) and a book was next to emerge in children's thinking. Reading had now become identified as a key aspect of the interpersonal routine described above, and books had become the focus. When asked what people did with books, children with this idea announced, for example, "They read, like this," and proceeded to demonstrate their ability. Some sat and silently turned pages in a book while others pointed out the pictures on a page, labeled objects and actions depicted in the illustrations, or asked questions.

Noah (3 years 11 months) immediately reached for a picture storybook on a table before him. He took the book in both hands, turned it right side up, and opened the book to the first page. He turned the pages one at a time and looked briefly at each illustration. When Noah reached the last page he closed the book.

When Corinne (3 years 9 months) was invited to read she nodded her head "yes," placed a picture storybook on the table before her, and spent quite a while looking at the cover. She opened the book to the first page and continued to silently turn the pages, one by one, from front to back. Unlike Noah, she spent a great deal of time looking at each illustration. When she finished she closed the book and smiled. Both Noah and Corinne showed that they understood that readers turn pages and look at pictures, often silently.

Keely (3 years 9 months) took a different approach. She picked up *I Am a Bunny* (Scarry, 1967), placed it right side up on the table before her, opened it to the first page and announced "Here we go!" Keely's posture and intonation changed. Cues provided by specific illustrations and her own experiences guided Keely's construction of a monologue that combined labeling, rhetorical questions, general information, and statements of personal preference:

Keely: Another picture of butterflies! Look at all those butterflies. Are they beautiful? [Pointing to one butterfly in the illustration] What color is this one?

Interviewer: Yellow and blue.

Keely: Why two colors? [Answering her own question] 'Cause that's the way they are! And what color are those birds? [Pointing to a bluebird] Blue! Those are seeds. Yeah. And look at those following him [the bunny]. . . . Look at the rabbit now. He just has that on [a hat] 'cause it's winter. Because that's when he—'cause if he doesn't have that on he's cold. I just wear a jacket, I don't want a hat. I just wear a jacket and I don't wear any hat!

The idea that readers must focus on a book had clearly emerged in all of these children, though their reading strategies varied. This idea persisted as children's understandings evolved.

- *Readers construct a sequenced account.*

Every child in our study developed the idea that readers construct a meaningful sequenced account in a unique style that is determined by the series of illustrated pages in a book. Children with this notion could also identify lists of words or letters or print on cards as "something you can read," but at this point they nevertheless thought that an account is created by the reader, who is guided to varying degrees by the illustrations that accompany the written text, and did not attempt to use their growing awareness of print to read. They were willing to read books, even books they had never seen before, because they were confident of their ability to invent an organized account. Dana (3 years 10 months) told us, "I can read it but I can't know the words. I know new [her own] words." Her strategy was to construct a story using the illustrations in the book as guides. As Megan (4 years 7 months) said, "You know what it's about from the pictures."

Brian (3 years 7 months) pointed to the print in a picture storybook when asked, "What part do you read?" but when asked where the story was he indicated the illustrations and proceeded to use them to read *Sammy the Seal* (Hoff, 1980) in this way:

Brian: The seal didn't have.
He calls hello to the dogs.
He looks in the stars.
He looks in the restaurant.
He looks at the goldfish.

Although Brian's account diverges considerably from the author's text, he used distinctive intonation and simple repetitive structures, characteristic of many children's books, and very different from his own rather complex conversational style. Brian showed a great deal of awareness of the stylistic markers of written language.

Taylor (3 years 7 months), when invited to read, chose *The Pooh Story Book* (Milne, 1965). Using the illustrations in correct sequence as guides, and with phrasing and intonation that accurately mimicked oral reading, she read to the interviewer:

Taylor: Once upon a time.
Bear.
It was raining and raining and raining.
A jar of honey.
There was something in the tree.
Honey.
And there was all bumble bees.
The end.

Taylor combined picture labels and details remembered from other Pooh books with the narrative style of children's books ("It was raining and raining and raining") to construct her own account. In addition, she included some traditional narrative conventions ("Once upon a time," "The end"). Though she ran her finger back and forth under the print when asked "Where does it say that?" she made no attempt to use print to guide her account.

Other tasks we presented to these children revealed increasing knowledge of letters and sight words. Significantly though, they never attempted to read to us by focusing on print. Instead, they consistently focused on constructing a sequenced account and equated reading with this activity.

- *Readers reconstruct a specific account.*

The idea that readers reconstruct an account that is unique to each particular book emerged next in children's thinking. However, to many children this meant that, although the meaning must remain the same, the choice of words need not be exact.

Taylor (5 years 8 months), for example, was able to print her name as well as the names of family members and friends. She had a growing vocabulary of sight words and some knowledge of letter/sound relationships. (When asked, for example, how she had correctly matched the word cards *DOG* and *BIRD* to pictures of a dog and a bird, she stated "'Cause *dog* starts with *D* and *bird* starts with *B* 'cause I have a dog.") However, Taylor gave no evidence of applying knowledge of this aspect of the written code to the task of reading stories. She understood reading to mean reconstructing a particular account, which is controlled by the illustrations. Taylor authoritatively told the interviewer "I can make up the words. It's the same story because it's the same book, but the pages don't say the same thing. The words change. When you say something it says something else. But it always says what the picture looks like."

Taylor's explanation attributed a specific account to each book but denied that fixed written language was part of reading. She believed that while her choice of words might vary, this would not alter the meaning as long as her version was consistent with "what the picture looks like."

In contrast, when asked to discuss her favorite book, Taylor said, "I can read it without my book," and continued:

Taylor: One day Arthur was standing at the table with his mommy and his daddy. He loved pancakes. And his grandmother said, "What cake do you want me to make for your birthday?"
"Chocolate, chocolate!" said Arthur.

Note that Taylor's account also included many stylistic markers of written language, including dialog markers.

Cordelia (4 years 1 month) told the interviewer, "Mommy reads the pages. She reads that the kid is going in the mud. She looks down here [pointing to the print in a book she was holding]. She reads the letters. She reads all the pages. I do it by myself. I can do *The Little Bears [sic]*." Not having the book at hand, she told the story from memory. Her narration employed several attributes of written language as well as storytelling conventions:

Cordelia: Once upon a time there were three little pigs *[sic]*. A mama, a papa and a baby. They made some porridge. Mama tried hers, and it was too hot. They went for a walk. Then

Goldilocks came. She tried the porridge but it was too hot. Then she went upstairs. Pap's bed was too soft, mama's bed was too slow. Baby's bed was just right. Then the bears came back! Then they went upstairs and the baby said, "Somebody's been sleeping in my bed, and there she is!" And then Goldilocks ran, and then they made more porridge, and that's the end.

Cordelia had developed the idea that each book has a specific story and that some readers (her mother) refer to print to tell the story, but she could learn the story from others and simply retell it.

Clearly, both Cordelia and Taylor had acquired a great deal of knowledge about reading and about written language, yet they described their behavior as "reading" when there was no print for them to decode. They believed that the reader's primary task is to reconstruct a specific account. Children at this point in their developing conceptualization of reading may recognize that older readers use print to help them read; they see this as an optional, rather than an essential, strategy.

Other children in our study thought that a specific account must be constructed using particular words that must be memorized. Their strategy required collaboration with another reader who already knew the story. As James (6 years 1 month) told us, "The teacher reads us the book and we try to memorize it."

Jeffrey (3 years 11 months), when offered an unfamiliar book, told the interviewer, "I don't know how to read. I don't know the words, I'm not big enough. I'm 3. My Dad knows all the words." When asked which part of the book his dad would read, Jeffrey pointed to the illustration. Jeffrey's idea was that readers must say particular words when they read particular books aloud, but he did not understand that these words are embodied in the printed text. He believed that in order to master a specific and unfamiliar narrative one must be "big." The idea that reading comes with bigness was almost universally articulated by these children at some point and persisted, even as their ideas about the nature of reading evolved, reflecting their view that reading is a mysterious way of knowing written language, not a matter of decoding print into speech sounds. As Taylor put it, "The babysitter can read; she can drive."

- *Readers refer to print to reconstruct texts.*

Many of the children in our study eventually came to the idea that print provides cues to written language. At the point when children achieved this insight they were generally able to read and write their own names, family names, and a few sight words (e.g., *stop, go, no, love*). Most could "sound out" some simple unfamiliar words. However, these skills did not constitute reading in the minds of these young children because they did not yet understand that the nature of the reading task is to use multiple strategies to interpret the language encoded by print. Many children who had earlier expressed the view that stories would be revealed to them through "magic" or by their "being big" now invoked these same powers to explain how they would unlock the secrets of the written code and become fluent readers. Many claimed that they could not read when asked to do so. Others told us that readers memorize the text, referring to print to prompt their memories, while some abandoned their efforts to decode print because it hindered the process of revealing the meaning.

Jeffrey (4 years 4 months) pointed to the printed text on a page in an unfamiliar book and said that he could not read it because "I don't know these words." Jeffrey knew that readers refer to print. He had accumulated an exceptionally large amount of information about print by this point, though he was only 4, but he did not understand how to apply this knowledge to the task of reading.

Like Jeffrey, Noah (4 years 3 months) had developed the idea that readers read the print in a book. Explaining that he could not read, he pointed to the written text in the book he was holding and said, "You read the letters in it. You look at them. Maybe in kindergarten I'll know them. The teacher will tell us."

Calvin (6 years 2 months) believed that in order to reconstruct a text readers memorize the words and use print to guide page-turning or to prompt their memories. He selected *Stop!* (Cowley, 1982), a favorite beginning book, from his classroom library and said, "I can tell you the story in my head, or I can look at the book." He turned each page at precisely the correct point, reciting the text verbatim (even making his voice louder when the print got bigger), and used illustrations as well as some print cues to guide his recitation:

Calvin: Stop said the police officer, but the truck went on. Stop. Stop. Stop! Crash!

Calvin told us that it would not be possible to read a book that he did not "know." He knew that an important relationship existed between the written text and the language associated with a particular book. However, even near the end of his kindergarten year, when he had successfully completed a curriculum focused on letter/sound correspondences, Calvin, like Jeffrey, did not understand how his knowledge of sounds and letters could enable him to reconstruct the text of an unfamiliar book.

When invited to read, Dana (5 years 5 months) chose a book that was familiar to her, *Animals Should Definitely Not Wear Clothing* (Barrett, 1970). She turned the first few pages, scanning the written text and looking at the illustrations. Closing the book she pointed to the title and read:

Dana: A-ni-mm-als, animals . . . sh-oo-l-d . . . shoo-l-d? (Looking at the interviewer for assistance).

Interviewer: Should.

Intentionally skipping the first page of text, Dana announced, "I'm gonna just read it."

Text: Animals should definitely not wear clothing because it would be disastrous for a porcupine, because a camel might wear it in the wrong places . . . because possums might wear it upside down by mistake, and most of all because it might be very embarrassing. [The animal pictured in the illustration that accompanies the last line of text is a dog.]

Dana: I am a porcupine. I don't wear clothes. I am a camel. I don't wear clothes. . . . We are possums. We don't wear clothes. I am a puppy. Of course I don't wear clothes!

Dana knew that readers read print. She had mastered many of the skills necessary to decode individual words, and when asked, "What do you need to do to read?" she

responded, "You need to 'sound out.'" However, Dana also realized that laboriously repro-
ducing the sounds was impeding her efforts. Therefore, she chose to abandon the print and
"just read."

At this point these children knew that readers focus on print, but they had yet to fully
understand how readers decode and interpret the language encoded by print to reconstruct
written texts.

- *Readers reconstruct texts by using multiple strategies to interpret the language
  encoded by print.*

By the conclusion of our study, only 2 of the 18 children had developed the idea that
readers must accurately interpret written language in order to read. These children now
began to apply graphophonemic, syntactic, and semantic information, as well as cues provided by illustrations (or by collaborators), to interpret the language encoded by print.

When Cordelia (6 years 4 months) was interviewed at the end of her kindergarten year,
she offered to read *Eat Your Peas Louise* (Snow, 1985) to the interviewer. Cordelia's negotiation of this story demonstrates her understanding that readers use a variety of strategies
to read. She was clearly aware of letter/sound relationships, which she used to limit her
choices among contextually appropriate words. She told the interviewer, "You sound out
the letters, or you just know it." Cordelia further relied on her knowledge of context, content, and the stylistic devices of written language, cues provided by the illustrations, recognition of words, and the assistance of a collaborating adult (the interviewer). Significantly,
Cordelia had also come to believe that reading books would make her a more fluent reader:
"There's lots of books, and you try to read lots of books. I read to myself."

Cordelia began by running her finger under the book's title (although there was other
print on the cover) and read "Eat Your Peas Louise." As Cordelia continued to read, her
body language occasionally indicated a desire that the interviewer collaborate with her.
Assistance was offered only after enough time had elapsed for Cordelia to examine the text
but not lose a sense of the meaning. In order to be able to observe Cordelia's repertoire of
strategies as she negotiated the text, the interviewer did not coax Cordelia to employ one or
another strategy to decode.

Turning to the first page of the narrative Cordelia continued:

p. 3 text: Eat your peas, Louise. You will like good peas like these.

Cordelia: [Looking at the written text] Eat your peas, Louise. [Pausing and looking at the
illustration above the text for a cue] H-m-m [looks at the interviewer].

Interviewer: You.

Cordelia: [Looking at the written text] You will [looks at the interviewer].

Interviewer: Like.

Cordelia: [Running her finger under the written text] good peas like these.

In addition to the assistance offered by an adult collaborator, Cordelia used her knowledge
of letter/sound relationships to self-correct misread words:

p. 9 text: Eat them with your fork, or . . .

Cordelia: [Looking at the text] Eat these. No. Wait. [Self-corrects] Eat *them* [Rereads] Eat them with your fork or . . .

Cordelia referred to illustrations for cues to unfamiliar words. She also appeared to scan ahead as she read. In the following sample Cordelia read the first two words, looked at the illustration for additional information, continued reading but skipped the third word, and used information acquired from the illustration to read the fourth and fifth words in the sentence. Then, Cordelia reread the sentence, including the third word, to clarify meaning:

p. 10 text: Eat them with your spoon.

Cordelia: [Looking at the written text] Eat [looking at the illustration] them [looking at the illustration] your spoon. [Corrects herself and rereads] Eat them with your spoon.

Cordelia's knowledge of syntax, as well as her understanding that text is continuous and meaningful, had led her to include the preposition.

Cordelia used her knowledge of letter/sound relationships to read unfamiliar words in the next sample. However, she misread several words as she attempted to fit the text to the meaning as she understood it:

p. 13 text: But eat them up fast. It's way past noon. [The accompanying illustration is of a wristwatch indicating that the time is 12:50.]

Cordelia: [Looking at the written text, places her finger under *But*]. But. But eat them up fast. It's [pauses and looks at the illustration]. H-m-m. One? No. [Looks at the interviewer].

Interviewer: Way.

Cordelia: [Running her finger under the written text, word by word] way past night? [Looks at the interviewer].

Interviewer: Noon.

Cordelia: [Placing her finger under the word *noon*] noon.

Cordelia could tell time and thought (as she later told the interviewer) that the wristwatch in the illustration registered one o'clock. Therefore she misread *way* as "one." Note that the sound of the initial consonant supported Cordelia's initial prediction; however, the contradictory information provided by the final consonant caused her to doubt her interpretation.

Cordelia had attained several insights that led her to understand that in order to interpret the language encoded by print, readers employ multiple strategies. She knew that illustrations as well as written text provide information about the content and context of the story. She understood that written language has a characteristic syntax and grammar and employs special conventions. She knew that a relationship exists between letters and sounds and that specific written words represent specific spoken words.

Discussion

A primary purpose of our 3-year study of these 18 preschool children was to elicit children's changing thoughts about what readers do. Though children expressed their ideas in many different ways and reached various conclusions at widely different ages, we saw a consistent evolution of these ideas as each child slowly came to see an accurate interpretation of the language encoded by print as the key to reading. This was reflected both in changes in the way they approached the task of reading and in their perceptions of themselves as either readers or as "too little" to read. Although we did not explore the specific factors that contributed to these shifts in ideas, this would be an important avenue for further research.

The children's earliest ideas about reading (readers read storybooks) incorporated the notion that readers read organized, meaningful material. This idea continued to be central to their concept of reading through kindergarten.

Initially children focused on observable reading behaviors (turning pages, commenting on pictures), believing that this is all adult readers do. Consequently, they thought that by replicating these behaviors they were reading.

Eventually, they developed the idea that readers use information in the book to construct a sequenced account. A distinction between reading and, as one of our 3-year-olds put it, "doing letters" held for a period of time as children continued to elaborate their ideas about reading. Even when children knew that "sounding out" was required, they were swayed by the need to create a meaningful account. Once the idea that readers construct a sequenced, meaningful account evolved, it clearly dominated their conceptualization of the reading process.

When they came to understand that the sequence of meanings in a particular book is fixed, they also realized that the illustrations do not provide enough information to enable them to accurately reconstruct a specific account. Some children were now quite sure that in order to read they had to memorize texts, while others believed all would be revealed at a specific age or by "magic." Although a few children did memorize texts verbatim and believed that they were now reading, at this point in their development most simply said they could not read because they could not reconstruct the books' exact language.

By the end of our study, most of our young subjects had acquired significant reading-related skills. However, the majority of the children had yet to reach a clear understanding of the relationships between these skills and reading. The children who realized they would be able to read only by interpreting the language encoded by print, and who were able to use multiple strategies to undertake this process, were now well on their way to becoming fluent readers.

Implications for Beginning Reading Instruction

Our observations confirm that learning to read is a developmental process but show that a young child's age, word- and letter-level decoding skills, or other specific skills are not necessarily reliable indicators of what he or she understands reading to be and, therefore, of what intervention may be useful.

It is important for teachers to realize that a child's growth in ideas about what readers do and her/his growth in reading itself are interdependent. A fundamental goal of beginning reading instruction should be to move each child toward the understanding that readers reconstruct texts by using multiple strategies to interpret the language encoded by print and, at the same time, to make it possible for the child to do this by providing information that will enable construction of appropriate strategies. With this in mind we make the following recommendations regarding children's early literacy instruction.

1. Teachers of young children should initially assess a child's ideas about the nature of reading, written language, and the written code, as well as her/his reading strategies, and tailor reading experiences to that child's idea about what readers do.
2. Teachers should ask themselves what new information could cause a child to rethink or reinterpret what he or she believes and challenge each child's nonconventional ideas through demonstrations that contradict her/his current thinking. For example, frequent rereadings of a particular text help to build a child's knowledge of written language but may also promote the idea that reading is memorizing texts. If a child believes this is what readers do, then demonstrating that readers can and do read a variety of unfamiliar texts may contribute to a shift in the child's thinking.
3. Teachers should set expectations for a child's reading performance that always take into account the child's ideas about how readers read.

The child's idea of the nature of reading governs her/his efforts to read and should govern teachers' decisions about curriculum as well.

References

Bissex, G. (1980). *Gnys at work: A child learns to write and read.* Cambridge, MA: Harvard University Press.

Bloom, L. (1970). *Language development. Form and function in emerging grammar.* Cambridge, MA: Harvard University Press.

Bloom, L. (1973). *One word at a time.* Paris: Mouton.

Bowerman, M. (1973). *Early syntactic development.* Cambridge, England: Cambridge University Press.

Clark, M. M. (1984). Literacy at home and at school: Insights from a study of young fluent readers. In H. Goelman, A. A. Oberg, & F. Smith (Eds.), *Awakening to literacy* (pp. 122–130). Portsmouth, NH: Heinemann.

Cochran, O., Cochran, D., Scalena, S., & Buchanan, E. (1984). *Reading, writing and caring.* New York: Richard C. Owen.

deVilliers, P., & deVilliers, J. (1974). *Early language.* Cambridge, MA: Harvard University Press.

Downing, J. (1972, December). *A summary of evidence related to the cognitive clarity theory of reading.* Paper presented at the annual meeting of the National Reading Conference, New Orleans, LA.

Downing, J. (1986). Cognitive clarity: A unifying and cross-cultural theory for language awareness phenomena in reading. In D. Yaden & S. Templeton (Eds.), *Metalinguistic awareness and beginning literacy* (pp. 13–29). Portsmouth, NH: Heinemann.

Durkin, D. (1966). *Children who read early.* New York: Teachers College Press.

Dyson, A. H. (1984). Learning to write/learning to do school: Emergent writers' interpretations of school literacy tasks. *Research in the Teaching of English, 18,* 233–264.

Ferriero, E. (1978). What is written in a written sentence?: A developmental answer. *Journal of Education, 160,* 25–34.

Ferriero, E., & Teberosky, A. (1982). *Literacy before schooling.* Exeter, NH: Heinemann.

Ferriero, E., & Teberosky, A. (1984). The underlying logic of literacy development. In H. Goelman, A. A. Oberg, & F. Smith (Eds.), *Awakening to literacy* (pp. 154–173). Portsmouth, NH: Heinemann.

Fischer, K. W. (1980). A theory of cognitive development: The control and construction. *Psychological Review, 7,* 477–531.

Forester, A. D. (1986). Apprenticeship in the art of literacy. In D. Tovey & J. Kerber (Eds.), *Roles in literacy learning: A new perspective* (pp. 66–72). Newark, DE: International Reading Association.

Gibson, L. (1989). *Through children's eyes: Literacy learning in the early years.* New York: Teachers College Press.

Gotchall, S. M. (1995). Hug-a-book: A program to nurture a young child's love of books and reading. *Young Children, 50,* 29–35.

Gottlieb, A. (1994, October 23). What's on your mind kid? *New York Times Book Review,* p. 15.

Hall, N. (1987). *The emergence of literacy.* Portsmouth, NH: Heinemann.

Holdaway, D. (1986). Guiding a natural process. In D. Tovey & J. Kerber (Eds.), *Roles in literacy learning: A new perspective* (pp. 42–51). Newark, DE: International Reading Association.

Matthews, G. (1994). *The philosophy of childhood.* Cambridge, MA: Harvard University Press.

Morrow, L. M., & Rand, M. (1991). Promoting literacy during play and designing early childhood classroom environments. *The Reading Teacher, 4,* 396–403.

Neuman, S. B. (1991). *Literacy in the television age.* Norwood, NJ: Ablex.

Piaget, J. (1929). *The child's conception of the world* (J. & A. Tomlinson, Trans.). New York: Harcourt, Brace and World. (Original work published 1926).

Rossman, F. (1980). *Preschoolers' knowledge of the symbolic function of written language in storybooks.* Unpublished doctoral dissertation, Boston University, Boston.

Rozin, P., Bressman, B., & Taft, M. (1974). Do children understand the basic relationship between speech and writing? *Journal of Reading Behavior, 3,* 27–34.

Schickedanz, J. (1986). *More than the ABC's: The early stages of reading and writing.* Washington, DC: National Association for the Education of Young Children.

Smith, F. (1984). The creative achievement of literacy. In H. Goelman, A. A. Oberg, & F. Smith (Eds.), *Awakening to literacy* (pp. 143–153). Portsmouth, NH: Heinemann.

Snow, C., & Ninio, A. (1984). The contracts of literacy: What children learn from learning to read books. In H. Goelman, A. A. Oberg, & F. Smith (Eds.), *Awakening to literacy* (pp. 116–138). Portsmouth, NH: Heinemann.

Sulzby, E. (1985). Children's emergent reading of favorite storybooks: A developmental study. *Reading Research Quarterly, 20,* 458–481.

Taylor, D. (1983). *Family literacy.* Exeter, NH: Heinemann.

Teale, W. (1984). Home background and young children's literacy development. In H. Goelman, A. A. Oberg, & F. Smith (Eds.), *Awakening to literacy* (pp. 173–206). Portsmouth, NH: Heinemann.

Teale, W., & Sulzby, E. (1989). Emergent literacy: New perspectives. In D. Strickland & L. M. Morrow (Eds.), *Emerging literacy: Young children learn to read and write* (pp. 1–15). Newark, DE: International Reading Association.

Tough, J. (1977). *The development of meaning.* New York: John Wiley and Sons.

Children's Books Cited

Barrett, J. (1970). *Animals should definitely not wear clothing.* New York: Atheneum.

Cowley, J. (1982). *Stop!* Bothell, WA: Thomas C. Wright.

Hoff, S. (1980). *Sammy the seal.* New York: HarperCollins.

Milne, A. A. (1965). *The Pooh story book.* New York: E. P. Dutton.

Scarry, R. (1967). *I am a bunny.* Racine, WI: Western.

Snow, P. (1985). *Eat your peas Louise.* Chicago: Children's Press.

Research Based Answers to Questions about Emergent Literacy in Kindergarten

JUDI LUCAS LESIAK
Central Michigan University

Several questions school psychologists and teachers have regarding emergent literacy in kindergarten are addressed. Answers to questions are based on an extensive review of the literature. Answers include specific suggestions for encouraging kindergarten children's emergent literacy. © 1997 John Wiley & Sons, Inc.

Setting the Stage for Emerging Literacy Activities

What kind of environment/classroom settings are most appropriate for encouraging emergent literacy? The best kindergarten for children is a "child-centered" kindergarten in which "education involves the whole child and includes concern for the child's physical, cognitive, and social development. Instruction is organized around the child's needs, interests, and learning styles. The process of learning, rather than what is learned is emphasized" (Santrock, 1993, p. 291). The best practice for all children includes varied, informal learning activities within a specifically prepared environment. This does not mean a lack of structure because the teacher will plan specific activities for large groups, small groups, *and* individuals. It does mean that objectives will not be the same for all children and that workbooks and dittoes will be avoided. *Developmentally appropriate practice* means a concrete, hands-on approach to learning using activities that are age *and* individual appropriate as opposed to the use of paper-and-pencil activities presented to large groups of children (Santrock, 1993). In 1986 the National Association for the Education of Young Children (Bredekamp, 1987) published a position statement recommending appropriate practices for programs for four and five year olds. Appropriate teaching strategies recommended include: preparing the environment for children to learn through active exploration and interaction with others and materials; allowing children to select many of their own activities from a variety of prepared learning areas; having children work individually or in small groups most of the time; avoiding workbooks, dittoes, flashcards. These ideas also have been supported in a position paper from the Association for Childhood Education International (ACEI) (Moyer, Egertson, & Isenberg, 1987).

The way in which the learning environment is structured is important. The ACEI lists several principles that are important. These are summarized below.

✶Room arrangement should accommodate individual, small group, and large group activities.

✳ Learning centers or interest areas need to be clearly defined, differentiated (segregated), and be arranged to facilitate activity and movement.

✳ Materials should be displayed and arranged so that they are inviting, accessible, and changed as children develop.

Fisher (1991) portrays an excellent room arrangement that includes a variety of segregated learning center interest areas. Fisher's book is also an excellent reference for those readers who feel a bit uncomfortable with the whole language ideas to be presented under emergent literacy. Other excellent floor plans are presented by Morrow (1989) and Neuman and Roskos (1990). In addition, Bergman (1990) presents numerous learning center activities for kindergarten organized according to various physical areas (e.g., housekeeping, science, math, etc.). As Bergman points out, "Learning Centers can help to individualize the curriculum because activities planned can be accomplished on a variety of levels depending upon a particular youngster's interest and skill" (Bergman, 1990, p. xvi). Materials needed, how to get started, and how to extend and enrich activities are described for each activity in the book. For some activities, reproducible worksheets are given; however, most appear short and not "drill" oriented. Their use is of course up to the teacher. In addition to allowing for individualization in the center itself, individual instruction/attention can be given to children when others are using the centers.

Emergent Literacy

What *is* emergent literacy and how can it be encouraged? The emergent literacy perspective "represents a relatively recent way of thinking about the reading and writing development of young children" (Strickland & Morrow, 1988, p. 70). "Emergent literacy is concerned with the earliest phases of literacy development, the period between birth and the time when children read and write conventionally" (Sulzby & Teale, 1991, p. 728). Thus, literacy development begins much earlier than previously thought, is multidimensional and linked to the child's natural surroundings (both in the home and at school). "Literacy develops from real life settings in which reading and writing are used to accomplish goals" (Teale & Sulzby, 1989, p. 3). Rather than "getting a child ready" to learn to read, the emergent literacy perspective emphasizes the child's ongoing development. We no longer should speak of "reading readiness" or "prereading" but rather "literacy development" (Teale & Sulzby, 1989). It is important to note that reading and writing "develop currently and interrelatedly in young children" (Teale & Sulzby, 1989, p. 3). "Reading and writing are learned through active use. Young children are not interested in learning about literacy, they are interested in doing it" (Strickland & Morrow, 1988, p. 70). As children pretend to read and scribble messages on cards they are learning about language. These are the "foundations for conventional reading and writing and should be celebrated and encouraged at home, in preschools, and in the early years of formal schooling" (Searfoss & Readence, 1994, p. 58). The concepts of emergent literacy and developmentally appropriate activities mean we must abandon the traditional formal instruction often found in kindergartens (Durkin, 1987). "Traditional, formal reading instruction typical of first grade is simply inappropriate for young children. So is the worksheet dominated reading curriculum" (Teale & Sulzby, 1989, p. 5). Research by Taylor, Blum, and Logsdon (1989) and others supports a print-rich environment. Taylor et al. compared the emergent literacy skills of kindergarten children who were in "language and print rich" classrooms to those who were not. Many of the students in the study were from low income areas. Language and print rich classrooms had multiple and varied stimuli for reading and writing. Opportunities for reading were linked to ongoing classroom activities. Daily routines involved children in writing (e.g., signing in for the day). Results indicated that scores of children in the print rich environment were significantly higher on a written language awareness test, a test of concepts and two subtests (one measuring letter recognition and matching, one measuring school language) of a readiness test. Neuman and Roskos (1990) found that changing the environment in two preschool classrooms in a racially mixed early childhood setting to a literacy enriched play environment resulted in more purposeful, connected reading and writing behaviors.

Most authors recommend a separate reading center ("book nook," "library corner") and a separate writing center in addition to reading/writing activities provided in other centers (Morrow, 1989; Strickland & Morrow, 1989; Teale & Sulzby, 1989). Thus, "reading and writing should function as an integral part of every day's activities, rather than as separate instructional components" (Strickland & Morrow, 1988, p. 71). Neuman and Roskos (1992) studied the effects of placing literacy objects (e.g., books, signs, recipe cards, calendars, magazines, etc.) along with physical design changes (e.g., more sharply defining a play space such as the "library corner" or "office") on the literacy behavior of children ages three to five. Results indicated that children's uses of literacy objects became increasingly varied. Children in the experimental group spent more time with reading and writing activities in play. Simply providing a literacy environment may not be sufficient for some youngsters; some may need a gentle "nudge" to use the library corner, etc.

The reading center or library corner is a special place filled with an assortment of books (e.g., stories, fairy tales, fables, nursery rhymes, poetry, informational books). Newspapers and magazines should also be provided. It is very important to include familiar and predictable books. Martinez and Teale (1988) found that kindergarten children preferred familiar (i.e., books that have been read aloud by the teacher), predictable (i.e., books with repetitive, cumulative, or rhyming language patterns) and oversized (approximately 14" × 18") books. Kindergarten children were observed as they used the library corner in class. Familiar (read aloud once) and very familiar books (read aloud repeatedly) were preferred by children more than other books, almost twice and more than three times as much, respectively. Predictable books were preferred almost twice as much as nonpredictable books. Similar findings occurred with big books selected over small. Emergent reading (reenactment of books) was observed more frequently with familiar and predictable books.

Morrow (1989a) gives specific recommendations for the physical arrangement of the library corner. It should be large enough to accommodate five or six children, occupying approximately one third of the wall space on one side of the room with cozy chairs, pillows, rugs for sitting. Posters that encourage reading, available from the Children's Book Council (50 E. Huron St., Chicago, IL 60611), should be displayed. Numerous books, approximately five to eight per child, should be available with approximately 25 new books introduced every two weeks to replace others. A felt board with characters from stories and finger puppets will allow children to reenact stories. Ideas for a separate writing center are given in the section on writing.

Other centers in the classroom also should encourage reading and writing activities. For example, Strickland and Morrow (1989b) describe a veterinarian's office used with a unit on animals. The "waiting room" has books and magazines for pet owners to read, posters on animal care, a sign with the doctor's schedule, paper for writing prescriptions, etc. In another book, Strickland and Morrow (1989a) include several "Ideas you can use" sections providing suggestions for including reading and writing in other centers such as the "art gallery" or "bakery." Morrow (1989) gives suggestions for a music center, math center, science center, social studies center. Neuman and Roskos (1992) stress the need for varying play centers to fit children's experiences. For example, an "office" might be appropriate in one setting, a "restaurant" in another. Ideas for specific items they call literary props to place in centers are given by Neuman and Roskos (1990).

Reading to Children

How important is reading aloud to children? It is well known that reading to children is very important! "The single most important activity for building the knowledge required for eventual success in reading is reading aloud to children" (Anderson, Hiebert, Scott, & Wilkenson, 1985, p. 23). As Trelease (1989) puts it, "Reading aloud is the most effective advertisement for the pleasures of reading" (p. 201). But, this reading must begin long before children come to kindergarten. Research has shown that children who have fewer literacy experiences in preschool tend to be poorer readers later in school. For example, Scarborough, Dobrich, and Hager (1991) found that second grade students who were poor readers (i.e., scored 1.5 standard deviations lower than expected on reading tests) had less frequent preschool related experiences. Poor readers had less activities with books, were read to less frequently, and had parents who did less reading. Walker and Kuerbitz (1979) found that first grade reading achievement increased with frequency of story reading as preschoolers. Children who were read to "everyday" had generally higher achievement in first grade. Thus, it is important that kindergarten and preschool teachers make parents aware of the importance of reading to their children every day. Holdaway (1979) points out that "children with a background of book experience since infancy develop a complex range of attitudes, concepts, and skills predisposing them to literacy. They are likely to continue into literacy on entering school with a minimum of discontinuity" (p. 49). Rasinski and Fredericks (1990) give as their "candidate for the very best generic advice that any teacher could give any parent . . . Parents should read to their children" (p. 344). They suggest that parents schedule a particular time of day for reading so that it becomes part of the routine, talk about what is read and answer questions. Strickland and Morrow (1989c) concur. They suggest also that parents make children aware of print around them (e.g., point out labels, share the newspaper, etc.), visit the library regularly, let their child see them reading, make writing materials accessible. Numerous suggestions for books for young children are given by Cullinan (1989) (e.g., books for infants, Mother Goose and nursery rhymes, books for babies, nursery songs, participation books, etc.). Ollila and Mayfield (1992) cite several examples of programs involving parents in the child's emergent literacy/reading experiences. Research showing gains in reading because of parent programs is also reviewed. Needless to say, these programs are important at levels from preschool through the elementary grades. Enz and Searfoss (1996) give several ideas kindergarten teachers can use to involve parents (e.g., a coupon exchange box where children sort out coupons used at home, classroom lending library with books to go home, videotapes modeling storybook reading) and several activities encouraging emerging literacy that teachers can suggest to parents.

What about reading to children in kindergarten? The kindergarten teacher must read to children every day, at least once a day (Teale & Sulzby, 1989). What kinds of books? All kinds (see Cullinan, 1989). Big Books are especially useful for reading to children. "One of the most effective ways to get young children involved with print is through the use of Big Books. Enlarged texts allow groups of children to see and react to the printed page as it is being read aloud" (Strickland & Morrow, 1990, p. 342). Holdaway (1979) emphasizes the use of Big Books that can be used for "shared reading" similar to what was done in the home before entry into kindergarten. As when sitting next to an adult in the home, the child can see the print and pictures when Big Books are used. Appendix 1 lists publishers of Big Books. Smaller versions of the Big Books (e.g., companion versions) are available from many of these publishers; these can be placed in the library corner for individual use and emergent reading activities. Teachers can also make their own "enlarged" books.

When a book is read to children, Teale and Sulzby (1989) suggest previewing the book, establishing a receptive story listening context, briefly introducing the book, reading with expression and engaging children in discussion about what is being read. Strickland and Morrow (1990) suggest repeated readings where children read parts of the story in unison; teaching concepts of print by pointing to the text as it is read, pointing out text features such as repeated words or punctuation marks; using cloze activities where children predict words to fit sentences in the story. These ideas fit under what some writers call "interactive" reading, reading that involves social interaction between the child and adult (Morrow & Smith, 1990). As Roser and Martinez (1985) point out, adults assume three roles as they read to children: co-responders who initiate discussion, recount parts of the story, share reactions, relate experiences to real life and invite children's responses; informers/monitors who explain, provide information and assess understanding; directors who introduce the story, announce conclusions, and assume leadership. Mason, Peterman, and Kerr (1989) provide specific guidelines for reading to children with examples from different types of books (i.e., story books, informational books, and picture phrase books).

What does research show about these ideas for reading aloud? Combs (1987) found that kindergarten children at three "readiness levels" (below average, average, above average based on a school screening battery) read to with enlarged texts using some of the ideas presented by Teale and Sulzby (1989) and Strickland and Morrow (1990) showed significant differences in comprehension of stories when compared to children who listened to the teacher read regular size books in a traditional manner (i.e., read title, briefly explain the book, read story with a few pauses and a few questions). Children who were read the enlarged texts showed a significant increase in their ability to freely recall story elements. More evidence of attention during reading and emergent (pretend) reading afterward were noted for children read the enlarged texts. Morrow (1988) found that repeated readings of books resulted in more interpretative responses and more responses about print and story structure from four year olds. Comments and questions from children with low ability increased significantly with repeated readings. Trachtenbury and Ferruggia (1989) report a successful early reading experience for "transitional first graders" (i.e., not "ready" for grade one) using Big Books that were made using the children's "pretend" stories following repeated readings of a book. They also present sight word strategies, etc., that sprang from the use of the created Big Books. Nielsen (1993) investigated four models of group interaction with storybooks on the literacy growth of low achieving kindergarten students. A sample of 87 students participated in one of four story reading groups for three 20 minute sessions per week for 6 weeks. Students were divided into three literacy achievement levels using measures of story comprehension, story structure, and concepts about print. In Group One a different story book was simply read aloud for each of the 18 sessions; comments and questions were discouraged diplomatically. Group Two was read to using a directed reading activity format with pre and post discussion using teacher led questioning. The focus of story reading for Group Three was story structure with retelling with puppets and reenactment (activities that provided repeated experiences with the same story). Group Four experiences focused on concepts of print (e.g., letter, word, punctuation). Repeated experiences with the book were provided for by constructing a shortened version of the story on a large chart, rereading the chart focusing on concepts of print and then following along and illustrating individual facsimiles of the chart. Low achieving students in Group Three did significantly better than low achieving students in the other three groups and out performed average students in Group One achieving as well as high achievers in Group One. Low achievers also did better in Group Four.

Varying the size of the group for interactive storybook reading may be beneficial. Morrow and Smith (1990) studied the effects of story reading to kindergarten and first grade children in three settings: one-to-one, small group (three per group), and whole class (15 or more children). The adult readers in the study used many of the behaviors (roles) cited by Roser and Marinez (1985). Children who heard stories in the small group performed significantly better on probed and free recall comprehension tests than children in a one-to-one setting who performed better than the children in the whole class setting. Children in the one-to-one and small group settings also gave significantly more comments and asked more questions. Morrow and Smith point out that this does not mean that whole group reading should not be done, rather that settings should be varied.

Studies with children considered "at risk" for reading, though limited, indicate that incorporating emergent literacy ideas into classrooms with at risk children has positive results. Some studies have already been presented (Combs, 1987; Neilsen, 1993; Trachtenburg & Ferruggia, 1989). Otto (1993) investigated the effects of book reading with inner city kindergarten children. Children were introduced to a new storybook every 2 weeks for 14 weeks. Two copies of each book were placed in the library corner and then children were given personal copies of the book to take home and keep. Marked differences were found in book reading behaviors. Seventy-five percent of the children had higher scores on a measure of emergent reading behaviors. Most parents reported that children used their personal copies every day or several times per week accompanied by more interest in having stories read to them, telling stories, and in printing or trying to print. Sulzby, Branz, and Buhle (1993) found that when teachers in kindergarten used emergent literacy practices such as repeated readings of literature and encouraging reading emergently, low SES black and white children's developmental patterns were similar to nonrisk students; however, initially many students "adamantly" declared they could not read. Sulzby et al. concluded that teachers may experience more resistance from lower SES urban children and need to be patient and encouraging, "Sure you can do it!" Katims (1991, 1994) found that immersing children with disabilities (14 students, 1/3 mild to moderately mentally impaired, 2/3 learning, behavioral, and physical disabilities) (ages 4 to 6) in a literature rich environment which included repeated daily readings by adults of familiar and predictable books, assisted readings where children repeated sentences read or supplied missing words and interactive dialogues about story content resulted in more independent reenactments of books and a significant increase in scores on *Concepts about Print* (Clay, 1979, 1985), a measure of early literacy skills. Whitehurst, Epstein, Angell, Payne, Crone, and Fischel (1994) found interactive book reading at home and in the classroom as well as a classroom-based sound (phonemic awareness) and letter awareness ("letter of the week") program significantly affected the performance of four-year-old Head Start children on emergent literacy skills (e.g., printing first name, identifying sounds and letters, segmenting words).

Print Awareness/Concepts of Print

What do children need to learn about print? Young children must gradually come to understand the conventions of print that authors follow, i.e., to develop print awareness/concepts of print. Durkin (1993) lists several basic elements of print awareness:

1. Knowing the difference between graphic displays of words and graphic displays made up of nonwords.
2. Knowing that print is print no matter what medium was used to record it (e.g., pencil, crayon, finger marks in sand).
3. Knowing that print can appear on different kinds of surfaces (e.g., paper, cloth, metal).
4. Knowing that print can appear alone or with pictures and decorations.
5. Understanding that print corresponds to speech, word by word.
6. Understanding the function of empty space in establishing word boundaries.
7. Understanding that words are read from left to right.
8. Understanding that lines of text are read from top to bottom.

Research has generally indicated that print awareness is related to reading achievement (Reutzel, Oda, & Moore, 1989). The print awareness elements "are not developed one at a time or with one-day lessons. Rather, they are the product of many experiences with meaningful text spread out over time that may also result in some ability to read" (Durkin, 1993, p. 82). Some studies have indicated that children learn print awareness/concepts of print through an immersion in a print-rich environment and through shared reading using predictable books (Box & Aldridge, 1993; Reutzel et al., 1989).

Print awareness/concepts of print can be assessed informally (see Searfoss & Readance, 1994) or with a test such as the *Concepts about Print Test* (Clay, 1979, 1985).

Letter-Names

How important is knowledge of letter names? Substantial evidence is available that shows a high positive relationship between letter-name knowledge at entry into kindergarten or grade one and achievement in reading at the end of grade one (Badian, 1995; Blanchard & Logan, 1988; Bond & Dykstra, 1967; Chall, 1967; Samuels, 1971; Walsh, Price, & Gillingham, 1988). In other words, children who know the names of the letters tend to be children who succeed in reading. Does this suggest we should teach letter-names in kindergarten to children who do not know them? Is letter-name knowledge a prerequisite for learning to read? An inspection of basal reading series material for kindergarten or beginning grade one would lead one to certainly think so! The emphasis on teaching letter-names in kindergarten or before formal reading instruction is initiated is not new; it began shortly after the publication of the USOE First Grade Studies results (Bond & Dykstra, 1967) indicating the high predictive utility of knowledge of letter-names. However, research since then has suggested that *teaching* children letter-names has little effect on future success in reading (Blanchard & Logan, 1988). Samuels points out that "the mistake which some educators have made regarding letter-name knowledge and success in reading is to impute causation to correlational findings" (Samuels, 1971, p. 605). Venezky (1975) states that "a heavy emphasis on letter-name learning in either preschool or initial reading programs has neither logical or experimental support" (p. 19). But, Ehri (1983) criticized the teaching of letter-names studies for being too narrowly focused on the letter-*names* as opposed to letter-*names* and *sounds*. Thus, as Blanchard and Logan (1988) point out, we have a paradox here. "If students know the letter names before kindergarten begins they stand a good chance of learning to read without failure. On the other hand, if they have to be taught the letter names this will have little impact on predicting whether or not they experience future success in reading" (p. iv). Most writers feel that knowledge of letter-names is a result of the language experiences children have had before coming to school. "Knowledge of letter names is not important in itself so much as it is a reflection of broader knowledge about reading and language" (Anderson et al., 1985, p. 31). Many children who lack letter-name knowledge also "lack home and environmental language experiences necessary to avoid failure" (Blanchard & Logan, 1988, p. ix). This obviously is not true for all youngsters—some children have had numerous pre-reading literacy experiences and still have difficulty learning letter-names.

Despite the lack of research support for teaching letter names as a prerequisite to reading some writers, notably Donald Durrell have long argued that letter-names *are* important in reading and spelling because most letter-names contain the *sounds* of the letters (e.g., "s," "t") (Durrell, 1980). Durrell also points out that some words begin with letter-*names* (e.g., "bee" in beaver, "cee" in ceiling). Walsh et al. (1988) argue that "facility with letter names eases the process of learning to read . . . by vesting the symbols (letters) with immediate familiarity" (p. 110). In addition, letter-names are convenient labels. Venezky (1975) concurs but argues that they should not be overemphasized. Scott and Ehri (1990) point out that learning letter-names is important because when learning letter-names children learn to discriminate and remember shapes and learn many of the sounds commonly made by the letters in words. Their study with prereaders found that knowing letter-names enabled them to read words using phonetic cues (e.g., JRF as "giraffe," RM as "arm"). Groff (1984) reviews the research and beliefs of "teaching of reading" text authors and concludes that simultaneous teaching of letter- names and sounds appears to be the best approach. I concur but stress that instruction should be informal and not include workbooks and dittoes. Kindergarten teachers will have to work with first grade teachers to point out what research says about teaching letter-names to resist the emphasis placed on them in basal programs and the pressure to ensure that *all* children know *all* letter-names before grade one.

As with many skills attended to in a typical kindergarten program, children's knowledge about letter-names will vary (McGee & Richgels, 1989). Some children will know all or most letter-names, others will know only a few or none. Blanchard and Logan (1988) found a range of knowledge from 0 to 26. Over 50% of the kindergarten children (n = 107 children from racially and economically mixed backgrounds) knew 8 or less lower case letters; only 15% knew 20 or more letters. Informal activities can meet the needs of all children. I recommend including letter (both upper and lower case) activities in various centers in the room. Alphabet books can be placed in the library corner. See Appendix 2 for a list.

The writing center with its natural focus on letters can include manipulative letters (e.g., plastic letters, felt letters, blocks with letters) and an alphabet chart. Teachers can use "written language talk" in various contexts to focus attention on letters (e.g., letters in books, lettering on a truck, letters on a t-shirt) (McGee & Richgels, 1989). When talking about daily schedules, the teacher can read and spell the words (Schickendanz, 1989). McGee and Richgels also recommend talking about environmental print items, displaying children's names in the writing center so children can write notes to friends, singing alphabet songs, and playing games. "Children learn to recognize, name, and write alphabet letters as they engage in meaningful reading and writing activities with their parents, teachers, and other children" (McGee & Richgels, 1989, p. 224). Although some writers don't "approve" of the somewhat traditional idea of the "letter of the week" approach, I see little harm done when one letter is the focus of informal activities for a week.

Some informal, but direct, one-on-one instruction will be necessary for those children who enter kindergarten with little or no letter-name knowledge and who don't seem to be acquiring knowledge with the other activities. Initial one-on-one multisensory activities for learning the letter name/sound/written form can be done using letters in the child's name. The first letters that children often learn are related to names of people they know or stories they are familiar with. For example, Kristen's name begins with "K," just like in K-Mart (McGee & Richgels, 1989). Thus, this appears a logical place to start. See a description of the Slingerland Approach by Lesiak (1984) for a procedure for teaching the name, sound, and written forms of letters.

Phonemic Awareness

What is phonemic awareness and how important is it for learning to read? Research strongly suggests that phonemic awareness is an extremely important skill for reading (e.g., Backman, 1983; Bryant, MacLean, Bradley, & Crossland, 1990; Bryne, Freebody, & Gates, 1992; Catts, 1991; Cunningham, 1990; Foorman, Navy, Francis, & Liberman, 1991; Juel, 1988; Lenchner, Gerber, & Routh, 1990; Mann, 1993; Pratt & Brady, 1988; Share, Jorm, MacLean, & Matthews, 1984; Spector, 1992, 1995; Stanovich, Cunningham, & Cramer, 1984; Torgesen, Wagner, & Rashotte, 1994; Vellutino & Scanlon, 1987; Yopp, 1988). Phonemic awareness (also know as phonemic segmentation, linguistic awareness, linguistic insight, phonological awareness) begins when a child realizes that speech is composed of words (Pikulski, 1989). "Then awareness must spread to the individual sounds that compose words (e.g., The word "cat" has both 3 letters and 3 phonemes)" (Pikulski, 1989, p. 637). Lewkowicz (1980) identifies the following "phonemic awareness tasks" (note that many of these were assumed under auditory discrimination, analysis, blending in the past):

1. *Sound-to-word matching* (recognition, within a word, of a previously identified phoneme) (e.g., Does "fish" start with /f/?)
2. *Word-to-word matching* (recognition of the fact that a word has the same beginning sound or final sound or medial vowel sound as another word) (e.g., Does "fish" start with the same sound as "feather?")
3. *Recognition of rhyme* (recognition that a word is identical to another except for the portion preceding the stressed vowel) (e.g., Does "fish" rhyme with "dish?")
4. *Isolation* of a beginning, medial, or final sound (e.g., What is the first sound of "fish?")

5. *Phonemic Segmentation* (separately articulating all the sounds of a word in correct order) (e.g., What are the 3 sounds of "fish?")
6. *Counting the phonemes* in a word (How many sounds do you hear in the word "fish?")
7. *Blending* (e.g., What word is this /f/ /i/ /v/?)
8. *Deletion of a phoneme* (responding to a spoken word by pronouncing the new word that can be formed by omitting a designated phoneme) (e.g., Say "fish." Now say it without the /f/.)
9. *Specifying which phoneme has been deleted* (e.g., Say "meat." Now say "eat." What sound was left out of the second word?)
10. *Phoneme substitution* (e.g., Say "meat." Now say it with /f/ instead of /m/.)

"Evidence from both prediction and training studies favors a causal hypothesis: that explicit awareness of phonemic units in language is a necessary precursor to understanding that letters correspond to phonemes. In addition, a few studies have indicated that phonological awareness is augmented as a consequence of reading instruction" (Pratt & Brady, 1988, p. 319).

Phonemic awareness can be assessed informally using gamelike tasks described in Griffith and Olson (1992) or tasks presented by Yopp (1988, 1995), *The Yopp–Singer Test of Phoneme Segmentation*. The Yopp–Singer test measures the ability to separately articulate the sounds of a spoken word in order. Griffith and Olson present suggestions for assessing rhyme, blending, isolating sounds, segmenting sounds, deleting sounds with guidelines for performance using Yopp's studies as a guide. *The Lindamood Auditory Conceptualization Test* (Lindamood & Lindamood, 1971) is an individually administered criterion referenced test for subjects in prekindergarten to adult designed to assess the discrimination and manipulation of sounds using colored blocks. The *Test of Phonological Awareness* (Torgesen & Bryant, 1994) is a norm-referenced group test designed to identify children in kindergarten, grades one and two who have difficulty identifying sounds that are the same or different within dictated words accompanied by pictures (beginning of words in kindergarten, end of words in grades one and two). The *Phonological Awareness Profile* (Robertson & Salter, 1995) is an individually administered criterion-referenced test designed to assess six phoneme awareness tasks. The test appears most appropriate for students in grades kindergarten through early elementary.

Phonemic awareness training has been found to improve phonemic awareness and the reading performance of students of many ages and in many grades (Alexander, Andersen, Heilman, Voeller, & Torgesen, 1991; Bradley & Bryant, 1983; Bus, 1986; Byrne & Fielding-Barnsley, 1989, 1991; Cunningham, 1990; Hurford, 1990; Lie, 1991; Lundberg, Frost, & Petersen, 1988; Torgeson, Morgan, & Davis, 1992; Vellutino & Scanlon, 1987). Studies with students in kindergarten have shown positive affects on reading and/or spelling phonetically regular words and later reading and spelling achievement in grades one and two (Ball & Blachman, 1991; Bryne & Fielding-Barnsley, 1991; Cunningham, 1990; Lundberg et al., 1988; Torgesen et al., 1992).

Studies with "at risk" kindergarten students (including low achievers, learning disabled, low SES and language delayed students) have shown positive results from training in phonemic awareness (Blachman, 1994; Brady, Fowler, Stone, & Windbury, 1994; O'Connor, Jenkins, Leicester, & Slocum, 1993; O'Connor, Jenkins, & Slocum, 1995; O'Conner, Notari-Syverson, & Vadasy, 1996; Warrick, Rubin, & Rowe-Walsh, 1993).

Two studies (Blachman, 1994; O'Connor et al., 1995) found transfer to reading tasks. Blachman (1994) found training in kindergarten to result in higher reading achievement in grade one. O'Connor et al. (1993) found that learning disabled students in treatment groups improved compared to controls but that skill levels were not commensurate to their peers. They concluded that learning disabled students may need more intensive instruction.

The predictive and training studies support the need to give attention to phonemic awareness in kindergarten. An important note, teaching "phonics" should not be assumed to ensure the development of phonemic awareness (Byrne & Fielding-Barnsley, 1991; Spector, 1995). Children need to acquire letter-sound knowledge *and* phonemic awareness. Spector (1995) points out that phonemic awareness programs that incorporate segmentation and blending training with letter-sound instruction have had the most positive effects on reading achievement. There are numerous, informal, but structured, activities teachers can use when working with children to improve their phonemic awareness. Reading nursery rhymes, teaching short rhymes or songs are helpful. MacLean, Bryant, and Bradley (1987) studied preschool children over a time span of 15 months beginning at age 3 years, 4 months and found a significant relationship between knowledge of nursery rhymes and the development of phonemic awareness skills (detection and production of rhyme, segmenting sounds, detection and production of alliteration, i.e., using the same sounds as a stimulus word). Bryant et al. (1990), after studying children for two years (ages 4–7 to 6–7), concluded that sensitivity to rhyme leads to awareness of phonemes which affects reading and that rhyme makes a direct contribution to reading that is independent of the connection between reading and phonemic awareness. Griffith and Olson (1992) provide examples of books that contain text "that plays with the sounds in language" (p. 520).

Many of the training studies cited with kindergarten children (Lundberg et al., 1988; Cunningham, 1990; Ball & Blachman, 1991; Torgeson et al., 1992) used a combination of gamelike activities and exercises supporting the use of more direct but informal activities for teaching phonemic awareness. "The objective of any phonemic awareness activity should be to facilitate children's ability to perceive that their speech is made up of a series of sounds" (Yopp, 1992, p. 699). Yopp gives examples of activities for matching and isolating sounds, blending sounds, segmentation, sound addition or substitution. Tasks in isolating the initial phoneme should precede segmenting phonemes (Lewkowicz, 1980; Yopp, 1992). Stahl and Murray (1994) found phoneme isolation to be the easiest task for kindergarten and grade one students of four presented, followed by blending, deletion, and segmentation. Initially, using short, one syllable words for instruction focusing on single consonant sounds is recommended. Treiman and Weatherston (1992) found that children in preschool and kindergarten performed better on short words (e.g., bay) than long words (e.g., bones). Words without initial consonant clusters (e.g., bay) were easier than words with consonant clusters (e.g., brow). Ideas presented in Strickland and Morrow (1989a) include having children respond with their name to a rhyming word given by the teacher (e.g., "Whose name rhymes with wave?"), having children respond to the beginning sound of their names (e.g., "Whose name begins with /ssss/?") Other suggestions include activities where children respond to questions such as "What's the first sound in _____? If we change the /f/ sound in fat to an /s/ what word will we have?" Several authors have suggestions for teaching sound segmentation. Griffith and Olson (1992) suggest using "Elkonin" boxes (named after the Russian psychologist, D. B. Elkonin) in which the teacher slowly articulates a word and pushes a counter for each sound into a box; children imitate. For example, the card for "cat" would have three boxes and use three counters. Clay (1985) gives a similar procedure. Ball and Blachman (1991) in their training study used a "Say it and move it" activity. Students were given disks to move on a card for each phoneme. With tasks such as this, Lewkowicz (1980) suggests slow "stretched" pronunciation and that the child imitate the pronunciation. *Auditory Discrimination in Depth* (Lindamood & Lindamood, 1975) is a published program which uses colored felt squares or wooden cubes to signify how many sounds are in a word or how sounds change in a word.

Formal Reading Instruction in Kindergarten

Should formal instruction in reading be a part of the kindergarten program? It should be readily apparent at this point that I, along with many other authors, am opposed to a formal (sit down basal reader, workbooks, spiritmasters, black line masters) approach to reading instruction in kindergarten; rather, I support the activities suggested in the first several pages of this article. Numerous studies (Lesiak, 1978; Hayes & Cangelosi, 1985) have indicated that children can be taught to read in kindergarten and that the "lead" they gain in reading is maintained throughout the elementary grades, but in particular in the primary grades. Hanson and Farrell (1995) report a study investigating the effects of learning to read in kindergarten on high school seniors and found "clear consistent, and positive differences were associated with receiving reading instruction in kindergarten" (p. 909). Reading instruction in the studies varied (basal series, picture type reading readiness programs, language arts approaches). That research, however, has left an important question unanswered. What are the social and emotional effects of "formal" instruction in reading in kindergarten? Some research (Lesiak, 1978) has indicated that classroom behaviors and attitudes toward school were better in kindergartens without formal instruction in reading. Werner and Strother (1987) present case studies of two children, Michael, a preschooler pressured into learning to read by his parents with workbooks and flashcards and Jeff, an early reader who received positive reinforcement but no formal reading in preschool and kindergarten. Jeff's social/emotional adjustment and attitude toward reading differed greatly from Michael's who experienced a great deal of frustration and anxiety, had difficulty interacting with peers, and did not enjoy reading. Concern over the practice of pushing formal instruction in reading downward into kindergarten led several organizations including the International Reading Association to issue a position statement about pre-first grade reading instruction in 1977 (Strickland and others, 1977). That statement, which generally considers formal instruction inappropriate, also gave recommendations which fit the emergent literacy perspective. It is interesting to note, however, that recent surveys indicate the practice of teaching reading to kindergarten children has increased, probably as a result of pressure from first grade teachers and parents (Shepard & Smith, 1988). As stated previously, kindergarten teachers must work with first grade teachers and parents to share with them what professionals working with young children view as appropriate practices in educating young children. However, it must be pointed out that Hanson and Farrell (1995) conclude that the results of their study "provide full support for the policy of teaching reading in kindergarten" (p. 929). The program used in kindergarten in that study incorporated group instruction for approximately 20–30 minutes per day. Instruction in sight words and decoding skills followed by the reading of short stories was done. It would be interesting to see research comparing this program with a program focusing on the ideas presented previously!

So, what does a teacher do with a child who begins reading "conventionally" in kindergarten? Encourage that reading! Provide early reading books in the library corner. Answer questions about words. Simply respond to the child's initiative.

Early Readers

What about children who are reading when they enter kindergarten? Some children *will* enter kindergarten already reading (Durkin, 1966; Torrey, 1979; Thomas, 1985; Tobin & Pikulski, 1988). Most of these "early readers" have not had formal training in reading. Instead, they were read to frequently, had parents who simply answered questions about whole words, etc., may have had older siblings who assisted them as they "played school" (Durkin, 1966). Durkin also found that early readers had an early interest in writing, were interested in letters/numerals as they appeared in everyday surroundings. (Sounds like emergent literacy ideas!) What do we *do* with these early readers? Let them read! Provide many early reading books in the library corner. Chances are very good that these children will find peers wanting to listen to them read a story! Encourage this peer-to-peer interaction.

Writing

What about writing in kindergarten? An important center in the kindergarten classroom is the writing center (Teale & Sulzby, 1989). Sulbzy (1992) reviews research indicating that "children write with many forms prior to developing close to the adult concept that I call conventional writing" (p. 293). "At kindergarten, most children are still using emergent forms of writing such as scribble, drawing, nonphonetic strings of letters, or phonetic ("invented" or "creative") spelling and few have made the transition to conventional writing as their preferred writing form" (Sulzby, 1992, p. 290). We need to understand that kindergarten children can write. Martinez and Teale (1987) argue that it is destructive to assume "that children cannot write (that is, cannot compose) until they have mastered the mechanics and that the only way they should write is through conventional orthography" (p. 69). We are all aware of the push downward into kindergarten of conventional writing. Most basal writing series have kindergarten books with many introducing all the lowercase letters of the alphabet. However, I support informal approaches to writing in a literacy environment. Sulzby (1992) points out that we need to provide many opportunities in kindergarten for children to write and share their writing. This can be done by providing a rich literacy environment as opposed to sit-down lessons in handwriting; it is not known whether a "push" towards conventional writing is advantageous (Sulzby, 1992). Sulzby, Teale, and Kamberelis (1989) point out that children need to be "encouraged" or "nudged," not "pushed" or "pressured." For example, when the teacher knows a child can write in readable forms and still scribbles or uses nonphonetic strings, the teacher might say, "I like your story. It's great! Do you think you could write it so I can read it too?"

The writing center should be one utilized by children everyday. Martinez and Teale (1987) suggest introducing the center by writing a message on the board and explaining that even if most children cannot read the message, it is still writing. The teacher then tells the children that they will be writers in the writing center and even though others may not be able to read their writing, they can read their writing to others. Samples of writing by kindergarten children can be shown, from scribbles/drawings to random letters. Sulzby et al. (1989) suggest three tips to encourage writing: accept the forms of writing children use; make your request simple and straightforward (e.g., "Write a story." "Write a letter."), ask the child to read what he or she has written; Reassure (e.g., "Do it your way. It doesn't have to be like grown-up writing."). An adult (teacher, parent, community volunteer) is an important part of the writing center (Martinez & Teale, 1987). The adult can facilitate prewriting (e.g., discuss a topic with a child first), serve as an aid while children write (e.g., "Spell it the best you can."), be an audience for the child's writing and a record keeper noting progress. Children write stories, letters, signs, etc. They share their writing. Teale and Sulzby (1989) suggest a classroom post office to encourage writing of notes and letters. A connection is made to reading by having children read what they have written or write about something stemming from a story read by the teacher.

The writing center should contain a variety of writing instruments (e.g., crayons, pencils, pens, markers) and materials (e.g., lined and unlined paper, a chalkboard, slates, a typewriter, a computer, plastic letters to manipulate, materials for making books such as a stapler, paper for covers) (Sulzby et al., 1989; Teale and Sulzby, 1989). Martinez and Teale (1987) recommend unlined paper at first because it doesn't suggest how writing *must* be done. Sulzby et al. (1989) suggest moving to lined paper after children are writing in straight, regular lines. A note about pencils: research has indicated that young children prefer adult pencils and that they do not write better when using beginner's pencils (Askov & Peck, 1982). However, pencils with soft lead so that writing requires less pressure on the pencil are recommended.

As with reading, writing is also done outside the writing center. For example, children can write a grocery list or copy a recipe in the housekeeping corner, write prescriptions in the vet's office, write one's name (in one's own way) when checking out books from the library corner.

Speaking of writing one's name, how important is it for the kindergarten child to write his/her own name? Sulzby et al. (1989) suggest that writing one's name is important for showing ownership and point out that most kindergarten children will be able to write all or part of their first name in conventional orthography. They prefer learning in an emergent literacy approach as opposed to specific instruction in conventional writing. Harris (1986) found that most preschoolers who could not initially write any letters of their names could at least write one letter of their name after a five month period of being required to write names (in their own way) on artwork, waiting lists, etc. The teacher wrote the child's name in conventional writing next to the child's version.

What about children who are still using scribbles through most of kindergarten and have difficulty with the basic shapes (circle, square, triangle)? These children will be faced with formal handwriting instruction in first grade. I have worked with several kindergarten children whose fine motor skills are very poor and who need specialized instruction before they begin conventional writing. Informal instruction in learning the circle, square, and triangle is recommended because the movements needed to make these shapes ($\subset \supset / - \setminus /$) are those needed to write letters. Once the shapes are learned, the transition to learning letters in traditional first grade classrooms will be easier. Procedures adapted from those described several years ago by Kephart (1961) (See Appendix 3) are recommended. The steps use multisensory cues to teach the movements for and the making of the basic shapes. Teach proper pencil grip. Three sided pencil grips that can be placed on a pencil are helpful (One source: Michigan Produces, P.O. Box 24155, Lansing, MI 48909-4155). Use soft lead pencils or felt tip pens to allow the student to write without a great deal of pressure.

Summary

Several questions school psychologists and teachers might have regarding emergent literacy in kindergarten have been presented and answered. It is hoped that the many ideas and activities presented in response to these questions will help school psychologists and teachers as they work together to encourage emergent literacy in *all* students in kindergarten.

References

Alexander, A., Andersen, H., Heilman, P., Voeller, K., & Togesen, J. (1991). Phonological awareness training and remediation of analytic decoding deficits in a group of seven dyslexics. *Annals of Dyslexia, 41,* 193–206.

Anderson, R., Hiebert, E., Scott, J., & Wilkenson, I. (1985). *Becoming a nation of readers: The report of the Commission on Reading.* Washington, DC: The National Institute of Education.

Askov, E., & Peck, M. (1982). Handwriting. In H. Mitzel, J. Best, & W. Rabinowitz (Eds.), *Encyclopedia of educational research* (pp. 764–769). New York: The Free Press.

Backman, J. (1983). The role of psycholinguistic skills in reading acquisition: A look at early readers. *Reading Research Quarterly, 18,* 466–479.

Badian, N. (1995). Predicting reading ability over the long term: The changing roles of letter naming, phonological awareness and orthographic processing. *Annals of Dyslexia, 45,* 79–96.

Ball, E., & Blachman, B. (1991). Does phoneme awareness training in kindergarten make a difference in early word recognition and developmental spelling? *Reading Research Quarterly, 26,* 49–66.

Bergman, A. (1990). *Learning center activities for the full day Kindergarten.* West Nyack, NY: Center for Applied Research in Education.

Blachman, B. (1994). What we have learned from longitudinal studies of phonological processing and reading, *and* some unanswered questions: A response to Torgesen, Wagner, and Rashotte. *Journal of Learning Disabilities, 27,* 287–291.

Blanchard, J., & Logan, J. (1988). Editorial comment: Letter-naming knowledge in kindergartners: What's happening? *Reading Psychology, 9,* iii–xi.

Bond, G., & Dykstra, R. (1967). The cooperative research program in first-grade reading instruction. *Reading Research Quarterly, 2.*

Box, J., & Aldridge, J. (1993). Shared reading experiences and Head Start children's concepts about print and story structure. *Perceptual and Motor Skills, 77,* 929–930.

Bradley, L., & Bryant, B. (1983). Categorizing sounds and learning to read—A causal connection. *Nature, 301,* 419–421.

Brady, S., Fowler, A., Stone, B., & Winbury, N. (1994). Training phonological awareness: A study with inner-city kindergarten children. *Annals of Dyslexia, 44,* 26–59.

Bredekamp, S. (Ed.). (1987). *NAEYC position statement on developmentally appropriate practice in programs for 4- and 5-year-olds.* Washington, DC: National Association for the Education of Young Children.

Bryant, P., MacLean, M., Bradley, L., & Crossland, J. (1990). Rhyme and alliteration, phoneme detection, and learning to read. *Developmental Psychology, 26,* 429–438.

Bus, A. (1986). Preparatory reading instruction in kindergarten: Some comparative research into methods of auditory and auditory-visual training of phonemic analysis and blending. *Perceptual and Motor Skills, 62,* 11–24.

Byrne, B., & Fielding-Barnsley, R. (1989). Phonemic awareness and letter knowledge in the child's acquisition of the alphabetic principle. *Journal of Educational Psychology, 81,* 313–321.

Byrne, B., & Fielding-Barnsley, R. (1991). Evaluation of a program to teach phonemic awareness to young children. *Journal of Educational Psychology, 83,* 451–455.

Byrne, B., & Fielding-Barnsley, R. (1993). Evaluation of a program to teach phonemic awareness to young children: A 1-year follow-up. *Journal of Educational Psychology, 85,* 104–111.

Byrne, B., Freebody, P., & Gates, A. (1992). Longitudinal data on the relations of word-reading strategies to comprehension, reading time, and phonemic awareness. *Reading Research Quarterly, 27,* 140–151.

Catts, H. (1991). Early identification of dyslexia: Evidence from a follow-up study of speech-language impaired children. *Annals of Dyslexia, 41,* 163–177.

Chall, J. (1967). *Learning to read: The great debate.* New York: McGraw-Hill.

Clay, M. (1979, 1985). *The early detection of reading difficulties.* Portsmouth, NH: Heinemann Educational Books.

Combs, M. (1987). Modeling the reading process with enlarged texts. *The Reading Teacher, 40,* 422–426.

Cullinan, B. (1989). Literature for young children. In D. Strickland & L. Morrow (Eds.), *Emerging Literacy: Young children learn to read and write* (pp. 35–51). Newark, DE: International Reading Association.

Cunningham, A. (1990). Explicit versus implicit instruction in phonemic awareness. *Journal of Experimental Child Psychology, 50,* 429–444.

Durkin, D. (1966). *Children who read early.* New York: Teacher's College Press.

Durkin, D. (1987). A classroom-observation study of reading instruction in kindergarten. *Early Childhood Research Quarterly, 2,* 275–300.

Durkin, D. (1993). *Teaching them to read.* Boston: Allyn & Bacon.

Durrell, D. (1980). Letter-name values in reading and spelling. *Reading Research Quarterly, 16,* 159–166.

Ehri, L. (1983). A critique of five studies related to letter-name knowledge and learning to read. In L. Gentil, M. Kamil, & J. Blanchard (Eds.), *Reading research revisited* (pp. 143–153). Columbus, OH: Merrill.

Enz, B., & Searfoss, L. (1996). Expanding our views of family literacy. *The Reading Teacher, 49,* 576–579.

Fisher, B. (1991). *Joyful learning: A whole language kindergarten.* Portsmouth, NH: Heinemann.

Foorman, B., Novy, D., Francis, D., & Liberman, P. (1991). How letter-sound instruction mediates progress in first-grade reading and spelling. *Journal of Educational Psychology, 83,* 456–469.

Griffith, P., & Olson, M. (1992). Phonemic awareness helps beginning readers break the code. *The Reading Teacher, 45,* 516–523.

Groff, P. (1984). Resolving the letter name controversy. *The Reading Teacher, 37,* 384–388.

Hanson, R., & Farrell, D. (1995). The long-term effects on high school seniors of learning to read in kindergarten. *Reading Research Quarterly, 30,* 908–933.

Harris, S. (1986). Evaluation of a curriculum to support literacy growth in young children. *Early Childhood Research Quarterly, 1,* 333–348.

Hayes, B., & Cangelosi, J. (1985). Kindergarten reading instruction and students reading achievement trends. *Reading Improvement, 223,* 305–315.

Holdaway, D. (1979). *The foundations of literacy.* New York: Ashton Scholastic.

Hurford, D. (1990). Training phonemic segmentation ability with a phonemic discrimination intervention in second- and third-grade children with reading disabilities. *Journal of Learning Disabilities, 23,* 564–569.

Juel, C. (1988). Learning to read and write: A longitudinal study of 54 children from first through fourth grades. *Journal of Educational Psychology, 80,* 437–447.

Katims, D. (1991). Emergent literacy in early childhood special education: Curriculum and instruction. *Topics in Early Childhood Special Education, 11,* 69–84.

Katims, D. (1994). Emergence of literacy in preschool children with disabilities. *Learning Disability Quarterly, 17,* 58–69.

Kephart, N. (1961). *The slow learner in the classroom.* Columbus, OH: Merrill.

Lenchner, O., Gerber, M., & Routh, D. (1990). Phonological awareness tasks as predictors of decoding ability: Beyond segmentation. *Journal of Learning Disabilities, 23,* 240–247.

Lesiak, J. (1978). Reading in kindergarten: What the research doesn't tell us. *The Reading Teacher, 31,* 135–138.

Lesiak, J. (1984). Review of a multisensory approach to language arts for specific language disability children. *Techniques, 1,* 7–13.

Lewkowicz, N. (1980). Phonemic awareness training: What to teach and how to teach it. *Journal of Educational Psychology, 72,* 686–700.

Lie, A. (1991). Effects of a training program for stimulating skills in word analysis in first grade children. *Reading Research Quarterly, 26,* 234–250.

Lindamood, C., & Lindamood, P. (1975). *Auditory Discrimination in Depth.* Allen, TX: DLM.

Lindamood, C., & Lindamood, P. (1971). *Lindamood Auditory Conceptualization Test.* Austin, TX: PRO-ED.

Lundberg, I., Frost, J., & Petersen, O. (1988). Effects of an extensive program for stimulating phonological awareness in preschool children. *Reading Research Quarterly, 23,* 263–284.

MacLean, M., Bryant, P., & Bradley, L. (1987). Rhymes, nursery rhymes, and reading in early childhood. *Merrill-Palmer Quarterly, 33,* 255–281.

Mann, V. (1993). Phoneme Awareness and future reading ability. *Journal of Learning Disabilities, 26,* 259–269.

Martinez, M., & Teale, W. (1987). The ins and outs of a kindergarten writing program. *The Reading Teacher, 40,* 444–450.

Martinez, M., & Teale, W. (1988). Reading in a kindergarten classroom library. *The Reading Teacher, 41,* 568–572.

Mason, J., Peterman, C., & Kerr, B. (1989). Reading to kindergarten children. In D. Strickland & L. Morrow (Eds.), *Emerging literacy: Young children learn to read and write* (pp. 52–62). Newark, DE: International Reading Association.

McGee, L., & Richgels, D. (1989). "K is Kristen's": Learning the alphabet from a child's perspective. *The Reading Teacher, 43,* 216–225.

Morrow, L. (1988). Young children's responses to one-to-one story readings in school settings. *Reading Research Quarterly, 23,* 89–106.

Morrow, L. (1989). Designing the classroom to promote literacy development. In S. Strickland & L. Morrow (Eds.), *Emerging literacy: Young children learn to read and write* (pp. 121–134). Newark, DE: International Reading Association.

Morrow, L., & Smith, J. (1990). The effects of group size on interactive storybook reading. *Reading Research Quarterly, 25,* 213–231.

Moyer, J., Egertson, H., & Isenberg, J. (1987). The child-centered kindergarten. *Childhood Education, 63,* 235–242.

Neuman, S., & Roskos, K. (1990). Play, print, and purpose: Enriching play environments for literacy development. *The Reading Teacher, 44,* 214–221.

Neuman, S., & Roskos, K. (1992). Literacy objects as cultural tools: Effects on children's literacy development in play. *Reading Research Quarterly, 27,* 203–225.

Nielson, D. (1993). The effects of four models of group interaction with storybooks on the literacy growth of low-achieving kindergarten children. In D. Leu & C. Kinzer (Eds.), *Examining central issues in literacy research, theory and practice* (pp. 279–287). Chicago, IL: National Reading Conference.

O'Connor, R., Jenkins, J., Leicester, N., & Slocum, T. (1993). Teaching phonological awareness to young children with learning disabilities. *Exceptional Children, 59,* 532–546.

O'Connor, R., Jenkins, J., & Slocum, T. (1995). Transfer among phonological tasks in kindergarten: Essential instructional content. *Journal of Educational Psychology, 1995,* 202–217.

O'Connor, R., Notari-Syverson, A., & Vadasy, P. (1996). Ladders to literacy: The effects of teacher-led phonological activities for kindergarten children with and without disabilities. *Exceptional Children, 63,* 117–130.

Ollila, L., & Mayfield, M. (1992). Home and school together: Helping beginning readers succeed. In S. Samuels & A. Larstrup (Eds.), *What research has to say about reading instruction* (pp. 17–45). Newark, DE: International Reading Association.

Otto, B. (1993). Signs of emergent literacy among inner-city kindergartners in a storybook reading program. *Reading & Writing Quarterly, 9,* 151–162.

Pilulski, T. (1989). Questions and answers. *The Reading Teacher,* p. 637.

Pratt, A., & Brady, S. (1988). Relation of phonological awareness to reading disability in children and adults. *Journal of Educational Psychology, 80,* 319–323.

Rasinski, T., & Fredericks, A. (1990). The best reading advice for parents. *The Reading Teacher, 43,* 344–345.

Reutzel, D., Oda, L., & Moore, B. (1989). Developing print awareness: The effect of three instructional approaches on kindergartner's print awareness, reading readiness, and word reading. *Journal of Reading Behavior, 21,* 197–217.

Robertson, C., & Salter, W. (1995). *The Phonological Awareness Profile.* E. Moline, IL: Lingui Systems, Inc.

Roser, N., & Martinez, M. (1985). Roles adults play in preschoolers' responses to literature. *Language Arts, 62,* 485–490.

Samuels, J. (1971). Letter-name versus letter-sound knowledge in learning to read. *The Reading Teacher, 24,* 604–608, 662.

Santrock, J. (1993). *Children.* Madison, WI: Brown & Benchmark.

Scarborough, H., Dobrich, W., & Hager, M. (1991). Preschool literacy experience and later reading achievement. *Journal of Learning Disabilities, 24,* 508–512.

Schickendanz, J. (1989). The place of specific skills in preschool and kindergarten. In D. Strickland & L. Morrow (Eds.), *Emerging literacy: Young children learn to read and write.* Newark, DE: International Reading Association.

Scott, J., & Ehri, L. (1990). Sight word reading in prereaders: Use of logographic vs alphabetic access routes. *Journal of Reading Behavior, 22,* 149–166.

Searfoss, L., & Readence, J. (1994). *Helping children learn to read.* Boston: Allyn & Bacon.

Share, D., Jorm, A., MacLean, R., & Matthews, R. (1984). Sources of individual differences in reading acquisition. *Journal of Educational Psychology, 76,* 1309–1324.

Shepard, L., & Smith, L. (1988). Escalating academic demand in kindergarten: Counterproductive policies. *The Elementary School Journal, 89,* 135–145.

Spector, J. (1992). Predicting progress in beginning reading: Dynamic assessment of phonemic awareness. *Journal of Educational Psychology, 84,* 353–363.

Spector, J. (1995). Phonemic awareness training: Application of principles of direct instruction. *Reading and Writing Quarterly, 11,* 37–51.

Stahl, S., & Murray, B. (1994). Defining phonological awareness and its relationship to early reading. *Journal of Educational Psychology, 86,* 221–234.

Stanovich, K., Cunningham, A., & Cramer, B. (1984). Assessing phonological awareness in kindergarten children: Issues of task comparability. *Journal of Experimental Child Psychology, 38,* 175–190.

Strickland, D. and others (1977). *Reading and pre-first grade.* Newark, DE: International Reading Association.

Strickland, D., & Morrow, L. (1988). New perspectives on young children learning to read and write. *The Reading Teacher, 42,* 70–71.

Strickland, D., & Morrow, L. (Eds.). (1989a). *Emerging Literacy: Young children learn to read and write.* Newark, DE: International Reading Association.

Strickland, D., & Morrow, L. (1989b). Environments rich in print promote literacy behavior during play. *The Reading Teacher, 43,* 178–179.

Strickland, D., & Morrow, L. (1989c). Family literacy and young children. *The Reading Teacher, 42,* 530–531.

Strickland, D., & Morrow, L. (1990). Sharing big books. *The Reading Teacher, 43,* 342–343.

Sulzby, E. (1992). Research directions: Transitions from emergent to conventional writing. *Language Arts, 69,* 290–297.

Sulzby, E., Branz, C., & Buhle, R. (1993). Repeated readings of literature and low socioeconomic status Black kindergartners and first graders. *Reading & Writing Quarterly, 9,* 183–196.

Sulzby, E., & Teale, W. (1991). Emergent literacy. In R. Barr, M. L. Kamil, P. B. Mosenthal, & P. D. Pearson (Eds.), *Handbook of Reading Research: Volume II* (pp. 727–757). New York: Longman.

Sulzby, E., Teale, W., & Kamberelis, G. (1989). Emergent writing in the classroom: Home and school connections. In D. Strickland & L. Morrow (Eds.), *Emerging literacy: Young children learn to read and write* (pp. 63–79). Newark, DE: International Reading Association.

Taylor, N., Blum, I., & Logsdon, D. (1986). The development of written language awareness: Environmental aspects and program characteristics. *Reading Research Quarterly, 21,* 132–149.

Teale, W., & Sulzby, E. (1989). Emergent literacy: New perspectives. In S. Strickland & L. Morrow (Eds.), *Emerging literacy: Young children learn to read and write* (pp. 1–15). Newark, DE: International Reading Association.

Thomas, K. (1985). Early reading as a social interaction process. *Language Arts, 62,* 469–475.

Tobin, A., & Pikulski, J. (1988). A longitudinal study of the reading achievement of early and non-early readers through sixth grade. In J. Readance & R. Baldwin *Dialogues in literacy research* (pp. 49–58). Chicago, IL: National Reading Conference.

Torgesen, J., & Bryant, B. (1994). *Test of Phonological Awareness.* Austin, TX: PRO-ED.

Torgesen, J., Morgan, S., & Davis, C. (1992). Effects of two types of phonological awareness training on word learning in kindergarten children. *Journal of Educational Psychology, 84,* 364–370.

Torgesen, J., Wagner, R., & Rashotte, C. (1994). Longitudinal studies of phonological processing and reading. *Journal of Learning Disabilities, 27,* 276–286.

Torrey, J. (1979). Reading that comes naturally: The early reader. In T. Waller & G. MacKinnon (Eds.), *Reading research: Advances in theory and practice* (Vol. 1, pp. 115–144). New York: Academic Press.

Trachtenburg, P., & Ferruggia, A. (1989). Big books from little voices: Reaching high risk beginning readers. *The Reading Teacher, 42,* 284–289.

Trelease, J. (1989). Jim Trelease speaks on reading aloud to children. *The Reading Teacher, 43,* 200–206.

Treiman, R., & Weatherston, S. (1992). Effects of linguistic structure on children's ability to isolate initial consonants. *Journal of Educational Psychology, 84,* 174–181.

Vellutino, F., & Scanlon, D. (1987). Phonological coding, phonological awareness, and reading ability: Evidence from a longitudinal and experimental study. *Merrill-Palmer Quarterly, 33,* 321–363.

Venezky, R. (1975). The curious role of letter names in reading instruction. *Visual Language, 9,* 67–71.

Walker, G., Jr., & Kuerbitz, I. (1979). Reading to preschoolers as an aid to successful beginning reading. *Reading Improvement, 16,* 149–154.

Walsh, D., Price, G., & Gillingham, M. (1988). The critical but transitory importance of letter naming. *Reading Research Quarterly, 16,* 159–166.

Warrick, N., Rubin, H., & Rowe-Walsh, S. (1993). Phoneme awareness in language-delayed children: Comparative studies and intervention. *Annals of Dyslexia, 43,* 153–173.

Werner, P., & Strother, J. (1987). Early readers: Important emotional considerations. *The Reading Teacher, 40,* 538–543.

Whitehurst, G., Epstein, J., Angell, A., Payne, A., Crone, D. & Fischel, J. (1994). Outcomes of an emergent literacy intervention in Head Start. *Journal of Educational Psychology, 86,* 542–555.

Yopp, H. (1988). The validity and reliability of phonemic awareness tests. *Reading Research Quarterly, 23,* 159–177.

Yopp, H. (1992). Developing phonemic awareness in young children. *The Reading Teacher, 45,* 696–703.

Yopp, H. (1995). A test for assessing phonemic awareness in young children. *The Reading Teacher, 49,* 20–29.

Appendix 1: Publishers of Big Books

DLM
PO Box 4000
One DLM Park
Allen, TX 75002
800-527-4747

Gryphon House
PO Box 207
Beltsville, MD 20704-0207
800-638-0928

Steck Vaughn
PO Box 26015
Austin, TX 78755
800-531-5015

SRA
PO Box 543
Blacklick, OH 43004-0543
800-843-8855

Houghton-Mifflin
One Beacon Street
Boston, MA 02108
800-323-5663

Scholastic, Inc.
PO Box 7501
2931 East McCarty Street
Jefferson City, MO 65102
800-325-6149

Curriculum Assoc.
5 Esquire Road
E. Billerica, MA 01862-2589
800-225-0248

Rigby
PO Box 797
Crystal Lake, IL 60014
800-822-8661

Sundance
PO Box 1326
Newtown Road
Littleton, MA 01460
800-343-8204

Jamestown Publishers
PO Box 9168
Providence, RI 02940
800-USA-READ

Dale Seymour Publications
PO Box 10888
Palo Alto, CA 94303-0879
800-872-1100

Kaplan
PO Box 609
Lewisville, NC 27023-0609
800-334-2014

The Wright Group
19201-120th Avenue
Bothell, WA 98011-9512
800-345-6073

Appendix 2: Alphabet Books*

Alphabatics, Suse MacDonald
The Alphabet Tree, Leo Lionni
Animal Alphabet, Bert Kitchen
Anno's Alphabet, Mitsumas Anno

*Most of these books are available from Perfection Learning, Logan IA 51546.

Applebet: An ABC, Clyde Watson
The Bird Alphabet Book, Jerry Pallotta
A Caribou Alphabet, Mary Beth Owens
Clifford's ABC, Norman Bridwell
Curious George Learns the Alphabet, H. A. Rey
The Dinosaur Alphabet Book, Jerry Pallotta
Ed Emberley's ABC, Ed Emberley
Farm Alphabet Book, Jane Miller
The Flower Alphabet Book, Jerry Pallotta
The Frog Alphabet Book, Jerry Pallotta
The Furry Alphabet Book, Jerry Pallotta
Guinea Pig ABC, Kate Duke
Harold's ABC, Crockett Johnson
The Icky Bug A Book, Jerry Pallotta
The Most Amazing Hide-and-Seek Alphabet Book, Robert Crowther
The Ocean Alphabet Book, Jerry Pallotta
Q is for Duck, Mary Elting & Michael Folsom
What's Inside? The Alphabet Book, Satoshi Kitamura

Appendix 3: A Mulitsensory Sequence for Handwriting (Adapted from Kephart, 1961)

1. Movement (student makes movement in the air) (K)*: if necessary guide his hand or use template (T) (Large shapes are used). An auditory clue (A) can be added at steps 1–3 by talking student through the movements (e.g., down, up and around).
2. Template against chalkboard (student traces template with finger) (K,T,V) (Large shapes are used.)
3. Tracing to develop visual control; proceed in small steps

   a. Large form drawn, enclosed with template, child traces with finger (V,T,K)
   b. Remove template, trace form with finger (V,T,K)
   c. Trace form with chalk (V,K, minimum T)
   d. Trace in air to copy (K)
   e. Reduce visual cues for tracing

4. Copy form (visual data is now in a different position)
5. Reproduction (memory)
6. Practice size variations
7. Move to paper and pencil

Integrating Sources

1. Of the emergent literacy issues raised by the authors in this section, which ones are supported by the research of Lesiak? Which issues are yet to be implemented and examined?

2. How might Lesiak respond to children's ideas about the nature of reading?

3. Strommen and Mates suggested that "a fundamental goal of reading instruction should be to move each child toward the understanding that readers reconstruct texts by using multiple strategies to interpret the language encoded by print and . . . providing information that will enable construction of appropriate strategies." How would Lesiak respond to these concepts?

Classroom Implications

1. It is now clear that the parent plays a crucial role in a child's early progress toward literacy. What are some ways educators can encourage parents to act purposefully?

2. Given what you know about emergent literacy, do you still think there is a place for "readiness" books in a kindergarten classroom? Explain.

3. The concept of emergent literacy has major implications for the way children are assessed in the primary grades. Describe a few of them.

Annotated Bibliography

Beach, S. A., & Young, J. (1997). Children's development of literacy resources in kindergarten: A model. *Reading Research and Instruction, 36,* 241–265.

> *This article proposes a classroom model for the development of various types of literacy resources as a foundation for their success in various different instructional programs. Implications of this research are suggested for emergent literacy programs.*

Clay, M. M. (1991). *Becoming literate: The construction of inner control.* Portsmouth, NH: Heinemann.

> *This text traces the changes that occur over time in young children's literacy development. The emphasis in this reference is on the role the individual child plays in the literacy changes.*

Henriques, M. E. (1997). Increasing literacy among kindergartens through cross-age training. *Young Children, 52,* 42–47.

> *This article describes the advantages of the use of older tutors working with kindergartners in literacy development. Specific information is provided on the selection and training of tutors, as well as format and evaluation of classroom instruction.*

Ketner, C. S., Smith, K. E., & Parnell, M. K. (1997). *Journal of Educational Research, 90,* 212–220.

> *Reports on research that investigates consistency between teacher beliefs and classroom practice related to emergent literacy learners. Discusses teacher beliefs that result from preservice programs, inservice teacher programs, and teachers' experiences in classroom instruction.*

Lysaker, J. (1997). *The relational dimensions of literacy.* (ERIC Document Reproduction Service No. ED 409 543).

> *A single-subject study that examines ways in which personal relationship contributes to literacy development. Discussion focuses on limitations of effective instruction placed by reviewing literacy learning as cognitive and linguistic processes, rather than personal and social tasks.*

McGee, L. M., & Purcell-Gates, V. (1997). So what's going on in research on emergent literacy? *Reading Research Quarterly, 32,* 310–318.

> *This article reviews the current thinking in the field of emergent literacy, noting that much of this work deals with sociocultural factors opposed to cognitive development. An excellent bibliography of related references is also included in this material.*

Strommen, L. T., & Mates, B. F. (1997). What readers do: Young children's ideas about the nature of reading. *The Reading Teacher, 51,* 98–107.

> *This article describes the results of a three-year longitudinal study that describes the changing nature of young children's perceptions of what the term reading means to them. Of particular importance are the implications of this research for preschool and kindergarten teachers.*

Valencia, S. W. (1997). Authentic classroom assessment of early reading: Alternatives to standardized tests. *Preventing School Failure, 41,* 63–70.

> *This summary of various types of current assessment of young children's reading concludes that the best measure of language development are various measures of informal student learning as opposed to the use of standardized tests. This is a particularly strong article in that the author presents a wide variety of assessment procedures for emergent readers, beginning readers, and developing readers.*

Wood, J. M. (1997). Inside "Reading Rainbow": A spectrum of strategies for promoting literacy. *Language Arts, 74,* 95–106.

> *This discussion evaluates the television show, "Reading Rainbow" with particular attention given to the development of early literacy. Findings, according to the author, indicate that the philosophical literacy base of this program reflects prevailing beliefs about literacy development of young children.*

You Become Involved

1. Reflect on what you remember about your own personal experiences in learning to read and write. What specifically do you recall about emergent literacy activities and your family? What memories do you have of your first experiences in school with literacy? Are they generally positive or negative? Commit your remembrance to writing and consider sharing it with a colleague.
2. Talk with colleagues about how they encourage parents to help their children's development of a variety of literacy abilities. What are some of the problems you have faced in developing a positive home/school relationship?
3. Review a commercial reading program and note how it encourages students to develop early literacy abilities. What are some specific activities that are included to help with this process? Are there ways in which the program falls short?
4. During conferences, ask parents what they are doing in their homes to foster literacy development? Document both their successes and problems. See if you can discern patterns related to socioeconomic status.

8

CONTENT LITERACY

There are three stages in the development of ability to read:
1. The acquisition of the working knowledge of the mechanics of reading. The child should acquire this knowledge through his reading work in Grades I, II, and III.
2. The development of skill and fluency in reading through extensive oral and silent reading. This skill should be developed in grades IV and V, and during this period the mechanics of reading should become automatic and unconscious.
3. Independent reading for information, appreciation, and enjoyment. The reading work of grades VI and VII should be of this type.
—*GEORGIA DEPARTMENT OF EDUCATION (1926)*

Subject matter textbooks pose the biggest challenge for young readers being weaned from a diet of simple stories.
—*BECOMING A NATION OF READERS (1985)*

The best thing about textbooks is, they don't break when you drop them.
—*NIKKI, A VIDALIA, GEORGIA, FIFTH-GRADER QUOTED IN* TEACHING THROUGH TEXT *BY MCKENNA AND ROBINSON (1997)*

The realization that students in the middle and secondary grades may experience difficulty with assigned materials is hardly new. Historically, teachers associated the problem with a need for remediation on the part of some students. Their difficulties, it was assumed, were the result of deficiencies in basic reading skills. Clearly, this has been the case for some students. A more modern appraisal of the situation, however, involves an awareness that content classrooms present unique demands that may place even good readers at risk. Content reading assignments tend to rely on prior knowledge of content and on reading skills specific to certain areas (for example, the ability to interpret charts in social studies). Teachers who do not take these factors into account and simply assign materials to be read without adequate preparation of students are often unhappy with the results. Not surprisingly, a large majority of states now require a course in content area reading of those seeking certification at the middle and secondary levels.

Misconceptions about Content Literacy

Certification regulations have not been universally applauded by teachers (Misulis, 1994). Many continue to view with suspicion the suggestion that they take into account the reading needs of their students. Stewart and O'Brien (1989) surveyed high school teachers to find out why their reactions tend to be so negative. They identified three principal reasons given by these teachers for resisting what they perceived to be "content area reading":

1. Many teachers feel inadequate to contend with the reading problems they face in their classes.
2. Many believe that literacy activities would infringe on subject matter time.
3. Many deny the need for content are literacy techniques.

We suspect that a large number of elementary teachers would offer an additional reason: Literacy needs can be addressed at other times during the day (in a language arts block, for example). These arguments miss two important points about the nature of content literacy techniques. First, such techniques are always integrated with content; they are not taught separately. The use of graphic organizers to teach a cluster of technical vocabulary is one example; the use of a reading guide covering a textbook chapter is another. This means they require no *extra* time. Rather, they represent alternative ways presenting content in the first place. Second, they are designed to enhance content learning and not to improve general reading ability. If the latter occurs, it is a by-product (Hadaway & Young, 1994; McAloon, 1994).

As You Read

Richard Vacca, former president of the International Reading Association, offers a plea in behalf of the continuing reading development of adolescents. His reasons are compelling, and he identifies teachers—both English and content—at the middle and secondary levels as holding the key to improvement. Andrea Guillaume, on the other hand, suggests that the underpinnings of content literacy can be established in the primary grades. We have attempted to present alternative approaches to the same problem, one stressing remediation and the other prevention.

As you read these articles, be mindful of these questions:

1. What has the National Assessment of Education Progress revealed about the state of adolescent literacy in the United States?

2. How can the willingness of English teachers to tackle this problem be contrasted with the attitudes of content specialists?
3. How might IRA's Commission on Adolescent Literacy play a future role in improving the picture?
4. What techniques might primary teachers use to foster content learning from textual materials?

References

Becoming a nation of readers. (1985). Washington, DC: The National Institute of Education.

Manual for Georgia teachers. (1926). Atlanta: Georgia Department of Education.

McAloon, N. M. (1994) It's not my job! *Journal of Reading, 37,* 322–334.

McKenna, M., & Robinson, R. (1997). *Teaching through text* (2nd ed.). White Plains, N.Y.: Longman.

Misulis, K. E. (1994). Nuturing the growth of content teachers in content area reading instruction. *Reading Improvement, 31,* 125–128.

Stewart, R. A., & O'Brien, D. G. (1989). Resistance to content area reading: A focus on preservice teachers. *Journal of Reading, 32,* 396–401.

Let's Not Marginalize Adolescent Literacy

RICHARD T. VACCA

For the February/March 1997 issue of *Reading Today,* I wrote an article on "The Benign Neglect of Adolescent Literacy." As president of the International Reading Association I expressed concern over what I perceive to be the apparent neglect of older literacy learners at all levels of U.S. society. I borrowed the oxymoron "benign neglect" from a phrase attributed to Daniel Moynihan, who served as a presidential adviser to John F. Kennedy in the 1960s. Moynihan, now a senator from New York, advised Kennedy to implement a policy of benign neglect in Southeast Asia during the early stages of the Vietnam conflict. As it turned out, there wasn't anything benign about U.S. foreign policy in Southeast Asia in the 1960s. Nor is the way we care for or attend to the literacy needs of older learners at a crucial time in their transition to adulthood by any means benign.

I welcomed the opportunity offered by the editor of JAAL to revisit the issues I raised in the *Reading Today* column, if for no other reason than to continue a conversation on the state of adolescent literacy in the United States. Although I am not familiar in an authoritative way with how other countries make policy or plan literacy curricula for older learners, I suspect that the neglect of adolescents' literacy learning extends to other countries as well, if the anecdotal accounts I have received from colleagues around the world mean anything.

When I speak about neglect, I am not referring to the work of reading and English teachers who labor under extraordinary conditions to provide the best possible language and literacy instruction for adolescents. Rather, the neglect to which I refer is more pervasive in nature, manifesting itself through educational policy, school curricula, and a public mindset on literacy that doesn't appear to extend beyond learning to read and write in early childhood and elementary school.

Research funding for adolescent literacy, for example, is minuscule in relation to the big bucks federal and state agencies spend on early literacy and early intervention research. The U.S. Department of Education in all likelihood will call for research on early literacy up to the third grade as it prepares to fund the next national reading research center. Although I applaud the funding of research for early literacy, what is the implicit message that is being signaled? As one of my colleagues noted in a personal communication, "While I support literacy dollars being spent on younger children, I am disappointed that the young adolescents in our middle and secondary schools are now moved out of the picture—sidelined, so to speak, at the very time when middle grades education seems to be taking off in the country."

I am not arguing against early literacy development. Quite the contrary. We need to continue to place high educational priority on family literacy and early intervention programs for beginners who need intensive instructional support. We need to continue to support research and development that will help us to better understand young children's literate behavior, how they develop literacy skills and strategies, and how to achieve some sem-

Source: From Vacca, Richard T. (1998, May). Let's not marginalize adolescent literacy. *Journal of Adolescent & Adult Literacy, 41*(8), 604–628. Reprinted with permission of Richard T. Vacca and the International Reading Association. All rights reserved.

blance of balance between direct and holistic instruction within meaningful contexts for literacy learning.

My concern is that the local and national debates over how children learn to read and write—played out in the media and reduced to a "war" between the proponents of phonics and the proponents of whole language—has bifurcated literacy by focusing almost totally on early development in elementary school, while putting on hold the literacy needs of older learners in middle and high schools. Political leaders and literacy reformers can't get beyond their fixation on a program of national testing and a literacy policy designed for 8-year-olds. Moreover, the public debate over literacy remains stuck on "phonics versus whole language" rather than critical literacy as the key instructional issue facing our nation's schools.

Let's not marginalize adolescent literacy, pushing it to the edges of public debate and policy, at a time when the literacy development of early adolescents and teenagers is more critical than ever. One needs only to consider the results of the most recent national assessments of reading and writing to recognize that we cannot afford to marginalize literacy learning at *any* level of development. The National Assessment of Educational Progress (NAEP) in Reading (Campbell, Donahue, Reese, & Phillips, 1996), for example, supports what many teachers already know about their students. The majority of U.S. children and adolescents (around 60%) are capable of reading at a basic level of performance—reading for details, identifying main ideas, and recognizing relationships among ideas. Fewer than 5% of students surveyed in Grades 4, 8, and 12 perform at an advanced level where they are required to examine, extend, and elaborate the meaning of literary and informative texts (Campbell, Donahue, Reese, & Phillips, 1996). Likewise, the most recent results of the NAEP in Writing (Applebee, Langer, Mullis, Latham, & Gentile, 1994) report that all students, even in Grade 12, had considerable difficulty moving beyond minimal performance to more elaborate writing tasks that require a higher level of coherence and detail to support points made in the writing.

NAEP Reading and Writing represent specific indicators of literacy performance and should be interpreted cautiously. Cut-off scores to determine basic, proficient, and advanced levels of performance are arbitrarily determined and also should be interpreted with caution. Yet the results of national assessments such as these are often used to set educational goals and priorities by policy makers from President Clinton and U.S. Secretary of Education Richard Riley to state and local politicians and members of school boards. What the results of NAEP Reading and Writing clearly indicate is that we need a literacy agenda that recognizes and values the developmental nature of reading and writing across all age groups, not one that is preoccupied almost totally with the literacy learning of young children.

Why Adolescent Literacy Is Critical

In the 30 years that I have been associated professionally with adolescent literacy, I have never seen the potential to marginalize the development of older literacy learners more evident than it is today. The current debate over how children learn to read and write serves only to magnify the lack of attention and commitment given to adolescent learners and their literacy needs. I am beginning to wonder whether there is a political and public mindset that literacy learning is critical only in early childhood. The faulty and misguided assumption,

"If young children learn to read early on, they will read to learn throughout their lives," results in more harm than good.

The International Reading Association/National Council of Teachers of English *Standards for the English Language Arts* (1996) underscores the importance of preparing students at all grade levels for the literacy demands of today and tomorrow. Literacy expectations have accelerated in this century and are likely to increase dramatically in coming decades. When the process of developing national standards began, IRA and NCTE recognized that, "To participate fully in society and the workplace in 2020, citizens will need powerful literacy abilities that until now have been achieved by only a small percentage of the population....Being literate in contemporary society means being active, critical, and creative users not only of print and spoken language but also of the visual language" (*Standards for the English Language Arts,* 1996, p. 5). The IRA/NCTE Standards underscore the importance of language and literacy in use. Students throughout the grades must learn how to use language and literacy clearly, strategically, critically, and creatively.

Early childhood literacy programs help children to develop a sense of competence and confidence as literacy learners. Not only are they expected to develop automaticity and fluency with print, but they are also in the process of becoming more strategic in their ability to use literacy to comprehend, compose, converse, and think critically about text. As children make the transition into middle childhood and adolescence, literacy use becomes increasingly more complex and demanding. Instructional programs place a high premium on strategy learning as students become more sophisticated in their use of language to comprehend, compose, converse, and think critically about texts.

Adolescents use literacy in complex and meaningful ways to shape and reshape their identities. The editors of *Reconceptualizing the Literacies in Adolescents' Lives* (Alvermann, Hinchman, Moore, Phelps, & Waff, 1998) weave together a collection of research reports and essays by literacy researchers and educators who grapple with notions of what counts as literacy among adolescents. In doing so, they inquire into and reflect upon the multiple literacies of adolescents in and out of school, many of which go unnoticed and remain hidden in school contexts. How important are the literacies in adolescents' lives? Very.

The possibilities for adolescents to use literacy in print and nonprint contexts are unprecedented. Technological changes, brought about by the digital forces of the computer, are transforming the way we communicate and disseminate information. Highly interactive and engaging electronic texts are transforming the way we think about literacy. Moreover, a healthy resurgence of print media has resulted in a veritable motherlode of fiction and nonfiction books for adolescents about every topic imaginable.

Yet the literacies in adolescents' lives cannot be limited by conventional notions of texts. Texts, as Neilsen (in press) explains, represent sets of potential meanings and signifying practices: "A novel in English class, for example, is a text; so, too, is the conversation about such a novel in which the students and teachers engage . . . and so, too, are teen 'zines, mall cultures, and television sitcoms." Adolescent literacy development is of critical importance because it helps to shape the core strategies by which adolescents learn to negotiate meaning and think critically about the texts in their lives, whether in the context of school or the world outside of school.

Let me illustrate the importance of literacies in adolescents' lives—the lessons I learned as an adolescent literacy educator—by sharing a story or two.

How and Why I Became an Adolescent Literacy Educator

I was 23 years old, still very wet behind the ears, when I began my doctoral studies at Syracuse University in 1970. I chose Syracuse on the strength of its secondary reading program. My experiences with middle and high school students convinced me that there was much that I didn't know about how adolescents become literate and use reading and writing in meaningful ways. I was fortunate enough to study with Hal Herber and Margaret Early, two of the most prominent scholars in the field of reading. They taught me well. Each mentored me in different ways. Hal Herber reinvented the concept of "reading in the content areas" and pioneered the use of instructional strategies in content area learning situations. Margaret Early, one of the most eloquent voices ever on matters related to adolescent literacy, viewed reading as a process that must be thought of and taught as such. Both were powerful advocates of literacy instruction for older learners and were pivotal in making reading beyond the elementary school a legitimate area of study within the field.

I had been teaching English in a high school just outside of Albany, New York, prior to entering the doctoral program at Syracuse. One of my students during my first year as a teacher, Johnny Palcheo (whose name has been changed to protect the innocent), did my auto mechanical work whenever my 1960 Chevy died on me, which was often. Johnny was just 2, maybe 3, years younger than I when I first started teaching. In the days before special education, and the identification of children and youth as "learning disabled," Johnny and others of his academic ilk were known as NR students. NR stood for nonregents, meaning that students classified as NR would not earn a regents diploma from the State of New York upon graduation. But NR could have easily stood for NOT REAL. He was one of the forgotten young men and women at school, who largely went unnoticed, except when they got into trouble. Johnny couldn't read well; he couldn't write well either; but he knew how to take apart a carburetor and replace a timing belt with his eyes closed.

As it turned out, Johnny didn't graduate from high school, regents diploma notwithstanding. He dropped out of school and went to work at his uncle's garage full time. During that first year as a teacher, I taught two NR classes, two regents classes, and one advanced regents class. Johnny and his friends would do a number on me whenever I tried to introduce any topic that required reading and writing. I battled back the best I could, but often to little avail. In those days, I was light on teaching strategy and heavy on exhortation and intimidation. The more I urged them to learn with texts, the more they resisted. And the craziest part of it all was that these tougher-than-nails kids respected me. Some even liked me.

I was tough on Johnny, always challenging him to do better. There was a measure of respect between the two of us. And even though it's been more than 27 years since I last saw him, I won't soon forget our encounter. Just before I left my English teaching position, my Chevy had to be towed into Johnny's uncle's garage for repair. I remember telling Johnny I was moving to Syracuse to work on my doctorate. "Whattya goin' for?" he asked, "You want to be a doctor?" I told him that I wasn't going to be a "doctor doctor," the medical kind, but that I was going to study reading and become a college teacher. "Man," he said, "You read good already." Then he added somewhat wistfully, somewhat defiantly, "F___ reading. Reading robbed me of my manhood."

Reading robbed me of my manhood. The words, 27 years later, still haunt me. They have been a kind of motivation for me in my own work with students and teachers.

When I began teaching in the 1960s, society was too quick to write off low-achieving students like the Johnny Palcheos of the world. There was a time, I don't know if it exists anymore, when the workforce could absorb a kid like Johnny. There was a place for him in his uncle's garage. But that was during an era when cars had carburetors. Today, survey research shows that most Americans spend more time reading and writing in the workplace than they do anywhere else. In today's society, there are a small and shrinking number of jobs requiring little or no literacy. Ask car mechanics today if they could survive without being able to read various manuals for the kinds of high-tech, high-performance cars that are produced.

When Johnny dropped out, sad to say, I was relieved. Sometimes kids like Johnny can become the hard-core recalcitrants in school (sometimes out of school) who make the life of a teacher tougher than it has to be. In my naïveté, I took solace in the adage, "Out-of-sight, out-of-mind."

While it may have been easy to write off low-achieving students, it's just as easy, especially today, to lull oneself into believing that if so-called average or above average students can read the words with some degree of fluency and accuracy, they can read effectively enough to handle the conceptual demands inherent in texts. Often they have trouble learning with texts because, in many cases, they were never shown how. What I learned in my early days as a teacher was that average and above average students—kids who were most like me in high school, promising students who sometimes worked hard and sometimes didn't—also struggled with texts.

Although they had developed fluency, the ability to read print smoothly and automatically, they didn't know what to do with texts beyond just saying the words. Today, we might describe such readers as not having sufficient "strategy awareness" to know when and how to use learning strategies to think deeply with texts. One of the dilemmas facing most adolescents in an academic context, then and now, is that few effectively learn how to use reading and writing to explore and construct meaning in the company of authors, other learners, or teachers.

When I first began teaching, I deluded myself into thinking that I was teaching these kids what they needed to know and be able to do. However, I soon realized that they often read just enough to answer the questions I asked or circumvented reading altogether. At least the kids in my NR class were genuine in their resistance to reading. I knew where I stood with them. But the kids in my regents classes were somewhat disingenuous. They went through the motions and played school the best they could.

So for one class period each day, I sought the safe haven of my advanced regents class. I thoroughly enjoyed working with students who seemed to know how to use texts as a springboard to solve problems and explore the significance of what they were reading. These kids were good academicians—high achievers—who knew how to play school well. But frankly, outside of school, literacy was not prominent or significant in many of their lives. They knew how to read and write, but often chose not to. Many years later, my wife and I witnessed our daughter, Courtney, playing school with the best of them. In her pre-adolescence, she loved to read books, but the older she got, the less she engaged in reading outside of an academic context. Reading and writing were tools that she could rely on when she needed to use them, but little else.

These remembrances remind me of why I became a literacy educator. While I can look back over the past 30 years and recognize the knowledge base that has developed to support the teaching of literacy beyond the elementary school, I also recognize that unless we take seriously the role that literacy plays in adolescents' lives, not much will change in the way we plan and enact curriculum that will support and extend their literacy development.

Prospects for the Future of Adolescent Literacy

The proposed National Reading Initiative, which resonated well with the public during the 1996 U.S. presidential election campaign, calls for a massive voluntary school and community effort in which every child in the U.S. will be reading at grade level by the end of third grade. The initiative, proposed by President Clinton, was well-timed politically, but is currently mired in the legislative process. In the meantime, local and national debates continue to revolve around the merits of phonics and whole language programs. But where's the debate over what happens to young children's literacy development beyond fourth grade? Since the 1960s we have learned much about the literacy needs of older learners. The literacy development of a 12-year-old in a middle school or a 17-year-old in high school remains as critical a concern to society as the literacy development of a preschool child or a child in the elementary grades.

Middle and high school reading and English teachers are the last instructional front in an adolescent's development as a competent and proficient user of language and literacy. Yet reading teachers and specialists are an endangered species in middle and high schools, except in situations where their positions are mandated by state law. The first academic teaching position cut from a school district's budget is usually that of the middle or high school reading teacher or specialist. With the exception of students who struggle as readers, few if any curricula provisions are made for the majority of adolescents.

Content area teachers, of course, are in a strategic position to influence adolescents' uses of literacy for academic learning. Yet content area teachers often resist literacy practices, despite taking a preservice or inservice course as required for teacher certification (O'Brien & Stewart, 1992; Vacca & Vacca, 1995). Without a middle or high school's long-term commitment to professional development and organizational change, it is very difficult for teachers to sustain the use of content area literacy practices in their instructional repertoire.

Are the prospects for adolescent literacy bleak? Or promising? I would suggest the latter. As adolescent literacy educators, we need to continue to advocate for and make public the literacy needs of adolescents. In 1997, IRA created the Commission on Adolescent Literacy to advise the Board of Directors on policies and priorities related to literacy learning in middle and high schools and the literacies in adolescents' lives. The Board charged the Commission on Adolescent Literacy to make recommendations concerning future directions for the field of adolescent literacy. The Commission's work is in the early stages of planning and goal setting. Yet as an association of literacy educators, IRA recognizes that we need to advocate as strongly for the literacy needs of adolescents as we do for younger children. As a society we can ill afford to marginalize adolescent literacy by putting all of our eggs in the basket of improved literacy in early childhood.

References

Alvermann, D., Hinchman, K., Phelps, S., & Waff, D. (Eds.). (in press). *Reconceptualizing the literacies in adolescents' lives.* Mahwah, NJ: Erlbaum.

Applebee, A., Langer, J., Mullis, I., Latham, A., & Gentile, C. (1994). *NAEP 1992 writing report card.* Washington, DC: U.S. Department of Education, Office of Educational Research and Improvement.

Campbell, J., Donahue, P., Reese, C., & Phillips, G. (1996). *NAEP 1994 reading report card for the nation and the states.* Washington, DC: U.S. Department of Education, Office of Educational Research and Improvement.

Neilsen, L. (1998). Playing for real: Performative texts and adolescent identities. In D. Alvermann, K. Hinchman, S. Phelps, & D. Waff (Eds.), *Reconceptualizing the literacies in adolescents' lives* (pp. 1–12). Mahwah, NJ: Erlbaum.

O'Brien, D., & Stewart, R. (1992). Resistance to content area reading: Dimensions and solutions. In E. Dishner, T. Bean, J. Readence, & D. Moore (Eds.), *Reading in the content areas: Improving classroom instruction* (3rd ed., pp. 30–40). Dubuque, IA: Kendall-Hunt.

Standards for the English Language Arts. (1996). Newark, DE: International Reading Association.

Vacca, R., & Vacca, J. (1996). *Content area reading,* (5th ed.). New York: HarperCollins.

Learning with Text in the Primary Grades

ANDREA M. GUILLAUME

The day before yesterday, my 3-year-old son Zachary asked me, "What do our bodies look like on the inside?" As a science lover, I relish the opportunity to explore the natural world with children. In this instance, though, actual exploration was not feasible. Instead, Zachary and I talked some about our own ideas, then I suggested that we take out our book about human bodies. His enthusiastic response? "Yes! The giant book!" Together we turned the heavy cardboard pages of our human body big book and pored over the diagrams and descriptions to gain an answer to Zachary's question. I was struck by the power of text to help us find answers to personally relevant questions.

This article provides a rationale for providing learning-with-text experiences for primary-grade children, lists 10 general approaches to foster primary-grade content area reading, and gives a sample lesson that promotes comprehension of text and content matter.

A Rationale

Five compelling propositions urge us to learn with text in the primary grades. First, knowledge is power. The more ways we have of gaining information to build knowledge, the more empowered we become. Literate people can use various resources to learn about the world and important ideas, can communicate with others, and can make informed decisions. Reading is one of the most efficient and flexible ways of learning. Through reading, we bring our prior experiences with the world and with the printed word to a text and use our knowledge and reading strategies to answer our questions. Classroom experiences in content area reading are of particular importance for dependent readers in that reading can occur with the structure and support that enable dependent readers to move toward independence. Reading is a powerful tool.

Second, content area reading is not the sole territory of those who are already proficient readers. Teachers of children of all ages have the important job of helping learners interact with text to produce meaning. Those who suggest that primary-grade teachers help children *learn to read* while upper-grade teachers help children *read to learn* deprive students at both levels of learning opportunities. Even young children can learn through text, and older readers should continue to refine their skills and find new ways to understand text. For this reason, content area reading should begin in the primary grades. As Olson and Gee (1991) suggest, learning to learn from text takes many experiences with text. Rich experiences with primary-level texts build a foundation of skills and habits that will help readers as they face more—and more sophisticated—texts in later years.

Third, the content areas—science, social studies, mathematics, the arts—fuel questions. How did Egyptians make mummies? Are there volcanoes on Venus? What do our

Source: From Guillaume, A. M. (1988, March). Learning with text in the primary grades. *The Reading Teacher, 51*(6), 476–486. Reprinted with permission of Andrea M. Guillaume and the Interntional Reading Association.

bodies look like on the inside? The content areas build motivation and purpose for reading: We read to know (Baghban, 1995).

Fourth, language, including reading and writing, permeates all of the content areas. Language can encourage careful thinking, support student participation, and motivate creative decision making. Reading and writing experiences thus belong from the very beginning across all subject areas (Dickson, 1995).

Finally, content areas provide a meaningful context for the reading/language arts goals teachers hold as dear. Content areas naturally embed skills like decoding into meaningful situations (Bristor, 1994; Romance & Vitale, 1992).

In sum, content area reading experiences help young children develop one of the critical attributes of a literate, responsible citizen: the ability to process and analyze information (Dickson, 1995). Given the strong rationale for primary-grade content area reading, how can teachers help young students learn to learn with text?

Ten Big Ideas

Teachers can provide potent content area reading experiences through the environments they create and through general approaches to content study. Fueled by the whole language movement, rich literacy programs have in recent years moved away from focusing solely upon textbooks to exploring texts of many kinds. (See Figure 1.)

FIGURE 1   A Variety of Texts for the Primary-Grade Content Area Library

- **Textbooks**
  Assigned textbooks are a mainstay in classrooms across the grades, and they become increasingly prevalent thought the grades. Because they *explain* rather than *tell* a story through narrative, textbooks can present comprehension challenges. Technical vocabulary and high concept load also make them slower going than storybooks.

- **Trade Books**
  Trade books are often also expository. However, trade books typically include richer detail and more imaginative presentation than do textbooks. Their content tends also to be more focused and of greater depth (Ross, 1994).

- **Fiction with Content Information**
  Fictional literature across the curriculum is popular, in part because the narrative structure flows smoothly and is familiar to young children. Fiction often treats content area information fairly, but care must be taken to ensure that selections encourage better understanding of topics rather than perpetuating faulty content ideas.

- **Other Kinds of Print**
  Newspapers, interactive software, and magazines written for young children (e.g., *Zoobooks* and *Ranger Rick*) provide accurate information about topics of great interest to young children. Their format is also appealing.

Each kind of text can be a powerful resource for helping children learn to read and read to learn. How can text, no matter its kind, be incorporated in meaningful ways throughout the primary-grade program? Ten big ideas reflect the literature on content area reading and learning.

1. *Access and build prior knowledge.*   One powerful determinant of what we will learn in a given situation is what we already know. In reading, the unique experiences that each child brings to the classroom affect transactions with the text. Limited background knowledge confounds comprehension. This is especially true in classrooms where students' background knowledge and literacy experiences are highly divergent, as is the case in classrooms where some or all students are learning English as a second language (Schifini, 1994) or where dependent readers are present (Tierney & Pearson, 1994). Schifini's (1994) five general strategies for accessing prior knowledge (see Figure 2) are helpful with diverse groups of children.

An additional technique particularly useful for accessing young children's knowledge is drawing. Primary-grade children are usually eager to draw, and their drawings can spark

FIGURE 2   Strategies for Accessing and Building on Prior Knowledge

- **Visuals:** Begin a lesson by having groups inspect pictures in texts or from magazines. Ask questions that prompt children to observe and then draw inference: "What are the people in the picture doing?" "What do you notice about their clothing?" "Where might they live?" Because observations spring from prior experience, children's answers to such questions provide insight into their current content knowledge.

- **Manipulatives and multimedia presentations:** Generate discussions by providing historical artifacts, posters, replicas, or real-life objects like rocks or leaves. Well-chosen objects invite conversation and personal connections. Consider prompts that ask students to make observations and that can build the store of background information: "What do you notice about the squid?" Have you ever seen one before?" "This is a model of a dinosaur tooth. How might your size compare to that of this dinosaur?"

- **Sharing experiences with students from diverse backgrounds:** Poems, music, and works of art allow for diverse responses. Group students heterogeneously, then prompt them to consider differences in opinion. For example, a teacher might say, "This is a song that African American slaves memorized in order to ride the underground railroad to freedom. As you listen, think about whether escaping slaves did the right thing. Did those who helped them? You'll share your ideas with your group in a bit."

- **Writing experiences:** Focus prior knowledge through factstorming, brainwriting, quickwrites, journal entries, and structured writing prompts. For instance ask students to make a 2-minute list of all words that come to mind when they hear the word *water*, then build a class idea bank. No doubt these words will resurface as students read about the water cycle.

- **Linking prior knowledge to new concepts and ideas:** Use charting strategies like semantic maps and K-W-L (Know, Want to learn, Learned; Ogle, 1986) charts to help discover what children bring with them to a lesson and to set a purpose for reading (for examples of charting in the content area of science, see Guillaume, Yopp, & Yopp, 1996).

conversations that reveal what they know. Early drawings can later serve as helpful tools to reflect on what children have learned through hands-on activities and reading experiences. Figure 3 provides Zachary's interpretations of crickets as he studied them at home. Note that his drawings indicate scientific understandings (the head is separate from the body, the legs—6 in all—are jointed, both crickets have cerci on their back ends, but only the female has an ovipositor) as well as some concepts still under development (the body has only two segments, only two eyes appear, and the crickets carry eggs on their backs). Information from students' drawings can thus provide teachers with direction for the kinds of experiences that will help children build accurate conceptions of the content.

Classroom reading experiences also serve to build background knowledge for future reading experiences. The texts children read and create in the classroom can serve as resources for future learning experiences.

2. *Provide hands-on experiences prior to reading.*   Perhaps because of the high vocabulary load of content areas, it is tempting to assign vocabulary activities before children have had sufficient opportunities to build concepts. Instead, interactive experiences like science activities, map making, cooperative discussions, and film viewing should be provided early in the lesson sequence so that children develop ideas and relationships among concepts and can use terms flexibly to express content-related ideas. Thus, building common experience before reading can help to remove one potential stumbling block for dependent readers: concept deficiencies. Hands-on experiences become part of the current knowledge store that children bring to bear on their readings, and subsequent reading experiences can help children attach labels to newly formed concepts.

For example, when a group of first graders and I studied the paper-making process, we began by making our own paper (American Forest Foundation, 1994). We blended soggy recycled paper in a blender, swished the pulp through screens in dishpans, pressed out extra water, then removed our damp new paper for drying. This messy and memorable activity allowed children to build a shared experience that they later recalled as we read a brief content area book on paper making. Instead of building rote recall of terms like *pulp, rollers,* and *metal screen* students drew from their recent experience to connect vivid understandings to new vocabulary terms.

FIGURE 3   A Young Child's Drawing of Crickets

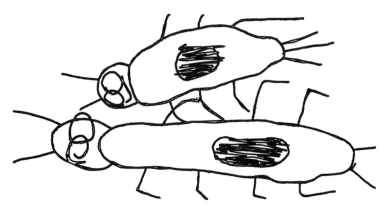

3. *Read aloud.* [An adult's enthusiastic oral reading can have a mighty influence on children in developing a listening vocabulary, a recognition for the cadence of the language, and an appreciation for the powerful meanings that print can convey. This holds true for content area selections as well.]In fact, for kindergartners, read-alouds may provide much of the content area reading experience. In addition to narrative text, teachers' read-alouds can include nonfiction and fiction with content information. Some specific suggestions for content area read-alouds are given in Figure 4.

4. *Read for a purpose.*   School is a place where students often subsume their own purposes to those of the teacher (Jackson, 1968). However, reading, like all tools, should be used to construct something useful or to enjoy or improve life in some way. When students set personally meaningful purposes for their reading, motivation and task persistence increase, and the idea that reading is a tool, not an end in itself, is reinforced.

In fact, when readers' purposes fail to match those of an author, breakdowns in comprehension are likely (Tierney & Pearson, 1994). Tierney and Pearson suggest that teachers can help dependent readers find reading purposeful by choosing highly motivating text or functional text that requires a reader response. Treasure maps and directions to science experiments are examples.

Strategies like the K-W-L chart (Ogle, 1986) and Manning and Manning's (1995) 3W2H strategy can also effectively support purposeful reading. In 3W2H, the reading experience begins with students' questions:

W1: What is your question?
W2: What do you already know about the topic?
W3: Where can you find the answers?
H1: How are you going to record your ideas?
H2: How are you going to share your findings?

I recently used an anticipation guide (Yopp & Yopp, 1996) to help set purposes for reading as a class of second graders and I made fossils. The guide served to prompt students' existing ideas, encourage discussion, and spark student questions about fossils. In the antic-

FIGURE 4   Suggestions for Reading Aloud in the Content Areas

- For very young students, read science-based stories, then supply materials so students can experiment with the topics of the books. Keep the books on hand for reference (McMath & King, 1993).

- For all grade levels, choose read-alouds that show vivid examples of the content and that build appropriate attitudes related to that content (Richardson, 1994).

- Read a passage aloud as a fluent model, then allow children to read it alone or to a partner. This is especially helpful for building fluency for dependent readers.

- Use content area readings, including realistic fiction and biographical works, as your read-alouds in math, science, and social studies.

- Include content area texts of all kinds for your Sustained Silent Reading period.

ipation guide, students checked "agree" or "disagree" for such statements as, "Fossils are made by people in a factory," and "We know all there is to know about dinosaurs." After we discussed students' responses, pairs of more and less dependent readers read an informational text on fossils. Before releasing partners to read, we studied the table of contents, and I suggested that they select portions of the text that addressed points of interest from our earlier discussion. Students with questions about how fossils are made, for instance, could read specific sections of text to meet that purpose. Our postreading conversation was enriched as children talked excitedly about the portions of the text they had selected.

5. *Provide access to content area materials.*   Print-rich environments encourage the joy of pursuing one's own interests through the freedom of selecting what one reads (Smith & Johnson, 1994). Richardson and Morgan (1994) note that many young children choose nonfiction materials as often as they choose fiction, and young readers may even be more likely than older students to read for information. Thus, <u>rooms stocked with varied nonfiction books and print materials allow learners to engage in purposeful communication that is contextually embedded.</u> In addition to magazines and software, all three types of content area texts (textbooks, trade books, and realistic fiction) belong in the classroom (Manning & Manning, 1995). Helpful sources for locating content area materials include Kobrin's (1995) *Eye Openers II: Children's Books to Answer Children's Questions About the World Around Them* and professional journals, which frequently recommend high-quality trade books. For instance, the National Science Teachers Association's journal, *Science and Children* publishes an annual listing of outstanding science trade books for elementary students. Additionally, the children's own content area writings serve an important role in the classroom library stacks: Children can reread their writings for continued practice and appreciation of their new knowledge.

Providing a variety of materials at different reading levels and across many topics allows students to read at their individual levels (Ross, 1994), make choices about what they read, and thus build their strengths and curiosities (Schifini, 1994), aspects of a literacy program considered essential for dependent readers (Manzo & Manzo, 1995).

6. *Encourage efferent and affective responses.*   Although school life focuses primarily on the cognitive domain, the affective domain cannot be ignored. Affect captures attitudes inherent in the subject areas, like curiosity in science or the ability to view historical events from different perspectives in social studies, and reinforces them in reading. In social studies, affect is essential for bringing about change in preconceptions and prejudice (Lickteig & Danielson, 1995). Additionally, affect may motivate children to read in the content areas, where, as in science, reading may be devalued in favor of experimentation as a way of learning (Dickson, 1995). Affect, including the will to continue reading, can in part determine whether one will become an independent reader.

Because cognition and affect are essential in learning, reading experiences need to capture both domains by allowing learners to respond in both efferent (cognitive) and aesthetic (affective) ways (Rosenblatt, 1991; Ross, 1994). Too, children should be allowed at least occasionally to choose the type (efferent or aesthetic) of their response and the form of their response. One example of an efferent response is a bookmaking activity wherein students write nonfiction books after studying content like the local community, geometry, earthquakes, or sharks. Gaylord (1994) provides a wealth of bookmaking strategies that can be used for content area writing across the curriculum.

As aesthetic responses, children can choreograph a dance; compose poetry; or write persuasive letters to appropriate legislators, companies, or individuals. Figure 5 contains a diamante poem that the first graders composed after their experiences studying the process of paper making. To aid the class in composing this poem, I put a diamante on a different topic (seeds) on the chalk board. We studied the structure of "Seeds" before writing our own diamante about trees. Children who were quick to discern patterns in text led us in the activity; others listened quietly, perhaps supplying single-word ideas. After reading and rereading our poem together aloud, I was ready to move on. However, students who listened silently as we initially analyzed "Seed" began, upon seeing the two similar poems side by side, blurting out important discoveries about the structure of the two works: "They both have no periods! Or capitals!" "They both have two lines of *ing*-words!" A whole-class activity intended to capture our aesthetic response to paper making also provided an unexpected opportunity to study text structure.

7. *Encourage discussion.* [Discussion allows for finding main ideas, summarizing, and providing the redundancy (revisiting ideas and text) that may otherwise be neglected (Manzo, 1991). Participating in peer discussion can also build upon students' prior knowledge to enhance their reading experiences.]

Some informal principles guide my use of discussion with primary-grade students. First, students must have opinions, ideas, or experiences related to the topic. Second, the discussion question or task must allow for multiple responses rather than for a single convergent or factual one. Third, the climate of the classroom must encourage the risk-taking necessary for children to share personal ideas. Finally, young children need structured opportunities and friendly teacher support to share their ideas in the classroom.

Manzo and Manzo (1995) share a discussion strategy that illustrates the use of each of these principles: the discussion web graphic developed by Alvermann (1991). The discussion web graphic has been used successfully with children as young as kindergarten (as a whole-class activity), and its use is supported by research. For the graphic, a central yes/no question related to the reading is posed in the middle of the responses. In partners, students respond in writing to the question, providing responses on both the left ("yes") side of the paper and on the right ("no") side. Figure 6 displays a web graphic two boys completed

FIGURE 5　A Diamante Poem Composed by First Graders after Studying Paper Making

		tree			
	big		green		
	standing	waving		falling	
shade	treehouse		pine		home
	crumbling	ironing		drying	
	ripped		colorful		
		paper			

before studying Bash's (1993) *Shadows of Night: The Hidden World of the Little Brown Bat.* After pairs have completed their discussion webs, one partner group joins another so that, in teams of 4, students defend their positions and reach group consensus. One member of the team then reports to the class, sharing both the consensus and dissenting viewpoints. The teacher monitors carefully throughout the writing and discussion phases in order to extend thinking and challenge students' misconceptions, especially those that may impair comprehension. The web in Figure 6 suggests that the authors hold many accurate concepts about bats and that the teacher's job may focus upon supplying readings and discussion to address misconceptions that arise from folklore and the media.

   8. *Connect reading and writing.* For all students, content area writing can facilitate long-term memory of the content, can increase metacognitive skills and complex thinking, can foster recognition of text structure, can facilitate decoding and comprehension, and can increase learning in every content area (Armbruster, 1992; Richardson & Morgan, 1994). Informal classroom writing experiences can also serve affective purposes by fostering curiosity, alleviating anxiety, and promoting confidence.

   Content area writing experiences may be most successful when they address varied audiences, are of consequence to the writer, and take a variety of forms. As a closure to our recent lesson on magnetism, second graders composed their own magnet books. Although the content (magnetism) was predetermined and the number of pages was dictated by the folded-page format I selected (Gaylord, 1994), all other decisions were left in the hands of the authors. The divergence of the results surprised me: One student wrote a comic book about Magnet Man, the Man of Steel, and another wrote a how-to book on induced magnetism. Also, Figure 7 shows the difference in the level of sophistication of text produced by two authors, Kay and Randy.

   Although the amount of text and the usage of writing conventions vary widely between these two students' works, both authors produced accurate information about a scientific phenomenon, and both students' texts could be used for future individualized reading instruction.

FIGURE 6   A Completed Discussion Web Graphic

- They have fangs and may bite you.
- They're scary.
- They can give diseases to cows, pigs, and other animals like people.
- Their claws can stick onto people or walls or anything.
- I had a bad dream that one bit me on the leg and I never saw my family again.
- When it comes to bats. Dracula's a pain in the neck.

yes ← **Are bats bad?** → no

- They teach us about echolocation.
- They really don't bother people much.
- They keep bugs away from us by eating them.
- They're good parents. They hold their babies and feed them milk.

FIGURE 7   Contrasting Examples of Second-Grade Students' Nonfiction Writing (Original Spellings)

The Magnet Book illustrated by Kay K. words by Kay K.	by Randy A. About Magnet. How they Science
If you stick a magnet in your shert and put one in the top they stik to you shirt.	Magnets cen go throw metal.
Magnitism can travel throgh cardbourd. For example put the magnet on cardboard and hold on the cardboard.	there are aku cins fo magnet *[There are all kinds of magnets.]*
If you tack a nail and rub a magnet next to it the nail by itself can pick up metal.	Magnets cat go thero everytheing *[Magnets can't go through everything.]*
And thats how you can use magnets.	

9. *Use general strategies or heuristics.*   Heuristics are effective in increasing comprehension and in moving students toward independent reading. Although some are too formal or complicated to be appropriate for primary-grade learners, others provide useful formats for guiding content area reading instruction, especially when the teacher leads students through the process. Two promising examples include the previously discussed 3W2H (Manning & Manning, 1995) and Manzo's (1991) Listen, Read, Discuss (LRD). During LRD, students:

Listen to the teacher discuss the content.

Read content text aided by the background experience of the teacher's words.

Discuss: What did you understand best? Least well? What questions or thoughts did this raise for you about the content or reading strategies?

LRD can be varied to meet students' interests and needs. Examples include varying the input for listening, providing a purpose for reading that requires critical or creative expression or application, and discussing which portions of the text struck readers as inconsiderate (poorly written or poorly organized). Teachers may hold postreading discussions on teaching and learning strategies or create research teams that allow students to delve into a topic in greater depth.

10. *Use pre-, during-, and postreading activities.*   Although proposed content area reading frameworks differ (e.g., Richardson & Morgan, 1994; Singer & Donlan, 1989), frameworks each suggest that teachers need to prepare students for readings, guide them through readings, and then extend the reading experience. Use of pre-, during-, and postreading strategies offers dependent readers support to activate and maintain relevant schema (Tierney & Pearson, 1994). Explicit instruction about the framework helps children see that it can generalize to other texts and settings as well. Figure 8 presents a brief sampling of activities—many of which are particularly helpful for dependent readers—that can take

FIGURE 8   Sample Strategies for Pre-, During-, and Postreading Activities in the
Content Areas

Prereading Strategies:	**During-Reading Strategies:**	**Postreading Strategies:**
Access and build prior knowledge. Prepare students to read.	Build conceptual understanding, reading fluency, and comprehension.	Synthesize and summarize content area information, build comprehension, and extend the reading experience.

• Brainstorm. • Factstorm (list all the facts we know about the content). • Brainwrite (individuals create their own brainstorming lists, then pass their papers to peers, who review and add to the lists). • Create graphic organizers. Use charts that match the text's structure (compare and contrast? description?). • Listen to one another's stories. • List student questions. • Provide concrete experiences. • Set a purpose for reading. (What are we looking for?) • Preview the text: How is it organized? Does it have charts? An index? How can we find particular topics in it?	• Vary reading structures (Smith & Johnson, 1994): Paired reading, kaleidoscope reading, taped readings, literature circles, large-group discussion. • Find patterns in text structure. • Help children study text features. • Use simple notetaking strategies. • Expand on the charts used during prereading. • Use reading guides. • Pause to ask who, what, where, when, why, how. • Incorporate visual imagery and partner discussion. • Try guided reading/ thinking activities. • Learn vocabulary in context. Include general terms with specific connotations in current usage and specific, technical terms. Connect to earlier hands-on experiences.	• Retell the passage. • Compose group or partner summaries. • Write structured expository paragraphs or journal paraphrases. • Try language experiences in whole groups for writing (for example, ABC books on the content). • Reflect on what text features were helpful and which ones seemed rude. • Use reading-to-learn experiences as a means to an end; in some way, use what is learned through reading. • Bridges back to real life to ensure that reading experinces have relevance. • Reflect on the answers found to children's earlier questions. • Ask for students' new questions.

children into, through, and beyond their content area readings while addressing vocabulary, content ideas, and text features and structures.

Figure 9 gives a sample primary-grade content area lesson that illustrates how the framework can be used to address vocabulary, concepts and relationships, text features, and text structure and to provoke efferent and affective responses. This lesson, used successfully with learners of many ages, embodies each of the 10 ideas related to content area reading.

FIGURE 9   A Sample Science Content Area Reading Lesson for Primary Grades: Crickets

Prereading Activities
1. Teacher shares a personal story of wildly chasing crickets that interrupted her sleep. She elicits cricket stories from students.
2. Children close their eyes and visualize a cricket. When they open their eyes, compose a 30-second sketch of a cricket. Teacher circulates to check prior knowledge. (Did each child draw an insect? What notable features are apparent?)
3. The class constructs a semantic map on crickets: Cricket bodies, what they do, what they need, other information.
4. Teacher records questions and uncertainties in a different color.
5. Children fold a paper in fourths and record one cricket question related to each of the four sections of the semantic map in each fourth. Teacher models for students who need support.
6. Teacher distributes hand lenses and crickets (from tropical fish store), one per student pair. Students make observations to begin to answer their questions.
7. The class revises its map based upon observations (e.g., "crickets have four eyes; crickets have two pairs of wings; females and males look different"). They review their questions to determine which remain unanswered.
8. Teacher distributed text on crickets (one is available from the author in English or Spanish). The class studies text features (e.g., diagrams, headings, boldfaced terms) and notices that the organizational headings match the categories of their semantic map.

(Analysis: These activities allow children to respond affectively to the topic, connect the topic to their prior experiences, explore specific concepts related to the content, engage in hands-on activity to build background knowledge, set a purpose for reading, and examine text features and structure to gather information quickly.)

During-Reading Activities
1. Dependent readers listen to the text and follow along on their own copies as the teacher reads text aloud. A cross-age tutor may read the text, or students may listen to a taped reading by a fluent model.
2. Less dependent readers may meet in hetereogeneous pairs to partner read the text. They may take responsibility for reading only a section of text, then retell and summarize the information for the class.
3. Independent readers can silently read the material, focusing on sections that address their recorded questions.
4. The class takes simple notes, including words and drawings, upon their folded question papers.
5. Students attach vocabulary terms from the text to their observations. Examples of terms include *ovipositor, cerci, stridulation,* and *compound eye.*

(Analysis: These activities provide support for students as they read for a purpose.)

Postreading Activities
1. Students examine the initial cricket drawings and compose new drawings to correct inaccuracies and add detail.
2. The class revises the semantic map.
3. Students analyze the text for its friendliness and make a list of the next set of cricket questions to be addressed.
4. Students select a writing activity to capture their knowledge and response to the cricket experience. Examples include pop-up cards with a single student-composed sentence, group paragraphs, and cinquain poems.

(Analysis: Students reflect on their knowledge gains, analyze the reading experience, and respond through writing to the experience. This aids comprehension and solidifies content knowledge. The purpose is set for future reading endeavors.)

Summary and Conclusions

Trade books, textbooks, realistic fiction, and other print sources all have a place within the primary-grade classroom for content area reading. Exposure to abundant informational resources provides young students with the valuable opportunity to read for the purpose of learning about their worlds and to answer their questions. Primary-grade teachers can use content area reading experiences to help children learn, to build a foundation for getting meaning from text, to encourage the use of reading as a powerful tool to gain information, and to help children develop and respond to important ideas. Although time and effort are necessary to collect materials and develop content area learning experiences, teachers can draw on other resources to enrich their literacy programs. Students can bring materials from home, the librarian may provide assistance, and financial support may be available through sources like parent-teacher organizations or grant funds. Teachers can also work with colleagues to develop or implement meaningful content area reading experiences. They can listen to young students' questions about the world and work together with students to find answers to those questions and get meaning from the printed word. When primary teachers encourage content area reading, they

- provide a meaningful context for reading instruction.
- help children develop lifelong skills for gaining information.
- encourage comprehension, the exploration of big ideas, and connections among ideas.
- nurture students' quest to know and to seek answers to their important questions.

References

Alvermann, D. E. (1991). The discussion web: A graphic aid for learning across the curriculum. *The Reading Teacher, 5,* 92–99.

American Forest Foundation. (1994). *Project Learning Tree: Environmental education activity guide.* Washington, DC: Author.

Armbruster, B. B. (1992). Content reading in RI: The last 2 decades. *Reading Teacher, 46,* 166–167.

Baghban, M. (1995, July). *Content reading: Is there any other kind?* Paper presented at the annual meeting of the National Council of Teachers of English International Conference, New York. (ERIC Document Reproduction Service No. ED 385 824)

Bash, B. (1993). *Shadows of night: The hidden world of the little brown bat.* San Francisco: Sierra Club.

Bristor, V. J. (1994). Combining reading and writing with science to enhance content area achievement and attitudes. *Reading Horizons, 35,* 30–43.

Dickson, B. L. (1995). Reading in the content-areas. *Reading Improvement, 32,* 191–192.

Gaylord, S. K. (1994). *Multicultural books to make and share.* New York: Scholastic.

Guillaume, A. M., Yopp, R. H., & Yopp, H. K. (1996).

Accessible science. *Journal of Educational Issues for Language Minority Students, 7,* 67–85.

Jackson, P. W. (1968). *Life in classrooms.* New York: Holt, Rinehart & Winston.

Kobrin, B. (1995). *Eye-openers II: Children's books to answer children's questions about the world around them.* New York: Scholastic.

Lickteig, M. J., & Danielson, K. E. (1995). Use children's books to link the cultures of the world. *The Social Studies, 86,* 69–73.

Manning, M., & Manning, G. (1995). Reading and writing in the content areas. *Teaching K–8, 26,* 152–153.

Manzo, A. V. (1991). Training teachers to use content area reading strategies: Description and appraisal of four options. *Reading Research and Instruction, 30,* 67–73.

Manzo, A. V., & Manzo, U. C. (1995). *Teaching children to be literate: A reflective approach.* Fort Worth, TX: Harcourt Brace.

McMath, J., & King, M. (1993). Open books, open minds. *Science and Children, 30,* 33–36.

Ogle, D. (1986). K-W-L: A teaching model that develops active reading of expository text. *The Reading Teacher, 39,* 564–570.

Olson, M. W., & Gee, T. C. (1991). Content reading instruction in the primary grades: Perceptions and strategies. *The Reading Teacher, 45,* 298–307.

Richardson, J. S. (1994). A read-aloud for science classrooms. *Journal of Reading, 38,* 62–63.

Richardson, J. S., & Morgan, R. F. (1994). *Reading to learn in the content areas.* Belmont, CA: Wadsworth.

Romance, N. R., & Vitale, M. R. (1992). A curriculum that expands time for in-depth elementary science instruction by using science-based reading strategies: Effects of a year-long study in grade four. *Journal of Research in Science Teaching, 29,* 545–554.

Rosenblatt, L. (1991). Literature—S.O.S.! *Language Arts, 68,* 441–448.

Ross, E. P. (1994). *Using children's literature across the curriculum* (Fastback 374). Bloomington, IN: Phi Delta Kappa Educational Foundation.

Schifini, A. (1994). Language, literacy, and content instruction: Strategies for teachers. In K. Spangenberg-Urbschat & R. Pritchard, (Eds.), *Kids come in all languages: Reading instruction for ESL students* (pp. 158–179). Newark, DE: International Reading Association.

Singer, H., & Donlan, D. (1989). *Reading and learning from text* (2nd ed.). Hillsdale, NJ: Erlbaum.

Smith, J. L., & Johnson, H. (1994). Models of implementing literature in content studies. *The Reading Teacher, 48,* 198–209.

Tierney, R. J., & Pearson, P. D. (1994). Learning to learn from text: A framework for improving classroom practice. In R. B. Ruddell, M. R. Ruddell, & H. Singer (Eds.), *Theoretical models and processes of reading,* (4th ed., pp. 496–513). Newark, DE: International Reading Association.

Yopp, H. K., & Yopp, R. H. (1996). *Literature based reading activities* (2nd ed.). Boston: Allyn & Bacon.

Integrating Sources

1. Vacca suggests that the key to the problem of adolescent literacy lies with teachers in the middle and secondary grades, while Guillaume encourages primary teachers to start their children down the road of content literacy. Are these two views contradictory, or are they complementary? Explain.

2. Reread the quote at the beginning of this chapter from a 1926 teacher's manual. The point at which children are expected to become proficient learners from this text is grades 6–7. Can this view be reconciled with that of Guillaume? Are present-day educators setting the literacy bar too high too soon?

3. Vacca describes the popular movement toward early intervention programs as involving a danger of "putting all of our eggs in one basket." What is the extent of this danger in your view?

Classroom Implications

1. Describe three ways you might incorporate more reading and writing into content instruction.

   a.

   b.

   c.

2. Describe an action research study that might convince a resistant content teacher (not you, of course) that content literacy activities can improve content learning.

Annotated Bibliography

Alvermann, D. E., & Moore, D. W. (1991). Secondary school reading. In R. Barr, M. Kamil, P. B. Mosenthal, & P. D. Pearson (Eds.), *Handbook of reading research* (Vol. II, pp. 951–983). White Plains, NY: Longman.

This is an extensive research review of effective practice in content area settings, with additional focus on actual practice.

Armbruster, B. B. (1993). Readings about reading to learn. *The Reading Teacher, 46,* 598–600.

An annotated list of references related to content literacy instruction for elementary classroom teachers is included.

Cooter, R. B. (1993). A think-aloud on secondary reading assessment. *Journal of Reading, 36,* 584–586.

The current role of literacy assessment in secondary reading content classes is discussed, and suggestions are made for effective changes in these procedures.

Daisey, P., & Shoryer, M. G. (1992). Perceptions and attitudes of content and methods instructors toward a required reading course. *Journal of Reading, 36,* 624–629.

This reviews the results of a survey of university student attitudes in relation to a content area reading course. Results are divided into seven categories based on changing ideas of the purpose for content literacy instruction.

Feathers, K. M. (1993). *Infotext: Reading and learning.* Portsmouth, NH: Heinemann.

This text describes students who have difficulty learning from information text and suggests specific strategies for help with these problems. An excellent bibliography of related references is included.

Flood, N., et al. (1993). Teaching the whole enchilada: Enhancing multiculturalism through children's literature in the content areas. *Reading Horizons, 33,* 359–365.

This article suggests that the integration of content disciplines (social studies, mathematics, art, etc.) can best be accomplished through the use of thematic units. This article includes examples of various types of thematic units based on the theme of Mexico. It also includes a current bibliography.

Frager, A. M. (1993). Affective dimension of content area reading. *Journal of Reading, 36,* 616–622.

The importance of the affective element in the development of content literacy is discussed. Also suggested are classroom strategies to enhance the affective behavior of students' reading in content classes.

McKenna, M. C., & Robinson, R. D. (1990). Content literacy: A definition and implications. *Journal of Reading, 34,* 184–186.

This article introduces the term content literacy, *which is now widely accepted. The authors define the concept as "the ability to use reading and writing for the acquisition of new content in a given discipline."*

Mosenthal, P., & Kirsch, I. S. (1993). Profiling students' quantitative literacy abilities: An approach with precision. *Journal of Reading, 36,* 668–674.

An approach to helping content area students improve their quantitative literacy ability is discussed.

Reinking, D., et al. (1993). Developing preservice teachers' conditional knowledge of content area reading strategies. *Journal of Reading, 36,* 458–469.

A model for preservice teachers' implementation of effective literacy strategies is presented.

Schumm, J. S., et al. (1992). What teachers do when the textbook is tough: Students speak out. *Journal of Reading Behavior, 24,* 481–503.

This article reviews the opinions of a group of middle and high school students on what content literacy teachers do when the textbooks are difficult to read. Suggestions are given to facilitate the effective reading of these literacy materials.

You Become Involved

1. Locate a content textbook at any grade level published more than 25 years ago. Contrast it with a present-day text in the same area designed to be used at the same level. As you contrast the two, you might use the following questions as guidelines:

   a. Does the reading level of the material seem appropriate for the intended readers?
   b. How well is the content of the material likely to reflect the background of the students?
   c. Is the material well organized? What devices have the authors used to make the organization visible to students?
   d. What devices appear as comprehension aids? In which text is there better use of charts, marginalia, diagrams, boldface and italics, and other aids?

2. Recall your own personal experiences with literacy in the content areas. Were they positive or negative? What do you think made the difference in your reaction to your past experience? Some possible reasons include the instructional activities of your content teachers, the materials that were used, or perhaps your individual background of experiences related to a particular content subject.

3. Visit a high school content classroom and note the literacy activities taking place. In what ways are reading and writing incorporated in the students' learning activities? If you note few examples, ask the teacher why literacy activities are not used more often. Do you agree with the answer(s)?

9

EARLY INTERVENTION

Reading instruction ought to begin with
the first day of the child's school life.
—*HARRY WHEAT (1923)*

The attainment of a given chronological or mental age (such as six
and one half years) does not insure success with reading activities.
—*EMETT BETTS (1946)*

All schools, but especially schools that serve large numbers of
children who arrive with few experiences with books, stories,
and print, need effective early-intervention programs in
place. A successful early-intervention program would likely
involve reorganizing classroom instruction to better focus on
literacy instructional needs of all children and the development of a support program that provides targeted children with
added instruction in the specific areas identified as problems.
—*CUNNINGHAM AND ALLINGTON (1999)*

Overview

Machiavelli, a Renaissance political theorist, suggested that when political problems are just beginning, they are difficult to detect, but easy to remedy. After they
have entrenched, however, they are easy to detect but difficult to remedy. The educational equivalent of Machiavelli's principle is what Stanovich (1986) has called
the *Matthew Effect*—the notion that the gap between the highest and lowest achievers is narrow in the lower grades but expands as the children grow older. The idea
that this gap can be much more easily bridged in the primary grades has occasioned
the widespread interest in early intervention programs in the area of literacy.

   Cost effectiveness constitutes one of the primary rationales for early intervention programs. To make their case, Robert Slavin and colleagues (1991) tell the
hypothetical story of a town plagued by a contaminated water supply. Some 30 per-

cent of the children regularly become ill and some die as a result. The town spends a great deal in medical costs, and then one day an engineer proposes a water treatment plant that would virtually irradicate the disease. But the plant would cost more than the hospitalization, some argue, and besides, 70 percent of the children never become ill to begin with. Can an expensive intervention be cost effective in the long run by reducing the need for remedial services? And what about the human cost in unrealized potential as students fail to achieve and eventually drop out?

The movement toward early intervention is easy to understand. It offers an approach to the gravest problem faced by literacy educators, an approach that salvages human lives at a point when they are most likely to be saved.

As You Read

Reading Recovery remains one of the most popular and effective early intervention programs yet introduced. One testimony to its success has been the large number of similar programs that have appeared in this country, usually with lower price tags. As you read the Askew and colleagues' review of early literacy intervention, consider the following:

1. Consider the three levels of professional training. How practical do you find them?
2. What roles does assessment play in an effective program?
3. Why is individual instruction crucial?

Barbara Taylor and colleagues have developed another early intervention program, one that is research based, empirically validated, and multifaceted. In these respects it is similar to Reading Recovery. As you read, keep the following questions in mind:

4. How is individualization accomplished in a small-group setting?
5. What is the role of cross-age tutoring?
6. Are the results sufficiently positive to warrant such a program?

References

Betts, E. A. (1946). *Foundations of reading instruction.* New York: American Book Company.
Cunningham, P. M., & Allington, R. L. (1999). *Classrooms that work: They can all read and write* (2nd ed.). New York: Longman.
Slavin, R. E., Madden, N. L., Karweit, N. L., Dolan, L., & Wasik, B. A. (1991). Success for All: Ending reading failure from the beginning. *Language Arts, 68,* 404–409.
Stanovich, K. E. (1986). Matthew effects in reading: Some consequences of individual differences in the acquisition of literacy. *Reading Research Quarterly, 21,* 360–407.
Wheat, H. (1923). *The teaching of reading.* Boston: Ginn.

Helping Struggling Readers

Linking Small-Group Intervention with Cross-Age Tutoring

BARBARA M. TAYLOR   KAREN JUSTICE-SWANSON
BARBARA E. HANSON   SUSAN M. WATTS

Providing the best reading instruction possible for children who are struggling academically remains a major responsibility for educators. Although the overall level of reading achievement in the United States has remained fairly stable since 1970 (Mullis & Jenkins, 1990) and is relatively high in international comparisons (Elley, 1992), we still have too many children and adolescents reading at low levels, which has a negative impact on their success in school (Williams, Reese, Campbell, Mazzeo, & Phillips, 1995). Recent data from the National Assessment of Educational Progress (NAEP) reveal that two fifths of the 1994 sample of fourth graders (age 9 to 10) failed to demonstrate even a basic level of reading ability. We also know that students who are struggling in reading come disproportionately from families of poverty (Mullis, Campbell, & Farstrup, 1993; Puma, Jones, Rock, & Fernandez, 1993) and that the gap in performance between middle- and lower- income children is not closing substantially.

Over the past 10 years we have learned a considerable amount about what works to improve the reading ability of young children at risk of reading failure. Early reading intervention programs, the most notable of which are Reading Recovery (Pinnell, 1989) and Success for All (Madden, Slavin, Karweit, Dolan, & Wasik, 1993), which focus on accelerating students' learning to prevent failure as opposed to remediating problems as they occur, have been found to be very effective (Hiebert & Taylor, 1994; Pikulski, 1994; Slavin & Madden, 1989). Programs that provide extensive one-on-one tutoring (Wasik & Slavin, 1993) and small-group models have also been successful (Hiebert, Colt, Catto, & Gury, 1992; Taylor, Short, Shearer, & Frye, 1995).

First-grade (age 6 to 7) early intervention programs have been widely incorporated into schools around the U.S. For example, Reading Recovery is now in more than 1,000 schools in more than 40 states (Shanahan & Barr, 1995). The rapid influx of programs as well as numerous recently published books and articles focusing on early reading intervention suggest that getting children off to a good start in reading is essential and that early intervention is a key factor in making this possible (Pikulski, 1994).

However, first-grade reading intervention alone is not sufficient. Educators have recently begun asking questions about what needs to be done to sustain the effects of early intervention and to help children, whether they did or did not receive first-grade interven-

Source: From Taylor, B. M., Hanson, B., Justice-Swanson, K., & Watts, S. M. (1997, November). Helping struggling readers: Linking small-group intervention with cross-age tutoring. *The Reading Teacher, 51*(3), 196–209. Reprinted with permission of Barbara M. Taylor and the International Reading Association. All rights reserved.

tion, who are struggling readers beyond the age of 6 to 7 (Hiebert, 1994; Hiebert & Taylor, 1994; Shanahan & Barr, 1995). Recent research on Reading Recovery, for example, indicates that the impressive learning levels achieved through the program are not sustained in subsequent grades to the level one would hope (Hiebert, 1994; Shanahan & Barr, 1995), that 10 to 30% of the children receiving the program in first grade (age 6 to 7) are not successfully discontinued (Shanahan & Barr, 1995), and that the high cost of the program may limit the number of children served out of the total who need help (Hiebert, 1994; Shanahan & Barr, 1995). Based on these findings, it is clear that even in elementary schools fortunate enough to have Reading Recovery, there are older children in Grade 2 and beyond who are in need of extra help in reading.

The purpose of this article is to describe Webster Magnet School's 2-year effort to go beyond early reading intervention. Webster Magnet, located in a large midwestern U.S. city, is a K–6 (ages 5 through 12) school with 1,100 children from diverse backgrounds. Of the student population, 56% are students of color and 49% receive subsidized lunch. Webster is a magnet school in a low-income neighborhood but attracts many middle-income students from nearby neighborhoods.

In October, 1994, 50% of the students age 7 to 8 at Webster scored in the lowest quartile on the Metropolitan Achievement Test (1993). Reading Recovery was in its first year of operation at Webster, but it was clear that there would continue to be many 7-year-olds in need of special reading help. In response to this need to work with low-achieving readers, an effective, cost-efficient intervention program was developed. The program was supplemental to the non-ability-grouped regular reading program, which used a basal reader series and sets of trade books.

As a first step, the authors designed a small-group extension of the Early Intervention in Reading program (Taylor, Frye, Short, & Shearer, 1992) that could be implemented as a 7-week enrichment class for students age 7 to 8. This particular delivery model was used because it fit well with the enrichment model of the school in which children select specialty classes such as band, computer, and Spanish. For some of the children, the intervention program was supplemented with a cross-age tutoring program involving 9- to 10-year-olds as tutors in an attempt to maximize the effectiveness of the intervention.

As a follow-up to the 1994–95 project, willing teachers incorporated the reading intervention into their regular classroom routines the following year. This phase was developed to counteract the difficulty schools have in keeping innovative programs going; typically, they are introduced, are effective for a few years, and then die out (Allington & Walmsley, 1995; Slavin & Madden, 1989). Furthermore, effective instructional strategies within classrooms are needed to sustain the effects of intervention programs that are external to the classroom.

Research Base for the Reading Intervention Program

The reading intervention program developed at Webster was based on a number of instructional components found to be effective in fostering reading growth: repeated reading, coaching children in the use of strategies to foster independence in reading, writing, and one-on-one tutoring. Repeated reading was emphasized because this has been found to be an effective technique to build word recognition rate, accuracy, fluency, and reading comprehension (Adams, 1990; Dowhower, 1987; Samuels, 1979). The repeated reading in the second-grade intervention program resembled the Shared Book Experience technique (Holdaway, 1981) described by Reutzel, Hollingsworth, and Eldredge (1994) in which children read intact stories repeatedly, first in a group with teacher support and then individually or with a partner.

The emphasis on coaching children to read for meaning and to become independent in word recognition through the use of decoding and self-monitoring strategies has been discussed as an important aspect of Reading Recovery (Clay, 1993; Pinnell, 1989) as well as in the small-group Early Intervention in Reading program (Taylor et al., 1992). As Clay (1991) explains, to become an independent reader, a low-progress reader will need help in learning to detect and self-correct word recognition errors, to become aware of and able to use a repertoire of effective strategies for working on text, and, perhaps most importantly, to do these things within the context of reading for meaning.

The importance of writing in learning to read has also been stressed by Clay (1991) and others (Adams, 1990; Clarke, 1988; Ehri, 1989). Through writing, children learn to hear the sounds in words and to spell these sounds with letters. They also learn to pay attention to letter order, learn about regular sound-letter sequences in words, and learn to write and read frequently occurring words. Thus, sentence writing has been identified as an important component in many successful early intervention programs (Clay, 1993; Hiebert et al., 1992; Pikulski, 1994; Pinnell, 1989; Taylor et al., 1992).

The effectiveness of one-on-one tutoring by trained teachers in preventing reading failure has been documented in a recent review by Wasik and Slavin (1993). Sixteen studies evaluating five programs, including Reading Recovery and Success for All, found substantial positive effects for tutoring by trained educators. However, one of the biggest drawbacks to such models is the expense (Hiebert, 1994; Shanahan & Barr, 1995; Wasik & Slavin, 1993). A community volunteer tutoring program in Virginia directed toward young students at risk of reading failure, in which the tutors are carefully trained, has had impressive results (Invernizzi, Juel, & Rosemary, 1997). Cross-age tutoring programs (Heath & Mangiola, 1991; Labbo & Teale, 1990; Limbrick, McNaughton, & Glynn, 1985) have also been effective in increasing elementary students' reading achievement. In addition to benefiting the younger children who are tutored, older students who are themselves struggling readers have benefited when they serve as tutors (Devin-Sheehan, Feldman, & Allen, 1976; Labbo & Teale, 1990).

The Reading Intervention Program

Participants

In 1994–95 teachers of second-grade students (age 7 to 8) were asked to identify approximately one third of their students who they felt would benefit from the reading intervention program that would be offered twice during the year as an enrichment class by the building reading coordinator. Children scheduled for the fall enrichment session also participated in the cross-age tutoring program in which fourth-grade students (age 9 to 10) served as tutors.

The teachers identified 31 children whose mean score on the fall Metropolitan Achievement Test 7 (MAT7, 1993) was at about the 10th percentile. In October a project assistant listened to these children (who also received Chapter I help) read from *Tiger Is a Scaredy Cat* (Phillips, 1986), an easy reader at the primer level, and verified that none of the children could read this with 90% word recognition accuracy. Twelve children who did not have conflicts with other requested enrichment classes were scheduled for the fall reading intervention class (intervention plus tutoring group), and 7 were scheduled for the spring class (intervention-only group). The remaining 12 children made up a control group. They did not receive tutoring.

Materials

The reading material for the intervention program consisted of picture books and easy readers selected for their appeal to 7- and 8-year-old children and their appropriateness to the intervention model that was being used. The books were categorized into 6 levels (A–F, see Appendix A).

Books in Levels A–D were picture books that were fairly easy for the younger children to read. Level A books were only 40–60 words long and consequently could be read successfully by almost all of the children at the end of 3 days of choral, partner, and individual repetitive reading. Levels B, C, and D books progressively increased in length. However, picture clues or some repetition in the text allowed the children to read these books successfully also (with 90% word recognition accuracy or better) by the end of the 3-day cycle of choral, partner, and individual repeated reading. Levels E and F books were easy readers selected so the children could practice independent, as opposed to choral, reading. Level E books were easier than Level D books, but the children were asked to read the Level E books on their own the first time, whereas Level D books were read to them first and then read chorally before they were read independently.

Instruction

For 45 minutes each day for 7 weeks, the children met for the reading intervention class taught by the building reading coordinator. For 20–30 minutes of each class, the children engaged in a 3-day cycle of activities pertaining to the intervention program (see Figure 1 and Appendix B). The group spent 3 days reading a book from one of the six levels identified in Appendix A. During the first 5 weeks the children read picture books from Levels A–D in which choral and partner reading of the book was initially stressed, followed by independent reading. During the last 2 to 3 weeks of the session the children read easy readers from Levels E and F in which initial independent reading of the book was stressed, followed by partner reading. This allowed the children to demonstrate to themselves that they could independently read a book they had never read before. The teacher circulated among the children as they were reading independently or in pairs to coach them in reading for meaning and in the use of decoding and self-monitoring strategies (see Figure 2).

For partner reading, the children were taught and reminded as necessary to be good helpers who gave hints, but did not automatically tell a word when their partner was stuck. They were encouraged to give their partner the first sound of the word or to tell their partner

FIGURE 1   Timeline for 3-Day Cycle of Intervention Activities

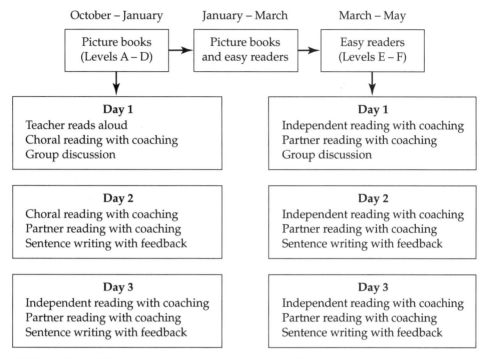

Children also read intervention story to tutor on 1 or 2 days out of 3.

FIGURE 2   Decoding and Self-Monitoring Strategies Emphasized in the Reading Intervention Program

Word Attack Strategies
Think about what would make sense.
Try to think of a word that starts with _____ that would make sense.
Look for a familiar rhyming part.
Sound out the word and think about what would make sense.
Use picture clues.
Read past the word and come back to it.

Self-Monitoring Strategies
Check to see if the word you come up with looks like what is on the page and makes sense.
Go back to a word you had trouble with if the sentence isn't making sense.

to look at the pictures for a clue. For example, to help David with *eating,* Joseph pointed to a picture clue and said, "What is he doing? What am I doing?" as he pretended to eat. On another word Joseph helped David by saying, "You read that word already, /c/–/an/."

In addition to these reading activities, the 3-day cycle included discussion and writing. The purpose of the sentence writing was to engage the children in a comprehension activity related to the story, to refine their phonemic awareness, and to help them to continue to develop their word analysis skills and knowledge of symbol-sound correspondences, especially for vowel sounds. The writing was typically based on a teacher prompt, such as "What are things that keep you from going to sleep?" or "Tell about a place you can go to be alone" in response to *Marmalade's Nap* (Wheeler, 1983), a story about a cat who could not find a quiet place to take a nap. (See Figure 3 for additional examples of prompts.) As each child finished writing his or her sentence, s/he read it to the teacher who gave feedback on one or two words not spelled correctly by directing the child's attention to a word that had a sound missing or to a word in which the vowel sound wasn't represented with an appropriate spelling. For example, if the child wrote *friend* as *fred,* the teacher would ask the child to say the word and try to figure out what sound was missing. Usually, the child could come up with the missing sound and the letter that represented that sound. If not, the teacher assisted the child. The purpose of this activity was to help the children refine their phonemic awareness. Or, if the child wrote *box* as *bax,* the teacher would ask the child to say the word slowly and try to figure out what other vowel spelled the sound heard in *box.* A child who finished the writing activity before the others either wrote another sentence or read from one of the earlier books in the program.

FIGURE 3   Examples of Prompts for Sentence Writing in the Reading Intervention Program

---

Sam's Cookie
Who/what is someone who made you angry and why?
What is a favorite snack or treat? When do you eat it?
What is something that makes you scared and why?

Lady With the Alligator Purse
Write a sentence about something in the story that couldn't really happen.
What was a part of the story that you thought was funny?
Tell about something that happened to you or someone in your family that was funny.

George Shrinks
If you were as little as George, what would you like to do?
Tell about a picture you like.
What would happen to George if he were as big as a giant?

Is Your Mama a Llama?
Tell us about your mother or grandmother.
Tell about something you lost and where you found it.
Tell why you likes a favorite picture . Describe a favorite picture.

For the last 15–20 minutes of the enrichment class, the group engaged in other activities that involved language development and research skills. For example, the fall class created a calendar for the following year. They researched seasonal activities, holidays, and special events, and then students selected one month and developed a page of activities and pictures for the calendar. The spring class worked on shorter term projects that involved weekly art and writing activities centered around spring.

The Cross-Age Tutoring Program

Participants

The younger children (age 7 to 8) in the fall enrichment session left their regular classroom twice a week for 25 minutes to participate in the cross-age tutoring program. Once the fall 7-week reading intervention class was over, these children continued to participate in cross-age tutoring through mid-April. The reading coordinator prepared the younger children for the book from the intervention program that they would be reading to their tutors (age 9 to 10) during a 10- to 15-minute period once a week.

The 12 older children selected as tutors met three criteria: (a) they had been identified by their teachers as being behind in reading and likely to benefit from the tutoring experience, (b) they did not have scheduling conflicts with other enrichment classes, and (c) they were able to read a 3 basal reader with at least 85% word recognition accuracy.

Materials

The reading materials for the cross-age tutoring program consisted of books from the intervention program (see Appendix A). Also, the tutors read picture books to the younger children. A few of their favorites were *Miss Nelson Is Missing* (Allard & Marshall, 1977), *Another Mouse to Feed* (Kraus, 1980), and *The Cloud Book* (dePaola, 1975). The tutors also read aloud nonfiction material by authors such as Gail Gibbons and Joanna Cole.

Instruction

During the fall and winter enrichment sessions, the 12 older children in the tutoring class met for 45 minutes each day for 14 weeks with one of their teachers and the reading coordinator. This program was patterned after a similar cross-age tutoring program developed by Heath and Mangiola (1991). The children spent Mondays and Tuesdays getting ready to tutor. Their teachers modeled how to be a good coach who would hint but not immediately tell a child a word. There was considerable discussion about good word recognition strategies to teach the younger children to use (see Figure 2). Students kept an ongoing list of these strategies in a journal and referred to this as they were practicing or actually tutoring. The children also practiced reading the same books the younger children would be reading to them.

The tutors also chose a picture book to read to the young partners. They practiced reading this to themselves and to a classmate in the tutoring class. At the same time, they practiced being good coaches if someone got stuck on a word. They also planned with their teachers an extension activity focused on comprehension and based on the picture book they would be reading aloud. For example, one week the tutors prepared a character sketch activity. They helped their young partners identify a main character in the picture book and listed character traits. In another activity, tutors and their partners made a story map in which they decided on the main idea and listed supporting details. The tutors also regularly listed generic and specific questions for discussion in their journals so they could refer to them when working with their partners.

On Wednesdays and Thursdays, the children and tutors met for 25 minutes during the tutors' enrichment class time. Each day the younger children read the book they were working on in their intervention program to their tutor. The tutors would coach with prompts such as, "Look at the picture" or "It starts with / p /." One example was Tom, helping Nate who was reading, "And most of all because it might be very . . . " (Barrett, 1970). Tom said, "Sound it out in chunks." Nate replied with, "Em . . . Embarrassing," and Tom said, "Yup," as he smiled and nodded his head. Tara helped Amber by covering up the end of the word and saying, "Sound this first part out." After Amber said, "Wal-," Tara covered it up and said, "Now say this last part." Amber said "-rus" and then "walrus."

Across the 2 tutoring days, the tutors read the picture book they had practiced to their young partners. They used the questions in their journals to have discussions about the story, talked about words with which the younger children might be unfamiliar, and then engaged the younger children in the comprehension extension activity related to the picture book.

Following the tutoring sessions on Wednesdays and Thursdays, the tutors had oral debriefing sessions on what went well and what were problems or concerns pertaining to the tutoring sessions. The children often reported that they liked working with their young partners and that their partners read well. They also frequently mentioned problems such as their partners talking too softly, not paying enough attention, or not sitting still. The teachers shared positive things they had noticed as the partners worked together and helped the tutors think of ways to solve problems that arose.

On Fridays the tutors wrote a letter to an adult mentor (one of the authors or the project assistant), using their debriefing discussions to help them decide what to write about. They typically would write about what had gone well that week when they met with their young partners, what problems they had had, and how their partners were doing in reading. The mentor wrote back by Monday of the next week, praising the tutors for their efforts, giving advice, asking questions, and providing encouragement.

After the fall and winter enrichment sessions were over, the tutors continued to meet with their young partners once a week for 25 minutes through mid-April. The reading coordinator brought them a copy of the partners' intervention book in advance so the tutors could practice reading it. They also selected a picture book from the tutoring project collection and practiced reading this book in their regular classroom in preparation for reading it aloud to their young partners.

Results and Discussion

In May a project assistant listened to the younger children read independently to determine whether or not they were able to decode second-grade material. First the children were asked to read a segment of a story from *Frog and Toad All Year* (Lobel, 1976), which was considered to be at a beginning level for most 7- to 8-year-olds. If they could read this with at least 90% word recognition accuracy, they were also asked to read a passage from *How My Parents Learned to Eat* (Friedman, 1984), which was from the 2^2 basal, but which had not yet been read in the regular reading program. Those who could not read the passage from *Frog and Toad All Year* with at least 90% word recognition accuracy were asked to read a passage from *The Three Wishes* (Aardema, 1989), which was in the 1^2 basal.

In May, 75% of the students in the intervention plus tutoring group, less than 30% in the intervention-only group, and none in the control group could read the passage from the 2^2 basal with at least 90% word recognition accuracy. The reading levels in May for children in all three groups are in Table 1. A Yates-corrected chi-square test revealed that significantly more children in the intervention plus tutoring group than in the control group were reading on grade level by the end of second grade ($X^2 = 11.38, p < .001$).

The means and standard deviations on fall Grade 2 and Grade 3 raw scores from the reading subtest of the MAT7 (1993) are shown in Table 2. An analysis of covariance on the Grade 3 scores, with the Grade 2 raw scores serving as the covariate, revealed a significant difference among groups, $F(2.24) = 3.66, p < .05$. Further comparisons revealed that the mean score of the intervention plus tutoring group was significantly higher than that of the control group, $F(1.24) = 6.45, p < .05$. The mean difference between the intervention plus tutoring and intervention-only groups approached significance, $F(1.24) = 3.85, p = .06$. In other words, after controlling for any differences in fall Grade 2 reading scores between groups, we found that the intervention plus tutoring group scored significantly higher on the MAT7 in fall of Grade 3 than the control group.

In May, the project assistant also listened to the tutors read independently. Each child read from *Rufus M.* (Estes, 1944), a story at the end of the fourth-grade basal reader, which they had not read before. Students in the tutoring class were reading below grade level at the beginning of fourth grade; their mean word recognition score on a narrative passage from the 3^1 basal was 94.3%. In May of Grade 4 all 12 children could read the narrative passage from the end of the fourth-grade basal with at least 95% word recognition accuracy ($\bar{x} = 98.5\%$). In addition, in the fall the 12 children in the tutoring group had a mean raw score on the reading subtest of the MAT7 corresponding to the 12th percentile. In the fall of the following school year, the children in the tutoring group had a mean raw score on the MAT7 corresponding to the 19th percentile.

TABLE 1   Number of 7- to 8-Year-Old Students Able to Read at Various Levels with at Least 90% Accuracy (May, 1994–95 Study)

Group	n	Primer or Lower	1^2	2^{2*}
		Highest Level Read		
Intervention plus tutoring	12	2	1	9
Intervention only	7	4	1	2
Control	12	10	2	0

*All children could also read from *Frog and Toad All Year* with at least 90% accuracy.

TABLE 2   Student Score on the MAT7 in the Fall of Grade 2 and Fall of Grade 3 (1994–95 Study)

Group	n		Grade 2 (age 7–8) Raw Score	Grade 2 (age 7–8) Percentile Rank	Grade 3 (age 8–9) Raw Score	Grade 3 (age 8–9) Percentile Rank
Intervention plus tutoring	10	$\bar{x}$	34.50	(12)	41.40	(19)
		SD	7.79		7.41	
Intervention only	7	$\bar{x}$	35.00	(12)	32.57	(11)
		SD	8.54		12.30	
Control	11	$\bar{x}$	31.91	(9)	29.36	(8)
		SD	6.43		10.60	

Note: Two intervention plus tutoring children and one control child are missing because they moved between second and third grade. Their pretest standardized reading scores were 28, 41, and 28, respectively.

Together, the oral reading and standardized test results suggest that both younger and older students made progress in reading during the school year. Compared with a control group, younger children who received the 7-week intervention and 21-week cross-age tutoring programs made significant gains in reading ability. Furthermore, 75% of the children in the combined reading intervention/tutoring program who entered second grade unable to read at a primer level could decode a passage from a grade-level (2^2) basal with 90% accuracy or better by May. None of the control group children could read this well, and only two of seven children in the intervention-only group could read at this level.

The 7-week intervention class that started in the spring without a one-on-one component was not sufficient to improve the reading ability of students arriving unable to read. Since the impact of this intervention is confounded with the fact that it took place relatively late in the year and did not include opportunities for one-on-one reading practice, further study is needed to determine whether an intervention plus tutoring program beginning in the second half of the school year can be effective.

On the other hand, the 7-week intervention program commencing in the fall and supplemented with a 21-week cross-age tutoring program was effective. The fact that we were able to help such a high proportion of nonreaders reach grade level in decoding ability by the end of the year with this particular intervention package is encouraging, particularly because the program did not take a great deal of student time and, relatively speaking, did not require much instructional time provided by teachers. This intervention was also relatively inexpensive. Approximately US$30 per child was spent on books for the intervention and tutoring projects. Averaged out across the year, the two intervention programs required approximately one sixth of the reading coordinator's time, resulting in a total instructional cost of about US$400 per child served. The reading coordinator was free to work with additional enrichment classes during the year and to spend the majority of her time on her primary responsibilities, which involved teacher training and support, working with parents, and providing administrative assistance to the principal.

Adaptations to Classroom Instruction

Although the results of the 1994–95 project were positive for many of the children who participated, we wanted to determine if it had any major impact on classroom instruction at Webster. As we describe below, the project did, in fact, lead to important changes at the school.

The Reading Intervention Program within Regular Classrooms

During the 1995–96 school year, the reading intervention program was used in classrooms as supplemental instruction for all 7- to 8-year-olds. One of the teachers, who had piloted the program in her classroom the previous year, assumed the role of mentor to the other second-grade teachers. After meeting with the teachers to explain the program, she invited them to her room to observe several times in the fall before they began using the program. During the year, the teachers came to the mentor teacher or to the reading coordinator with questions as they arose. In addition to discussing the program at grade-level meetings and informally over lunch, the teachers met as a group with the reading coordinator and one of the other authors on a monthly basis to discuss their successes and concerns pertaining to the program.

In November each teacher selected a group of five to six struggling readers (reading below the primer level) to meet for 20 minutes a day. The group spent 3 days on a story, following the cycle of activities described previously (see Figure 1). A project assistant went to five of the classrooms once a week to coach the children individually as they read from their current intervention story. In two of these five classes the children also received help once a week through the cross-age tutoring program. In three others, a parent volunteer listened to the children read once a week.

One of the greatest challenges to teachers in providing the intervention program within the classroom was finding the time to do so. Four teachers taught the small-group lesson following the regular reading lesson while the other children in the room were engaged in independent reading, writing, or other projects related to the regular reading program. Another teacher taught her group while the other children were completing practice activities related to their math lesson. As they finished, they moved into independent reading and writing activities. This teacher actually met with all of her students in small groups each day on a literacy activity, so everyone had time to finish independent math work and to engage in independent reading and writing activities. One teacher reported that a trial-and-error process was needed to find a time that worked for him to provide the supplemental instruction. The after-reading class time didn't work, but he found that a 20-minute period directly after lunch worked well. During this time, the other children read independently.

Of 42 children in six classrooms with the yearlong intervention, 5 (or 12%) were reading on a 2^1 level and 19 (or 45%) were reading on a 2^2 level in May. All of the children had been reading below the primer level in September. Although the incidence of children reading on grade level by May was not as high as in the 1994–95 project, the results were encouraging as compared with the reading levels of control students from the previous year. Furthermore, teachers were very positive about the program. One teacher reported, "I really liked the program because it easily fit into the daily schedule. It worked; it got kids reading." Another said, "I liked it a lot. The poor readers really improved. The kids felt special to be in the group, and they felt very good about themselves." An added bonus of the program was that it made the teachers more aware of the importance of emphasizing reading strategies with all children.

The participating teachers plan to continue using the program, and as they become more experienced with it, we hope to see even more struggling young readers reading at grade level by May. Additionally, in the future, teachers plan to start the intervention in September instead of November to increase effectiveness.

The Cross-Age Tutoring Program within Regular Classrooms

Two fourth-grade teachers worked with two second-grade classrooms to provide the tutoring class within the classrooms. After meeting with the reading coordinator who explained the tutoring program, these two teachers identified six struggling readers for the program. These children met with the reading coordinator for two 30-minute sessions that focused on how to be a good tutor. The tutors practiced reading picture books aloud to a peer or to the reading coordinator in these initial sessions. Then, the classroom teachers helped their tutors prepare for each week's tutoring session.

On Mondays, the teachers gave the tutors the second-grade intervention book to practice and then gave the tutors time to select a picture book to read aloud to their second-grade partners. For 15–20 minutes on Tuesday through Thursday, the tutors practiced reading their picture books independently and with another tutor or with a parent volunteer. On Friday, the tutors met with their second-grade partners for 25–30 minutes for the tutoring session in the reading coordinator's room. On the following Monday, as they met to prepare for the next week's read-aloud book, the tutors discussed with their teacher what went well and what were problems to be solved pertaining to the previous week's tutoring session.

Teachers were positive about the tutoring program. One second-grade teacher reported, "Not all of my kids in the intervention program have a tutor, but I think they all should. Those who do are better readers. It really helps them with their learning." One of the fourth-grade teachers said, "The program helps the students improve in self-confidence in their reading. Their fluency and comprehension are improving. It puts them in the role of expert." Another said, "Many of the tutors show an increased responsibility with their own work because of the tutoring. They're building self-esteem and improving oral reading and vocabulary skills."

Conclusions

We are pleased that the combination of the reading intervention enrichment class and cross-age tutoring program carried out in this project made important differences in the reading ability of struggling readers at Webster, an urban school with high numbers of 7- to 8-year-olds in need of extra help in reading. Furthermore, the tutors, who were themselves behind in reading, made progress as measured by their ability to read from a fourth-grade basal and by their performance on the MAT7 (1993) at the beginning of fourth and fifth grades. We are equally pleased that the project was incorporated into other classrooms the following year. Thus, a number of teachers at Webster made significant changes in what they were doing for their struggling readers in the regular classroom.

It is important to point out that the reading coordinator was instrumental in developing and piloting the reading intervention and cross-age tutoring programs. Furthermore, she provided invaluable leadership in supporting and encouraging teachers who decided that they wanted to implement the intervention and tutoring programs in their classrooms. She provided materials for teachers, facilitated initial and ongoing staff development, and arranged for meeting times for children participating in the tutoring program. We do not believe the program would be operating without her support.

Beyond the need for a staff member in this essential leadership position, the two programs do not require much money to operate. What both programs do require are commitment and collaboration among classroom teachers. Second-grade teachers must find the time for 15–20 minutes of daily reading intervention if they are doing this themselves within the classroom. Fourth-grade teachers must find the time to help their students prepare for each week's tutoring session if they are playing major roles in the tutoring program. Also teachers must work together to find a time once or twice a week for their students to work together in the cross-age tutoring program. Most importantly, teachers must share the belief that these supplemental programs are worth the effort and that their struggling readers can make significant gains in their reading ability.

Changes at Webster have not occurred overnight and, in many ways, are just beginning. We believe that lasting change can be made only when classroom teachers, other staff, and administrators are willing to spend the time required to build support for struggling readers into the fabric of daily school life. As Allington and Walmsley (1995) so clearly state, there really is no "quick fix" for students who find learning to read difficult. Nonetheless, with little extra in the way of resources, but with the willingness to try, classroom teachers and a reading coordinator at Webster are working together to provide supplemental instruction for struggling readers that is having a positive impact on children's reading ability. We believe this type of schoolwide effort is essential in preventing reading failure in elementary schools.

References

Adams, M. J. (1990). *Beginning to read: Thinking and learning about print.* Cambridge, MA: MIT Press.

Allington, R. L., & Walmsley, S. A. (1995). No quick fix: Where do we go from here? In *No quick fix: Rethinking literacy programs in America's elementary schools* (pp. 253–264). New York: Teachers College Press.

Clarke, L. K. (1988). Invented versus traditional spelling in first graders' writing: Effects on learning to spell and read. *Research on the Teaching of English, 22,* 281–309.

Clay, M. (1991). *Becoming literate: The construction of inner control.* Portsmouth, NH: Heinemann.

Clay, M. (1993). *Reading Recovery: A guidebook for teachers in training.* Portsmouth, NH: Heinemann.

Devin-Sheehan, L., Feldman, R. S., & Allen, V. L. (1976). Research on children tutoring children: A critical review. *Review of Educational Research, 46,* 355–385.

Dowhower, S. L. (1987). Effects of repeated reading on second-grade transitional readers' fluency and comprehension. *Reading Research Quarterly, 22,* 389–406.

Ehri, L. C. (1989). Movement into word reading and spelling: How spelling contributes to reading. In J. Mason (Ed.), *Reading and writing connections* (pp. 65–81). Boston: Allyn & Bacon.

Elley, W. B. (1992). *How in the world do students read?* The Hague, Netherlands: International Association for the Evaluation of Educational Achievement.

Heath, S. B., & Mangiola, L. (1991). *Children of promise: Literate activity in linguistically and culturally diverse classrooms.* Washington, DC: National Education Association.

Hiebert, E. H. (1994). Reading Recovery in the United States: What difference does it make to an age cohort? *Educational Researcher, 23(9),* 15–25.

Hiebert, E. H., Colt, J. M., Catto, S. L., & Gury, E. C. (1992). Reading and writing of first-grade students in a restructured Chapter 1 program. *American Educational Research Journal, 29,* 545–572.

Hiebert, E. H., & Taylor, B. M. (Eds.). (1994). *Getting reading right from the start: Effective early literacy intervention.* Boston: Allyn & Bacon.

Holdaway, D. (1981). Shared book experience: Teaching, reading, using favorable books. *Theory Into Practice, 21,* 293–300.

Invernizzi, M., Juel, C., & Rosemary, C. A. (1997). A community volunteer tutorial that works. *The Reading Teacher, 50,* 304–311.

Labbo, L. D., & Teale, W. H. (1990). Cross-age reading: A strategy for helping poor readers. *The Reading Teacher, 43,* 362–369.

Limbrick, E., McNaughton, S., & Glynn, T. (1985). Gains for underachieving tutors and tutees in a cross-age tutoring programme. *Journal of Child Psychology and Psychiatry, 26,* 939–953.

Madden, N. A., Slavin, R. E., Karweit, N. L., Dolan, L. J., & Wasik, B. A. (1993). Success for All: Longitudinal effects of a restructuring program for inner city elementary schools. *American Educational Research Journal, 30,* 123–148.

Mullis, I. V., Campbell, J. R., & Farstrup, A. E. (1993). *Reading report card for the nation and the state.* Washington, DC: U.S. Department of Education.

Mullis, I. V., & Jenkins, L. B. (1990). *The reading report card, 1971–80. Trends from the nation's report card.* Washington, DC: U.S. Department of Education.

Pikulski, J. J. (1994). Preventing reading failure: A review of five effective programs. *The Reading Teacher, 48,* 30–39.

Pinnell, G. S. (1989). Reading Recovery: Helping at-risk children learn to read. *Elementary School Journal, 90,* 160–183.

Puma, M. J., Jones, C. C., Rock, D., & Fernandez, R. (1993). *Prospectus: The Congressional Mandate Study of educational growth and opportunity. The interim report.* Washington, DC: U.S. Department of Education.

Reutzel, D. R., Hollingsworth, P. M., & Eldredge, J. L. (1994). Oral reading instruction: The impact on student reading development. *Reading Research Quarterly, 29,* 40–65.

Samuels, S. J. (1979). The method of repeated reading. *The Reading Teacher, 32,* 403–408.

Shanahan, T., & Barr, R. (1995). Reading Recovery: An independent evaluation of the effects of an early instructional intervention for at-risk learners. *Reading Research Quarterly, 30,* 598–996.

Slavin, R. E., & Madden, N. A. (1989). What works for students at risk: A research synthesis. *Educational Leadership, 64*(5), 4–13.

Taylor, B. M., Frye, B. J., Short, R. A., & Shearer, B. (1992). Classroom teachers prevent reading failure among low-achieving first-grade students. *The Reading Teacher, 45,* 592–597.

Taylor, B., Short, R., Shearer, B., & Frye, B. (1995). First grade teachers provide early reading intervention in the classroom. In R. L. Allington & S. A. Walmsley (Eds.), *No quick fix: Rethinking literacy in America's elementary schools* (pp. 159–176). New York: Teachers College Press.

Wasik, B. A., & Slavin, R. E. (1993). Preventing early reading failure with one-to-one tutoring: A review of five programs. *Reading Research Quarterly, 28,* 178–200.

Williams, P. L., Reese, C. M., Campbell, J. R., Mazzeo, J., & Phillips, G. W. (1995). *1994 NAEP reading: A first look.* Washington, DC: U.S. Department of Education.

Children's Books Cited

Aardema, V. (1989). *The three wishes.* Boston: Silver Burdett & Ginn.

Allard, H., & Marshall, J. (1977). *Miss Nelson is missing.* Boston: Houghton Mifflin.

Barrett, J. (1970). *Animals should definitely not wear clothing.* New York: Macmillan.

dePaola, T. (1975). *The cloud book.* New York: Holiday House.

Estes, E. (1944). *Rufus M.* New York: Harcourt, Brace, Jovanovich.

Friedman, J. R. (1984). *How my parents learned to eat.* Boston: Houghton Mifflin.

Kraus, R. (1980). *Another mouse to feed.* New York: Simon & Schuster.

Lobel, A. (1976). *Frog and toad all year.* New York: Harper & Row.

Phillips, J. (1986). *Tiger is a scaredy cat.* New York: Random House.

Wheeler, C. (1983). *Marmalade's nap.* New York: Knopf.

Appendix A: Children's Books in the Reading Intervention Program

Level A (40–60 words)

(Used in weeks 1–2 of enrichment class and in October with regular classroom model)

Title	Author
Who Is Coming?	Patricia C. McKissack
Sam's Cookie	Barbo Lindgren
Things I Like	Anthony Browne
Flying	Donald Crews

Level B (60–90 words)

(Used in weeks 2–4 of enrichment class and in November and December with regular classroom model)

Title	Author
Ten, Nine, Eight	Molly Bang
Marmalade's Nap	Cindy Wheeler
Sleepy Bear	Lydia Dabovich
The Cake That Mack Ate	Rose Robart
The Lady With the Alligator Purse	Nadine Bernard Wescott

Level C (90–120 words)

(Used in weeks 5–7 of enrichment class and beyond and in January with regular classroom model)

Title	Author
Sheep in a Jeep	Nancy Shaw
George Shrinks	William Joyce
Animals Should Definitely Not Wear Clothing	Judi Barrett
Hooray for Snail!	John Stadler
Who Is the Beast?	Keith Baker

Level D (120–200 words)

(Used in weeks 6–7 of enrichment class and beyond and in February and March with regular classroom model)

Title	Author
The Happy Day	Ruth Krauss
Which Witch Is Which?	Deborah Guarino
Is You Mama a Llama?	Pat Hutchins
Mr. Gumpy's Outing	John Burningham
The Little Mouse, the Red Ripe Strawberry, and the Big Hungry Bear	Don Wood and Audrey Wood

Level E (easy readers)

(Used in weeks 5–7 of enrichment class and beyond in January and February with regular classroom model)

Title	Author
My New Boy	Joan Phillips
So Sick!	Harriet Ziefert & Carol Nicklaus
Tiger Is a Scaredy Cat	Joan Phillips
Wake up Sun	David Harrison

Level F (easy readers)

(Used in weeks 6–7 of enrichment class and beyond in March, April, and May with regular classroom model)

Title	Author
Fox All Week	Edward Marshall
Four on the Shore	Edward Marshall
There Is a Carrot in My Ear and Other Noodle Tales	Alvin Schwartz
Mouse Tales	Arnold Lobel
Frog and Toad Together	Arnold Lobel
Frog and Toad Are Friends	Arnold Lobel

Appendix B: Intervention Procedures

Levels A–D (October–March)

Day 1   Teacher reads story, perhaps to the whole class.
Group reads story twice with the teacher.
Group discusses the story.

Day 2   Group reads story as a group once with the teacher.
Partners take turns reading the story once while the teacher circulates to provide coaching.
Children write individual responses in complete sentences to a question on the story posed by the teacher and then share these with the teacher.
The teacher provides individual feedback focusing on children's ability to represent all sounds and to represent short vowel sounds correctly in one or two selected words in their sentences.

Day 3   Children read the story individually, and partners take turns reading the story as teacher circulates to provide coaching.
Children write individual responses to the new question posed by the teacher.
The teacher provides individual feedback to the sentences as in Day 2.

Levels E –F (January–May)

Day 1   Teacher reads story first, only if necessary. This is phased out so that the emphasis is on reading independently.

Children read to themselves first then read in pairs. The teacher coaches individuals. Group discusses the story

Day 2   Children read to themselves and then in pairs. The teacher coaches individuals. Children write individual responses to the story and share these with teacher.

Day 3   Children read to themselves and then in pairs. The teacher coaches individuals. Children write individual responses to the story and share these with teacher.

A Review of Reading Recovery

BILLIE J. ASKEW
Texas Woman's University

GAY SU PINNELL
The Ohio State University

IRENE C. FOUNTAS
Lesley College

MARIBETH C. SCHMITT
Purdue University

CAROL A. LYONS
The Ohio State University

Reading Recovery is an early intervention program designed to assist the lowest achieving children in first grade who are having difficulty learning to read and write. Children meet individually with a specially trained teacher for 30 minutes each day for an average of 12–20 weeks. The goal is for the children to develop effective reading and writing strategies. During this relatively short-term intervention, these children make faster than average progress so that they can catch up with their peers and continue to work on their own within an average group setting in the regular classroom.

Reading Recovery is also available to children whose initial reading instruction is in Spanish. Descubriendo La Lectura (DLL), or Reading Recovery in Spanish, is now well established in a number of sites across the United States. Information within this publication applies to Descubriendo La Lectura as well as to Reading Recovery.

The key to the successful implementation of the program resides in the training model. The two-tiered process begins with an intensive series of post-masters graduate level courses for teacher leaders at a university training center recognized by the North American Trainers Group. The teacher leader training model involves (a) a study of the program procedures that includes working daily with students across the course of a year; (b) an in-depth study of the theoretical foundations upon which the procedures are based; (c) comprehensive study of seminal and recent theories and research focusing on the reading and writing processes; (d) training in the process of working with adult learners; and (e) training in management and administrative services required to successfully implement the program. Following successful completion of the training year, teacher leaders return to their school districts to train teachers who will work with the lowest-achieving first-grade readers.

Training at the second tier, or teacher training, is also a year-long commitment. Teachers enroll in a graduate level course taught by a certified teacher leader. Through clinical and peer-critiquing experiences, teachers learn to observe and describe student and teacher behaviors and develop skills in making moment-to-moment decisions to inform instruction.

The research-based professional development courses for teachers and teacher leaders focus on analyzing children's reading and writing behaviors and relating those behaviors to more general theories of literacy and learning. Teachers-in-training and teacher leaders-in-training build theoretical models of literacy learning that they use to guide their work with children. Through on-going required professional development classes, Reading Recovery teachers and teacher leaders continue to refine and further develop their skills to effectively teach children who are"at risk" of failing to learn how to read and write.

Reading Recovery is an effective safety net within a comprehensive approach to solving education problems. No classroom program in the first grade will be adequate for all children. Each educational system has two problems to solve: (a) how to deliver good first instruction in literacy and (b) what kind of supplementary opportunity should be provided for children who are low achieving even in a good instructional program.[2] Acting as a safety net within a good instructional literacy program, Reading Recovery can be part of a strong, comprehensive approach to bring all students to literacy.

Reading Recovery provides a window of opportunity for the lowest achieving children to accomplish the goal of literacy for all children. In this section, we discuss seven important realities that policy makers, administrators, and all educators need to know about Reading Recovery in order to accomplish this goal.

1. Reading Recovery has one clear goal: "to dramatically reduce the number of learners who have extreme difficulty with literacy learning and the cost of these learners to educational systems."[3]

Reading Recovery addresses the needs of a particular group of students—those first graders who score lowest on measures of achievement in reading and writing. It helps the majority of those children work successfully in the classroom program. It is not designed

Training for Reading Recovery Professionals on Three Levels

Teachers	Teacher Leaders	Trainers
• enables teachers in apprenticeship for one year to learn to design a series of lessons tailored to the specific needs of an individual child and to make effective, moment-by-moment decisions. • supports effective teaching of the hardest-to-teach children. • provides a way for teachers to continue to study and learn and consult teacher leaders about children whose learning is puzzling.	• provides for expert professionals called teacher leaders to train and support Reading Recovery teachers; advise on all aspects of delivery of the program in a school, a district, or a consortium of districts; and create understanding at all levels of the potential and limits of Reading Recovery. • creates teacher leaders who carry out local training programs, support a local implementation of quality, and guide the instruction of the most difficult children.	• provides a third level of leadership of university-based professors as trainers who prepare the teacher leaders at university centers, advise about new developments, and provide guidance on issues that may facilitate or impede the delivery of effective programs. • creates and maintains a trainer network that actively guides all Reading Recovery programs through any necessary adaptations and adjustments to the program that may need to occur over time as knowledge and society change.

The training for Reading Recovery professionals acknowledges that at each level of training the roles of professionals, as well as their use of theory, are different.[4]

to raise the overall achievement of an age cohort but rather to reduce the numbers of children who are having extreme difficulty. It cannot guarantee progress in spite of unsatisfactory subsequent teaching, nor is it intended to be a model for changing classroom instruction.

2. Reading Recovery is an investment in the professional skills of teachers.

If we can focus our energies on providing this generation of teachers with the kinds of knowledge and skills they need to help students succeed, we will have made an enormous contribution to America's future.[5]

A recent large-scale study revealed that every additional dollar spent on raising teacher quality netted greater student achievement gains than did any other use of school resources.[6] Few educational programs offer a more powerful teacher education process than Reading Recovery with a full academic year of intensive training.

The training of Reading Recovery teachers is provided by specially trained Reading Recovery teacher leaders who have been prepared in a year-long residential program at a recognized university training center. Teachers also train for an academic year while they work with children and fulfill other professional responsibilities. In the United States, graduate-level university credit is awarded for successful completion of the Reading Recovery teacher training program. Training continues after the initial year, with a built-in renewal system to update teachers on new ways to be effective in their work.[7]

Reading Recovery training sessions involve extensive use of a one-way glass screen through which teachers watch each other work with children as they put their observations and analyses into words. In their conversations, they articulate their questions and dilemmas. The process challenges assumptions about children's learning; teachers think critically about the art of teaching. They "need to become more flexible and tentative, to observe constantly and alter their assumptions in line with what they record as children work. They need to challenge their own thinking continually."[8]

Reading Recovery teachers learn to make teaching decisions "on the run" while teaching. Research on Reading Recovery teaching[9] indicates that Reading Recovery teachers seem to know "just what to do" in response to individual children. No time is wasted because the teacher is working from what the child knows and finding powerful examples that will help these initially struggling learners make leaps in learning.

The key is extensive, rigorous training that allows the teacher to develop a repertoire of actions and decisions and then to adjust each child's program to help make the most of her or his knowledge base and strengths. Clay[10] cites educator Pearson's comments about the implications of teacher education in Reading Recovery:

Reading Recovery has managed to operationalize that vague notion that teachers ought to reflect on their own practice. That behind the glass play by play analysis and the collegial debriefing with the teacher after her teaching session represent some of the best teacher education I have witnessed in my 28 year history in the field.

A body of research[11] indicates that Reading Recovery teacher training has a powerful and long lasting impact on the teachers who participate. The skills and knowledge teachers develop in Reading Recovery contribute to their ongoing learning and result in an impact on children across time. There is at least anecdotal evidence that these learnings also influence their work in other settings.

There is also evidence that the communication between Reading Recovery teachers and classroom teachers supports literacy teaching in a school. In a change study,[12] classroom teachers cited the benefits of collaborating about individual children with a knowledgeable colleague. The investment in the professional skills of Reading Recovery teachers, then, appears to go beyond their work with individual children.

3. Reading Recovery is a research-based approach to helping children who are the lowest achievers.

Reading Recovery has a strong research base. The structure and design of the program are consistent with a large body of substantial research on how children learn to read and write. In addition, empirical studies have been conducted on the outcomes of the program itself.

- Reading Recovery is based on the best of current knowledge about how children become literate.

Reading Recovery has its roots in Marie Clay's studies of young children's reading and writing behaviors in the 1960s.[13] Clay's basic research in classrooms and clinics, along with intensive studies in other disciplines, became available in the United States through academic publications in the 1970s. Clay also designed and tested observation techniques that have been widely used by classroom teachers and researchers. These instruments comprise *An Observation Survey of Early Literacy Achievement.*[14]

Clay's observation instruments are useful for classroom teachers, reading teachers, evaluators, and researchers because of their sound measurement qualities. All of the tasks were developed in research studies. They have the qualities of sound assessment instruments checked for reliability, validity, and discrimination indices. This work has led to research by others in the United States,[15] Australia, and England.[16] A unique feature of Reading Recovery is that every teacher, every day, records the detail of every lesson with every child. Similar teacher observations provide sound research data for inspection and analysis of the changes that occur as individuals work through their series of lessons.

A second research program was undertaken by Clay to explore this question: "What is possible when we change the design and delivery of traditional education for the children that teachers find hard to teach?"[17] A number of studies explored this question, beginning with the development project in 1976 and followed by field trials, follow-up studies, replication studies, analyses of lesson content, monitoring studies, and subgroup studies.[18] The Ministry of Education has monitored the New Zealand program nationally since 1984.[19]

Therefore, Reading Recovery is built on a foundation of more than 30 years of research about how young low-achieving children take on the process of reading and writing. Because Reading Recovery is a dynamic program, it has changed in response to growth in understandings about how children learn to read and write while remaining grounded in a sound, well developed theory. For example, teaching for phonemic awareness and visual analysis were significant aspects of the program from its beginning. Differences in subsequent editions of the published materials for Reading Recovery training[20] continue to reveal refinements in the procedures as more research information becomes available.

Change in Reading Recovery is a deliberate, careful, ongoing process based on continuous research. Over the years, refinements in practice have been based on current research in language and literacy learning and teaching as well as on research and evaluation directly related to the program.

Changes in Reading Recovery practice are gradually assimilated through required, ongoing professional development at all levels of training. The implementation of programs and training courses for professionals are constantly under scrutiny, with studies designed to test different models of delivery. Because of the dynamic nature of the underlying theory and its responsiveness to new knowledge arising in related disciplines, as well as the ongoing evaluation of student outcomes and training schemes, elements of Reading Recovery are revised when appropriate.

As knowledge changes around us, Reading Recovery professionals must continue to ask what new discussions of theory and research are relevant for a preventative approach to early intervention. One important example which supports that approach was provided by Vellutino and his colleagues.[21] By comparing the cognitive abilities and experiential deficits of children who were easy and difficult to remediate, they were able to recommend that

> *to render a diagnosis of specific reading disability in the absence of early and labor-intensive remedial reading that has been tailored to a child's individual learning needs is, at best, a hazardous and dubious enterprise* [22]

Reading Recovery professionals have contributed to the advance of understanding by their contributions to research projects as diverse as applying Vygotskyan theory to early literacy instruction (Hobsbaum, Peters, & Sylva on tutoring early writing)[23] and school improvement (Hill, Rowe, & Crevola on providing a safety net for children with difficulties in a thrust to provide improved classroom instruction).[24]

- Research on Reading Recovery is ongoing.

In the United States and other countries, researchers continue to examine different questions and to design and conduct studies that inform the teaching and implementation of Reading Recovery.[25] For example, U.S. researchers have implemented empirical studies that compare Reading Recovery with other approaches, as well as qualitative studies probing aspects of teaching, learning, and implementation. Notable studies are included in Section 3 and in the list of references.

4. Reading Recovery teacher leaders and administrators at every site systematically collect and report data on every child to a central national evaluation center.

"Replication is important in all sciences because it is through replication that scientists verify research results."[26] Reading Recovery replicates its effect at the level of individual subjects, and the same results are achieved again and again with different children, different teachers, and in different places. Altogether, if a result is seen consistently across time and across locations, we can predict with some confidence that the results will occur. Hiebert, who was critical of initial Reading Recovery research and evaluation studies, has stated that "a high percentage of Reading Recovery tutees can orally read at least a first-grade text at the end of Grade 1 ... Once a program is in place, there appears to be considerable fidelity in the results."[27]

Unique to Reading Recovery, evaluation data are collected on the implementation of the program for every child. By the end of the 1996–1997 school year, data had been reported to the National Data Evaluation Center (NDEC) for Reading Recovery as well as to the U.S. Department of Education on 436,249 children. The more replications a program can document, the more reliable the results, and the more confidence researchers have in the procedures and interventions that produced those results.[28]

General Procedures for Data Collection:

1. In consultation with classroom teachers, the Reading Recovery teacher identifies individual students who need a check on performance, administers six assessments, and selects the lowest children.
2. The Reading Recovery teacher fills out a computer scan form with vital data on each child and entry scores.
3. The Reading Recovery teacher provides daily lessons to each child selected.
4. As children exit the program, the Reading Recovery teacher records exit scores on the scan form.
5. As new children enter the program, each child's entry data are recorded on a new scan form.
6. At the end of the first grade year, all children are again tested and their scores recorded on scan forms.
7. A separate scan form is completed to report contextual variables for the Reading Recovery site.
8. Scan forms are checked by district officials and sent to the National Data Evaluation Center (NDEC) for Reading Recovery. Scan forms report the end-of-year status of each child (for example, whether service was successfully discontinued because the child met performance criteria).
9. Data are analyzed and aggregated at the National Data Evaluation Center for Reading Recovery.
10. Results are sent back to each site so that local reports may incorporate the information into their local decision making.
11. Each site reports local data to local officials, to university training centers, and to appropriate school officials and policy decision makers.
12. A national report is prepared and published annually.[29]

At every step of the process, data are checked and verified.

- Measures used in Reading Recovery

Measures used in *An Observation Survey of Early Literacy Achievement*[30] and the Spanish version *Instrumento de Observación de Logros de la Lecto-Escritura Inicial*[31] are used by classroom teachers and Reading Recovery teachers to inform their teaching. These measures provide a reliable and valid way to assess young children's literacy knowledge and to detect evidence of progress in the early stages of literacy learning.

The Survey is comprised of six literacy tasks with established validity and reliability (see *An Observation Survey of Early Literacy Achievement*). The neutral observer records exactly what a child does on each reading or writing task with appropriate coding categories. The survey tasks have four characteristics in common with good measurement instruments. They provide

- a standard task
- a standard way of administering the task
- ways of knowing when we can rely on observations and make reliable comparisons
- a task that is like a "real world" task, relating to what the child is likely to do in the classroom (establishing validity).

An Observation Survey of Early Literacy Achievement

Measures in *An Observation Survey of Early Literacy Achievement* are listed below, with information on reliability provided in Endnotes. Measures in Spanish vary only in the number of items for some tasks.

1. *Letter Identification.*[32]   Children are asked to identify 54 characters, the upper and lower case standard letters as well as the print form of *a* and *g*.
2. *Word Test.*[33]   Children read a list of frequently occurring words. Three alternative lists are available for testing and retesting.
3. *Concepts About Print.*[34]   The examiner reads a short book and invites children to perform a variety of tasks to find out what the child has learned about the way spoken language is put into print. Two versions are available, *Sand* and *Stones*. The test reflects important concepts to be acquired by children in the beginning stages of learning to read. As children move from nonreading to reading, changes occur in the scores on this measure.
4. *Writing Vocabulary.*[35]   Children are asked to write all of the words they can within a maximum 10-minute limit. Within guidelines for testing, examiners are permitted to prompt as needed.
5. *Hearing and Recording Sounds in Words.*[36]   The examiner reads a short sentence or two and asks the child to write the words. Children's scores represent every sound recorded accurately in this assessment of phonemic awareness and/or orthographic awareness.
6. *Text Reading.*[37]   Children are asked to read a series of increasingly more difficult texts that they have not seen before. The tester provides a minimal, scripted introduction and records reading behaviors using a running record. The texts used for Reading Recovery testing in the U.S. are not used in instruction, nor were they created for Reading Recovery. Texts were drawn from established basal systems and have, over the years, been shown to be a stable measure of reading performance. Texts represent escalating gradients of difficulty.

The criteria for a child's successful completion of a Reading Recovery program include the ability to read texts that have

- long stretches of print with few pictures.
- full pages of print without pictures.
- complex story structures that require sophisticated ways of understanding.
- complex ideas that require background knowledge to understand and interpret.
- many multisyllable words.
- new words to decode without help from illustrations.
- some vocabulary words that are unfamiliar.

The text reading measure is not an equal interval scale; that is, there are smaller differences in the beginning levels than at upper levels. For beginning readers, it is necessary to look at the reader's progress in more detail.

- Criteria and process for discontinuing service to children

Reading Recovery provides one-to-one instruction until a child's performance shows behavioral evidence that the extra help can be discontinued. Educators involved in the program often talk about the child being able to perform within average or above average levels in classroom literacy instruction, and that is true. In classrooms where the average text reading level is too low to support the child's continued growth, discontinuing levels will need to be higher than the average. *Therefore, there is another important criterion for discontinuing.* The child must have a self-extending system for literacy. This means that the child is able to use a variety of flexible strategies for problem solving in reading and writing text. It is expected that the child will continue to improve in reading and writing skills and will learn from reading and writing in regular classroom instruction.

Discontinuing Reading Recovery service is a carefully considered decision that is collaboratively made by the classroom teacher, the Reading Recovery teacher, and other members of a Reading Recovery team. In schools, the team typically includes the building administrator, Reading Recovery teacher, classroom teachers, and others. The team communicates closely with the teacher leader, who operates across many schools.

At the Time of Discontinuing, a Systematic Process Is Followed:

1. Through consultation between the classroom teacher and the Reading Recovery teacher, the child is recognized as performing successfully in the classroom. The child is able to read and write within expected average ranges or a little above average at that point of time in the school year.
2. A trained assessor, someone different from the Reading Recovery teacher who has been working with the child, administers the range of assessments. (Observation Survey)
3. Through consultation, the educators involved decide whether the child is independently using reading and writing processes with comprehension, rapid word solving, and fluency.
4. Reading Recovery tutoring is discontinued; data are recorded on scan forms; and the child's family members are informed.
5. The Reading Recovery teacher monitors the child's progress regularly until the educational team is assured that the child is continuing to make progress at a satisfactory rate.

- Every child is counted!

The national data set includes data on every single child who enters the program, regardless of program outcome. In the early days of data collection, Reading Recovery implementers attempted to define a "program" for a child in order to determine the effect of the treatment. If a child had instruction for only a few days or a few weeks, it was difficult to say that the program had time to work. Therefore, "program" children were defined for research purposes as children having at least 60 Reading Recovery lessons. While the status of *all* children served by the program has always been documented locally and sent to the National Data Evaluation Center, national reports were published related to two groups: (1) the children who discontinued from the program; and (2) children who had the opportunity for a full program (both discontinued and not discontinued).

Reporting practices have changed to more clearly describe the action taken for each child served by Reading Recovery. Status categories, beginning in the 1998–1999 school year, are as follows:

- children who successfully discontinued from the program
- children who had complete programs of 12–20 weeks (with an opportunity to participate for 20 weeks) who were recommended for assessment and consideration for longer-term assistance or other actions to support the child
- children who moved during their programs
- children remaining in the program at the end of the school year without time for completion of program

Exceptions to these categories are extremely rare and are carefully documented with a narrative explanation.

Educators involved in Reading Recovery are concerned about the number of children who have insufficient time to complete the program before the school year ends. Efforts are under way in many sites to extend the school year for these children, to increase the effectiveness and efficiency of current programs, and to consider flexible use of resources to provide more teaching time within the school year.

5. Reading Recovery has two positive outcomes.

The results for children in Reading Recovery can be viewed in two important ways. Both outcomes represent actions that benefit the child.

- Positive Outcome #1: The child no longer requires extra help, and service is "discontinued."

Discontinuing is a systematic process by which a child is determined to no longer need Reading Recovery teaching in special 30-minute sessions. The child is an independent reader and writer who needs only a good classroom literacy program to continue to make progress.

- Positive Outcome #2: A recommendation is made for additional assessment. Appropriate school staff members collaborate to plan future learning opportunities for the child.

Even children who do not make the accelerated progress needed for discontinuing (they do not "catch up" with peers or meet criterion measures) make progress in Reading Recovery. Moreover, positive subsequent action is initiated to help such children keep making progress. Educators have learned much about the child through the Reading Recovery diagnostic processes and can take action to recommend future actions to support the child.

Reading Recovery evaluation data show that the large majority of children served in the program experience the first outcome; a smaller proportion are in the second category. Instead of waiting or allowing children to struggle, educators in Reading Recovery assume responsibility that something positive is going to happen for every child coming into the program. A secondary outcome of the process is that people work together to identify children who might be at risk and provide the necessary extra support at a critical time. There is recognition that *everyone* is responsible for every child.

6. Well-planned implementation determines the success of Reading Recovery.

Smart administrators protect their investment by assuring a high quality implementation of Reading Recovery. Consideration must be given to the processes involved in "opening up" the existing system to accommodate and support this innovation.

Implementation factors include the following:

Shared Ownership. In order to sustain an innovation, basic understandings about the purposes, rationales, and processes of the innovation must be shared.[38] In addition to shared understandings, ownership must be felt by the stakeholders who collaborate to provide the structures for successful implementation within the system. All stakeholders must be perceived to have a responsibility for the success of each child served.

Level of Coverage. Each school or system must determine the number of children needing the service. A school or system has reached full coverage or full implementation when there is sufficient Reading Recovery teacher time to serve all children defined as needing the service in the school or in the system. Systems move to full coverage over several years. It is only at the stage of full coverage that a dramatic decrease in the number of children with literacy difficulties will be realized.

Partial implementation is a temporary condition and a period that reveals all the implementation difficulties. It is a time for persistence and a focus on individual success stories. As schools move toward full coverage, many problems disappear.

Flexible staffing plans support full implementation. Schools with a significant number of trained Reading Recovery teachers have the capacity to serve all needy children within a flexible staffing framework.

Informed Administration. As with any school or system commitment, the role of the administrator is critical. In Reading Recovery, the system-level administrators and the school-level administrators must be knowledgeable and collaborative in working with all stakeholders on behalf of the children needing the intervention service.

Continuous Attention to Quality in Training and Teaching. As stated earlier, Reading Recovery is an investment in teachers and teacher training. Selection of the highest quality teacher leaders and teachers is essential for a successful program. Initial training at both levels must be strong. An important feature of Reading Recovery is the ongoing nature of training through continuing contact sessions. The quality of these sessions will also impact the success of the program.

Administrators are cautioned to refrain from stretching the roles of the Reading Recovery teacher leaders and teachers beyond their training expertise and beyond their ability to continue to perform their primary role successfully. When this happens, program results may suffer.

Sustained Focus on the Goal of Reading Recovery and Its Attainment.   All stakeholders must retain the focus of Reading Recovery—to reduce dramatically the number of children unable to work within average levels within their classrooms. There is a temptation to focus on other worthy goals that may interfere with the primary goal of supporting successful performance of children.

Examination of Data to Uncover and Solve Problems.   Each school and each system involved in Reading Recovery will benefit from a careful examination of student outcomes. This exploration will document the program's effectiveness as well as identify problem areas in implementation that need to be addressed.

Implementation is important in any venture. "The failure to institutionalize an innovation and build it into the normal structures and practices of the organization underlies the disappearance of many reforms."[39] "In too many cases, where ideas deserve consideration, the processes through which they were implemented were self-defeating."[40]

In Reading Recovery, factors related to establishing a new program in a school and district context are not ignored. Although implementation issues are still being examined and refined, a structured process exists to assist local educators in implementing a consistent, high quality program.

7. Reading Recovery is a not-for-profit program that involves collaboration among schools, districts, and universities.

Reading Recovery is not an independent business venture; it is partnership between school, districts, and universities. In the United States, the name "Reading Recovery" has been a trademark and/or service mark of The Ohio State University since December 18, 1990, when action was taken to identify sites that meet the essential criteria for a Reading Recovery program.

In the educational system, true innovation is difficult to achieve. Innovations appear to come and go with little lasting impact. Any time an innovation is adopted, it inevitably means that there must be adjustments in the system. In the case of Reading Recovery, for example, educators had to provide for one-to-one teaching time and space, for a long initial training and ongoing training of teachers, for a special facility so that the observation of lessons could take place, and for the transportation of children for "live" lessons. All of these requirements meant changes in the usual way of doing things.

Most innovations fail; that is, they have no lasting effect. When innovations are introduced into a system, one of three things is likely to happen:

- Because of the difficulties involved in change, the educational innovation is adopted but is rejected before a true test is made.

- The innovation is adopted in a half-hearted way so that the characteristics that provided the benefit are "watered down" or eliminated altogether.
- The innovation is adopted but after a short time is, itself, changed so that the system is accommodated.

When one thinks of the possibilities listed above, it is easy to see why innovations vary so widely from place to place.

The trademark for Reading Recovery is not a guarantee of high quality but it does contribute to consistency of implementation across sites that are far-spread geographically and exist in many different kinds of communities. The essential characteristics of Reading Recovery implementation are clearly described in a set of standards and guidelines.

On an annual basis, programs are granted a *royalty free* license to use the name. Every district that has a Reading Recovery program is reviewed annually to determine if the district has met standards for program quality. A list of registered sites is reported annually to the U.S. Department of Education.

Reading Recovery sites are part of a network that depends on regular contact with a university training center as well as examination of the data sent annually from each site. When an emergency situation exists (such as temporary loss of personnel), educators at a site may work with the Standards and Guidelines Committee of the Reading Recovery Council of North America for a temporary waiver on a given requirement. There is an attempt to work with sites toward improving the implementation plan; however, ultimately, Reading Recovery must be provided as specified. Some site officials at this point make the decision not to comply and no longer claim to have a Reading Recovery program in the district; a small number [fewer than a dozen] have had the right to licensure removed for noncompliance.

These actions are taken so that the benefits of Reading Recovery's high quality can be provided to children and to protect districts' investment in Reading Recovery training and implementation. The reason for using the trademark and monitoring program quality is to ensure the integrity of the program.

Reading Recovery is a non-profit program. There are strict controls that prevent individuals and commercial organizations from using the name Reading Recovery to promote a program that does not comply with Standards and Guidelines of the Reading Recovery Council of North America.[41]

Responses to Some Common Misconceptions

In today's debates over literacy and schooling, claims and counter claims are aired, often without regard for accuracy. "Expert" opinion offers a bewildering maze for educators to negotiate. Here, we clarify several issues that have caused confusions about Reading Recovery.

1. Reading Recovery is not aligned with any classroom approach.

Designed to offer extra help, Reading Recovery procedures are based on research about how children learn to read and write. The procedures represent highly effective approaches that Reading Recovery teachers use in response to the *individual* child's needs.

Reading Recovery provides additional one-to-one support for children who need more intensive teaching for strategic processing behaviors than any classroom approach can provide. The strategies learned by Reading Recovery children are helpful during reading regardless of the instructional method used in the classroom. Therefore, Reading Recovery is effective in any school regardless of the approach used in the classroom, provided that approach is well taught.

2. Reading Recovery teachers DO teach children about letters, sounds, and words.[42]

Reading Recovery teachers give specific and explicit attention to letters, sounds, and words, both while reading and writing extended text and as direct instruction.

In a comprehensive review of research on beginning reading instruction, Marilyn Adams, referring to Reading Recovery, acknowledged that the "importance of phonological and linguistic awareness is explicitly recognized."[43] She also stated that Reading Recovery, along with several other programs, is "designed to develop thorough appreciation of phonics."[44]

Consistent with Adams' analysis, subsequent research by Stahl, Stahl, & McKenna[45] reported that all students in the Reading Recovery group made gains in letter identification, phonemic awareness, and dictation tests, variables which were not stressed in Reading Recovery lessons, and all made significantly greater improvement in phonological processing tasks than unserved 'at-risk' students....

The program encourages meaning-making and problem-solving with print. Decoding is purposeful. Children need to use connections between letters and sounds and their knowledge of how words work in order to problem solve words while maintaining meaning. Recognizing this critical aspect of reading, Reading Recovery professionals understand:

- Phonemic awareness and its importance in beginning reading and writing.
- The alphabetic principle and orthographic knowledge and their importance in beginning reading and writing.
- The child's need to:
  - hear phonemes in words
  - associate letters with sounds
  - recognize and use spelling patterns
  - apply this knowledge in reading
  - apply this knowledge in writing
  - expand this knowledge to all the purposes for which it can be used in all levels of literacy processing.

3. Reading Recovery is not a classroom program and is not a program for groups.

Misconceptions are revealed through comments such as "Reading Recovery in the classroom" or "Reading Recovery in groups." *Neither is possible.*

Reading Recovery is not an approach that can be generalized to classrooms or small group teaching. Rather, it is a program in which the teacher works from the individual child's knowledge and responses in a one-to-one setting. When children are taught in a group, *the teacher has to choose a compromise path, a next move for "the group." To get results with the lowest achievers the teacher must work with the particular (and very limited) response repertoire of a particular child using what he knows as the context within which to introduce him to novel things.*[46]

To prevent literacy problems, individual teaching for some children is needed.[47]

Classroom teaching calls for a comprehensive approach, including a wide range of literacy-related activities with whole groups, small groups, and individuals in a variety of subject areas. Reading Recovery is a specific approach to prevent literacy problems and is targeted to a limited number of learners within a classroom program.[48] Reading Recovery provides supplementary instruction which is not intended to supplant the literacy program of the classroom.

4. The design of Reading Recovery calls for service to the lowest achieving children.

There are at least two rationales for taking only the lowest achieving children in Reading Recovery. First, at entry to the program, the rate and level of progress cannot be reliably predicted for any child. Therefore, the most extreme cases are selected and the program serves as a period of diagnostic teaching. Second, if the lowest achievers are not selected, the school will never clear the children with literacy difficulties from its rolls, and these children will return to haunt the program in subsequent years.[49] Any system or school not serving the lowest children is out of compliance with the standards and principles underlying Reading Recovery implementation.

Children in first grade who are receiving regular classroom instruction and who are not receiving another literacy intervention are eligible for Reading Recovery services. These children include those involved in a range of special services including ESL and special education.[50] For example, national data indicate that about 10% of those served are identified as ESL.

5. Children are not arbitrarily "dropped" from Reading Recovery service.

Critics have argued that children are dropped from the Reading Recovery program in early lessons because of predicted failure. The design of the program calls for a full program with an opportunity for up to 20 weeks for all children. When an exception is made, it is usually because of a report a specialist has made with alternative recommendations. These decisions are made at the school level and involve the school team and the site's teacher leader. Any school or school system arbitrarily removing children from Reading Recovery service is out of compliance with national standards and principles underlying program implementation.

6. Reading Recovery continues to expand.

Information from the National Data Evaluation Center (NDEC) shows continued expansion of Reading Recovery in the United States. As indicated in Table 1, Reading Recovery's growth in most categories approximated 10% from one school year to another.

TABLE 1   Program Growth in the United States from the 1995–1996 Academic Year to the 1996–1997 Academic Year

Categories	1995–1996	1996–1997	% Increase
Teacher Leaders	625	667	7%
Teachers	14,153	15,843	12%
Districts	2,939	3,241	10%
Schools	9,062	9,815	8%
Data as of 11/15/97			

In the fall of 1997, the number of teacher leaders-in-training was 17% higher than in the previous year. Teacher leaders are the key personnel in preparing Reading Recovery teachers. Therefore, the addition of these 133 teacher leaders-in-training will further extend the opportunities for expansion in subsequent years.

Endnotes

1. Reference to Clay as quoted in Askew, B. J. (under review)
2. See Clay, M. M. (1990; 1996).
3. Quoted from Marie Clay's implementation visit to North Carolina, 1994.
4. See Clay, M. M. (1994b). *Literacy Teaching and Learning.*
5. See Linda Darling-Hammond (1996), p. 194.
6. Cited in Darling-Hammond (1996).
7. See Smith-Burke, M. T. (1996) and Ashdown, J. (1996).
8. See Clay, M. M. (1997). *Handbook,* p. 663.
9. See Wong, S. D., Groth, L. A., & O'Flahavan, J. F. (1994) and Elliott, C. B. (1994).
10. See Clay, M. M. (1997). *Handbook,* p. 663.
11. See Alverman, D. E. (1990); DeFord, D. E. (1993); DeFord, D. E., Lyons, C. A., & Pinnell, G. S. (1991); Geeke, P. (1988); Lyons, C. A., Pinnell, G. S., & DeFord, D. E. (1993); Power, J., & Sawkins, S. (1991).
12. See Blackburn, D. J. (1995).
13. See Clay, M. M. (1996). *Unpublished doctoral dissertation.*
14. See Clay, M. M., *Observation Survey* (1993).
15. See Fountas, I., & Pinnell, G. S. (1996) and Johnston (1997).
16. See Hobsbaum, A., Peters, S., & Sylva, K. (1996).
17. See Clay, M. M., *Guidebook* (1993), p. 97.
18. See Clay, M. M., *Guidebook* (1993).
19. Kerslake publishes annual New Zealand results.
20. There have been three widely used editions of a guide describing Reading Recovery teaching procedures, all by M. Clay: *The early detection of reading difficulties* was published in 1972, with revised editions in 1979 and 1985. Those editions included guides for the Observation Survey. A revised edition of Reading Recovery training materials, entitled *Reading Recovery: A guidebook for teachers in training* appeared in 1993 in the same year as a separate volume, *An observation survey of early literacy achievement.* All were published by Heinemann Education, Auckland, New Zealand, and Portsmouth, New Hampshire.
21. See Vellutino, F. R., Scanlon, D. M., Sipay, E. R., Small, S. G., Pratt, A., Chen, R., & Denckla, M. B. (1996).
22. See Vellutino, F. R., Scanlon, D. M., Sipay, E. R., Small, S. G., Pratt, A., Chen, R., & Denckla, M. B. (1996), p. 632.
23. See Hobsbaum, A., Peters, S., & Sylva, K. (1996).
24. See Hill, P. W., & Crévola, C. A. M. (1997).
25. See Askew, B. J. (1993); Blackburn, D. J. (1995); DeFord, D. E. (1993); DeFord, D. E. (1994); Dorn, L. (1994); Elliott, C. B. (1994); Frasier, D. F. (1991); Handerhan, E. C. (1990); Lyons, C. A. (1991; 1993; 1994b); Lyons, C. A., & White, N. (1990); Pinnell, G. S. (1997); Pinnell, G. S., Lyons, C. A., Bryk, A., DeFord, D. E., & Seltzer, M. (1993).
26. See Frymier, J., Barber, L., Gansreder, B., & Robertson, N. (1989), p. 228.
27. See Hiebert, E. H. (1994), p. 21.
28. See Lyons, C. A. (1998).
29. Executive Summaries (annual) are available from the Reading Recovery Council of North America.

30. See Clay, M. M. (1993). *Observation Survey.*
31. See Escamilla, K., Andrade, A. M., Basurto, A. G. M., Ruiz, O. A., & Clay, M. M. (1996) and Escamilla (1994).
32. Reliability: 100 urban children aged 6:0, 0.97, split-half (Clay, 1966). Validity: Correlation with Word Reading for 100 children at 6:0, 0.85 (Clay, 1966).
33. Different word tests are used in New Zealand and the United States. The New Zealand test is the *Ready to Read Word Test.* In the U.S., words were drawn from a Dolch word list. Reliability: 107 urban children, Autumn, 1990, Cronbach Alpha = 0.92 (Clay, 1993).
34. Reliability: 40 urban children aged 5:0 to 7:0 in 1968, 0.95, KR (Clay, 1970). 56 kindergarten children in Texas 1978. Test-retest reliability coefficients 0.73–0.89, and corrected split-half coefficients 0.84–0.88 (Day & Day, 1980). Validity: Correlation with Word Reading for 100 children at 6:0, 0.79 (Clay, 1966).
35. Reliability: 34 urban children aged 5:6 in 1972 (Robinson, 1973), 0.97 test-retest (reported in Clay, 1993). Validity: correlation with reading; 50 urban children aged 5:6 in 1972 (Robinson, 1973), 0.82 (reported in Clay, 1993).
36. Reliability: Test-retest coefficients from 0.73–0.89 on a New Zealand population (Clay, 1985). For a U.S. population, Cronbach alphas procedure indicated reliability coefficient of .96 (Pinnell, McCarrier, & Button, 1990). Also a U.S. population, corrected split-half coefficients ranging from 0.84 - 0.88 on a U.S. population of 403 subjects (Pinnell, Lyons, DeFord, Bryk, & Seltzer, 1994). Validity: Correlation with Word Reading for 100 children at age 6.0, correlation coefficients 0.79 (Clay, 1966). For a U.S. population, Cronbach alphas procedure indicated reliability coefficient of .96 (Pinnell, McCarrier, & Button, 1990).
37. Reliability: For U.S. population, 402 children, person separation reliability = .83, item separation reliability = .93 utilizing the Rasch rating scale analysis by Wright & Stone (1979). The person separation reliability is equivalent to a Cronbach's alpha coefficient. (Pinnell et al., 1994). Validity: This type of measure has proved to be a valid and reliable test of reading progress in other research (Clay, 1966, 1979; Robinson, 1973; Wade, 1978).
38. See Fullan, M. (1985).
39. See Fullan, M. & Miles, M. (1992), p. 748.
40. See Sarason, S. B. (1991), p. 99.
41. See Standards and Guidelines (1998).
42. A concise statement on phonological awareness and Reading Recovery may be obtained from the Reading Recovery Council of North America.
43. See Adams, M. (1990), p. 420.
44. See Adams, M. (1990), p. 421.
45. See Stahl, K. A. D., Stahl, S., & McKenna, M. (under review).
46. See Clay, M. M. (1993). *Guidebook*, p. 8.
47. See Pinnell, G. S. (1993).
48. See Fountas, I. C. & Pinnell, G. S. (1996).
49. See Clay, M. M. (1994c).
50. See Lyons, C. A. (1994a) and Lyons, C. A., & Beaver, J. (1995).

References

Adams, M. (1990). *Beginning to read: Thinking and learning about print.* Cambridge, MA: MIT Press.

Allington, R. L., & McGill-Franzen, A. (1989). Different programs, indifferent instruction. In D. Lipsky & A. Garther (Eds.), *Beyond special education* (pp. 3–32). New York: Brookes.

Allington, R. L., & Walmsley, S. R. (1995). *No quick fix: Rethinking literacy programs in America's elementary schools.* New York: Teachers College Press.

Alverman, D. E. (1990). Reading teacher education. In W.R. Houston, M. Haberman, & J. Sikula (Eds.), *Handbook of research on teacher education: A project of the Association of Teacher Educators* (pp. 687–704). New York: Macmillan.

Ashdown, Jane (Spring, 1996). The challenge of continued learning. *Network News,* 1–4.

Ashdown, J., & Simic, O. (1998). *Reading achievement and its relationship to attendance: Evidence from an early intervention program.* Paper presented at the annual meeting of the American Educational Research Association, San Diego.

Askew, B. J. (1993). The effect of multiple readings on the behaviors of children and teachers in an early intervention program. *Reading & Writing Quarterly: Overcoming Learning Difficulties, 9,* 307–316.

Askew, B. J. (under review). Reading Recovery in the context of schooling.

Askew, B. J., & Frasier, D. F. (1994). Sustained effects of Reading Recovery intervention on the cognitive behaviors of second grade children and the perceptions of their teachers. *Literacy, Teaching and Learning: An International Journal of Early Literacy, 1,* 7–28.

Askew, B. J., Wickstrom, C., & Frasier, D. F. (under review). An exploration of the literacy behaviors of children following an early intervention program.

Askew, B. J., Kaye, B., Wickstrom, C., & Frasier, D. F. (in progress). Subsequent literacy performance of former Reading Recovery children: Two longitudinal studies.

Blackburn, D. J. (1995). *Changes in a Chapter 1 program when Reading Recovery was implemented: Its impact on one district*. Denton, TX: Unpublished doctoral dissertation, Texas Woman's University.

Barnes, B. L. (1996–1997). But teacher you went right on: A perspective on Reading Recovery. *The Reading Teacher, 50*, 284–292.

Browne, A., Fitts, M., McLaughlin, B., McNamara, M. J., & Williams, J. (1996–1997). Teaching and learning in Reading Recovery. Response to "But teacher you went right on." *The Reading Teacher, 50*, 294–300.

Center, Y., Wheldall, K., Freeman, L., Outhred, L., & McNaught, M. (1995). An experimental evaluation of Reading Recovery. *Reading Research Quarterly, 30*, 240–263.

Clay, M. M. (1966). *Emergent reading behavior*. Unpublished doctoral dissertation. University of Auckland Library.

Clay, M. M. (1970). Research on language and reading in Pakeha and Polynesian children. In D. K. Bracken & E. Malmquist (Eds.), *Improving Reading Ability Around the World*. Newark, DE: International Reading Association.

Clay, M. M. (1979). *The early detection of reading difficulties*. Auckland, New Zealand: Heinemann.

Clay, M. M. (1979). *Sand—the Concepts About Print Test*. Auckland, New Zealand: Heinemann.

Clay, M. M. (1979). *Stones—the Concepts About Print Test*. Auckland, New Zealand: Heinemann.

Clay, M. M. (1982). *Observing young readers; Selected papers*. Portsmouth, New Hampshire: Heinemann.

Clay, M. M. (1985). *The early detection of reading difficulties*. Second edition. Auckland, New Zealand: Heinemann.

Clay, M. M. (1987). Implementing Reading Recovery: Systemic adaptations to an educational innovation. *New Zealand Journal of Educational Studies, 22*, 35–58.

Clay, M. M. (1989). Concepts about print: In English and other languages. *The Reading Teacher, 42*(4): 268–277.

Clay, M. M. (1990). The Reading Recovery Programme, 1984–88: Coverage, outcomes and education board district figures. *New Zealand Journal of Educational Studies, 25*, 61–70.

Clay, M. M. (1991a). *Becoming literate: The construction of inner control*. Portsmouth, NH: Heinemann.

Clay, M. M. (1991b). Reading Recovery surprises. In DeFord, D. E., Lyons, C. A., & Pinnell, G. S. (Eds.), *Bridges to Literacy: Learning from Reading Recovery* (pp. 57–76). Portsmouth, NH: Heinemann.

Clay, M. M. (1993a). *An observation survey of early literacy achievement*. Portsmouth, NH: Heinemann.

Clay, M. M. (1993b). *Reading Recovery: A guidebook for teachers in training*. Portsmouth, NH: Heinemann.

Clay, M. M. (1994a). An early intervention to prevent literacy learning difficulties: What is possible? *The Running Record, 6*, 4–5.

Clay, M. M. (1994b). Reading Recovery: The wider implications of an educational innovation. *Literacy, Teaching and Learning, 1*, 1994, pp. 121–143. Reprinted from Clay, M. M. (1993c). Reading Recovery: The wider implications of an educational innovation. In A. Watson & A. Bandenhop (Eds.), *Prevention of reading failure* (pp. 22–47).

Clay, M. M. (1994c). Report on meeting on Reading Recovery implementation. Raleigh, North Carolina.

Clay, M. M. (1996). Is Reading Recovery aligned with a specific approach? *Council Connections: A Newsletter of the Reading Recovery Council of North America, 2*, 1.

Clay, M. M. (1997). International perspectives on the Reading Recovery program. In J. Flood, S. B. Heath, & D. Lapp (Eds.), *Handbook of research on teaching literacy through the communicative and visual arts* (pp. 655–667). New York: MacMillan Library Reference USA (a project of the International Reading Association).

Clay, M. M. (1997). Letter to the Editor. *Reading Research Quarterly, 32*, 114.

Clay, M. M., & Cazden, C. B. (1990). A Vygotskian interpretation of Reading Recovery. In L. Moll (Ed.), *Vygotsky and education: Instructional implications and applications of sociohistorical psychology* (pp. 206–222). New York: Cambridge University Press.

Clay, M. M., & Tuck, V. (1991). *A study of Reading Recovery subgroups: Including outcomes for children who did not satisfy discontinuing criteria* (Technical Report). Auckland, New Zealand: Ministry of Education.

Clay, M. M., & Watson, B. (1982). An inservice program for Reading Recovery teachers. In M. M. Clay (Ed.), *Observing young readers* (pp. 192–200). Portsmouth, NH: Heinemann.

Condon, M., & Assad, S. (1996, Winter). Demonstrating the cost effectiveness of Reading Recovery: Because it makes a difference. *The Network News, 12*, 14.

Coopers & Lybrand (1994). *Resource allocations in the New York City Public Schools*. Coopers & Lybrand, L. L. P, 1251 Avenue of the Americas, New York, New York, 10024.

Cunningham, P. M., & Allington, R. L. (1994). *Classrooms that work*. New York: Harper Collins Publishers.

Darling-Hammond, L. (1996). What matters most: A competent teacher for every child. *Phi Delta Kappan, 78*, 193–200.

Day, H. D., & Day, K. (1980). *The reliability and validity of the Concepts About Print and Record of Oral Language*. Resources in Education, Arlington, VA: (ERIC Document Reproduction Service No. ED 179 932)

DeFord, D. E. (1993). Learning within teaching: An examination of teachers learning in Reading Recovery. *Reading & Writing Quarterly: Overcoming Learning Difficulties, 9,* 329–350.

DeFord, D. E. (1994). Early writing: Teachers and children in Reading Recovery. *Literacy, Teaching and Learning: An International Journal of Early Literacy, 1,* 31–57.

DeFord, D. E., Lyons, C. A., & Pinnell, G. S. (1991). *Bridges to literacy: Learning from Reading Recovery.* Portsmouth, NH: Heinemann.

DeFord, D. E., Tancock, S., & White, N. (1990). *Teachers' models of the reading process and their evaluations of an individual reader: Relationship to success in teaching reading and judged quality of instruction* (Technical Report, Vol. 5). Columbus, OH: The Ohio State University.

Dorn, L. (1994). *A Vygotskian perspective on literacy acquisition: Talk and action in the child's construction of literate awareness.* Denton, TX: Unpublished doctoral dissertation, Texas Woman's University.

Dudley-Marling, C., & Murphy, S. (1997). A political critique of remedial reading programs: The example of Reading Recovery. *The Reading Teacher, 50,* 460–468.

Dunkeld, C. (1991). Maintaining the integrity of a promising program: The case of Reading Recovery. In DeFord, D., Lyons, C., & Pinnell, G. S. (Eds.), *Bridges to literacy.* Portsmouth, NH: Heinemann.

Dyer, P. C., & Binkney, R. (1995). Estimating cost-effectiveness and educational outcomes: Retention, remediation, special education, and early intervention. In R. L. Allington and S. A. Walmsley (Eds.), *No quick fix* (pp. 61–77). Newark, DE: International Reading Association.

Elley, W. (1992). *How in the world do students read?* The Hague: International Association for the Evaluation of Educational Achievement (IEA).

Elliott, C. B. (1994). *Pedagogical reasoning: Understanding teacher decision making in a cognitive apprenticeship setting.* Denton, TX: Unpublished doctoral dissertation, Texas Woman's University.

Escamilla, K. (1994). Descubriendo la Lectura: An early intervention literacy program in Spanish. *Literacy, Teaching and Learning: An International Journal of Early Literacy, 1,* 57–85.

Escamilla, K., Andrade, A. M., Basurto, A. G. M., Ruiz, O. A., & Clay, M. M. (1996). *Instrumento de observación de los logros de la lecto—escritura inicial.* Portsmouth, NH: Heinemann.

Fountas, I. C., & Pinnell, G. S. (1996). *Guided reading: Good first teaching for all children.* Portsmouth, NH: Heinemann.

Frasier, D. F. (1991). *A study of strategy use by two emergent readers in a one-to-one tutorial setting.* Columbus, OH: Unpublished doctoral dissertation, The Ohio State University.

Frater & Staniland (1994). Reading Recovery from New Zealand: A report from the Office of Her Majesty's Chief Inspector of Schools. *Literacy, Teaching and Learning, 1,* 143–162.

Frymier, J., Barber, L., Gansneder, B., & Robertson, N. (1989). Simultaneous replication: A technique for large-scale research. *Phi Delta Kappan, 71,* 228–231.

Fullan, M. G. (1985). Change processes and strategies at the local level. *The Elementary School Journal, 85,* 391–421.

Fullan, M. G., & Miles, M. B. (1992). Getting reform right: What works and what doesn't. *Phi Delta Kappan, 73,* 744–752.

Gaffney, J. S., & Anderson, R. C. (1991). Two-tiered scaffolding: Congruent processes of teaching and learning. In E. H. Hiebert (Ed.), *Literacy for a diverse society* (pp. 184–198). New York: Teachers College Press.

Gaffney, J. S., & Paynter, S. Y. (1994). The role of early literacy interventions in the transformation of educational systems. *Literacy, Teaching and Learning: An International Journal of Early Literacy, 1,* 29–42.

Geeke, P. (1988). *Evaluation report on the Reading Recovery field trial in Central Victoria, 1984.* Australia: Centre for Studies in Literacy, University of Wollongong.

Glynn, T., & McNaughton, S. (1992). Early literacy learning: A tribute to Marie Clay. *Educational Psychology, 12* (3 & 4), 171–176.

Handerhan, E. C. (1990). *Reading instruction as defined by "successful" teachers and their first grade students within an early intervention program.* Columbus, OH: Unpublished doctoral dissertation, The Ohio State University.

Herman, R., & Stringfield, S. (1997). *Ten promising programs for educating all children: Evidence of impact.* Arlington, VA: Educational Research Service.

Hiebert, E. H. (1994). Reading Recovery in the United States: What difference does it make to an age cohort? *Educational Researcher, 23,* 15–25.

Hill, P. W., & Crévola, C. A. M. (1997). The literacy challenge in Australian primary schools. Incorporated Association of Registered Teachers of Victoria: Seminar Series No. 69.

Hobsbaum, A. (1995). Reading Recovery in England. *Literacy, Teaching and Learning, 1,* 21–39.

Hobsbaum, A., Peters, S., & Sylva, K. (1996). Scaffolding in Reading Recovery. *Oxford Review of Education, 22,* 17–35.

Holland, K. E. (1991). Bringing home and school literacy together through the Reading Recovery program. In DeFord, D. E., Lyons, C. A., & Pinnell, G. S. (Eds.),

Bridges to literacy: Learning from Reading Recovery (pp. 149–170). Portsmouth, NH: Heinemann.

Iversen, S. J., & Tunmer, W. E. (1993). Phonological processing skills and the Reading Recovery program. *Journal of Educational Psychology, 85,* 112–126.

Jaggar, A. M., & Simic, O. (1996). *A four-year follow-up study of Reading Recovery children in New York state: Preliminary report.* New York: New York University Reading Recovery Project, School of Education.

Jaggar, A. M., & Smith-Burke, M. T. (1994). *Follow-up study of Reading Recovery Children in Community School District #2, New York City.* New York: Reading Recovery Project, School of Education, New York University.

Johnston, P. (1997). *Knowing literacy: Constructive literacy assessment.* York, ME: Stenhouse Press.

Kelly, P., Klein, A., & Pinnell, G. S. (1994). Reading Recovery: Teaching through conversation. In D. Lancy (Ed.), *Children's emergent literacy: Social and cognitive processes.* Westport, CT: Praeger.

Kerslake, J. (1996). *A summary of the 1995 data on Reading Recovery.* Research and Statistics Division Bulletin, No. 5. Ministry of Education, Wellington, New Zealand.

Learning disabilities—A barrier to literacy instruction. (1995). Washington, DC: International Reading Association.

Levin, H. (1989). Financing the education of at-risk students. *Educational Evaluation and Policy Analysis, 11,* 47–60.

Lyons, C. A. (1989). Reading Recovery: A prevention for mislabeling young at-risk learners. *Urban Education, 24,* 125–139.

Lyons, C. A. (1991). A comparative study of the teaching effectiveness of teachers participating in a year- long and two-week inservice program. In J. Zutell & S. McCormick (Eds.), *Learning factors/teacher factors: Issues in literacy research and instruction* (pp. 367–675). Fortieth Yearbook of the National Reading Conference. Chicago, IL: National Reading Conference.

Lyons, C. A. (1993). The use of questions in the teaching of high-risk beginning readers: A profile of a developing Reading Recovery teacher. *Reading & Writing Quarterly: Overcoming Learning Difficulties, 9,* 317–328.

Lyons, C. A. (1994a). Reading Recovery and learning disability: Issues, challenges and implications. *Literacy, Teaching and Learning: An International Journal of Literacy Learning, 1,* 109–120.

Lyons, C. A. (1994b). Constructing chains of reasoning in Reading Recovery demonstration lessons. In Kinzer, C. K., & El, D. J. (Eds.), *Multidimensional aspects of literacy research, theory and practice* (pp. 276–286). Forty-third Yearbook of The National Reading Conference. Chicago, IL: National Reading Conference.

Lyons, C. A. (1998). Reading Recovery in the United States: More than a decade of data. *Literacy Teaching and Learning: An International Journal of Early Reading and Writing, 3,* (1) 77–92.

Lyons, C. A., & Beaver, J. (1995). Reducing retention and learning disability placement through Reading Recovery: An educationally sound cost-effective choice. In R. Allington & S. Wamsley (Eds.), *No quick fix: Redesigning literacy programs in America's elementary schools* (pp. 116–136). New York: Teachers College Press and the International Reading Association.

Lyons, C. A., Pinnell, G. S., & DeFord, D. E. (1993). *Partners in learning: Teachers and Children in Reading Recovery.* New York: Teachers College Press.

Lyons, C. A., & White, N. (1990). *Belief systems and instructional decisions: Comparisons between more and less effective teachers.* Technical Report: The Ohio State University.

Moore, M., & Wade, B. (1994). Reading Recovery: Parents' views. *English in Education, 27,* 11–17.

Moore, P. (1997). Models of teacher education: Where Reading Recovery teacher training fits. *Network News* (Fall), 1–4.

Moriarty, D. J. (January 25, 1995). Our Reading Recovery results: "Conclusive." *Education Week,* 36.

Moriarty, D. (1996). Report to the Massachusetts superintendents' task force on special education. Medford, MA: Medford Public Schools.

Moriarty, D. (1997). A message to Congress: Redefining special education. *Network News, 1,* 16–17.

Office for Standards in Education (1993). Reading Recovery in New Zealand: A report from the office of Her Majesty's Chief Inspector of Schools. London: HMSO. Reprinted (1995) in *Literacy, Teaching and Learning, 1,* 143–162.

Pinnell, G. S. (1989). Reading Recovery: Helping at-risk children learn to read. *The Elementary School Journal, 90,* (2), 161–183.

Pinnell, G. S. (1994). An inquiry-based model for educating teachers of literacy. *Literacy, Teaching and Learning: An International Journal of Early Literacy, 1,* 29–42.

Pinnell, G. S. (1997). Reading Recovery: A summary of research. In J. Flood, S. B. Heath, & D. Lapp (Eds.), *Handbook of research on teaching literacy through the communicative and visual arts* (pp. 638–654). New York: MacMillan Library Reference USA. (a project of the International Reading Association).

Pinnell, G. S. (1997). Letter to the Editor. *Reading Research Quarterly, 32,* 114.

Pinnell, G. S., Fried, M. D., & Estice, R. M. (1991). Reading Recovery: Learning how to make a difference. In DeFord, D. E., Lyons, C. A., & Pinnell, G. S. (Eds.), *Bridges to literacy: Learning from Reading Recovery* (pp. 11–36). Portsmouth, NH: Heinemann.

Pinnell, G. S., Lyons, C. A., DeFord, D. E., Bryk, A., & Seltzer, M. (1993). Comparing instructional models for the literacy education of high risk first graders. *Reading Research Quarterly, 29,* 8–39.

Pinnell, G. S., McCarrier, A., & Button, K. (1990). *Teachers' applications of theoretical concepts to new instructional settings.* Report No. 8, Early Literacy Research Project, Sponsored by the John D. And Catherine T. MacArthur Foundation. Columbus, OH: The Ohio State University.

Pinnell, G. S., Lyons, C., & Jones, N. (1996). Response to Hiebert: What difference does Reading Recovery make? *Educational Researcher, 25,* 23–25.

Power, J., & Sawkins, S. (1991). *Changing lives: Report of the implementation of the Reading Recovery Program on the North Coast.* Northern Rivers: University of New England.

Reading Recovery in Massachusetts. (1996). Cambridge, MA: Lesley College.

Robinson, S. M. (1973). *Predicting early reading progress.* Unpublished master's thesis, University of Auckland.

Rogoff, B., Matusov, E., & White, C. (1996). Models of teaching and learning: Participation in a community of learners. In D. R. Olson & N. Torrance (Eds.), *The handbook of education and human development* (pp. 388–414). Oxford, UK: Blackwell.

Rowe, K. J. (1995). Factors affecting students' progress in reading: Key findings from a longitudinal study. *Literacy, Teaching and Learning: An International Journal of Early Literacy, 1,* 57–110.

Rozzelle, J. (Fall, 1996). Reading Recovery: Does it work? *The National Dropout Prevention Newsletter, 9* (4), 7.

Sarason, S. B. (1991). *The predictable failure of education reform: Can we change course before it's too late?* San Francisco: Jossey-Bass.

Shanahan, T., & Barr, R. (1995). A synthesis of research on Reading Recovery. *Reading Research Quarterly, 30,* 958–996.

Slavin, R. E., & Madden, N. A. (1989). Effective classroom programs for students at risk. In R. E. Slavin, N. L. Kar-

weit, & N. A. Madden (Eds.), *Effective programs for students at risk* (pp. 23–51). Boston: Allyn & Bacon.

Slavin, R. E., Karweit, N. L., & Wasik, B. A. (1992). Preventing early school failure: What works? *Educational Leadership, 50,* 10–19.

Smith-Burke, M. T. (1996). Professional development for teacher leaders: Promoting program ownership and increased success. *Network News,* 1–4.

Stahl, K. A. D., Stahl, S., McKenna, M. C. (in press). The development of phonological awareness and orthographic processing in Reading Recovery.

Standards and Guidelines of the Reading Recovery Council of North America. (1998). Columbus, OH: RRCNA.

Sylva, K., & Hurry, J. (1995). Early intervention in children with reading difficulties: An evaluation of Reading Recovery and a phonological training. *Literacy, Teaching, and Learning, 2* (2), 49–68.

Vellutino, F. R., Scanlon, D. M., Sipay, E. R., Small, S. G., Pratt, A., Chen, R., & Denckla, M. B. (1996). Cognitive profiles of difficult-to-remediate and readily remediated poor readers: Early intervention as a vehicle for distinguishing between cognitive and experimental deficits as basic causes of specific reading disability. *Educational Psychology, 88,* 601–638.

Wade, T. (1978). *Promotion patterns in the junior school.* Unpublished diploma's thesis. University of Auckland, Auckland, Australia.

Wasik, B. A., & Slavin, R. E. (1993). Preventing early reading failure with one-to-one tutoring: A review of five programs. *Reading Research Quarterly, 28,* 179–200.

Wilson, K., & Daviss, B. (1994). *Redesigning education.* New York: Henry Holt & Co.

Wong, S. D., Groth, L. A., & O'Flahavan, J. F. (1994). *Characterizing teacher-student interaction in Reading Recovery lessons.* Universities of Georgia and Maryland, National Reading Research Center Report No. 17.

Wright, B. D., & Stone, M. H. (1979). *Best test design: Rasch measurements.* Chicago: Mesa Press.

Integrating Sources

1. Have Taylor and her colleagues produced a program that solves the cost dilemma of early intervention? Explain.

2. Would Reading Recovery and Taylor's program complement each other if they adopted simultaneously? Explain.

Classroom Implications

Without singling out any particular intervention program, assume that an elementary school must choose between a *pull-out* intervention program (one in which children leave the classroom for specialized instruction during the day) and a *push-in* program (one in which specialists enter the classroom and provide assistance). What are the pros and cons of these general approaches? Use a chart like this one to list them.

	Pros	Cons
Push-In		
Pull-Out		

Next, judge the relative advantages and disadvantages of each general approach. Does one of the two appear to have a distinct edge? Can you suggest ways of overcoming the disadvantages you have ascribed to each approach?

Annotated Bibliography

Fountas, I. C., & Pinnell, G. S. (1996). *Guided reading: Good first teaching for all children.* Portsmouth, NH: Heinemann.

This book describes how techniques popularized through Reading Recovery can be applied in small-group settings. Guided reading instruction is the basis of literacy group activities, an approach designed to make the expertise of Reading Recovery teachers go further. The techniques described here can be used in any primary classroom, however.

Hiebert, E. H., & Taylor, B. M. (Eds.). (1994). *Getting reading right from the start: Effective early literacy intervention.* Boston: Allyn and Bacon.

This edited volume presents useful descriptions of research-based approaches to early literacy intervention. In the mix are important elements that research suggests should be part of such programs if they are to have an impact educators desire.

Pikulski, J. J. (1994). Preventing reading failure: A review of five effective programs. *The Reading Teacher, 48,* 30–39.

Not only does Pikulski contrast five important early intervention programs (including Reading Recovery and Success for All), he also distills common elements that appear to constitute their "active ingredients."

Wasik, B. A., & Slavin, R. E. (1993). Preventing early reading failure with one-to-one tutoring: A review of five programs. *Reading Research Quarterly, 28,* 178–200.

This article examines the research evidence substantiating five tutoring-based intervention programs and extracts important conclusion about how they work and why.

You Become Involved

Chances are, your school or district has either implemented an early intervention program or is considering doing so. Even if it has already committed a particular approach, questions are likely to linger concerning its effectiveness and cost. In either event, the following options may help you to contribute to the dialogue.

1. Interview a specialist associated with an intervention program. Before you do, create a list of questions that organize what you would like to know about how the program works.
2. Visit web sites that tell you about early intervention programs. Conduct a net search that yields current web sites featuring schools that have implemented particular programs. Follow up with e-mail if you have questions.
3. While you're online, visit the site of the Center for the Improvement of Early Reading Achievement at **www.ciera.org**. This federally funded center conducts and compiles research into effective approaches to beginning reading instruction. It is frequently updated and offers many features for classroom educators, such as publications and online links.

10

WRITING

Composition is, for the most part, an effort of slow diligence and steady perseverance, to which the mind is dragged by necessity or resolution.
—*SAMUEL JOHNSON (1759)*

Research suggests that the finer points of writing, such as punctuation and subject-verb agreement, are learned best while students are engaged in extended writing that has the purpose of communicating a message to an audience.
—BECOMING A NATION OF READERS *(1985)*

Writing is an essential ingredient in any good reading program. At the same time, writing needs no justification for its existence. It is important in its own right. For without the ability to write our thoughts, we are less human.
—*FRANK MAY (1998)*

Changes and Issues in Writing

Few areas of literacy instruction have undergone more sweeping changes over the past 25 years than writing. Several important trends have characterized this period and have led to a transformation in the way educators have come to view the role of writing.

1. *Emphasis on process.* Insights into the approaches used by skilled writers have led to a refocusing of instruction from the final product to the process through which it was produced. Consequently, *process writing* instruction is now an everyday activity in many classrooms and at virtually every grade level. While authorities differ slightly on the nature of the stages, there is general agreement that they include the following: (1) drafting, (2) revising, (3) editing, (4) proofing, and (5) publishing. Nancie Atwell's approach to the "writers' workshop" has

become a popular means of facilitating children as they move through various stages of the writing process, but there are other viable approaches as well.

2. *Emphasis on learning.* It is now undisputed that writing can cause knowledge to become organized and coherent. Writing is for this reason now recognized as a means of reinforcing and extending learning (Myers, 1984). The phrases, *writing to learn* and *writing across the curriculum,* are testaments to its usefulness as a learning tool.

3. *Emphasis on reading.* The *reading-writing connection* has emerged as one of the more important insights of the twentieth century. Reading and writing are now viewed not as opposite processes, but as complementary activities. In particular, an early emphasis on writing facilitates learning to read (e.g., Adams, 1990). Through the years, important approaches to beginning reading instruction have made writing a central component. These include Montessori's techniques and the language experience approach. The success of a writing emphasis on the reading development of some children led Patricia Cunningham to make writing one of the "four blocks" in her own highly popular approach to language arts instruction (see Cunningham & Allington, 1999).

4. *Emphasis on word processing.* Word processing software is now firmly established in the workplace and is increasingly evident in classrooms. As David Reinking (1995) has put it, the most relevant instructional question will soon become not *whether* to incorporate word processing but *how* to incorporate it. Still, hardware limitations have meant that word processing, as an integral part of writing instruction, is a trend that is still in its early stages, particularly in elementary schools.

These trends, which together suggest a heightened interest in writing instruction, have given rise to a host of issues. The following list captures some of the more important controversies, though other issues could undoubtedly be added. Those that follow underscore just how difficult these issues tend to be.

1. *Time.* Granted, writing can help young children learn to read and can assist other children in organizing and solidifying what they learn. But writing takes time. What is the proper balance between classroom time devoted to writing activities and to other means of engaging learners? And what about the teacher time? Given that children's writing must be *read,* how much writing can feasibly be assigned and evaluated?

2. *Attitudes.* Many children lack a natural inclination to engage in writing. In fact, studies suggest a steady worsening of attitudes toward writing into the secondary years (Kear, Coffman, & McKenna, 1997). Good writing is, after all, nearly always taxing, as our rather startling quotation from Samuel Johnson, one of the most gifted writers of the eighteenth century, clearly indicates. How can teachers effectively motivate their students to engage in meaningful writing?

3. *Assessment.* Evaluating writing is anything but straightforward. Rubric systems, consisting of descriptive rating scales devoted to various aspects of writing are now used extensively and help make the process systematic. However,

many questions remain. What is the proper balance between assessing mechanics and content? How can the sensibilities of developing writers be spared the inhibiting effects of candid criticisms?

4. *Electronic transformation.* Word processing has already drastically altered the landscape of writing instruction, and changes are still under way. The use of spelling and grammar checkers, for example, can heavily support a student who is deficient in the mechanics of writing. Will the assessment of writing mechanics be permanently distorted by the use of these devices? As such devices become increasingly part of the prefered method of writing, both at home and in the workplace, does it matter that an individual's mechanical deficiencies may be remedied by their continual use? Moreover, such support extends well beyond mechanics. Access to a variety of electronic sources, such as encyclopedias and Internet documents, now makes copying and pasting from a variety of sources a simple matter. At what point do documents constructed in this way amount to plagiarism? For that matter, will plagiarism continue to have any real meaning in an electronic future? (For a provocative view that our traditional notions of plagiarism must give way, see Reinking [1996].) Finally, writing in electronic environments makes options available that have no place in traditional writing. For example, incorporating animation and hypertextual links to other documents are changing what it means to write. How must writing instruction change to accommodate these options?

As You Read

In light of the multitude of issues that presently confront writing instruction, we have chosen to narrow our focus to one of the most important: process writing. We offer two perspectives on the issues involved in making process writing successful. Both of the authors are clearly committed to the approach and speak to some of the impediments they perceive.

Jim Hoffman includes process writing amid a gallery of good ideas that have met with bad fates. He contends that this approach, together with writers' workshop, is so popular that is has become institutionalized in some places. Along the way, he offers a useful thumbnail history of writing instruction over the past few decades.

1. Describe how process writing developed.
2. What does Hoffman view as the greatest dangers of mandating process writing?

Barbara Carney discusses the role of process writing in a content environment. As you read this article note the following:

3. How is Carney's definition of process writing different or the same as Hoffman's?

4. What do you believe are the strengths and weaknesses of process writing, especially as it might be used in the classrom?

Jane Hansen discusses how writing can be used as one form of literacy assessment in the classroom setting.

5. What are some of the ways writing can be used as one form of literacy assessment?
6. What do you see as some of the strengths and weaknesses of this use of writing?

References

Becoming a nation of readers. Washington, DC: The National Institute of Education.

Adams, M. J. (1990). *Beginning to read: Thinking and learning about print.* Cambridge, MA: MIT Press.

Cunningham, P. M., & Allington, R. L. (1999). *Classrooms that work: They can all read and write* (2nd ed.). New York: Longman.

Johnson, S. (1759, January 6). *The Adventurer, No. 38.* In W. J. Bate, J. M. Bullitt, & L. F. Powell (Eds.), *The Yale edition of the works of Samuel Johnson. Volume II, The Idler and the Adventurer.* New Haven and London: Yale University Press.

Kear, D. J., Coffman, G. A., & McKenna, M. C. (1997, December). *Students' attitudes toward writing: A national survey.* Paper presented at the meeting of the National Reading Conference, Scottsdale, AZ.

May, F. B. (1998). *Reading as communication, Fifth edition.* Upper Saddle River, NJ: Merrill.

Myers, J. W. (1984). *Writing to learn across the curriculum.* Bloomington, IN: Phi Delta Kappa.

Reinking, D. (1995). Reading and writing with computers: Literacy research in a post-typographic world. In K. A. Hinchman, D. J. Leu, & C. K. Kinzer (Eds.), *Perspectives on literacy research and practice: Forty-fourth yearbook of the National Reading Conference* (pp. 17–33). Chicago: National Reading Conference.

Reinking, D. (1996). Reclaiming a scholarly ethic: Deconstructing "intellectual property" in a post-typographic world. In D. J. Leu, C. K. Kinzer, & K. A. Hinchman (Eds.), *Literacies for the 21st century: Research and practice: Forty-fifth yearbook of the National Reading Conference* (pp. 461–470). Chicago: National Reading Conference.

Process Writing and the Writer's Workshop

Excerpt from When Bad Things Happen to Good Ideas in Literacy Education: Professional Dilemmas, Personal Decisions, and Political Traps

JAMES V. HOFFMAN

When one door is shut, another opens.
DON QUIXOTE—CERVANTES

Over my 25 years of experience in education, starting out as a classroom teacher in Milwaukee, Wisconsin, USA, in 1969 and following a winding road that has taken me to my adopted home of Texas, I have seen many changes in the field of literacy education. I have lived through every imaginable curiosity ranging from ita, to words in color, to colored glasses, to learning styles, to the Wisconsin Design. I managed my way through each of these trials with the hope that we had surely lived through the worst of times, only to find out that things can get worse: state-mandated minimum skills assessments, dyslexia screening for every student at every grade level every year, teacher merit pay tied to student gains on standardized tests. We never seem to run out of bad ideas in education.

But I can live with bad ideas. A little adversity keeps us on our toes, gives us something to react to as a profession, provides us with a platform from which to launch our crusades, and unites us despite our differences. Bad ideas are not always easy to deal with, but at least we can take comfort in the fact that our target deserves to be terminated. What I have more difficulty accepting is, with apologies to Harold Kushner (1983), when bad things happen to good ideas. Here we encounter a professional dilemma. Shouldn't good ideas triumph and endure? That's the way it happens in the movies. Why shouldn't it be that way in our professional lives as well? In this brief essay, I will attempt to explore this puzzling part of our daily reality. I will begin by grounding my comments in two well-known innovations that most educators have embraced with enthusiasm. Each of these exemplifies, for me, the "good gone bad" dilemma. I will then use two examples to open a broader discussion of the issues involved in change and innovation.

Source: From Hoffman, J. V. (1998, October). When bad things happen to good ideas in literacy education: Professional dilemmas, personal decisions, and political traps. *The Reading Teacher, 52*(2), 102–112. Reprinted

Dilemma 1: Process Writing and the Writers' Workshop

The terms *process writing* and *writers' workshop* have become commonplace in the professional literature and in the discourse of practicing teachers. While it is next to impossible to pinpoint a specific point in time when these terms were introduced to the field or to identify a single source for them, the ideas are rooted in the work of a number of scholars conducting research in the late 1970s and early 1980s. Certain roots are to be found in the work of those attempting to create theoretical models of the writing process. The Flower and Hayes (1981) model, for example, reveals and reflects the highly interactive and conceptual nature of various components of the writing process. Other roots are found in the work of those investigating the early writing of young children (e.g., Clay, 1975; Ferriero & Teberosky, 1983; Teale & Sulzby, 1986). Here we find evidence for the developmental nature of the writing process and the progress that young children make as they explore increasingly complex forms of representation. The research of Donald Graves (1983) and his associates (e.g., Atwell, 1987; Calkins, 1986) has been seminal in uncovering some of the ways in which teaching and curriculum might be aligned using a process perspective to support developing writers.

No doubt the development of strategies for the holistic assessment of writing products was also influential as a separate root. Holistic assessment strategies provided the basis for documenting excellence in writing from a strong psychometric base (see Freedman, 1991). Finally, the roots of the process movement are to be found in the writing of those who have been critical of traditional instruction (e.g., Frank Smith, 1981). Such critics challenge the status quo for its lack of sensitivity and appreciation for children's abilities as language users and language learners.

Descriptions of the elements of a writers' workshop vary from one author to another. Typically, a writers' workshop offers opportunities for students to engage in the writing of texts that reflect their own interests and choices. Writers are encouraged to think freely as they explore early drafts. Teachers play an important role in creating the conditions and providing the resources that encourage risk taking on the part of students. Teachers engage in direct instruction through minilessons that help students extend their control over conventions used in writing. Peers are a critical part of the workshop model as well. They offer support and feedback to their writing colleagues. Peers may engage alternatively as coauthors, editors, or audience in a writers' workshop. Publishing (in the sense of targeting a broader "public" audience for the texts written) is also crucial to the writing process approach and writers' workshop. As writers look to share their writing with an "external" audience (e.g., through a class newspaper, through a literary collection, through writing displayed in the hall, through books catalogued in the library), they learn the importance of using the conventions of writing that are shared within that broader community. Student writing is evaluated for growth and may become part of the portfolio that documents development, flexibility, process, and diversity in style.

The writing process approach and the writers' workshop model began to spread initially through traditional channels such as preservice and inservice programs, professional journals, and conferences. Also influential in the growth of the movement were the workshops and research conducted through the national network of writing centers often referred to as the National Writing Project (Gray, 1988). By the mid-1980s publishers and policy makers took note of the movement and began to act. The translations and transformations offered by these groups were substantial. Many state curricula for the teaching of writing were rewritten during the middle and late 1980s to reflect a process perspective. In an effort to offer more authentic forms of assessment many states redesigned or created new tests that included holistic scoring of writing samples. Publishers responded by developing new programs that reflected the process perspective.

Consider the state of Texas as an example of the evolution of the movement into policy and published curriculum. In the mid-1980s, the Texas Education Agency mandated that writing be taught using a process approach. The five steps of the writing process (drafting, revising, editing, proofing, and publishing) were identified as essential to the teaching of writing. The Texas textbook adoption for English in the early 1990s required that state-approved texts employ the writing process approach as the basic model of instruction. Publishers responded with programs that represented a significant departure from the skills-based and skills-driven instructional programs of the past.

Unfortunately (and perhaps even tragically) the translation of the writing process into a published English curriculum did not reflect a great deal of the spontaneity and child-centeredness so valued in the process writing model for teaching. The writing process became proceduralized to the point that the five steps in the writing process became identified with the 5 days of the week: drafting on Monday, revising on Tuesday, editing on Wednesday, proofing on Thursday, and publishing on Friday. The fact that the entire class might march along this same path in unison was a reality driven by management and pacing concerns. One wonders if the children in the state of Texas, like Eric Carle's Very Hungry Caterpillar, might not go home at the end of the week with a very bad stomachache (for writing).

References

Atwell, N. (1987). *In the middle: Writing, reading, and learning with adolescents.* Portsmouth, NH: Heinemann/Boynton Cook.

Calkins, L. (1986). *The art of teaching writing.* Portsmouth, NH: Heinemann.

Clay, M. (1975). *What did I write?* Portsmouth, NH: Heinemann.

Ferriero, E., & Teberosky, A. (1983). *Writing before schooling.* Portsmouth, NH: Heinemann.

Flower, L., & Hayes, J. R. (1981). A cognitive process theory of writing. *College Composition and Communication, 32,* 365–387.

Freedman, S. W. (1991). *Evaluating writing: Linking large-scale testing and classroom assessment* (Occasional paper #27). Berkeley, CA: University of California, Center for the Study of Writing.

Graves, D. (1983). *Writing: Teachers and children at work.* Exeter, NH: Heinemann.

Gray, J. R. (1988). *National writing project: Model and program design.* Berkeley, CA: University of California, National Writing Project.

Kushner, H. (1983). *When bad things happen to good people.* New York: Avon.

Smith, F. (1981). Myths of writing. *Language Arts, 58,* 792–798.

Teale, W., & Sulzby, E. (1986). *Emergent literacy: Writing and reading.* Norwood, NJ: Ablex.

Process Writing and the
Secondary School Reality

A Compromise

BARBARA CARNEY

Incorporating the process approach to writing into my English classroom has been the biggest challenge of my 20-year teaching career. I first had the opportunity to experiment with the process approach about 15 years ago in a one-semester composition elective. Students could choose to take this course in addition to their required English class, which already involved a significant amount of writing. The elective offered practice in a variety of different types of writing, and, because it was usually a smaller group, more individualized attention.

I felt success with the process approach in the elective almost immediately, but when I attempted to adapt it to writing in my 11th-grade English classroom, where literature, vocabulary, and grammar units had to be covered in addition to composition, I found that the constraints of time and curriculum made the change much more difficult. I felt strongly that I wanted to make it work because of the consistent positive reaction of my elective students to the difference that the elements of the process had made in their writing. Over the years, their comments have served as the impetus for the change to process in my English classroom.

Experimenting in the Composition Elective

When I started teaching composition, students were accustomed to being assigned specific topics, hearing a lecture involving the best approaches to writing certain types of papers, reading models, creating an outline for approval, and doing most of the actual writing for homework. Most of the papers required by the English curriculum at that time were formal, multi-paragraph papers, so more informal, personal writing was offered in the elective. I began to give these students more of a voice in choosing their topics. I encouraged them to write and revise during class. Over the first few semesters, I developed a writing workshop approach similar to that described by Stephen Zemelman and Harvey Daniels (1988, *A Community of Writers,* Portsmouth, NH: Heinemann, 89–99). After a general assignment was discussed, most students were motivated to choose their own topics and work at their own pace. At the beginning of the period, they would come into the classroom, find their writing portfolios, and get started. I held conferences at a table in the classroom with individuals while the rest of the class wrote. Only the final drafts of each paper were graded, and I always had a sense of how close everyone was to finishing, so I could set the due date for the final draft at a comfortable time. The atmosphere was relaxed and positive.

Source: From "Process Writing and the Secondary School Reality: A Compromise" by Barbara Carney, 1996, *English Journal, 85,* (6), pp. 28–35. Copyright 1996 by the National Council of Teachers of English. Reprinted with permission.

The number of students taking the elective grew larger each year, and it became difficult to meet with them individually as often as I wanted. I also realized that their insights could help each other. I did some research on training peer tutors and became aware of the benefits to everyone that writing response groups can produce. After working with a group for the first time, Laura, who had seemed reluctant to share, wrote about the experience: "It was very helpful reading our papers aloud in discussion groups because we could hear our mistakes and spot each other's weak paragraphs or sentences."

The most dramatic outcome of using process for me was that my role changed from director to facilitator. The students, mostly seniors, saw the class as an opportunity to express their opinions and to receive input as they were writing rather than waiting for my evaluation of their final draft. They actually showed appreciation for my responses, rather than being threatened by them. Even more surprising, many students indicated that being expected to write multiple drafts was the most beneficial part of the course. Tim, a senior, wrote in his final evaluation:

> *The most helpful aspect I felt was the numerous revisions of the papers. This allowed me to see what I was doing wrong and correct it before receiving a final grade. It was also helpful to have other students read my papers and comment on them.*

I know now that many teachers of writing have found success with a similar approach in their classrooms.

Adapting to the Required English Course

I became more and more aware that this interaction and flexibility was possible because the elective composition course was devoted entirely to writing. I was excited to have developed such a positive situation in this one course, but for the rest of each day in my required 11th-grade English classes I faced the dilemma confronted by secondary English teachers. How can we fit the process approach into our large and regimented classrooms? Is it possible to allow the time-consuming activities for writing, revising, and conferencing with all of the other constraints demanded by our curriculum, not to mention the interruptions by activities, testing, and guidance? What about the students who are not motivated; can they be expected to work at their own pace, be interested enough to come up with ideas, or complete a paper without a deadline? If they don't enjoy writing one draft, how can we expect them to revise?

The unwieldy nature of the writing process seems impossible to conform to a regimented English environment where literature, research, vocabulary, communication skills, and grammar are demanded in addition to writing. Yet, today, the process approach is commonly accepted by the secondary community and is expected in writing instruction, even though its inherent spontaneity continues to appear incongruous with the short daily chunks of time and the demands implicit in the secondary classroom.

What has evolved in my 11th-grade English class is a compromise. I fell so strongly about the benefits of the process approach to my students that I decided to attempt to force this abstractly shaped peg into the square hole of a classroom period. I listened to my students to determine the most important elements of the writing workshop approach, and although I have had to make some sacrifices to make it work, I feel that the strengths remain.

The Necessary Compromises

Student Ownership

The first compromise is that of total student ownership of the assignment. Our strong, sequential curriculum requires certain types of writing at each level 9–12. It does allow for some flexibility, however, and I try to give students as much choice as possible within its parameters. For example, a character analysis might be required, but students may choose the character and determine an appropriate thesis for analysis. Writers might choose a person or place to describe for a descriptive piece or a precept from *Poor Richard's Almanac* they would like to relate their own lives. I think it is very important to give writers the experience of choosing a topic not only so they feel some ownership, but because deciding what to write about is a big part of the writing process: if we assign topics, we are not teaching what the process is all about. I believe that the process of selecting a topic, narrowing and refining it, should be the responsibility of the writer as far as the curriculum will allow. Although they do not "discover a subject" (Donald Murray, 1968, *A Teacher Teaches Writing,* Boston: Houghton Mifflin, 27) in the purest sense, my students do experience a wide range of subjects, approaches, and audiences.

Spontaneous Writing

The second major compromise involves the spontaneity of the process. Writing during class time that continues from one day to the next isn't possible because of time constraints, but I wanted my English students to learn the value of meaningful revision. Their reticence to write and revise led me to consider setting required deadlines for each draft. Spontaneity is destroyed by this approach, but I feel it is worth the sacrifice. Before I required the process, I had the strong feeling that when I collected final drafts, I was actually collecting first drafts in a pretty disguise, mostly because students did not allow the time they needed to develop a paper before the final draft was due.

I realize that setting deadlines flies in the face of process theory because it does not allow for individual writers to work at their own pace. It is, however, an answer for teachers who wish to more efficiently monitor the progress of their students, and it requires the writer who might otherwise be reluctant to do so to revise. Forcing the process allows writers to see what they are capable of through revision. As unbelievable as this may sound, my students continued to point to multiple drafts as the main reason for their success as writers. "The thing most helpful in this class was writing so many rough drafts before our final copy. Doing this helped me realize how important it is to not only write one copy of a paper," Heather wrote. For many it meant a change in attitude about writing. When asked about whether his attitude about writing had changed after taking the elective course, Nick said, "Yes, my attitude has changed. I found out that writing was not as bad and as hard as I always thought it was. There is always room for improvement and so I keep writing. I hope I keep getting better."

Retaining the Best of the Writing Process

Despite these compromises to the writing process' spontaneity and student ownership, my new plan for English contained the elements that my writing students consistently found to be the most helpful: writing multiple drafts and receiving a response at each stage of the process. Another important technique that is implied by the process approach is waiting until the end to deal with mechanics and grammar.

Ironically, critics of the process approach see postponing error correction as a shift in the emphasis on correctness; they believe that student writers are learning to write using poor grammar and incorrect mechanics. This does not need to be the case. Teaching students that editing is the final stage in the process should not lessen its significance. Postponing error correction does not mean putting it off altogether. If students are told that they are responsible for the editing process, then they must be held accountable in the final evaluation.

I first learned about emphasizing the editing stage from Lucy Calkins, who describes a special editing table in her 2nd grade classroom where students go to edit when their papers are ready (1986, *The Art of Teaching Writing,* Portsmouth, NH: Heinemann, 206). I try to maintain this same separation in a figurative way by asking students to wait until the editing stage to address grammar and mechanics.

The success I have felt with this approach is a result of my students focusing more on development of their content in the earlier stages of writing. They have learned that revision is not just error-correction. As they begin to write and revise, they look more carefully at what they are saying without the constraints of how they are saying it.

When asked if waiting to think about editing until later in the process had changed her writing, Karen said, "Yes, I just think about development, paragraphing, and support and later change wording and punctuation. It makes me feel more organized while writing papers and helps me concentrate on one thing at a time." A number of students said that this approach helped to reduce their anxiety about writing. Chris responded, "I am more relaxed when starting a paper." Jen said, "Yes, I think my writing has improved since I concentrate on only the important things first." Thinking about what type of writing happens at which stage created an entirely different way of thinking and talking about writing in my classroom.

Training Students to Understand the Process:
HOCs and LOCs

Now I begin each school year training all of my students using a framework from the NCTE TRIP booklet by Thomas Reigstad and Donald McAndrew (1984, *Training Tutors for Writing Conferences,* Urbana, IL: ERIC, 11–19). I ordered the booklet as part of my research on training peer tutors but have found it invaluable when talking about the type of writing that is done in each stage of the process. Reigstad and McAndrew provide a hierarchy, of writing concerns and when they should be addressed.... The High Order Concerns (thesis or focus, appropriate voice or tone, organization, and development) are dealt with first and in this sequence. If a writer's focus in a draft is unclear, organization confusing, or tone inappropriate, these weaknesses must be addressed before any discussion of spelling or word choice can take place. The Low Order Concerns (problems with sentence structure and variety, punctuation, spelling, and usage) are dealt with simultaneously, near the end of the process.... Usually, we emphasize the HOCs when looking at the first two drafts; punctuation, spelling, and usage at the editing stage; and sentence structure and variety somewhere in the middle. It's especially rewarding when awkward language dissolves because the writer hears it while reading during a peer conference.

Labeling writing priorities helps to demystify the composing process and allows student writers to focus on one concern at a time instead of trying to do everything at once. *High* and *low* may not be the most appropriate terms, but they do emphasize the idea that good writing is much more than correct writing. When I first read about waiting to edit, I didn't think it would make much difference, but retraining students to look at the priorities in their writing first continues to have the single biggest impact on my teaching of writing.

HOCs and LOCs

High Order Concerns	*Low Order Concerns*
1. focus/thesis	*1. sentence structure*
2. appropriate tone	*2. variety*
3. organization	*3. punctuation*
4. development	*4. spelling*
	5. usage

Reigstad, Thomas J. and Donald A. McAndrew, 1984. *Training Tutors for Writing Conferences.* Urbana: NCTE, 11–18.

How It Works: The Writing Process in My English Classroom

My attempt to develop the process approach comfortably in my English classroom has evolved into a predictable framework of activities at each stage of the process: prewriting, drafting, revising, editing, and publishing. . . . Although the type of assignment may change the approach, my students know what type of class session a writing workshop day will be. Each activity is designed to take a class period of 45 minutes or less; these periods are usually a few days apart to allow time for the writing outside of class that is needed for the next stage. These days add an enjoyable diversity to our more structured literature and vocabulary classes which usually involve more teacher-centered activities.

How Each Stage Is Usually Handled

Managing Process Activities in the Classroom

1. Prewriting-	class as a whole or individual brain-storming topic slips responded to by teacher & revised
2. 1st Draft-	response by writer
3. 2nd Draft-	response by writing partner
4. 3rd Draft-	response by teacher
5. Editing Draft-	response by teacher or partner or both
6. Final Draft-	response by writer evaluation by teacher

Prewriting: The Very Beginning

The idea behind the general assignment, a character analysis, for example, is introduced before prewriting begins. When reviewing our agenda for the next week, I might say:

You'll see that on Friday we are beginning a piece of writing in response to a character in The Crucible. *Choose one character from the play that interests you. Your homework for Friday is to know the character you will write about. You will be answering questions about the character in class on that day.*

Prewriting is done during class on the same day the written assignment is given, requiring students to write immediately. The goals of the final paper are described in detail on the sheet so students can return to them later, but on this first day I discuss the general focus needed to begin prewriting. For clarification, the assignment can be written in stages, and I delineate requirements for each stage of the process.

Prewriting is completed on the assignment sheet so that the writer has everything needed to begin on a single page. My goal is to have my students leave class with a sufficient start so that determining a specific focus on their own is not so difficult. A series of general prompts initiate prewriting. Using about five prompts is best and easier to look at quickly in a class period. For example, in the character assignment, students might be asked to list the character they have chosen, character traits and motivation, something puzzling that the character does, a physical trait that is significant, a conflict that is important or confusing, or an interesting relationship with another character.

I always do prewriting with the class as a whole, reading each prompt aloud and pausing, circling their desks, checking to see that they are writing, answering individual questions, encouraging them to do more. Everyone writes quietly, and I can sense from the beginning those who may be having difficulty with the assignment. Sometimes I collect this sheet, but usually I prefer the students keep it to use for determining a focus for their paper.

If I sense that students are ready by the end of the period, the exercise can be concluded by asking them to write an idea for a preliminary (topic or thesis) sentence stating the focus of the paper. This may also be due in the next day or two. Either way, asking students to write during class provides a concrete start that makes beginning a first draft a more palatable experience.

Determining a Specific Focus

Before beginning their first draft, student writers need to create a focus. Invariably, prewriting has led some to wonderful, original topics that I would not have offered had I assigned them. However, I have learned from experience that some guidance is necessary to avoid problems that result from a focus that is too general or inadequate.

Depending on the assignment, I may ask students to write their ideas in a formal thesis statement form, or in a sentence that simply states the focus, such as, "I will be describing my grandfather reading as he sits on the back porch." I always collect these on a form that facilitates my reading and grading them. These sheets are completed before the student comes to class and collected at the beginning of the period.

The process of drafting and revising actually begins with these topic slips. I try to return them as soon as possible with my responses. Often, a large percentage will be returned with my request to revise, and writers will not receive full credit for this stage until their attempts at revision are successful. Student writers often begin with a topic idea that is incomplete or too shallow to culminate in a meaningful analysis. Sometimes a grueling process of revision occurs as a result of my demanding an acceptable topic. I will not tell students what to write, but I do encourage them to be more specific or in-depth.

Starting: The First Draft

Once a focus has been established and goals for the assignment are clear, the students begin the drafting process on their own time. With the guidelines on the written assignment and my responses on their topic sheet, they should be ready to start. The first draft is due in class in a reasonable amount of time after I have returned the focus sheets. (Longer assignments may be broken up at this point. First draft of the introduction could be due.) I emphasize that this draft is *first* and not *rough* and although there may be mechanical errors, it must be legible. The first draft is responded to during class, but not by me. I initially used student peer responders with the first draft, but found that many papers were not ready for someone else's perusal, so now I have the writer look carefully at the first draft before anyone else does.

I may address the class as a whole and ask them to look for certain things in their own drafts, but usually I ask each writer to analyze his or her text at this stage by answering a few questions in writing, such as: Why did you choose this subject? What is the mood that you hope to create? This allows individuals to read and answer the questions at their own pace. It also gives me time to circulate and check to see that each student has a draft.

Giving credit for completed drafts is tricky in a large class without collecting them, but I am able to check quickly as I circulate the room, making note of who has nothing and who has only a partial draft. I do feel it is important to give credit for completing drafts as well as the final piece of writing in order to place value on the process as well as the product.

Questions for the writer at this early stage should reflect the High Order Concerns only: focus, tone, organization, and development. The questions should guide students' careful rereading of their own draft and often reinforce assignment priorities. We often conclude this activity by writing goals for what will be changed to improve the second draft. The vehicle for answering these questions could be a writing a journal, or part of a portfolio, or on a sheet of paper that the student can keep. The responses and drafts may be collected, but the student will need both to continue with the paper. Allowing writers to use these written thoughts to continue their work reinforces the idea that the activity is designed to help them and is not done for the teacher. Both the first draft (labeled D1) and the question sheets are saved and turned in with the final draft, so the students know the teacher will be seeing them eventually.

I have learned to limit my involvement in the early stages of the paper. In fact, teachers who "correct" drafts are missing the benefits of waiting and also are encouraging more dependence on their input. Reading every draft of each student creates an unhealthy dependence on the teacher's comments. Writers need to learn to see ideas that need to be developed or confusing passages without the approval of the teacher. My students appreciate that they should make some effort before I see their work and know that they will have the opportunity to react to my responses before the final paper is evaluated.

One final note: there is always the concern that students may not take this stage seriously and come to class with a paper that is carelessly written, knowing that it will not be carefully scrutinized. The benefits of getting this fresh start outweigh my concern for the unmotivated at this point. It reinforces the idea that the students are writing for themselves and planning to revise—two key elements of the process approach. It is also less threatening; many students who are intimidated by writing find this approach more relaxing, and many need the time to put the basics down on paper and then add to them in a second draft.

Revising: The Second Draft

The second draft always involves some type of collaboration. Students are assigned a due date soon after the first draft was due and the same procedure of credit is applied. This time another student—a writing partner—will respond to the draft, as I circulate and check that they have completed both drafts. They must, of course, have both their first draft (labeled D1) and their second draft (D2) with them. Partnering can provide an opportunity for a varied audience, and questions may be raised that might not be otherwise. Writing groups can also be effective, but the variety of responses takes much longer. My goal is to have each writer get a complete response by the end of one class period, so using partners has proven to be the most efficient approach.

Training Peer Tutors

Over the years I have experimented with training students and pairing them. I have found the most success with pairing students with similar ability levels. I also sometimes allow the students to choose their own partners. This adds to their comfort level when sharing their writing, and it may make for a more pleasurable experience. On the other hand, if I am less concerned about student comfort and more about writing focus, I choose opposite-sex partners of similar ability. Pairing can vary with assignment as well. It can be beneficial for students to be paired with another writer with a similar topic, or one who holds a contrasting point of view. Students who do not have a draft completed on this day forfeit the advantage of working with a partner and are asked to write quietly on their draft during conferences.

A variety of methods may be used to conduct the conference, but students must be trained in some general guidelines before these will be effective:

Peer Conference Guidelines

1. Writer reads out loud as partner reads silently.
2. Partners sit beside each other with paper between them.
3. The writer holds the pen.
4. The tone of the conference should be respectful and positive.

The first rule that I feel strongly about is reading the paper out loud. The writer should read the paper aloud while the responder reads silently, with the paper in between them. In order to facilitate this, students need to sit next to each other, not across from each other. Sometimes getting students to move and to read aloud is the most difficult part of the training. Asking students to read their work to someone else requires them to make a commitment that handing a paper over does not make. Also, they frequently hear their words in a different way when they are read out loud, and more meaningful revision occurs as a result of what they hear.

Another priority is that we show respect to the writer. The tone of each conference should be thoughtful and positive. Students can be very critical, so sensitivity must be encouraged. Looking for the good qualities in a piece can reinforce what students know about good writing. Also, the writer has ownership; as a result, I ask partners not to mark anything on the writer's paper during a conference, and I don't either. Only the writer has the right to make changes. The writer should listen carefully to suggestions and write them down, but the writer may choose to disagree with what was suggested. I feel this writer-centered approach has a real psychological advantage. Young writers see their papers as their own work, not what they have been told to do. Ultimately, the writer alone has the responsibility.

Once partners are assigned and students understand the general rules, I try to determine how directive I need to be to lead the partners through a successful conference. Possibilities include specific questions for the partner to answer about the writer's paper or an open discussion of each of the four HOCs followed by the writer listing what was learned from the conference and what will be revised as a result. Another approach I sometimes use to facilitate meaningful discussion is to ask the writer to write down three questions before the conference to guide the partner's listening. *(Does the second paragraph make sense? How can I make the beginning more interesting? Do I give enough examples?)* This technique enables the writer to *direct* the conference.

While the partners are meeting, my role is to see that the rules of the writer-centered conference are being followed and to oversee everyone's progress. I listen to what is being said and try to get around to all partnerships. Student conferences can give the teacher meaningful feedback as to the progress of the assignment. Clarifications can be made to the class as a whole based on questions that arise in the partnerships.

Teachers who question the value of students' responses to each other can have students answer questions about the draft they have listened to, collect the drafts and question sheets, and evaluate the partner's written responses. I have found that students do well with this exercise, and I believe they make more of an effort with their writing knowing that a peer is going to be listening. Although it takes preparation, the single period that a partner conference takes is well worth the time. The training can be a benefit all year.

The Third Draft: Teacher Response

In order for the process to be given the proper emphasis, the teacher should respond to a draft at least once before it is turned in for final evaluation. By waiting until a later draft, I feel I am giving validity to the students' responses and encouraging less dependence on what I say. I usually collect the third draft, where there is still need for meaningful revision, and my role is not seen only as error-checker.

With a shorter assignment, I comment on HOCs and identify LOCs in the third draft. (An ideal approach is to respond to HOCs separately, then focus on LOCs in a later editing draft, but there is only time for this on major papers.) By giving helpful suggestions before evaluating the paper, I believe I have changed my students' perception of my role in the process—from critic to helper. While the teacher who spends hours writing on a final evaluation is also trying to help students become better writers, this approach is perceived as being less helpful because the grade has already been given.

If I am dealing with editing on this draft, too, I also identify any errors by underlining or circling (never correcting) them. The writer is responsible for correcting any errors in the paper. Sometimes I put a check in the margin by a line that contains an error so the writer can identify it. These drafts are especially helpful to peruse when giving a paper a final evaluation, especially if problems were noted and ignored.

Editing: A Separate Draft

As mentioned earlier, separating the editing stage is crucial for students' understanding of writing as a process. A separate draft, preferably done on a computer, should be labeled as the editing draft. The draft can be collected by the teacher and returned on a day when there is time for clarification during class. Another effective method is to have students meet for an editing conference with the same writing partner. The paper still is read out loud by the writer, but both should scrutinize the paper for errors only (LOCs). If the writer misses a correction, the partner can interrupt to point it out. If I have indicated a problem on the draft that students do not recognize, they can work together to determine what the problem is or use the resource materials in the room to help them. For anyone who has attempted to teach traditional grammar or spelling and seen little transference to writing, this class session can be a rewarding experience. Students who have a context for concern about mechanics will discuss them meaningfully.

Publishing: The Final Stage

The final draft should reflect the sum of effort that is made in the stages of the process before it. Students should feel pride in their end result. Publishing parties, where a celebration takes place on the day the paper is due and writers share their final products, can reinforce this pride. If time does not allow for taking another class period on the due date, I ask students to answer a few questions on a cover sheet. . . . These may reflect on the content of the paper as well as their revision process and frequently add insight to the paper itself.

Final Character Analysis Cover Sheet

Your Name _____

Your Character _____

Your Writing Partner(s) _____

Read all of the questions first. Consider your answers carefully. Answer concisely in complete sentences.

1. What conflict or dilemma (involving your character) interested you the most? Why?

2. What insight into the character did you gain from writing this paper? Did any of your attitudes change?

3. Describe your organization (the order of discussion and paragraphing). Did this change as you revised?
4. How did responses of others affect your writing? Explain.
5. If you could continue working on this piece, what would you do?

When I collect the final drafts, my students turn in everything for my perusal—all the question sheets and drafts—so these must be arranged carefully. I evaluate the final copy with the use of a rubric with categories that emphasize the HOCs and LOCs and our goals for the assignment. Then everything is placed in each student's Working Portfolio where they will record further reactions. Taking time to look back and reflect on their work from the beginning enables students to see their own thinking process and to learn from it. Another meaningful technique is to have students revise the final copy after it has been graded so that they have a clean copy for their final portfolios. This reinforces the idea that writing continues to be an on-going process even after the so-called last draft has been completed. If students are interested, these revised final copies can be used in a class publication.

Conclusion

The use of the process approach can be intimidating at first, but it is possible to incorporate it successfully within a demanding secondary English curriculum. With preparation workshop techniques like peer conferencing, reading out loud, and self-reflection can occur meaningfully within a single period. While addressing the different stages during class does take more time than assigning a paper and collecting it two weeks later, there can be time for this work within traditional curricula. For instance, our high school's English curriculum has fewer literature requirements than it did 20 years ago because of the increased emphasis on composition. In addition, we probably finalize fewer papers in a year as a result of requiring the process, although my students do much more writing. As Jeff commented, "The one thing I found the most helpful in my writing was the time we spent on each paper. Instead of just going from one paper to another quickly, we spent time on each paper, which made it more helpful."

As for my role, I don't believe I have to spend more time with the papers outside of class than I did before, and I feel the time that I spend with the drafts is much more meaningful. I do collect and respond to at least two drafts instead of just the final one. However, I see more immediate results from my comments in the earlier drafts, and the writing has improved so much by the final draft that there are fewer weaknesses to identify, so grading papers is more rewarding than frustrating. I cannot imagine ever returning to the traditional method of teaching writing after experiencing what the process approach to writing has done for me and for my students.

Evaluation

The Center of Writing Instruction

JANE HANSEN

I heard an 11th-grade U.S. history student read this piece of writing to his class:

The Romanian Revolution of 1989

It happened exactly 200 years after the French Revolution. This event marked me and all other Romanians for life. I will never forget those bloody and heroic days of December 1989. We were actually living history. After 45 years of communist tyranny, we were free. We paid a high price, with the lives of young children and young men and women that were there with flowers and candles in their hands against the tanks and the bullets that wanted to crush them. But, on December 22, the people were victorious. The women and children put red and white carnations in soldiers' barrels and the army fought with the people. I still remember that last decree, at 8 a.m., when president Nicolae Ceausescu declared a state of emergency, and at 12 p.m. that same day a voice came on the radio saying: "We're free! Romania is free! The tyrant is gone!" Everybody was crying. They were crying for the dead, they were crying for the living. It was time now for the Romanians to shine, to show the world that we were a courageous and proud nation.

Silence. For a short time after John reads, the class sits in wonder. Then Meg breaks the quietness, "You were *there?*"

"Yes. Well, my family wasn't right there. We were in the mountains skiing, but we came down as soon as we heard."

The questions continue, and John tells more of his story. He goes back to after World War II when his grandfather spurned the communists. His story sheds light upon history throughout the last 50 years, and the students hear history in the making.

The response of this class speaks to the theme of my article: Evaluation as the center of writing instruction. When I use the word *evaluation* herein I refer to its root, which is *value.* Evaluation is the act of finding value in a piece of writing. My view of evaluation differs from our customary actions of giving tests and determining whether students have met certain criteria.

In the first section I focus on the importance of finding value in the content(s) of a piece of writing. In the second section I focus on evaluation as a way to promote a writer's growth, and finally, I write about teachers who find value in themselves as learners.

Source: From Hansen, J. (1996, November). Evaluation: The center of writing instruction. *The Reading Teacher, 50*(3), 188–195. Reprinted with permission of Jane Hansen and the International Reading Association. All rights reserved.

Evaluation: To Find Value in the Content(s)

Several facets of writing are important, but writing research over the last 2 decades or so has forced many of us to concentrate more on the content(s). In previous decades we learned all too well how to focus on the mechanical skills. Although we will not stop teaching students when to use effective conventions, we now realize that a perfectly punctuated paper written about noncompelling information is a paper with little, if any, value. In this section I will give a glimpse of what we do in classrooms to find value in (a) the content(s) of our students' writing and (b) the content(s) of literature.

To Find Value in the Content(s)
of Our Students' Writing

What does the author say that is important? In his short composition about the Romanian Revolution, John wrote about a scene of tremendous value. His classmates knew, beyond doubt, that John had written about something of significance to him and, also, to them. Their responses showed him that they valued what he wrote.

Their many questions remind me of an incident that happened in one of our research projects several years ago. A second-grade girl shared a draft of her writing with a small group, and later in the day, she asked Leslie Funkhouser, her teacher, if she could read it to the entire class. In explaining why she wanted to do this, she said, "When I shared it with my small group this morning, they asked me lots of questions. They were interested in it, so I think the class will be, also."

The questions the listeners ask show they find value in a piece of writing. These listeners are playing the role of readers. If the scene had been different, they could have all read a copy of the draft and then asked the author the same questions. Or the scene could have been between only two children. Or the scene could have been a conference between the child and the teacher.

Whatever the situation, a writer receives response when s/he offers her/his writing to others, and some (or much) of this response is an exploration of the content. The writer finds out what is of interest in her/his draft. The responders may begin by telling the writer what they learned, and then they may go into questions, a sequence I often hear in classrooms. Regardless of the order of the response, or whether it follows a free-flowing nature, the main role of the listeners/evaluators is to find value within the information or narrative the writer shares. The writer expects various listeners to find value in different parts of her/his writing, and this diverse response helps the writer consider whether a section is unclear or whether the possibility of different interpretations adds to the value of the writing.

To Find Value in the Content(s) of Literature

The task of finding value applies as well when we read a piece of literature written by a professional. We respond to a book in the same way as we do to the writing of our classroom writers. We want our students to think of themselves as writers; we treat them as closely as we can to the way we treat professionals. We try to see all writers as persons of value. When we read a book to our students, we value their responses to the writing. The unexpectedness and diversity in their responses often surprise us, and this we treasure.

Noted children's author Lois Lowry (1994) is one of many writers from whom we learn the importance of varied interpretations of a piece of writing. In her acceptance speech for her second Newbery award she gives examples to show that the meaning of her story lies not in *The Giver,* her 1994 winner, but within the readers. A boy wrote, "I was really surprised that they just died at the end. That was a bummer..." (p. 421). In contrast, one girl wrote to Lowry, "I love it. Mainly because I got to make the book happy. I decided they made it" (p. 421). As a professional writer, Lowry wants us teachers to know that she values varied responses to her work.

Similarly, Ellen Goldsmith (1995) writes about the great differences parents and teachers find in the messages of children's books. She meets with groups in which both parents and teachers participate and says, "It is not surprising that a range of responses emerges. What is interesting and seems important to me is that these perspectives have never created a polarizing atmosphere. Rather, . . . the room seems to grow larger" (p. 561).

The room seems to grow larger. To place value on the various responses to a piece of writing is to place value on the individuals in the classroom. This honor we give to each other not only gives us insights into text, but allows the community of readers and writers to emerge. They expect and respect differences.

Invariably, one of our students will say something that surprises us. I come to a discussion curious to know what stories I will hear. The students have thought about the characters in the books and themselves. As James Moffett (1992) writes, "The ultimate referents are in us, the readers... meaning is only implied..." (p. 63). Various students make connections I wouldn't have thought of if I were to read a book 10 times.

In my classes at the University of New Hampshire, I often use picture books to illustrate what we do to place value on the many contents in a piece written by a professional. I read to the teachers who are my students. One book I particularly like is *Whistle Home* written by Natalie Honeycutt and illustrated by Annie Cannon (New York: Orchard Books, 1993).

In this book a small child's aunt comes to spend the day while Mother goes away for several hours. The child and Aunt Whistle spend a delightful day picking apples with the dog, but the child worries that Mother will not return. Finally, at dusk, they watch the headlights on Mother's pick-up truck approach from afar, and the book ends with warm hugs.

When I finish reading the last page I pause and then say, "What are you thinking about now?" or "What were you thinking while I read it?" I receive all sorts of responses. People tell stories of their own childhoods when they didn't want their parents to leave, and of their own children. They tell stories of themselves as grandparents who often are the ones left with the children. They tell about their dogs. One woman said, "I wonder if some time in the past Father left and never came back."

These responses are interesting because they are similar to students' responses when a classmate shares a piece of writing. These responses are important because they represent a huge, yes, a huge change in what we do as reading teachers. These responses turn the word *evaluation* inside out. They stand in stark contrast to the kind of discussion we used to engineer when we called a group of children together to discuss a story.

We used to call them together to check their comprehension. We thought our questions would motivate students to read. Now, however, what we want is for students to find books themselves the motivators. We want a student to continue to read a book because s/he is dying to find out what will happen next, not because s/he fears a comprehension question. Happily, the scene where the teacher calls a group of children together to ask them questions to find out whether they read and understand a story is dying. It is such a relief to see this scene gradually disappear.

Here I am, someone who collected data for her dissertation on reading groups where she asked students comprehension questions! I finished that dissertation in 1979, and now I feel as if I did it a century ago.

What I have learned about the importance of seeking varied responses has changed what I believe about reading instruction. If I could wave a magic wand over the world of reading instruction, I would eliminate comprehension questions with one huge, magical sweep of my hand!

Evaluation: To Promote Writing Growth

Evaluation goes beyond the act of finding value in the content(s) of what we write and read. It has many other aspects, one of which is the role evaluation can play in helping students' writing grow.

In general, we have not thought of evaluation as a means to encourage growth. Instead, we typically use assessments after we complete a unit, to take a backward look in order to determine whether students have grown or have learned the content. However, within writing instruction, we collect daily information from the writers in our classroom in order to take a forward look, so we can decide what to teach each student in the most effective way possible. We ask them what help they want and provide it. In order to tell us what they need, our writers evaluate themselves, a skill we teach them.

As a starting point, we want our students to become articulate about what they do well. We help each student learn to answer this question, "What do I do well as a writer?"

To answer this question, students first need to consider themselves writers. The students write frequently and often reflect on what they do effectively. For example, a student lives in northern New Hampshire, where a moose wanders in the woods near his house, so he writes about this large, ungainly creature. The child chooses to share it because it shows what he does well as a writer. In this case, Justin is the classroom authority on flashbacks. He likes this technique in literature and often uses it in his writing. As he begins to read to the class he says, "I used a flashback again. It's not all that hard, you know. . . ."

Once a writer can show what s/he does well, the writer moves to a more specific question, "What's the most recent thing I've learned to do as a writer?"

This is similar to the first, but it's necessary to consider this slight variation. Some writers need to look carefully at their present self to see what they've learned recently. Some, unfortunately, don't think they are learning anything at the present time. Our students need to be very aware of what they are learning right now as writers so they have a sense of forward momentum.

In many classrooms, children compare two pieces of writing to help them see their growth. In February I was in a first-grade classroom where the children had their writing from September and February spread out before them. They were having the best time celebrating what they'd learned that year as writers! The knowledge that they are moving forward enables them to see themselves as writers who can continue to move forward.

Once students see themselves as writers who are constantly getting better, they start to think ahead. We hear them say, "I think I'll write a poem," or "I think I'll put a title on my next piece," or "How do you know where to put quotation marks?" They start to think ahead to what they might do to become better writers. It's time to point out to these students that they are setting goals, a valuable act of learners. Here are two additional questions for them to use as evaluators: "What do I want to learn to do next to become a better writer?" "What do I plan to do to work on this?"

These questions help students maintain their forward movement and adopt the role of curriculum designers, but it's difficult for some students to set goals. They look too far ahead and set grandiose, long-term goals. However, as Marie Clay (1991) has so adeptly taught us, students need to become aware of problem-solving strategies to use in their immediate and short-term work. They need to develop good habits from the beginning of their careers, so they don't need to "recover."

The teacher needs a great deal of knowledge to help students set realistic goals. S/he must have a general notion of the various strategies writers use. S/he knows, for example, that if a child writes in strings of letters with an occasional isolated word, it may make sense for a child to set as a goal, "I want to learn to make spaces between my words."

However, this isn't the only goal for the child to consider. The child must know of more than one possible goal in order to be able to make a decision about what to work on next to make her message more accessible to herself and others. This child could also be interested in making pictures that enhance her text, or she may want to learn when to use a contrasting color crayon to highlight words of exclamation. The teacher's task is to help the child generate possible goals and choose one to work on.

Each student decides what s/he wants to learn next. When I enter Ellen's Grade 3 classroom or Terry's Grade 10 classroom during writing workshop and stop beside a student who's writing, he'll be able to tell me what he's working on: "I'm working on *was* and *were*. I never know for sure which one to use."

This ability to set goals extends what we know about the element of choice in writing instruction. We have moved beyond the simple thought that students need to choose their own topics to a belief that they need to work consciously on becoming better writers. They work on specific skills and strategies within the topics they want to explore and via the genres that fit their topics and goals. Choice of goals, topic, and genre all place students at the best advantage to use self-evaluation to advance their writing skills.

In an elementary-secondary research project in Manchester, New Hampshire (Hansen, 1994), we gradually came to realize the necessity of another question, "What do I plan to do to work on my goal?" The plan helps to make the goal concrete, attainable. Students create a strategy(ies) they may use as they work on their goal.

For example, the writer who is learning when to use *was* and *were* tells me about his plan. "I have five *wases* and three *weres* on this page. I'm gonna ask Bud or Xiao Di if they're right." This young writer has a strategy to draw upon when he needs to use *was* or *were* in his writing. In time, he will not need to call upon his friends.

Another student I pause beside says, "I'm working on a story for my kindergarten buddy. They like stories with repetition. I'm trying to think of something for this teddy bear to say over and over on every page. Would it work for him to repeat, 'I love honey'?"

I say I think so, and ask this student where he came up with that idea. He shows me his plan and explains part of what he is doing to learn how to write for his kindergarten buddy. "I asked the kindergarten teacher to lend me 12 books that her students like. I read them, and some of them had patterns so I decided to try that." Often what our students do to stretch themselves as writers is something they've learned about from analyzing the work of professionals. They try what other writers have tried.

Another writer says to me, "I decided I wanted to learn about Bosnia. That's why I'm reading *Zlata's Diary* (written by Zlata Filipovic, New York: Penguin, 1994). Have you read it?" I have, but this student has much more knowledge of Bosnia than I have. She can draw a map, freehand, of the various regions and reads the news about Bosnia every day without fail. She has gone back to World War I and World War II to trace the history of the conflict. She has interviewed local Bosnian refugees.

These students know what they're doing. They not only set goals, they create plans, lists of what they'll do as they work toward their goals. They determine, in conjunction with their teacher and other students, the processes they plan to explore to become better writers.

Teachers often ask me, "But how can I manage a classroom in which my students are all working on various goals and plans?" Well, I don't mean to convey that this is easy! But the classroom environment we create makes it possible for our students to work on their various plans. Everyone has as large a block of time to read, write, and study as possible as often as we can arrange. During this time we mill, conferring with students, teaching very direct lessons on the spot. Similarly, during this workshop time, while they work, the students may confer with each other if need be. Periodically we interrupt this workshop to give the students opportunities to share their work when they want to celebrate or request help. We provide time for both all-class and small-group shares. Some students are more comfortable in small groups than large ones.

The students who evaluate regularly have a final question to answer, "What do I intend to use as documentation to show my journey and what I learned?"

The child who is working on *was* and *were* intends to put at least two pieces of documentation in his portfolio: an old piece of writing in which he incorrectly used those two words and a new piece of writing in which he used them correctly in every instance. He has two friends in the class who understand this *was* and *were* business. They help him. He will become unconfused about them, he is convinced.

The girl who's studying Bosnia plans six items for her documentation: (1) some of the sketches she draws as she reads *Zlata's Diary,* a book with no illustrations, (2) some clippings from the daily newspaper with information of particular interest to her highlighted, (3) her notes from her study of the history of Bosnia, (4) a transcript of her interview, (5) a final piece of writing about everything she has learned, and (6) her self-evaluation of her work and her growth as a person.

Writing is complex for many of these students. It encompasses many aspects of literacy, including reading, sketching, and interviews. They become enmeshed in complicated issues. Their growth is multifaceted and their evaluations reflect that. Tom Romano (1995) ends his most recent book with these words, "Writing is a worthy human experience. . . . We grow and become more complicated as our literacy evolves. Our lives are enriched by the doing. Never forget that" (p. 198).

Evaluation promotes this complicated growth on the part of writers who write frequently. Evaluation encourages writers to continue to write. We must never forget that.

Evaluation: To Rethink the Role of the Teacher

The teachers of these students who evaluate themselves, their writing, one another's writing, and the books they read play very different roles than many of us played several years ago (Emig, 1983). It is still very difficult for some of us to envision a reading group where students talk about what they read instead of answer comprehension questions, and it's difficult to envision a classroom in which students all work on their own goals. As we learn about these new teaching procedures, we alter our classrooms.

The one change that affects our students more than anything else is when we start to think of ourselves as the number one learner in the classroom. Ron Kieffer (1994) writes about an exploration of portfolio use with elementary, secondary, and college teachers. Over the course of a few years, their close look at themselves as evaluators moved them from a focus on assessment to a focus on themselves and their students as learners.

Similarly, Doug Kaufman (1995), a researcher in a fourth-grade classroom, writes about his decision to learn a new teaching strategy. He learned the value of letting a conversation with children follow its natural course, rather than guiding the discussion with questions. When he shared an item from his portfolio with a small group of children, he didn't ask them what connection they thought it might have to the fact that he became a reader. He asked them what the photo made them think of. They wondered why his father wasn't in a family photo. When he said his father was killed in Vietnam, a Vietnamese girl in the group started to talk about Vietnam for the first time all year. This led to a change in the interaction patterns in the entire classroom. When this teacher, and others, place value on the act of trying something new, they start to look for evidence that their students are trying to learn something new, which expands the traditional role of evaluation. No longer is evaluation limited to an assessment of what students have learned.

I now serve as a researcher in the same project as Doug Kaufman, but I collect my data in the classroom of Kathy Mirabile, the woman who teaches 11th-grade U.S. history to John, the young man from Romania. When Kathy's students started to create their family histories, she started also. She began by going to visit her dad, a gentleman in his 80s.

Two hours later, she was leaving her dad's house and her dad was saying, "Kathy, can we do this family history together? I want to learn about my grandparents. I never knew who they were, you know." Kathy shared this with her students the next day. They know she's on the verge of learning something new (Graves, 1990). She's in this with them, and they are all in the midst of uncovering family information, family stories.

As they uncover the stories in their families, they are amazed by how much U.S. history they create by weaving together their own stories. Kathy's students are finding more value in U.S. history than many of her students did in previous years, and she is a teacher who has won national awards for her teaching. To have her students' family histories contribute to the content of her class is something she has never tried before.

As a teacher Kathy asks herself the questions I shared earlier: "What is the most recent thing I've learned as a teacher?" "What do I want to learn next in order to become a better teacher?"

As a professor, I try to do likewise. Last fall I asked to teach freshman composition for the first time ever. In our first class session, on the first day of the semester, on their first day in college, my class of 20 excited, nervous young people sat in a circle with this gray-haired professor. I probably reminded them of their grandmothers! You can imagine how excited they were about having to take this English class.

I decided to read them the piece of my writing that follows. As it turned out, they referred to my narrative throughout our course. It not only surprised them, but it showed them that I expected them to write nonfiction that was interesting to read. (Freshman composition at the University of New Hampshire is a nonfiction writing class.) They learned from the overall setting that I expected them to share with each other and that I assumed we would enjoy this class. I showed them what I value as a writer and as an instructor.

This is the piece of writing I read to my class on that first day:

Have a Safe Trip

I am a freshman in college, I've never been to California, and I want to go there for Christmas. My roommate's boyfriend plans to visit his mother in Solvang, a town about halfway up the state and my aunt lives in Los Angeles. I hope to spend the holidays with her.

I ask my parents if I can go, and they say no. I go.

Four of us take turns at the wheel as we drive nonstop from Des Moines, Iowa, where we are college students, to my aunt's doorstep. On my first leg of driving, I sneak us through a snowstorm in Kansas. The windshield wipers of David's old VW don't work so I reach outside the window to keep a 6-inch circle clear. Sheets of ice cover the roads. Once I spin us 180 degrees, but the flat terrain saves us. I simply steer our bug back onto the road and proceed.

Just outside Albuquerque I drive through a construction area, and our VW emerges from potholes looking like a Fannie Farmer dipped chocolate. Not a trace of green paint peeks through the mud. We ride inside our new brown bug and happen upon a roadblock. A highway patrolman motions with his machine gun for me to stop and roll down my window. We've been up for many hours and feel giddy, but he doesn't appreciate our giggles. "Out!" he shouts. We stand while he and his comrades search our suitcases and Christmas gifts. He lets us go.

After the holidays, on our way back to Iowa I speed through a small Nevada town on New Year's Eve. Blue lights flash behind me as the policeman studies my license: Minnesota. He studies my college ID: Iowa. He studies the car registration: California. He studies us, wrinkles his brow, and silently returns my papers. "Be careful," he says as he shakes his head. He lets us go.

I start to fall asleep as I drive across Utah. A siren wakes me. "You're weaving," he says. We change drivers. He lets us go.

When my roommate drives us over the Rockies, amidst patches of ice on the road, one spins us. We will either fly off the cliff on one side of the road, or into the mountain on the other. We fly in, stuck in the snow with no shovel, but we do have a metal can of cookies. We eat them and scoop ourselves out.

A week after we return I get a ride north to Minnesota to visit my parents for a late Christmas. I tell them about my quiet, sunny holidays with my mother's sister. My dad shows me the short-term insurance policy he needlessly took out on me for the trip.

I asked my students to respond, "What did you learn about me? What's on your mind? What else would you like to know?"

My students asked me if I'd ever gotten any other tickets in my life. I told them I had and told them a bit about a few of those occasions. They asked other questions, curious to know about this professor. They shared their own stories about driving, hunting, and leaving home. The next time we met, they read narratives of their experiences to the class. They responded to each other, finding value in not only what their classmates wrote, but in the writers themselves.

I listened carefully to their interactions and their writing. I wondered what to do next to improve their compositions and their ability to work together. I evaluated the situation, myself, and my students all the time!

We all grow for our own reasons. We set goals and accomplish them as best we can. We all have our stories to tell about ourselves, our students, our writing. Our stories show what we value. We challenge ourselves to listen to our own narratives, to hear what we value. We work hard to create a match between our beliefs and what we teach, say, and write. It may take us as long to figure out the frustrations we experience with evaluation as it will take Romanians to orient their future, but we will work at it.

References

Clay, M. M. (1991). *Becoming literate: The construction of inner control.* Portsmouth, NH: Heinemann.

Emig, J. (1983). The composing processes of twelfth graders. In D. Goswami & M. Butler (Eds.), *The web of meaning: Essays on writing, teaching, learning, and thinking* (pp. 61–96). Portsmouth, NH: Boynton/Cook.

Goldsmith, E. (1995). Deepening the conversations. *The Reading Teacher, 38,* 558–563.

Graves, D. (1990). *Discover your own literacy.* Portsmouth, NH: Heinemann.

Hansen, J. (1994). Literacy portfolios: Windows on potential. In S. Valencia, E. Hiebert, & P. A. Afflerbach (Eds.), *Authentic reading assessment: Practices and possibilities* (pp. 26–40). Newark, DE: International Reading Association.

Kaufman, D. (1995). The value of blabbing it, or how students can become their own *Go.* In L. Rief & M. Barbieri (Eds.), *All that matters: What is it we value in school and beyond?* (pp. 109–118). Portsmouth, NH: Heinemann.

Kieffer, R. (1994, December). Portfolio process and teacher change. *NRRC News: A Newsletter of the National Reading Research Center,* 8. Athens, GA: University of Georgia.

Lowry, L. (1994). Newbery Medal acceptance. *The Horn Book, 70,* 414–422.

Moffett, J. (1992). *Detecting growth in language.* Portsmouth, NH: Heinemann.

Romano, T. (1995). *Writing with passion: Life stories, multiple genres.* Portsmouth, NH: Heinemann.

Integrating Sources

1. Summarize the similarities and differences between Hoffman and Hansen in their approaches to the teaching of effective writing strategies in the classroom setting.

2. What do you think are the strengths and weaknesses of these writing ideas in the classroom setting? Be able to defend your answers.

3. Summarize the similarities and differences between Hoffman, Carney, and Hansen in their approaches to the teaching of effective writing strategies in the classroom setting.

Classroom Implications

1. Are Hoffman's concerns over process writing mandates justified? If they are absent in your state, would they have a positive impact on instruction there?

2. Based on the material in this section on writing, what do you think are the most important qualities of an effective classroom writing program?

Annotated Bibliography

Atwell, N. (1998). *In the middle: New understandings about writing, reading, and learning* (2nd ed.). Portsmouth, NH: Boynton/Cook, Heinemann.

The second edition of Atwell's acclaimed book provides ideas and rationale for process writing instruction, writer's workshop, and other current approaches. Lots of ideas for teachers at a range of levels (not just middle school).

Graves, D. H. (1994). *A fresh look at writing.* Portsmouth, NH: Heinemann.

Graves places his views on writing in historical perspectives as he provides innumerable suggestions for teachers who wish to employ a process approach.

Petrosky, A. R., & Bartholomae, D. (1986). *The teaching of writing: Eighty-fifth yearbook of the National Society for the Study of Education* (Part II). Chicago: University of Chicago Press.

Contains a variety of views on writing instruction, and the contributors touch on a range of issues, including rationale, theories, evaluation, and instructional practice.

Reinking, D., McKenna, M. C., Labbo, L. D., & Keiffer, R. D. (Eds.). (1998). *Handbook of literacy and technology: Transformations in a post-typographic world.* Mahwah, NJ: Erlbaum.

This book presents numerous current perspectives from a number of leading authors regarding ways in which computers are changing the very nature of reading and writing and how instruction is being transformed as a result.

White, E. M. (1994). *Teaching and assessing writing: Recent advances in understanding, evaluating, and improving student performance* (2nd ed.). San Francisco: Jossey-Bass.

This book aims at instructors across disciplines as well as language arts teachers. It examines assessment issues in detail and strikes a useful balance between theory and practice.

You Become Involved

1. Inventory your own focus on writing. Review lesson plans over the span of a week and determine how much time you have apportioned to writing. Do the results surprise you? Are you satisfied?
2. Interview a sample of your students about what they like most and least about writing. Do the results agree with your predictions?
3. Visit the web site of the National Center for the Study of Writing and Literacy. Even though the mission of the Center is over, the site still houses information concerning research findings **http://www-gse.berkeley.edu/research/NCSWL /csw.homepage.html**

INDEX